RANDALI

Taking Up THE SWORD

A STORY *of a* SPECIAL AGENT *in the* DIPLOMATIC SECURITY SERVICE

outskirtspress
DENVER, COLORADO

Taking Up the Sword
A Story of a Special Agent in the Diplomatic Security Service
All Rights Reserved.
Copyright © 2013 Randall Bennett
v2.0 r1.0

Cover Photo © 2013 JupiterImages Corporation. All rights reserved - used with permission.

Outskirts Press, Inc.
http://www.outskirtspress.com

ISBN: 978-1-4787-1204-6

Outskirts Press and the "OP" logo are trademarks belonging to Outskirts Press, Inc.

PRINTED IN THE UNITED STATES OF AMERICA

TABLE OF CONTENTS

INTRODUCTION

March 27, 2007, Baghdad, Iraq – When you could hear the whistling of the rocket overhead, you knew it was close enough that you were within seconds of being dead or being lucky again. The louder the whistling, the closer it was to the hole you were trying to find or make. The speed and force of the rockets made that sound when they were passing directly overhead and possibly coming down on top of you. The detonation and deadly blast that followed would take place only a second or two at most after you heard it and I knew it was my duty to respond to the blast site to help anyone who got hit and injured or to deal with anyone who was killed. On this day, we would not all be lucky.

As the Senior Regional Security Officer (RSO) or "Chief of Security" for all official and contracted Americans in Iraq during June 2006 to July 2007, it was my job to keep them safe and try to protect them all and to rescue them when they were in trouble. This year was turning out to be the most violent and death-ridden of the entire Iraq incursion. People were dieing all over the place.

The first in this series of 122 mm rockets launched at us from Saddar City about 12 kilometers away and across the Tigris River, slammed into the earth inside the Palace grounds, near the volley ball court next to Saddam's pool and by the DFAC (the cafeteria). The ground shook so hard and the blast was so loud, I thought it had been a direct hit on Saddam's Palace where I had my office in the north "classified" wing. As it was, it hit about 120 yards away from my office and 60 yards away from the tiny trailer I called home for the 3 or 4 hours of sleep I tried to get a night. But it still hit inside my Palace grounds where everyone walked around and tried to find some semblance of normality in this dangerous and surrealistic environment.

When the first rocket hit, me and a few members of my exceptional, dedicated and well-trained team of Diplomatic Security Special Agents, all of us trained as High Threat Tactical Operatives for war environments, began running for the Palace back exit to check on any American or Iraqi staff who might have been outside walking around in the kill zone. While running down the long Palace hallway, the second rocket hit 50 yards closer and left shrapnel and metal pieces of the rocket in the crater and in the pool. We continued running down the hallway to the east exit door but it sounded like they were "walking" the rockets in on us for precision targeting and that meant there was a spotter somewhere nearby. This was all happening in seconds. Almost the moment we reached the door to exit, the third rocket of the series hit a tree as it came down in front of the KBR housing office, thirty yards from the door we were exiting and where three of our good friends were. Instead of penetrating the ground, it detonated about six feet high because of the tree trunk and the concussive explosion and shrapnel blasted straight out at body height. It was at this moment we exited the building.

We ran with our first aid trauma kits as others were also making their way to the site. There was no way to know if another rocket was incoming but we had a greater duty to help our friends and we prayed another rocket would not hit the same spot again. It was our job, but besides that, it was the right thing to do. The one positive thing about being in a war zone is that many people end up having medical training and besides my team, there were nurses and medics joining us. There is never a greater venue for demonstrations of valor and courage by Americans than a war with injured or dieing friends.

There were three people down. First was the KBR Housing Manager and everyone knew her. She was the first friendly face you met when you arrived on the RSO's massively armored Rhino Bus at 0300 hours to your new Baghdad trailer park home after traveling for 2 or 3 days to get here. You felt lost and confused and seeing her made things seem almost normal. She was the absolute sweetest and most even-tempered person in the camp. She had also decided the day before that after 200 rockets falling on our area just this year, she had finished her long 3 years and wanted to go home. We began triage. She had screamed following the close rocket hit and dropped straight down but we initially couldn't find a mark on her body. We tried to bring her to consciousness but couldn't. Two people stayed with her and we called for one of our armored cars to get her to the CSH (Combat Surgical Hospital).

The second one was a big funny red-headed National Guard soldier. He always made everyone laugh and his personality was a morale builder for everyone in the Palace, which included many thousands of people. He had some serious shrapnel wounds and everyone did the best they could to stop the bleeding but his condition was such that he needed immediate surgery, if it was not already too late. We put him in one of our armored vehicles and sent him to the CSH as well.

Others were working on the third casualty, another soldier who had eight pieces of jagged metal shrapnel embedded in his main torso and we did what we could to stop the bleeding and get him prepared for the surgery he would undergo at the CSH.

We learned that our friend, the National Guard soldier, died in the car on the 6 minute drive to the CSH. His injuries had just been too severe. The sweet Housing Manager died about 20 minutes after reaching the CSH, without ever regaining consciousness. Though there was apparently one penetration from shrapnel in her lower back discovered at the CSH, the concussive effect of the blast had been so horrific and powerful, her internal organs had not survived. The other soldier with eight holes in him hung on and survived and eventually days later was shipped off for all the follow-up care he would need.

For those of us left behind to grieve, we held the memorial services, and all, many of us grown hardened men of many battles, cried for the loss of our friends openly and without shame.

For quite a few years, various people had been asking me to write my memoirs, telling me that it would make a good book. I always told them that I wouldn't even buy a copy and who would want to read about another person's life. But, after this attack, I am not sure why, but I decided to put my story to paper, even if it ended up being only for my family as a genealogical family reference.

I am a Special Agent for the U.S. Department of State's Diplomatic Security Service (DSS) and though my story may be one of our organization's more active ones, we are all a group of men and women who serve much of our time overseas doing things that books are written about and movies are made, without receiving recognition. We are the most elite and well-trained Special Agents you have protecting you and our country and that you have probably never heard of. I guess it's time you knew something about us and what we do in the jungles, deserts, mountains and exotic front and back streets of foreign countries, which all impacts on your lives without you ever knowing about it. This is one Agent's story. Mine. A man who discovered the perfect job that was designed and waiting for him, and who became a Special Agent for all the right reasons.

Dedicated To

My brilliant sister Barbara Bennett, for her support, encouragement and authorship excellence that inspired me to try and put my stories to paper

and

to the courageous DS Agents who daily risk their lives in their devotion to protect the World's Nations and Peoples.

Chapter One
AN INTRODUCTORY EXPLANATION

A truth is that no one can be truly happy sharing their life with another until they have obtained a sense of contentment with who they themselves are. And no individual's life can ever truly or fully feel satisfying without attaining a sense of knowledge of who and what you are (and maybe what you are capable of). Many of us, while still searching, growing and attaining that personal sense, find ourselves in a traditionally carved career trench that will take us to the end but without much joy or enlightenment and in many cases, preventing us from fully attaining that personal sense of "me" and thus not feeling fulfilled with who and what we are.

Although I had a sense even while young that I was rebellious but was a relatively bright and perceptive individual (albeit naïve), I also recognized some limitations and weaknesses. None of us like to admit to any weaknesses, but to find our place in life, we have to open our eyes, cast off that naivete and face who and what we truly are and are capable of - then seek to challenge and beat that. After all, as that great "old west" philosopher once said, "A man's got to know his limitations". One of my limitations that fortunately I realized and worked to overcome is that I get bored easily if I work one same thing too long, or in the same single location too long. I never thought there was any solution to overcoming that. But one day, when I happened to be aware of my "self", and had my eyes open to a fleeting moment of opportunity, I recognized and seized on a job offer and my life was turned around. Luck and self awareness. Luck might actually be the theme of my life though there were times when it was the bad kind.

I knew in myself that the selection of my life's mission needed to have a component of wildly varying challenge. The opportunity to literally protect, help, rescue and save others from dire circumstances fulfilled a part of me that then made me whole. It met a perceived need for self-fulfillment that eventually made me happy with who and what I am in life. For me, that is the way with being a Special Agent for the U.S. Department of State's Diplomatic Security Service. There is always something new and always a greater challenge. A Special Agent with DSS must above all be flexible and willing to accept assignments and missions that have never been anticipated before and to take challenges beyond one's wildest anticipations. That is one of the true strengths of DSS; it's personnel, with creative intelligence to derive solutions on the spot to threats that arise without warning and to possess a dynamic enthusiasm to love pursuing a successful resolution to threats that make the adrenaline jump off the charts.

My name is Randall Bennett and as I look back at the whole of it this past 25 years, it seems hard to believe I survived so many wonderful adventures in a single career and that I was afforded through DSS the opportunity to offer substantive contributions to preserving and saving American lives in foreign countries. For someone with my understandably job-necessary "A" type personality, what could be more gratifying or rewarding than to look back and see the faces of those people who have benefited and are here today possibly due to the direct or indirect action or intervention of myself and in some cases, various teams I have led or worked with. Of all the Special Agents I have known, whether in DSS or the FBI, CIA, Secret Service, DEA or DHS, I think I might be the luckiest and one of the most "road tested." Lucky in that I have had the career I have, and lucky to have seen and done the things I have in so many other countries of the world, and perhaps more than a little bit lucky and road-tested in that I have survived so many close calls and direct attempts by various nefarious elements to eliminate my number from the playing field.

During my 25 years, I have served in Gulf War 1 in my capacity as a Special Agent protecting the Ambassador and the Embassy in Kuwait. I worked three years through a civil war in Angola, where I regularly encountered the UNITA rebel leader, Jonas Savimbi and his forces, and caught the tail end of another war in Ethiopia, where I was present on the day when the country was overtaken by the rebels who finally entered Addis Ababa. I served as the Senior Regional Security Officer and Senior Security Advisor to Ambassadors Khalilzad and Crocker in Iraq from summer 2006 to summer 2007, and I have evacuated six Embassies or Consulates including Kinshasa, Zaire, Brazzaville, Congo, Addis Ababa, Ethiopia, and three separate times the Consulate General in Karachi, Pakistan, which is where I also became the American Investigator involved with tracking down and capturing the Al-Qaeda kidnappers and murderers of the Wall Street Journal Reporter Daniel Pearl. Again, I state that I have been the luckiest of Agents and men. I have operated in more than 50 countries, worked side by side with our most elite and elusive military special elements, trained thousands of foreign host-nation personnel to be better security officers and guards, and was the person who found Jose Padilla (The Dirty Bomber) and provided the information on capturing him so that he could be taken off the streets before he committed his act of terrorism. There have been so many more adventures as well and their memories will keep me entertained when I finally turn in my equipment and those who I have mentored take over the role.

Chapter Two

DSS Hiring and Training

At 36 years old, I began the career of my dreams. I didn't know at the time what the direction would be that DSS would take me, and there are certainly hundreds of different paths one might select or find themselves on in the Diplomatic Security Service, but I began as all Agents do, thinking that wearing my surveillance communication ear piece and special protective equipment with dark shades, while protecting famous and important dignitaries, was about the coolest thing a guy could do. It didn't take long to learn that sweating, freezing, or being rained on in an unbuttoned suit so that there was easy access to my weapon, or that standing "post" in a hallway while the dignitary carried out his negotiating responsibilities or relaxed in his suite, or that traveling to a foreign country whose name you have never heard of before and have a hard time pronouncing, and doing it on a moment's notice, was not the best pathway to develop my leadership and managerial skills, nor to try and rise through the ranks of the organization. It was certainly exciting and enlightening and culturally enhancing for awhile, but another path was to reveal itself to me soon. A path that would keep me living in various overseas locations for most of my career and allow me to pursue some of the worst enemies of the American people and our country.

Everything has to start somewhere. In the case with DSS, it all starts with the training and discipline. 37 years old was the maximum one could be to be accepted into the Federal Law Enforcement Service so at 36 years old, I was competing daily with men and women 10 to 15 years younger than myself. Fortunately, I have always believed in a strong physical discipline and when hired, I was competing in martial arts tournaments regularly and working out every day. Nevertheless, for someone who has been an athlete all their life, there are bound to be some serious and detrimental injuries being carried as baggage. I refused to submit to mine but they were and are relatively serious ones requiring substantial compensation and compromise to perform satisfactorily. Many years before, I came back from my military stint during the Vietnam War and took an interest in a new sport called Hang Gliding. A sport with no history or statistics leading to no insurance companies being willing to cover any individual or any company. It didn't matter. It was exciting, interesting, and a challenge that needed to be accepted. Unfortunately, one time a gust of wind swept me up to about 125 feet, turned me upside down and sent me speeding to earth to hit the side of a mountain, shattering my knee into 13 pieces and permanently breaking my ankle, leaving a broken bone realigning itself and intruding into the ankle socket, restricting rotation. Both injuries created a constant aggravating level of pain and still do but it became the norm and just a part of everyday life. Well, here we are back at DSS introductory Agent training in Glynco, Georgia, at the Federal Law Enforcement Training Center, known as FLETC, and needing to perform as well as much younger athletes without injuries. Obviously I must have but there are many other areas of training as well. Intensive time is spent learning law and legally enforceable statutes as one would expect. So much time is spent on firing weapons and becoming reflexively proficient that blisters form on the trigger finger. We learned water survival, and about dangerous home-grown American terrorists like some brutal motorcycle gangs. One of the truly fun but highly useful skills learned is Anti-Terrorist Driving. Learning to spin cars in circles and escaping in the opposite direction to avoid being killed by terrorists at a road block or ambush was absolutely inspiring. Additionally, an Agent learns about Counterintelligence aspects and Counterterrorist techniques. Due to the nature of the work and the locations one might work in, an Agent is instructed in Hostage Survival just in case things go horribly wrong. There are a plethora of subjects and they all augment the others. After a few months, the training then moved to various other sites in the States and our skills continued to be refined and enhanced. If an Agent fails any course or training element, they are asked to leave to find another more appropriate line of work. The pressure can be intense during the training probation period and even the te-nuring years but typically those applying to become a DSS Agent find this type of challenge to be exhilarating rather than stressful.

Upon completion of the approximate 6 months of training, which is frequently described as like "drinking from a fire hose", graduation takes place in a spectacular and beautiful room in the upper floors of the U.S. State Department and it is a meaningful event one does not forget. Then, to continue on the whirlwind that has been the format so far, and with great anticipation on the Agent's part, everyone receives their first assignment. Some will serve their first tour domestically at one of the Field Offices, others will take a position in the World Headquarters in Rosslyn, Virginia, and some now, because of the increased terrorist activity overseas and our increased efforts at world diplomacy, will be called to serve at one of the Embassies or Consulates in the many countries we are currently servicing.

Those new Agents lucky enough to be assigned to a foreign post-ing will carry our overseas title of Assistant Regional Security Officer (ARSO) and will work for the Regional Security Officer (RSO). I have been an ARSO and RSO and most recently in Spain, Iraq, Pakistan, and Thailand, the Senior Regional Security Officer (SRSO) since 1993. It is the path that has best met my interests, needs and skills. The RSO is responsible for all U.S. Mission security in the country he is assigned to and runs some 23 or so separate Programs. He is also the Senior Security Advisor to the Ambassador. Though it is a huge responsibility, it also af-fords the RSO the greatest opportunity to run his own show and utilize every ounce of judgment, training and experience he has compiled over his entire life. No two days are alike and every day new situations arise, requiring some fast dancing and thinking, and on occasion requiring consultation with headquarters if it is potentially politically "affecting." The opportunity to develop and refine ones leadership and managerial capabilities are maximized in an RSO capacity. The mentoring of new Agents has always been one of my primary interests and emphasis. Coming from a business background, I have always remembered the "learn, do, teach" management principle, which prescribes learning the posi-tion above you so you can advance, while doing well the job you have, and teaching your next in line your own job so that if you do move up, or out, he or she will be best prepared to assume the job and lead and manage properly.

My first assignment was for 2 years as an Agent in the Washington, DC, Field Office, referred to as WFO. Though I did complete a substantial number of Background Investigations to cement the precepts on basic investigative techniques, and performed what seemed an uncountable number of protective details on world leaders like the Secretary of State, Soviet Foreign Minister

Shevardnadze, Daniel Mitterrand, the leader of Turkish Cyprus Rauf Denktash, Yasser Arafat, the Prince of Morocco (now the King), and maybe 30 or 50 others, I was also fortunate to receive two long-term temporary duty assignments (TDYs) in other countries, which really sank the hook deep in my love for exotic overseas assignments.

Before I jump to my first long term TDY assignment, let me give you an idea of just a few of those who I provided protection to and some of the other assignments I had in my first year or two. It is pretty traditional for new Agents to do mostly protection work while learning the nature of the job.

On August 17-20, 1988, I protected the brother of the President of Afghanistan. He had fled his country with his wife and two sons who unfortunately got captured and taken back. He continued his emigration to the U.S. with only 2 rugs and 1 suitcase.

August 30, 1988, I responded to the Burmese Embassy and interviewed their Consular Officer and their Second Secretary. They had received threats of a national coup and to destroy their Embassy and behead them. I tracked down the initiator of the threat and another cohort. I reported this to my Washington authorities and shortly thereafter, the coup actually took place in their country with this individual being involved and it eventually became Myanmar .

September 8-9, 1988, I protected Iraqi Minister of Foreign Affairs, Sagoon Hammadi. In the middle of accusations of chemical warfare being carried out in Iraq, suicide squads had been sent to kill him. This was very high threat in the middle of the Iran/Iraq Peace talks.

September 21-28, 1988, I protected the Foreign Minister of the Soviet Union, Eduard Shevardnadze. We dealt with protests and threats and a crazy Russian man who hid inside some bushes across from the half-circular driveway into the State Department entrance. When our motorcade departed out the driveway, he jumped out and threw himself on the hood of Shevardnadze's car. He was lucky not to be shot. He later showed up again at the Soviet Embassy. We then drove him to New York City for the United Nations General Assembly meetings. We met constant crazies and groupies who wanted to know who we were and who he was. The FM had to return to Moscow early for some big political shake ups and gave me a bottle of Russian Vodka as a gift.

September 29-Octover 12, 1988, I worked the protective detail of Prince Sidi Muhammed of Morocco. He stayed in a 3-story suite in the Helmsley Palace, next to Michael Jackson's suite. I worked the night shift and it sucked, but we went out every night to clubs just protecting him and his entourage of 30 Moroccan college students. We even went to a party at the Palladium with the Prince, Michael Jackson, Yoko Ono, and Tony Bennett. We got back to the hotel most nights/mornings at about 0600 hours.

October 16 – November 03, 1988, I protected the Turkish Ambassador Elekdag. It went smoothly - he played tennis in the mornings and we met with the owner of Atlantic Records and went to a formal dinner and show that was a weapons convention like the movie "Deal of the Century" with Chevy Chase. Right up our interest alley.

Chapter Three
TDY Dhaka,
Bangladesh - 1988

The first long-term TDY came about one morning in WFO short-ly after my assignment there, when the Supervisor walked into the open work area and asked who wanted to go to Bangladesh for a four-month TDY. As I watched the other Agents maneuver-ing themselves out of the room at a fast pace, keeping their heads down and making no eye contact, I raised my hand. I had no idea where Bangladesh was or even what it was. The magic finger pointed my way and within days, I was packed and on a plane. After 44 hours of travel with almost no sleep, I arrived in Dhaka, Bangladesh, and was picked up at a furiously chaotic airport by the RSO. It was evening and he said before taking me to my quar-ters for the next four months, we were going to a party at one of the Embassy Officer's homes. I remember arriving, shaking hands with a lot of people, and then sitting on a couch and falling asleep until awakened at the end of the party and taken to my home in the sparsely populated (other than by huts and cardboard box homes) remote Gulshan district of outer Dhaka. Once there, I found out I was replacing one of our Agents who had been fly-ing home on the Pan Am 103 flight that crashed over Lockerbie,

Scotland, killing him and all others. The TDY assignment was called a Site Security Manager (SSM) and I was to be responsible for all security on-site for a new Inman-designed Embassy, which was in its final stages of construction. This was the beginning of my many fire hose-type challenge developments and I loved it. I knew nothing about being an SSM at that time. Since this is just the introduction to ever more challenging and high threat assignments, I will just mention a few of the "opportunities" that came my way during these four months.

I resided in a relatively nice little cinder block home next to the U.S. Navy Seabee contingent, who would be working construction security under my currently less-than-knowledgeable oversight. They allowed me to join in their meal fund and I ate all my meals in their home, cooked by a Bangladeshi man. The area was going to turn into an expensive suburb one day but for now, it was filled by deathly poor citizens in cardboard or plywood huts who survived on whatever they could. I purchased a little Moped Scooter and gave rides to the gaggle of little Bangladeshi kids who lived around us. This seemed to bond me to their parents, who would frequently look out for my welfare and on one occasion, a stranger drove into the "village" neighborhood and recklessly hit me on my scooter, sending me face-first into gravel, which crammed itself under my skin and into my face and cheeks. As I started to get up, as if it was in slow motion, I saw the neighbors moving into the area, picking up rocks and circling the stranger, who had mistakenly and dangerously gotten out of his car to check on me. I realized they were going to stone him for hitting me and had to take some quick action to deter the situation, pushing the man into his car and telling him to get away fast. In a way, it was touching to see their reaction to my being hurt and their loyalty to me. It was also scary to realize that they would stone a man for an accident. I took myself to the doctor who removed the pieces of gravel and gave me facial micro-stitches.

On another occasion, it was a Muslim holiday, which name escapes me but the neighbors came to my door and told me to join them and to bring my camera. Once I arrived just down the dirt street, it became obvious it involved a ceremony using a large bull. They told me I should photograph the entire ceremony. As they started "singing" and chanting, a senior man took a large knife and began to cut the throat of the bull. I was a bit stunned and lost my focus for a moment but they all reminded me quickly that I was to photograph the whole thing. I still have the photos but seldom feel the need to reflect on the brutal nature of that almost biblical-type sacrifice.

As the construction continued, we received large shipments of hundreds of crates filled with supplies and equipment. I hated the thought of throwing out the crate material so I established a weekly supply giveaway for all the locals. They lined up by the hundreds outside the fence and as one huge crate would be emptied, the next family in line would be security-checked and would rush in and claim it and take it back to their rice paddy to create a living space for themselves. In this way, very quickly the homeless subsistence of Bangladeshi living quarters became almost overnight a plywood city. This was good for awhile but poor Bangladesh is geographically located at the small end of a funneled convergence of all rain and snow runoff from the Himalaya Mountain range. We are talking about vast amounts of water. The winter runoff began and what seemed like almost the next morning, the plywood village had disappeared. The Ganges River had backed up all the way into the Gulshan neighborhood and we found ourselves looking at a large river running past our new

Embassy gate with large fish including purplish colored dolphins swimming by. The entire area was covered by water and we later learned that 125,000 people died from that year's runoff. It was the first tragedy that I encountered that was of such a magnitude. It was incomprehensible. The temporary village was gone.

Later, as the waters died down, we began work again and the day laborers began to line up to see if they would be selected that day to earn wages to buy food for their families. Also, the local entertainment began to return. Young barefoot Muslim girls would come by with square wooden boxes balanced on their heads. These were the "Cobra Girls." For generations, their families were Cobra handlers and the children from birth would be seated on the ground next to the moving Cobras, occasionally being struck. However, apparently, over the generations they had developed and passed on a resistance to the venom and since this Cobra Show was their "bread and butter", they didn't want the next generations to lose that inherited resistance. I watched the way they would place one hand on the tail of the cobra, wiggling their other fist in front of its face and as the Cobra struck in a flash, they were able to pull their hand out of the way in time (most of the time). I came to realize that they were sensing the initial muscle response in the tail and were able to react appropriately proactive. A few times, the girls allowed me to try this same technique with their snakes, though it seems quite foolish to me now, but I was successful at it. I also have my memorable photos holding the cobras and standing with the girls. It was all well worth the dollars I paid, and their families ate as a benefit.

Another of the serious and dangerous entertainments was the giant (6-8 foot long) meat eating Monitor Lizards. Brave young boys would catch them and put a collar and rope on them and walk them around like a pet for money. The collar was strong and the rope was long. These Monitors were savage and would attack anything including my steel wire perimeter fence, biting it with sharp ragged teeth meant for killing quickly. They were pre-historically fascinating. We had a Korean Contractor at the site and one day I accidentally learned that they were buying them as an exotic meat supplement when I walked into what was going to be an Embassy cashier's office and found myself standing next to a small four-foot beauty. I couldn't resist trying to pet it's back and as I would try, it would exhale and flatten itself so that I couldn't touch it. As I through several attempts demonstrated my capacity for selection into the Darwin Elimination Award of the year, a Korean man entered and yelled, "no, no, you die, you die." Well, that was the final awakening for me and I moved on, lucky once again to have kept all my digits and limbs.

The final vignette on Bangladesh has to do with one day when daily Bangla employee selection was at a bit of a stressful point and they all, about 1,000 of them, went on strike, sitting in front of my new Embassy structure. The Koreans had kicked one of the Bangladeshis to "motivate" him and the entire force went on strike. The Koreans, besides not understanding appropriate treatment and supervisory behavior, did not understand the significance of the insult with using one's foot against a Muslim. It is the ultimate derogatory action and they were all incensed and furious. As the day wore on, their speeches became more aggressive and they demanded the Korean be turned over to them. Having witnessed a neighborhood thief being caught and stoned to death on the spot, I knew there would be no forgiveness for the Korean man. Without advising me on his proposed action, the RSO for Bangladesh decided to rescue the Korean man who we had securely locked up in a brick shed across the street from the construction site. While I was dealing with the large mob, the RSO in his car stopped across the street from the angry mob and picked up the Korean man. The force of anger interpreted it to be a betrayal and an attempt to get the Korean man out to safety. About 200 men ran after the car but since they could not catch it, a hush fell and they all turned to look at me and my compound with a small Bangla guard force. Unfortunately there were stacks of bricks in front of the construction site fence and each one of them became a projectile intended to injure myself and my guards. One brick hit a guard on the head and I grabbed the small man and another injured guard and dragged them as I ran for cover. They came over the walls and started destroying the vehicles and small adjacent buildings. Eventually the majority ran off, leaving about 50 hardcore rabble rousers to continue their dissent. I had taken enough and decided it was time to pull a bluff since I had no weapon on this job site. I began to scream like a crazy man while I walked toward them pointing my finger at them. Most fled in confused fear. A few stayed stunned staring at me wondering if I was nuts. When all but a few had run, I grabbed the three leaders and had my guards help me secure them and tie them up for the local police. It was a unique encounter that greatly enhanced my fledgling experience base. The guard force company owner, who had ties to the President of Bangladesh, came and picked up the three trouble-makers. Later we learned that none of them were ever seen again and that their family "homes" were destroyed. This was a harsh way to learn a lesson about third world justice. In the future, should I turn over culprits to the local police or authorities if they are corrupt enough to get rid of them? How does one balance justice with ethical and humane judgment?

Chapter Four

TDY GABORONE, BOTSWANA – 1989

After being back in the Washington Field Office for 2 months and having been the Agent of the Month for most completed Investigations for one of those months, again, the supervisory call for volunteers came. This time he announced it would be a 4 month TDY to a place called Gaborone, Botswana. And, it would be as a Site Security Manager (SSM) again. How exciting. Another place I had never heard of. Not wanting to be a TDY hog, I waited and watched as the other Agents quickly found other tasks that required their immediate attention anywhere but right there and then raised my hand. The finger of fate once again pointed at me and told me to be packed and ready to go in 2 days. Yes! This is what I became a Special Agent with DSS for in the Foreign Service. Exciting new cultures and locations. Little did I know at the time that it would turn into a wonderful 9 months and that some aspects of it would change who and what I was and set the stage for additional martial arts activities that remain with me today. But then, in truth, probably any and all adventures take on a certain influence factor and change or evolve our personalities in some way. I suppose that is why "they" suggest that travel opens the mind and self awareness.

I arrived in Gaborone (pronounced Haboroney), and was immediately struck by the fact that it was relatively clean, friendly, dry and moderate in climate, and similar but cooler than my home in Arizona, and had public game parks around the tiny colorful and culturally rich town that I could go into anytime I felt like it and had a few minutes to watch the animals. How could any place be more accommodating? It was even alright to do a little walking around but you had to be alert to the lions and other big cats sneaking up on you and the Cape Horn Buffalo would chase you just because they always seemed mad. But to see the Giraffe and Elephants and Rhino in the wild is something no one should miss. These are not zoo potential animals. These are the real thing, too big to capture and place in a zoo. Though the Giraffe were too skittish to permit it, I literally could walk under the belly of the huge and gentle animals and the Elephants seemed the size of a small home. I was smitten big time by the Africa image.

The new Embassy, also an Inman-type structure, was about 9 months away from completion and sat on a piece of property next to the tall and imposing DeBeers Diamond headquarters. Immediately, I knew I had to make friends with them, even though their impression to everyone was cold and aloof. I went next door and spoke with their head of security and told him that I would like to take monthly photos from their roof of my compound to track the monthly construction development from a historical progression perspective. He went for it and so not only did I get great project development photos, but I got to go on their roof once a month (the tallest point in Botswana) and look around and pass by their steel-gated vault each time with shoe boxes lining their shelves marked with some type of indications of the diamonds present. Later, I took a tour of one of their mining operations and from the stringent security the likes of which I had never seen before, I realized how privileged I was to be permitted in their building.

My guards and construction surveillance team consisted of Botswanans on the perimeter and cleared Americans inside the building, watching all sensitive construction aspects. The Botswanans were very nice and as interested in learning about me as I was to learn about them and their culture and superstitions. Once, I tried to get them to work out with me, running and exercising on the compound and they adamantly told me that they never worked out because any exercise would make them sexually inadequate and reduce their virility. Interesting. An exact opposite of the belief we have that exercise makes us stronger and more virile. The Americans were all retired older men who had served with various U.S. Government Agencies overseas previously and now could still enjoy the adventure of exotic life while making some decent money as well. Once the foreign adventure bug bites you, it is very difficult to ever let it go and settle into a "normal" sort of American existence, mowing the lawn, going to the mall, poker or golf with the neighbor buddies. That type of life-change can only entertain for so long before the need for an "injection of exotic" takes over complete control of your mind and focus.

One of the American supervisors who worked for me overseeing the guard force was a Japanese-Hawaiian man who had a big impact on me. Ramon Lono Ancho was a silver-hair and bearded Jiu-Jitsu Master who held a ninth-degree ranking. Though he was in his late sixties, he could physically control anyone with his arm locks or joint manipulations. He was also a knife thrower, something I had always wanted to learn and that now I am known for having taught many people since. Besides the sense of respect and dedication that Ancho taught me, and the spiritual sense about life he conveyed in all things, we accomplished two things beyond the job itself. Ancho taught me the secrets I had always wanted to know about the technique for throwing knives and I became proficient at it. I am still throwing them today and passed on the teachings of Ancho to Marines, TDYers and other RSOs and Officers who came to the particular Embassy I was posted at. The second thing, and much more along the philosophy Ancho passed to me was the free Martial Arts classes we set up for anyone who wanted to come. I was already a third degree Black Belt Tae Kwon Do practitioner with quite a few years under my "belt", but Ancho was a born leader and was highly skilled. We were allowed to use a public hall and once we announced the free classes, we found there were 100 barefoot Botswanans who came from as far as 50 miles away, hitchhiking just to take the classes. It was inspiring to see their dedication and motivation and for 6 months, we continued the classes until the project was finished and we were forced to move on.

My posse of Botswanan guards had become close and reliable friends. When Christmas arrived, the work on the site was stopped while everyone went home for the holidays. Everyone except security. So, I had to devise something to keep my guards entertained and alert. I came up with the idea of an internal site Botswana Olympics. It would involve just the guards and me but I devised rough, on-the-spot events that I hoped would seem culturally interesting to them. The run was a disaster. I was the only one willing to exercise due to the superstition about loss of sex drive from exercising. I had fashioned a javelin and that was a real hit. We didn't go for distance. We went for targeting. They did pretty well and continued to practice with it after our Olympics ended. We found a round steel ball that we supposed had some-thing do with the construction site but what the heck, we had a shot put event. We also created a high jump standard and pit and a few other miscellaneous events involving knives and Frisbees. It was a nice Christmas and I have always appreciated their enthu-siasm and loyalty.

The people I met and worked with. The adventures I experienced. The game parks and friends. The peaceful and friendly beautiful town itself. Botswana was truly a unique experience and it sank the love of overseas life deep into my psyche. At the end of my 9 months, the Embassy was ready for move-in and I assisted with that. Then, I returned to Washington and prepared for my next onward assignment, which was to become one of the most in-teresting, career-enhancing and advancing tours of my life. But there were more protective details before I moved on.

August 25-September 15, 1989, I protected a Colombian Judge, who was under a death threat from the Colombian drug cartels. The threat was very high and very real. The Judge was terrified and we kept her in a safe house that was unknown. There was an international girls private school in the building also and they were very cute and would bring us chocolate chip cookies. The entire building was covered inside and out but we worried about the Judge and the girls.

September 26-28, 1989, I next worked protection for Shimon Peres, the Vice Premier and Finance Minister of Israel. I was the Advance Agent for sites we would visit and it was the first time I met the National Security Advisor Donald Rumsfeld. Working with a mix of Israeli Protective Agents and the Secret Service Agents made it a complicated detail to keep operational.

October 01, 1989, I handled the Advance for Foreign Minister Barre of Somalia. He went from the airport to his son's residence. The residence was palatial but inside the "apartment", it looked like Somalia with no cleanliness and in total disorder.

October 11-14, 1989, we protected Rauf Denktash, the President of Turkish Cypress. My protective positions switched every day. He was a kind, overweight man who reminded me of a friend from my business days. He didn't seem to generate interest from his speeches and left disappointed.

October 23-25, 1989, I protected the First Lady of France Danielle Mitterand. She was very nice, attractive, spoke little English. Danielle gave me a silver key chain with the Mitterand family seal on it.

I consider this entire two-year period discussed as my "warm up" period; my introduction by fire. Two long-term TDYs, a lot of protective details, good investigative experience, and my enthusiasm could not have been at a higher level. Now that the Field Office experience was over, I felt my path might begin to define a direction that I could follow throughout my career. In a sense, it was true. I was headed for the Mobil Security Division (MSD). It was the "action group" for DSS, dealing with evacuations, wars, incursions and coups. And the additional training I would receive in order to become an instructor in many courses I would later teach during the MSD trips overseas, would prepare me for anything that might come my way. It was just where I wanted to be.

Chapter Five
THE MOBIL SECURITY
DIVISION, 1990 - 1993

The Mobil Security Division, or MSD as it is called, is perhaps the most comprehensive and perfect training ground for being a Regional Security Officer (RSO) that there can be. During the few years that an Agent might be lucky enough to serve in MSD, he or she would travel on 30 or so TDY trips to different countries and encounter as many Embassies and Consulates, and have the opportunity to deal with such a diversity and density of unique situations from the mundane to life-threatening, creating the perfect training ground for becoming an RSO and running one's own Program Portfolio in a foreign country. While traveling to all these places and dealing with so many operational challenges as well as training assignments, the Agents also have the chance to gain valuable insight into the inner workings, politically and operationally, of the true Foreign Service overseas Mission. This orientation allows them to begin as an Assistant Regional Security Officer (ARSO), already understanding who does what and how the real work gets accomplished. That is critical knowledge if one hopes to efficiently and effectively succeed in an Embassy environment.

There were so many trips, so many adventures, and so many stories that come from an MSD tour, and mine was 3.5 years, that I will have to be selective and diverse on what I choose to represent in this book. I have picked a few of them.

MSD itself is or was at that time, divided into two separate components. One was the MTT or Mobile Training Team side. The MTT missions provided training to the Embassy Officers and employees, as well as local American business persons on security issues, personal protection issues and self-awareness considerations.

The SST, or Special Security Team, would be deployed when there was a specific identified threat that required a highly trained team to provide augmented protective capability to the Mission that the RSO at post did not have the resources for. This would include but not be limited to High Threat Protection, evacuations, war situations, coups, surveillance detection missions, hostage situation assistance, and many other scenarios.

It was also frequently seen where a Team would do both MTT and SST during the same operational deployment. In truth, being the instructor in a wide range of courses made one a better operational Agent and carrying out the operational missions definitely made one a better teacher.

THE MSD TRAINING PORTFOLIO:

Even though as a budding Agent-in-training we received some of the information that an MTT would teach, there is a significant difference in listening to the words versus delivering the message. We had to become Instructors in each subject we taught and we each taught them all at different times. The course list is too long to discuss each in detail but the training was thorough. A partial list of courses we became certified instructors in included:

- Firearms Instructor
- Surveillance Detection
- Attack Recognition
- Hostage Survival
- Anti-Terrorist Driving Instructor

- Personal Protective Measures
- Rape Awareness
- Pressure Point Control Tactics
- Defensive Tactics

Other courses were solely for our benefit to bring us to an awareness and operational capability level to deal with the dangers we might face such as SERE School (Survival, Evasion, Resistance, and Escape) given by the most elite Army Special Forces element; Tactical Assault and Hostage Rescue, and edged weapons training. Many additional months of training were involved in these courses but one was capably prepared for mostly whatever came up when the battery of courses was finished. Then it was time to put it all to use.

THE NELSON MANDELA U.S. TOUR

As an example of a domestic MSD assignment, when Nelson Mandela was released from his South African Prison, he was brought to the United States on a two-week whirlwind tour to solicit donations for the African National Congress Political machine. The notorious Winnie Mandela came along too as did a few new friends including Harry Belafonte and his wife Julie, to accompany a physically weak and tired Nelson. As he was being released, a threat was made against his life by a South African radical organization and it was thought that the attack might be attempted during his two-week tour in the U.S. Since MSD was the Premier DSS contingent, besides the over 200 Agents who

worked the protective detail, six of us from MSD were selected to be his "close-in" bodyguards, staying with him the entire
two weeks, and performing special protective functions to assure
his safety. I was one of the six selected and for the first time in
our organization's history, we donned dark jumpsuits (SWAT
Uniforms), carried our special weaponry, and were jokingly (and
I hope affectionately although DSS Agents are thick- skinned)
given the nickname of The DSS Ninja Turtles.

This one single protective detail involved 123 cars and twice that
number in Agents and auxiliary personnel. In some venue moves,
the first vehicle would be pulling into the next venue before the
final vehicle left the previous one. This detail was certainly the
most complex we had ever attempted before and there were some
bugs to work out such as in Miami, when all 123 cars were parked
under a stadium, with all Agents deployed throughout and waiting for him to come back from his speech. The Agent responsible
for escorting Nelson from the stage to the cars decided to be extra
careful and took him down a non-designated exit way, leaving all
Agents still up above waiting for him to come out. This Agent
put Mandela in the vehicle and told all the cars to "roll". No one
knows why really to this day. Fortunately, besides all the drivers,
there were two of us (Ninja Turtles) at the vehicles and when we
saw them begin to move, we dove into a car. Then, while entering
the freeway on the way to the next venue, we sent the other 120
cars back to get the Agents, while the other Agent and I stayed
with Nelson to protect him.

Nelson Mandela was greatly loved, and in two separate neighborhoods he wanted to tour through, we had hundreds of thousands
of people swamp our vehicles and bring us to a halt. He could
have been killed just from the overwhelming love they had for

him and the desire to get close to him. We eventually forced our way through and got him to his next appointment. It was a fascinating opportunity to get to meet him and spend time with someone who had achieved legendary status. He was a gentle man who had obviously endured many hard years and needed time to regain his strength. On several occasions, we were confronted with situations of serious health issues from his fatigue from his prison experience complicated by the stressful routine created for him by Winnie Mandela and the ANC.

Chapter Six

MOBILE SECURITY DIVISION – KINSHASA, ZAIRE EVACUATION – 1991

In 1991, The special Presidential Guards of then Zaire President (and harsh Dictator) for life, Mobutu, had requested a pay raise, and after a brief consideration based on his own personal greed, that pay raise was rejected by President Mobutu. The almost immediate ramifications of this decision caused the armed Presidential Guard Forces to march into the Capital City, Kinshasa, and begin to loot, kill, rape, and destroy the city. Kinshasa is a large city with universities, a commercial district skyline, many good restaurants and clubs, Embassies representing many foreign nations, and was bordered on one side by the huge, powerful and fast-moving Congo River and on the other by dense jungle, leading back to their original villages. On the other side of the river, and within distant view was the sister-city of the country then called "Congo", Brazzaville. Escaping from the rampage of the Presidential Forces did not normally include fleeing to Brazzaville because of the size and power of the river and sure death that would follow from drowning or on the rapids, visible from the violent whitewater on the rocks and the large number of smashed boats that remained crushed and splintered on those rocks. There was however, one large ferry that went back and forth from Kinshasa and Brazzaville but that was costly for locals and limited in capacity. Most of the hundreds of thousands of residents of Kinshasa simply fled back into the jungle. That left in the city a few thousand stranded "Expatriates" fearing for their lives and wondering what their course of action would or should be. There remained also a few thousand hard-core indigenous Zarois citizens hoping to reap benefits from what was left behind by others.

As the Officers in charge of the various Embassies began to organize their evacuation plans and to coordinate them with the French Embassy, which had the largest representation in-country due to the prior Colony status and history, the Mobile Security Division activated my team to respond to assist with the evacuation and then to stay behind and protect those remaining official Americans. I was to pick a large team to include various special military elements out of Fort Bragg and Norfolk, Virginia, to assist with specialized functions that would be needed, and to include a combination of the talent we had within MSD, which was substantial. Within 48 hours, we would be walking off that ferry onto the docks in Kinshasa fully equipped to handle whatever came our way.

Since the airport in Kinshasa had been shut down, we flew into Brazzaville and caught the ferry across with all our large plastic equipment cases and personal bags. We arrived to see the French Embassy coordinator reviewing her evacuation list and checking it twice. It was very obvious that there was a high level of stress on her part and so we went to work to quickly alleviate at least the part involving the Americans. This was a massive operation and not many people have prior experience dealing with this type or level of crisis. Everyone was standing and sitting around in the scorching heat and humidity that was beyond full saturation point, all beginning to show signs of frustration and anxiety, not to mention heat exhaustion. Water was being distributed and everyone was encouraged to drink a lot but under this type of oppressive heat complicated by the dehydration that comes through physical and mental stress, everyone was already behind the curve and so we monitored the mob for any potential serious heat fallout victims.

Once all seemed to be progressing well, we moved on to the Embassy and began to set up our operations center and to prepare all the equipment and personal weaponry that we would need to secure the venue and carry out our mission. We also met with the Ambassador - a bright, quick witted and humored, stately woman named Melissa Wells. She was in excellent spirits and obviously experienced and not easily fazed by any crisis or burden. She quickly made us feel welcome and confident that we would be supported in our mission "to protect and to serve" so to speak. We could tell this was going to be an interesting assignment but we had no idea at the time of the wide range and depth of activities that we would be involved in, nor of the unique and unusual threats that existed in the mostly abandoned city.

We later learned that we were fortunate to be working with this Ambassador. Melissa had a strong reputation in the State Department's Foreign Service for being essentially the first female to have accomplished many of the peaks previously held for the male population. She had been the first female to rise to the highest levels and to be awarded certain positions. It was obvious to all of us why. She was a dynamo. She remained as the single primary U.S. Embassy Government official in Zaire, responsible for all political "goings-on" and as the primary link to President Mobutu, who had moved onto his boat and gone up-river to keep from being assassinated by his own troops or other jealous political cronies. One of our primary jobs was to travel everywhere with Melissa and to keep her safe in a very unsafe and currently unknown environment.

The first thing our team would need was a place to stay that we could control. We used Embassy vehicles for our scouting and found an abandoned 13-room hotel nearby the Embassy and "commandeered" the entire facility; rooms, kitchen, lobby, TV room, and all access control points. We arranged with the owner for full-occupancy payment and he was thrilled to be receiving income during a total shut-down and evacuation of his city as well as to have us to protect his facility from any rampaging troops looking to do last minute holiday looting.

Next, other Allied Embassies had brought in their security special elements as well and we sought them out to establish a joint working agreement to unite our resources, manpower, and focus, in order to maximize our effectiveness at maintaining control of the security and well-being of the city of Kinshasa, since no police or host-country military were active or visible and only local neighborhood gangs were demonstrating any proactive behavior, which was lethal and brutal. Unfortunately, this proactive behavior was that they put cars and tires at the entry points to their neighborhoods and kept them burning to maintain a lockdown of anything and anyone still remaining in their segment of the devoid city. They patrolled with AK-47s and were proving themselves to be anxious to spend ammunition just for the fun of it and some individuals had already been killed and wounded. We would have to traverse these routes and would be doing so with great caution. We (being DSS and our special Delta Force and Seal Team 6 elements) first contacted the Brits, who had brought in their special SAS teams and it was easily agreed that more eyes, ears, resources and weapons was definitely the way to go. In addition, their Ambassador's residence was next door to ours (Melissa's) and we had a connecting gate between the two, which meant that from a protective oversight of our Ambassadors at night, we could jointly and more efficiently provide that function. We next moved a few doors down in the Diplomatic Quarter to the German Embassy. They had about a week after us, brought in their elite GS-G9 forces, and their reputation was also Sterling. Again, logically, the German forces saw the advantage and joined our joint task force.

Our resources were mounting and we were now in possession of various types of water craft for a river evacuation if necessary and helicopters that were available across the river should a more rapid departure be required. What we didn't have was a river docking facility or a helicopter landing pad (HLZ). Our own Avon watercraft had been somewhat neglected and needed some work on the engines. With the large team I was leading, we split up functions. I was so thankful for the talent and skills of our military brothers. The "water oriented" elements went to work on rebuilding the engines of the Avons and our "land oriented" talent began to layout what would be needed to create a solid and operational HLZ. Within a short time, we had built a state-of-the-art stairway and docking system down on the river's edge across from the Ambassador's home that still remains today and the HLZ was finalized, giving us capable evacuation options. We all signed our radio "call-signs" in the concrete HLZ pad (mine being Ronin) for historic reference (alright, it just seemed like the thing guys need to do) and we were in business. Many years later, someone who served there would show me pictures of that post that included shots of these two projects still intact. While these teams were working, others were performing relevant city-wide patrols, watching for signs of a resurgence of people and trouble. A couple of weeks later, we found that the Canadians had also brought in their Royal Canadian Mounted Police, who had additional water assets and we brought them into our team and evacuation and extraction plan.

I continued to go with the Ambassador whenever she had to go out to discuss politics or future restoration with those few remaining host-government officials. The Ambassador always tried to keep us guessing and had a wonderful sense of humor. She knew we prided ourselves on our careful watch of her every move and also that we put 100% effort into our role as her protectors. One day Melissa tried sneaking past us to the front door just to give us a diversion and as I look back, as a way of establishing a more personal bond and sense of unity and camaraderie with us. It was her way of entertaining us and showing us she considered herself as part of our security family. We all still look back on her occasional antics and feel that nostalgic twinge of close friendship. Melissa had also been given a Narwhale spike from some country previously and one day she put on one of our tactical vests, a tactical ball cap, grabbed her Narwhale Spike and snuck down to our control center by the front door and leapt into the room like she was attacking. After the initial shock and adrenaline, we all laughed until tears came. I still have a photo of her in that outfit and I treasure it. I became very close to Melissa and 12 years later, when I became the Senior Regional Security Officer for Spain, I found her retired and living on one of the Canary Islands. She and I would get together occasionally for dinner and Spanish wine and we would talk and laugh about that time. We still email after all these years. I learned a lot about leadership and character from Melissa and have tried to incorporate what I saw and what she taught me into my own management style.

We, in the general DSS Agent context of "we", always try to do good. That is the basic tenet we follow. We have certain specific responsibilities during an assignment but we naturally expand those as the situation evolves and there was a lot of evolving on this mission. Sometimes those judgment calls reach outside the normal or "known" call-of-duty parameters and play at our heart-strings. Certain things just cannot be permitted and we know them when we see them. One typically hot and sweaty day while on city patrol, we passed by a man near the almost abandoned outdoor ivory market area perched on the side of the street. He had a small cage and as we drove by, what caught our attention was what we thought was a baby Ape inside the cage. It hit each of us the same about a block later. We pulled the car over and looked at each other and without a word being spoken, knew what we needed to do. We turned around and drove back to where the man was squatting. We got out and were immediately horrified to see two large mother gorilla hands on the ground being sold for whatever someone would want them for. We had heard of them being used as ash trays but here was the truth staring us in our faces. In the cage was the tiniest baby gorilla I had ever seen in any pictures. We could only assume the mother was killed for her meat and hands and this sickly tiny infant was on sale as entertainment. This was just not right. The baby's nose was running, it had glassy eyes and it did not look well. We gave the man a few notes of currency less than he demanded but we were armed and unhappy at what we saw, and we took the baby gorilla. We knew that when Jane Goodall had been evacuated with her pygmy chimpanzees, she had left a young lady back at her animal care center to watch over the remaining animals and we went to see her. We took this precious baby gorilla, which was hugging one of the guys neck for dear life as a human baby would, but with more strength, into the office and asked her if she could help save this baby. She was overworked, understaffed, and a bit stressed but agreed, stating she would call us in a few weeks after she had stabilized the gorilla's health. We then went on about our business feeling we had made contact with something extremely special in our lives and feeling like we did something positive. Surprise! Several weeks later, the health administrator called us and told us we could pick up our baby gorilla – that it was in good health and in need of constant care she couldn't provide. We were torn between fear of responsibility for something so fragile and unknown and precious, and our desire to have further contact with this unique being. We rushed out the door and picked up our hairy little child, which we named BA, for Bad Attitude, which was also anything but the truth. He was the sweetest and most loving little creature we had ever encountered. We now had another resident at our hotel command center. BA rode with us on patrol for about a month, hugging our necks and making us fall in love with him. Can you imagine, all these war and action-hardened people who carried around a baby gorilla attached to their necks and would have fought to protect him. Our paternal instincts were screaming out.

It was a hard thing to do, but eventually we realized we could not keep him and looked across the river to Brazzaville to a special humane gorilla park we had heard rumors of. We made contact and then faced the problem of getting him across the river from one country into another, without going through bureaucratic nonsense that would have ended in the death or sale of BA. Well, again here comes that occasional need to make a decision based on what is ethically right even if the technical legal part comes into question, another decision that comes once in a lifetime (sometimes more apparently with our type of work) with no pre-planned preparation or guidance. The need to save BA and get him into caring hands that would ensure his long and peaceful life. We put BA into a large orange Diplomatic Courier bag and two team members stepped onto the ferry with "the BA Bag". We kept away from everyone and appeared hostile to keep them away from us with the top of the bag slightly open to give BA breathing room. We stepped off in Brazzaville, gave BA to the Gorilla Park folks and returned to our side of the river. Much later, I saw a National Geographic special on this Gorilla Park and they referenced how this baby gorilla had been saved and brought to them by a bunch of caring guys who confiscated him from bad people in Zaire. Perhaps not according to policy or procedure but a proper thing for us to do. One I will never regret.

Because of our first success on animal rescue, we were not so shocked at our next. The British Ambassador had decided he had endured enough and was leaving but would leave behind his (and our) SAS Team to maintain control of the Brit resources and Ambassador residence. He had two dogs. One was a feisty Doberman and the other, a lethargic but large lovable Bassett Hound named Fred. One day while on protective detail with my Ambassador, coming back from a meeting with President Mobutu, I received a radio call from my associated SAS Team Leader, who advised me that the Ambassador was leaving and could not take the dogs. Not wanting to leave the dogs to be killed and eaten by local inhabitants, he asked the SAS to "put the dogs down." The Doberman had been killed already when they called but he asked if we would want to take Fred. I advised the Ambassador in the back seat and she enthusiastically said to save

Fred. We drove to the British Ambassador's residence (next door and connected to the American Ambassador's residence) and took possession of this huge happy Bassett. We kept Fred roaming the grounds for awhile but worked on finding him an American family on the Brazzaville side who might want a great family mascot. After locating a family, even though Fred was substantially larger and more awkward than BA, we applied the same successful courier bag methodology to our delivery and gave him to the nice family and returned back across the river.

I have talked about crossing the river but without really conveying the serious danger of traveling in a ferry across that powerful current. When standing at the ferry dock (such as it was), one could see large uprooted trees and boats that had lost their engines and their passengers while in a panic to get the engines restarted, racing for the rapids out of control. Looking right from the dock is the terrifying whitewater rapids with all the destruction smashed across the large rock formations. The story was that never had a single boat or person survived the rapids. With that as background, what we also saw everyday at the ferry dock was astonishing, horrifying, and is an image that has never gone away. Citizens of Zaire, with no hope of jobs or a future of any kind wanted to get to Brazzaville, where of course, anyone would think that it must be better than what they were leaving. That is very seldom true with the exception of those immigrants who make it to the United States or other western nations, but nonetheless, they felt it was literally worth risking their lives to try. The individuals could seldom afford the ferry fee. The ferry however was tied by large manila lines to the dock and there were railings that might be grabbed as the ferry pulled away if the individual could leap 12 or 14 feet quickly and upward. What was witnessed on a regular basis though was that people could not hold onto the ropes or missed the railings and not being able to fight the force, would make it into the first part of the current and be swept off and down to be killed in the rapids. I witnessed a few very athletic young boys make the jump to the rail, which was athletically amazing, but I witnessed most miss the rail and fail to get anything but a quick and final trip to the rapids. A dozen would try at each crossing and to again visualize that brings back the same helpless sadness I felt then.

As we considered all options for the possible necessary covert evacuation of the remaining people at the Embassy and within our allied joint task group's Embassies, it was necessary to make periodic unauthorized and risky "test the water" river trips to evaluate the host-country's, (or at this time, "the enemy's") capabilities. We did this at night and with night vision goggles in the hopes that we would see them and they would not notice us with their large caliber machine guns mounted on their boats. There were a few close calls but we managed to avoid being captured or being faced with a firefight on the river in our little Avon escape boats. The talented Navy Seals had repaired the boat's engines and made everything operational and escape-ready. The Delta Force elements had evaluated the best overland-to-river escape routes and the other DIA military faction was monitoring everything to keep us current on the situational awareness. We felt we were prepared if it became necessary, and it might have at the drop of a hat. The potential for spontaneous volatility was always a factor. I carried a weapon for quiet operations in case we ran into threatening objections while trying to quietly escape with our American citizens.

One day while on patrol near the closed and abandoned university, two student-aged youth stepped out and hailed us. We cautiously encountered them to see what they wanted. They told us a story about disappearing students in the area. Their associates went out walking and simply never returned. Our first thought was nefarious government actions or insurgent activity. They felt quite strongly it was something more superstitious and historically prevalent in nature. Cannibals. Although up to that point in my life and career, Cannibals had never been something I had been trained or prepared for as a state-of-the-art modern Special Agent, this was Zaire and I certainly had seen some unusual things since my arrival. So, we began patrolling the areas around the university with more scrutiny and probed into the deep woods that surrounded it. On the third day, we entered some dark and dense woods not more than 100 yards off a normally trafficked street and found several men eating what could only and clearly be human parts. There were also human remains scattered around the camp site. We took them to the only local authorities around and there weren't many. As it turned out, due to the looting and destruction in the city, there was no food and these three men had no compunction about subsidizing their caloric intake by yanking young people off the sidewalk and taking them to their camp where they killed, cooked and ate them. As was becoming the rule rather than the exception, we, as developing DS Agents were encountering experiences that we had never even thought about and that were giving us a chance to use that flexible brain matter and add to the experience base.

As we were finishing our months in Zaire, President Mobutu had pretty much isolated and cast off almost every foreign-friend government he had with the exception of the United States, being Ambassador Melissa Wells. His dictatorial ways and bizarre unpredictable harsh behavior to include literally serving those he decided were his enemies to his friends at dinner parties as the main entrée, had caused everyone to abandon their hopes that he might agree to a more moderate and peaceful way. Finally, the U.S. had reached a point of no return and Melissa was directed to deliver a Demarche to Mobutu that mandated he either change his ways or he would find himself also without the friendship of America. President Mobutu was known to be quite a Xenophobe and that meant a delivery like that could be quite precarious to the messenger or messengers.

Melissa advised me that she and I were going to be picked up by one of Mobutu's helicopters, piloted by foreign contractors, and delivered onto the stern of his boat, which was currently far up the Congo River so that no enemies could get to him. His wife had a large farm up the river where their tribe held strength and when things got touchy, he would simply pack up his presidential boat and sail up to anchor off where he thought they could be safe while his thugs remedied the existing threat. The helo ride up the river was terrific and to see the true deep double and triple canopy jungle was fascinating. We flew over herds of animals and I was able to get a glimpse of raw Africa. On the way up, Melissa spoke to me almost apologetically and told me that the purpose of the trip was to deliver the Demarche. Up to this point, I thought it was just another political meeting like all the others that I tried to stay out of and just do my protective duty. She explained to me how Mobutu was Xenophobic (and what that meant) and how we were in his mind, the last bond of any friendship. Melissa's voiced concern was that apparently, as his only remaining link, if we told him "agree or lose us", he might react like he did frequently, with extreme violence. There was a concern that we actually might be kidnapped or that he might kill the messengers of this edict. That put my level of protective awareness on quite a different focus level, and in my mind, I began to make final contingency plans if things did go horribly wrong and he decided to take action against us.

We landed the helicopter on the stern of the classy old and large ship on this huge river as the ship was still steaming up the river, and I was taken to a waiting salon while the Ambassador was taken to Mobutu's meeting room. The salon was everything one might imagine when picturing a floating brothel, though appropriate in its own way. The room was done in dark wood paneling and red velvet with the center piece on the wall facing the seating area, being a picture of Mobutu in his personal signature hat of leopard skin. While waiting, for entertainment purposes I suppose, on three occasions, machine gun-armed Presidential Guards came into my room and put on their "war faces" and had stare-down sessions with me. They never said a word. It was just five minutes of facially-projected anger testing to see if I would look away or cower I suppose. Remember those staring contests as a kid? I always did very well and they were out of their league with me. I put on a big smile, locked on my 1000-mile kid stare and never blinked. It reminded me of the "right of passage" event but in a mild and only visually threatening way. I have to admit that with the third guy, I was getting tired of staring and almost folded. My smile wasn't as genuine either. After about 45 minutes and enough time to imagine many scenarios of troops storming into the room in different ways to take me to be shot and tossed over the side, the door opened, Melissa poked her head in, and we were off to return on the same helicopter back to Kinshasa.

The sun was setting as we started and we knew we wouldn't make back until it was totally pitch black, as it only can be in areas of no villages or public utilities. We relied on the pilots to know what they were doing. They did. They knew well enough that half-way back to Kinshasa, the Pilot made an unnerving exclamation that caught our attention. We looked through the opening and the pilot told us something no one should ever have to hear flying over the jungle in total blackout. "Where was all the fuel he had put into the helicopter?" The pilot advised us that we were essentially out of fuel and that he had personally been aware that there was enough prior to the flight. Unfortunately, after fueling, he had apparently gone off to do other things and someone must have had other plans for us. It seemed obvious that Melissa's thought that Mobutu seemed to have taken the news better than she had expected might have been a bit optimistic. Someone drained our fuel. Enough so that we would run out somewhere on the way back in the middle of country no one would ever get to or would never find us even if we were able to set the helicopter down in a rare cleared space. This was true, dense, triple canopy, dangerous jungle and it was nighttime. I had a handgun and 40 rounds. Not the best of odds.

As the pilot was conducting whatever machinations pilots under stress do, we were becoming more focused on trying to see anything outside the windows. On occasion, we could make out a white cap on the Congo River where it made contact with large boulders but otherwise, we prayed we would see the lights of Kinshasa before we became a brief white cap. The pilot knew the direction to fly, he just didn't think the fuel would make it to the landing zone, any landing zone. The next bit of happy news came when the pilot advised us that we should have been able to see the lights of Kinshasa by now and that apparently the electricity was out. Nice planning Mobutu – very thorough. This Pilot was excellent and determined to find a way to survive although he advised us we were essentially on fumes according to the gauge. Following the river, he knew he could spot the huge and deadly rapids near the city's edge and hopefully from there guess at the spot the HLZ was supposed to be. There were two problems; one, we were on fumes and two, surrounding the now invisible HLZ, there were huge tall trees. Hearing undesirable sporadic engine noises, we were hovering near where the pilot thought the HLZ must be. Down below in the pitch black, I spotted a tiny moving light and I pointed it out to the pilot who agreed we needed to take the only chance we had. He began to set down where the light was moving back and forth. Just as we touched down, the engine quit and we hit a bit hard. It was a jolt but we were actually on the HLZ. Off to the side was a man with a small laser light flashlight. One of my Team's Navy Seals had become worried that we were out late into the evening and when the city lights went out, he made his way to the HLZ and waited until he heard the engine and then began his signaling. He literally saved our lives with a single pocket-size laserlite flashlight. I will always remember and be thankful for that man who saved our lives and once again proved that I am one of the luckiest people on earth. Melissa got out, took a breath, and it was business as usual. She was terrific and a real role model for leadership.

Chapter Seven
MOBIL SECURITY DIVISION – PAKISTAN – 1991

Around the 1990 to 1993 period there were other trips, which kept me out of the U.S. more than 10 months of each year. There were many trips to exotic locations doing unique missions that would craft and design me as an Agent to deal with what would come my way in the future, including my first trips to Bogota, Colombia, Caracas, Venezuela, Rio de Janeiro, Sao Paulo, and Brasilia, Brazil, back to Brazzaville, Congo, Cairo, Egypt, Nouakchott, Mauritania, twice to Nairobi, Kenya, Amman, Jordan, Damascus, Syria, Riyadh, Saudi Arabia, Addis Ababa, Ethiopia, and even another trip back into Kinshasa, but this next chapter will discuss my first two-month mission into Pakistan, which included Islamabad, Peshawar, and my favorite city, Karachi. These trips each had their own adventures, romances, close calls and strong memories, but every trip has just too much information to cover it all.

This Pakistan trip was to be a mixed mission. We would be conducting training at each post, which fell under the MMT, or Mobil Training Team heading, but we would also be involved in

SST or Security Support Team activities, which meant active operations at some locations due to threats or concerns for the safety and security of personnel and or the Embassy and Consulates.

The first city we began in was the capital, Islamabad. At that time, Islamabad was a sleepy, calm, but glorious and beautifully constructed city designed to be just for the Government of Pakistan officials and the conducting of government business. The citizens lived in the old run-down sister-city called Rawalpindi (10 kilometers away) and had to drive over each day to work. The same architect who designed the government city-enclave in Brasilia, Brazil, designed Islamabad and there were strong similarities like the excessively wide open boulevards where almost no traffic was running. It was terrific. Moving around was easy and you could see a potential attacker a mile away. The Diplomatic Enclave within the city where many of the Embassies were located was right off the main boulevard, Constitution Avenue, and had what was then considered excellent security and "set-back". To go from the police-controlled entrances to the American Embassy at the back of the enclave was a mile and involved going through several police and guard checkpoints before reaching the virtually impenetrable fortress that was the Embassy. This Embassy had been built to withstand attacks out of paranoia from a past incident. In 1979, thousands of students acting on a rumor that the U.S. had bombed Mecca, marched on the Embassy and burned it down, killing two Americans. So, stronger, better, more robust security was the standard operating procedure with this facility and all other new Embassies under the Senator Bobby Inman guidelines. It is an excellent example of the way the new Embassies have been put together. More recently of course with the Global War on Terrorism, even more security has been built-in such as at our new Embassies in Kabul and Baghdad. It's an evolution and new harsher times call for stricter security.

Our concern in Islamabad was that a military officer assigned to the Embassy had recognized surveillance being done on him and some indications had been picked up that there might be a threat against his life. Obviously he needed to be watched and protected going to and from work and while at home. But, during the day, while he worked in the secure compound, we would use the time to conduct training for everyone to improve their security skills and level of awareness and response capabilities. For about 2 weeks we conducted a series of training courses from Surveillance Awareness to Attack Recognition; from Hostage Survival to Personal Protective Measures. We even taught a two-day self defense course and another on Rape Awareness. The self defense course was heavily designed to assist small women to defend themselves against a large aggressive man and involved a technique called Pressure Point Control Tactics, which work on the nerve motor control centers. Simply put, the bigger the muscles, the more nerve network growth in the muscles. The more nerve networks, the more sensitive to a pressure strike to those areas, temporarily collapsing the electronic signals to the body from the brain causing a temporary lapse of consciousness and a big man drops like a bag of rocks. We occasionally had complaints the second day of the course from husbands whose wives decided to try it out on their TV-engaged husbands who almost always missed a couple of minutes of their ball game while their systems came back on-line. No matter how many warnings you give people, they just have to try it out on their unsuspecting and possibly neglecting husbands.

In order to effectively carry out our primary mission we needed a cover. Training provided that. But we needed to allow the Pakistani intelligence to conduct their surveillance of us. They wanted to know what we were doing. We had been conducting operations for about a week and one day decided we would go back to the hotel early afternoon to make our appearance a little earlier. As we came down the hall toward my room, I noticed my door was ajar. We prepared for what we might find and burst through the door. Working at the main electronic console between the two beds were two Pakistani intelligence men. The console was pulled away from the wall and they were checking on some wiring and a device that could only be an audio monitoring system. The look on their faces told the entire story and we couldn't help but laugh as we walked out shaking our heads. For the week I had been in the room, there had been no night conversation, deep breathing, mumbling, or anything else and they were under the impression that the monitoring system was broken. These were the repair men. We felt sorry for them being caught red-handed but we never made a point of it. From that point on though, briefings to incoming American Embassy visitors included the caution about things said or done in the rooms.

Looking like the epitome of a gringo, it was hard to conduct covert surveillance detection in a city of dark, shalwar camise-wearing Pakistanis. We learned a lot on this mission. One thing was that we simply couldn't work outside among the people. We had to be mobil, or fixed inside a facility unobserved. As we sat in our vehicles, monitoring suspicious individuals from what we thought were discreet hidden parking places, curious Pakistanis would walk up to the car window and rest their heads against the window and stare at us in wonder at the foreignness of us I suppose. No matter where we went, it was like a George Romero movie with Pakistanis shuffling after us and mashing their fore-heads against the windows and just staring like the living dead.

We were forced to reconsider our entire modus operandi. We did succeed though and unfortunately that meant that the Officer had to leave the country for his own safety.

A DS Agent who was the junior Assistant Regional Security Officer (ARSO) in Islamabad invited us to his house for dinner and cordially and out of hunger we accepted. We arrived at his relatively palatial residence and discussed the carpets he had purchased and how his tour was going. He served us the food and we went back to our secluded home. During the night all four of us came down with horrible food poisoning and felt like we were going to die. Within 24 hours, three of us were recovering; very dehydrated and weak, but recovering. The fourth never recovered the balance of the trip and after a week, we were forced to get him out of bed and put him on a plane home. When we were able, we spoke to the ARSO and he confessed that he had purchased the food from a street vendor because it was cheaper and brought it home and served it to us. One less person on my Christmas list.

One of the most death-defying acts I have ever been involved in is not one of the four wars I have been in, not one of the 6 evacuations I have participated in, not one of the several government-overthrowing coups I have been through - it was the drive from Islamabad to Peshawar on the Grand Trunk Road. Within the few hours it took to go from Islamabad to Peshawar and/or back, my team faced what seemed like absolute and certain death numerous times and witnessed horrendous traffic deaths each time we traversed the suicide run. It was insanity. A new highway has been finished now but in the early 90s, this was known as the most dangerous road in the world.

We had finished our mission and our training in Islamabad and needed to drive to Peshawar to conduct similar training for the Consulate located there. We had made reservations to stay in the "colorful" and somewhat famous American Club in their few and tiny "guest rooms". The only problem was actually getting there. One could fly but it was on a small prop plane and everyone highly recommended that no one's lives should ever be considered so expendable that the flight should be given serious consideration. When driving was suggested, the response was just head shaking and mumbling. It seemed that getting to Peshawar was actually one of those "you just can't get there from here" types of options. Well, we knew people lived there and traveled there everyday and hey, we were professional anti-terrorist driving instructors. We taught the courses that kept people alive. Surely we could muster enough talent to go three hours to a Pakistani wild-west town. I would drive and my buddy would take the front passenger "death seat". I had no idea what we were in for.

The road was two lanes; one each direction, with down-sloping dirt shoulders that were unsafe to pull over on. Maniacal drivers who either had death wishes or simply did not know how to drive would attempt to pass someone on a shoulder and end up sliding or tumbling down the dirt shoulder to rest upside down against a tree. We witnessed this several times on a single run and never understood how others could keep trying it, witnessing the disaster of the other driver – but they did. Cars would also pass in the on-coming lane and many times ours or other cars and large trucks were coming head-on. If they could squeeze in they would try. If they didn't make it, they would be seen spinning off down the shoulder again to most likely disaster. The four of us in the car were so amazed and terrified at what seemed like a total lack of regard for their or other's lives (like ours), that we decided we needed to film our on-coming deaths. My friend held his camera on the dashboard and when cars or those brightly painted and decorated trucks would be coming directly at us in our lane with no hope of anyone's survival, he would begin clicking shots so someone would see what happened to us. It was a game of chicken but if we chickened, it meant the dirt shoulder and possibly the same result. It was a lose-lose situation and anyone who drove the Grand Trunk Road in those days knows exactly what I am talking about. The near-death incident that sticks out in my mind most clearly was when we looked ahead and saw three buses across the two lanes all coming directly at us, fighting for dominance and position with each other, staying shoulder to shoulder, half of each of the two outside buses running the shoulder and trying to stay on track, with the third bus running right down the center of the two lanes. We had no idea what escape option would work and knew for a certainty that this was our final moment. Our designated photographer began clicking our final death shots and we all began attempting humorous comments as our final expressions of false-courage. As the buses reached about 70 yards from our imminent collision, like an orchestrated ballet, the two outside buses veered off the road, both going to their outsides and literally left the ground and took flight off the shoulders. We witnessed the buses flying left and right and crashing on the ground at the bottom of the shoulder embankments while the bus in the middle moved into his lane and zoomed past us. It appeared to us that the bus in the middle exerted his brutal dominance and nudged the two buses, which then lost their final grip and took flight. Later we learned that some of the passengers had died. This happened everyday on the old Grand Trunk Road. We ended up making a total of four trips and it changed us forever.

Peshawar was certainly entertaining. Today it is considered one of the most dangerous places one should avoid going to. The training went well but while there, extra-curricular events took the most interesting award. Previously, an American Officer was playing on the one tennis court at the American Club and as he threw the ball up to begin a serve, a bullet obviously fired as a celebratory round, came down and creased his forehead, burying itself into the ground. He was OK but needed some medical treatment and some calm reassurance. That tennis court is now gone.

We ventured into precarious areas inside and outside of the city of Peshawar, which are all off-limits in today's world and to be honest, were sort of off-limits then as well. We wanted to see the real heart of Peshawar. We parked and then began walking around the seventh century market areas. We found ourselves in an area that traded in ancient coins, I suppose lost on the old Silk Road or around those regions. We began our evaluation and bargaining for coins that caught our eye, some as old as the Roman era. Some coins, with hand stamped primitive designs, were even older. We could tell we were in a more fundamentalist area and were keeping a close eye out for anyone or any group who began to venture too close to our group or who maintained an evil eye on us.

The environment seemed to close in and groups of long-bearded, head-turbaned men were beginning to send dagger looks at us, we realized our time was over and we needed to get out. As we closed our payments, we heard female voices speaking English. It hardly seemed likely since first, women weren't permitted in this men's market, and second, western women would have to be simple-minded or suicidal to come here. We turned and were faced with two blond-headed females without head cover, wearing short pants. This would seem to signal they fit both categories; they must be simple-minded and suicidal. They were trying to discuss coins with some men who were yelling at them and probably telling them to get away before their shops were cursed and burned. We took a quick 360 review of the street and saw an angry crowd of men coming down the street. It appeared the local Religious Police were about to sentence two western females to gang rape and stoning to death for their crime. We ran to the girls, grabbed them by the arms and told them if they hoped to live, they needed to run with us. We drew our handguns to signal to the crowd that their threat would cause consequences, and we ran for our parked car a block away up a crowded market street hill. The crowd of 40 or 50 men were running behind us but either only for angry show or not as quickly as we due to their running in sandals, (or because of the weapons) because they maintained the same distance between us. Nonetheless, they would be on us as we got into the vehicle and tried to flee from the area. We made it to the van we were driving and a stare down with weapons slowed them for a moment while I started the van and everyone jumped in and we drove out of the downtown and back to the relative safety of the American Club.

It turned out the two twenty-something girls were Canadian and were backpacking through the region. They had simply wanted to see classic historic downtown Peshawar. We were shocked and amazed they were still alive after the week they had been on the road. Today, they wouldn't last 2 hours alone. They hadn't had a hot shower for the week of travel so we let them use ours, and when they came out we bought them dinner for the cost of a stern lecture and an educational speech on local cultural prohibitions and on the foolishness of their actions. We convinced them that they would not live out the next couple of days in the Northwest Frontier Province and that if they ever wanted to see Canada again, they needed to get out of Pakistan. Fortunately, they listened. Perhaps being chased by an angry mob throwing rocks to stone them provided some basis for an understanding. We took them to the Peshawar airport the next morning and they flew to India where their backpacking would be acceptable, and though crime would be a serious concern, at least they would probably survive. I still have the coins I bought that day stored in a case I hardly ever see as I move from country to country on my assignments.

Some days after the Canadian incident, after we completed our training courses, we drove to the outer barrier of Pakistani-controlled Peshawar, which was clearly labeled "The Tribal Zone". Here, the road had a large sign posted overhead that stated, "You are entering the Tribal Zone. Pakistani law does not prevail here. Do not enter". This began the area controlled by the Tribal Afghan refugees who fled from the Russian invasion of Afghanistan and their law was Sharia (ancient traditional Koran – no rights for women, eye for an eye-type). They made their own rules and the Pakistanis left them alone since they were mostly life-long genetically programmed warrior tribes who had never lost a war in their history. Our luck was holding pretty well, we were armed, and we wanted to see the weapons shops a couple of kilometers into the Tribal Lands where they crafted their own and sold Russian – Afghan war memorabilia. I drove under the sign and symbolically, over a large speed bump that signaled a true division line. Over a week, we actually made several trips in to see the shops and witness the weapons creativity but this trip was significant.

We pulled into the dirt field where a row of rickety hand-made huts had been constructed to house the guns and their Afghan-keepers. They had 12-gauge shotgun pistols that must have really shook one up to fire them and old Enfield Rifles. They of course had AK-47s, some Chinese made and some crafted by the

Afghans themselves. Looking into the barrels of the Afghan weapons, we could see that they had not yet evolved the skill level of cutting rifling into the barrel to spin the round as it came out to maintain any rotation accuracy for any reasonable range of fire. They had pen guns and lighter guns and a variety of items that didn't even look like guns. The selection was diverse, wild, creative and mostly crap, but always interesting.

At one shop, I looked into the very dusty shelves and spotted what looked like a big round gouda cheese wheel of about 12 inches across and maybe 10 pounds. I asked the man what it was and he told me Hashish. I asked what something like that would cost and he said $5 dollars US. I stared stunned, knowing that this could not bode well for the fight against drug use and distribution. I looked at another wheel that was about half the size and asked him what that was. The reply was Opium. The cost was $10 US. This was not good news.

We moved onto another shop (the outdoor shops being only about 12 feet by 10 feet) and found the man sitting on the dirt floor in the center of his shop working on an AK-47. He had the barrel end braced on his thigh and was working on the trigger housing. As we watched him work, a shot rang out from his weapon and the young man fell backwards with a hole in his leg and blood pouring out. I will never forget the young man of perhaps 25, raising his head and looking up at us and saying in English, "dangerous job", and falling back again. His fellow gun makers were running over to lend assistance and it became immediately obvious that we needed to move back across the tribal border. We verified he was getting actual treatment and then made our way to the car and quickly drove the distance back to Pakistani-controlled Peshawar. As we crossed, we were met by a jeep of

Frontier Constabulary (FC) who knew we were in town and had been told to keep us safe but had lost us. They extolled the virtues of staying on this side of the invisible border and we thanked them for their oversight and guidance. We worked closely with the FC and I have great respect for their strength and toughness. Few will take on the FC in a fair firefight. I guess they are sort of the "Gurkhas of Pakistan".

Our last properly relatable incident in Peshawar had to do with the Pearl Continental Hotel. This was the only actual real hotel in town and one was met with a sign upon entering that stated, "Gunmen must check in their weapons at the counter". No one ever checked in their weapons. That year, my Christmas card to friends and family was me standing armed next to that sign. A classic. Well, remember that Peshawar has always been a more fundamentalist environment. One day, as a local tribal politician was passing through the hotel down a hallway to a conference room, he passed by a glass door that had a brief view to the out-side wall-enclosed pool and he saw a British woman lying at the pool in a revealing swim suit. He continued to his meeting but the significance of a woman revealing herself "in public" meant something different to him than it does to the rest of the world where individuals have rights and tribal leaders don't get to make up their rules at will. As he exited the meeting and walked back down the hallway, he turned through the glass door to the pool and walked up to the British woman. The only report we have heard is from another individual who was at the pool, but the tale is that he told the British woman he would have sex with her. She replied in a firm tone something to the affect that he might not have been born legitimately to an actual human female and he drew his pistol and shot her dead in the lounge chair. An official complaint was filed but as the courts and police reviewed it, it was decided that the woman had caused it by being in a provocative swim suit and no charges were filed against the tribal leader. It created quite a controversy for the westerners for awhile but the locals all seemed to accept it as a valid judgment. I understand that a barrier was later built to block the hallway view to the pool.

Our final destination in Pakistan was Karachi, a city that would years later become one of my favorite and most experience-filled assignments. This time, it was a training mission only. Karachi was then a city of 19 million inhabitants, at least. It is the 9th largest city in the world and most people don't know that. For westerners, 95 percent of the city is off-limits due to the Al-Qaeda and Taliban influence, though at the time of this trip, those groups were not formed yet as we know them today.

Karachi is manic. The traffic is as insane as any place on earth with no enforced rules including driving within lanes, passing on the sidewalks and cutting in at the head of the line at the stoplight. In the U.S., this violation of protocol would probably initiate an event of road rage leading to someone's serious injury or death. In Karachi, it leads to others then cutting in front of him until the entire intersection is blocked and no one can go anywhere in any direction until a tired, poorly paid, and minimally motivated police officer feels the need to saunter over and begin to fix what will become an hour or two of pure tragedy and lots of noise.

We needed to do Consulate General motorpool driver training and that created some intriguing challenges. Where could anyone find an open place to drive without interference to practice some new skills. The owner and Chairman of the guard company was a well-educated and reasonably powerful man of influence in Pakistan who can be frequently seen on Pakistan television or

CNN offering advice and guidance on politics and terrorism. I consider him to be my friend, and he remains a loyal friend to the principles of the United States, but even moreso to the U.S. Marine Security Guards (MSGs) who provide internal Embassy and Consulate security controls. He has a sweet spot in his heart for them ever since as a young Pakistani soldier working some operations in at that time enemy India country, he was being pursued by the Indian Intelligence who most certainly would have changed his life forever. He made it to the gates of the American Embassy and begged to be allowed in for his life's safety. The MSGs showed understanding and sympathy and allowed him to wait inside the gate and his life was probably saved. He has never forgotten that and looks after the MSGs who come and go in Karachi as if they were his own sons.

The point here is that in order to get something done, he was the man. I asked him if there was any place we could do "controlled reckless driving training", and he told us he had just the spot. He owned a large restaurant on the beach at the far end of a well-to-do area of Karachi and the road in front of it was four lanes wide. I wasn't sure how we could gain control of the road for four hours but he assured me it could be done. He was right. He used his influence and simply shut down the road and no one but us got to access it. As the old expression goes, "its good to be king".

In these days, Karachi was volatile and active, and probably sub-rosa there was a radical movement that we were unaware of as a nation. But, we self-drove around the inner city, something that would never be considered today unless you were suicidal. This was also my first real introduction to the beautiful and creative hand-knotted rugs of Afghanistan and I picked up a few and took them back to the U.S. with me. It was the beginning of an obsession and a hobby collecting carpets and Kilims, principally from Afghanistan and Iran, and primarily with tribal patterns rather than the floral patterns.

The full sensory blast of exotic culture and fully-engaged adventure and electricity one could feel in Karachi (and a few other places) left a permanent insatiable need within my system that has remained with me throughout my career and to a large degree dictated the countries I chose to serve in and the things I sought to experience. Perhaps this need was always in me, but that adventure gene was triggered or amplified through the experiences like Karachi, offered to me by the Diplomatic Security Service and I frequently thank my lucky stars.

Chapter Eight

MOBIL SECURITY DIVISION – ADVENTURES FOR ANOTHER TIME

Before I get on to my next selected story, I wanted to briefly mention a few interesting and exciting trips that further developed my learning curve and my exposure to understanding world cultural differences through the Mobil Security Division (MSD) tour.

MSD - Nouakchott, Mauritania – Most people have never even heard of the country of Mauritania, located on the west coast of Africa, and the Capital, named Nouakchott, sounding like a name only Dr. Seuss could invent to have something to rhyme with. But it is a real place and has perhaps the largest and most expansive beaches in the world. In this case, for all you beach lovers now considering heading to Nouakchott for you next seaside vacation, the beach not only runs for miles before you get to the water, but it also runs through your house, your food, and your electronic equipment at will. Nothing can stop those moving sands. Pretty much everything you take there will be left there. It will be ruined. It is also Muslim and has developed dangerous radical cells. My team went there to do Embassy-wide training;

for the guards, the drivers, and the American officers who needed their security awareness raised. The RSO there was enduring it well although all his belongings including his prized stereo were now soon to be abandoned, sand-infested desert junk.

The guards were men struggling to earn enough to feed their families one day to the next and they had suffered through hard lives – some with previous careers in the military, others just hungry motivated local boys. Sometimes in a country like Mauritania, the guard company options are severely limited by the number of companies the political leadership will allow to exist. There could be only one, which might coincidentally be owned by the President's brother. This guard group at the Embassy was the best in the country, mostly because our RSOs trained and made them that way. The cadre ranged from about 20 to 70 years old. Unfortunately, during one classroom session of training, the 70 year old died of natural causes. In a country as harsh as this one, he most likely was one of the oldest persons in the country. We held a service for him and then continued on with training after a half-day of reflection.

Mauritania is made up of many different tribal dialects. Those we were training represented at least seven of those dialects. Just to make one simple brief statement during training, seven translators had to convert it to their language and voice it to their people. In some cases, the translators didn't speak English so they had to wait for another translation and then convert it to their dialect. Worse, most of the translators all tried to speak at once. I would say one sentence and then, it was like the first day after the disaster at the Tower of Babel; everyone would start speaking trying to be louder than the guy next to him and it was complete gibberish throughout. That took us awhile to create a system they would accept with tribal status, deference's and jealousies. After my 4 second statement, chaos ruled for the next five minutes. The training was exhausting.

Sanitation was limited to say the least. When the training was over and the 150 guards had completed the courses, we had certificates to give to them. The guards were so touched that anyone would come to their country and try to help them, they all wanted to shake every team member's hand as we awarded them the certificates. We all remember looking at each other and after seeing what they did, and did not do with their hands from a hygienic perspective, we were a little nervous but true to proper form, we shook every hand and at the end, it felt like our hands no longer belonged to us but rather like sweaty, grimy, overly heavy objects that should be turned over for medical study at a clinic. The most significant point all joking aside, it was a very moving moment to see that they were so affected and felt so appreciative of being shown some personal attention.

MSD - Addis Ababa, Ethiopia – At the time I was called to hurredly prepare for a mission to Addis, the country had been in civil war for many years and the rebels had taken over the entire country with the exception of the Capital, and now had surrounded the city of Addis Ababa, preparing to assault it for the final coup de gras. We have an Embassy there and those people needed to be evacuated and the compound needed to be secured and retained to protect the remaining skeleton staff that would stay behind principally for reporting purposes. I got the assignment but was told that I would not be taking any of my regular team members. It would be only me and two Army Delta Force elements. Our three-man team was to get into the city before the airport was totally shut down in 24 hours and get to our Embassy, situated at a 10,000 foot altitude, ensure that our people were safely evacuated and then take over all protective aspects and seal off our facility in case the coup became bloody.

Our insertion into Addis Ababa went without incident, that is to say without anything but the normal incidents one expects to see in a very backward third world country airport such as airport police with machine guns throwing people to the ground and sticking the barrel of the AK-47s into their faces to make their point about wanting to check all their papers. Perhaps a little drastic for a document check but not beyond expectations. What I had to do was to make sure that my two Army Delta Force guys didn't overreact to what they might think was the signal to save their lives and fight back. I paid the police the appropriate "expediting fee" and we were on our way to the Embassy. It was just another moment in security diplomacy.

The city had the feel of a ghost town. Traffic was light and the roads were much too traversable for a normally traffic-jammed poorly-planned ex-Soviet satellite city. Obviously everyone was well aware that the rebels were preparing to enter the city and most had either hunkered down expecting a blood bath, or, if they were a known political figure, they had fled with whatever corrupt money they had stashed away during their tenure in office. It was clear that the current government (such as it was) did not think they had a chance of holding off the rebels.

As it turned out, the final siege was bloodless with no government resistance and the rebels were gracious and did not execute people to make their show of power. I requested a meeting with the new leadership, which was made up of a dozen different tribal representatives with one man whose name escapes me after all these years, who seemed to be the ultimate commander. Another U.S. Government Agency had a man on the ground and he served to be very useful in arranging the meeting and the two of us attended. My Delta Force guys were working on the perimeter security and had already designed a water cannon that we could use to disperse angry crowds in a non-lethal manner.

The new leadership "committee" was suspicious but receptive and agreeable to providing us with external perimeter security, access to them for discussions in the future, and a substantial protective detail for the Charge. Their concept of a protective detail varied slightly from mine. The new government of Ethiopia was essentially made up of farmers, young uneducated wide-eyed boys and some intelligenzia who had fled to the rebels to prevent being executed by the overthrown power. They acted as advisors and in some cases new "Section" leaders for the rebel-farmer Commanders and would eventually be the Ministers of Education and the Economic Sections. I liked them immediately and we hit it off and over the next two months had numerous agreeable meetings in the old gold-plated conference room of the one time ruler Haili Selassi, who had failed so miserably that he had ended up feeding the bulk of his zoo animals to his favorite lions, and now, even his lions were starving. The country was a disaster and various segments wanted to split off to become independent.

My most memorable and pleasantly humorous part of this trip was the protective detail for the Charge. One morning a side-paneled cattle truck arrived at the gate with 30 young farm boys with machine guns, standing jammed into the back like sardines, so tightly packed, that they were shoulder to shoulder and couldn't even raise their weapons up with their arms that were so firmly pinned to their sides. But, their enthusiasm and heart made up for it, sort of. I started treating them like the father they missed and wanted back in their lives and even though I spoke no words in their language except the greeting I learned, and they spoke only a few words of English, they would cheer and hug me each day when they saw me. I actually came to really care about them.

Not meaning to be abusive in my search for humor in life but finding it anyway, the Charge's motorcade travels fast from point A to point B. It's just how it's done to keep bad guys from getting too close. This cattle truck literally filled with 30 young boys with their AK-47s would have to really move to keep up and the boys would all be standing, squeezed together but without any support or bracing of their bodies except each other. The driver's enthusiasm and desire to perform well in his new leadership role working with the new American Father, exceeded his ability to drive and when I would get a radio call that the Charge was returning, I would walk outside the walls and across the street to watch the arrival. The Charge's car would come speeding up the hill and the boy-laden cattle truck would be racing to keep up. As the Charge's car sped through the gate, the cattle truck would come screeching and sliding to a stop outside the gate and the kinetic energy mixed with the inability for anyone to hold on to anything, being like sardines in a can, always a couple of boys and AK-47s would go squirting up into the air and come down on the dirt or the road, the boys rolling up and ready to go again, as their weapons crashed onto the ground. This was the closest thing I have witnessed to the old Keystone Cops cartoons but these good-hearted boys would all smile and come over for their daily family hug and hello to "Father". I am still touched thinking about these homeless boys in search of belonging.

Now that the "rebels" no longer were the rebels, and were in fact the new government, it became a political necessity to get them talking with the rest of the world to ensure that there was a uniformity to world human rights and that no serious abuses were taking place. Addis Ababa is the location of the regional United Nations operation with a beautiful UN building that had been vacant and inactive for some years. I had now been here about 6 weeks and felt that with the Embassy safe, the final assault was over and no blood had been spilt, it was time for me to call it a day and ask for a new assignment to move onto. After all, the next steps were political in nature. This was not to be the case. I was informed by my MSD Headquarters that our government was to send out a high-ranking negotiator, Ambassador Cohen, but that before he would (or could) come, I had to get all the local tribes in agreement to meet at the UN building and had to get a firm day and time established when they would all be present and ready. Then, I had to review the security for the venue and ensure that the entire gathering would be safe and without incident. I don't know if it strikes you the way it struck me at the time, but there was me and my two special military elements, and as I found out, one remaining security officer at the entire UN operation who was now the man in charge, and it seemed to me that I was being asked to practically set up a new nation's security force. Ah, that seemingly impossible challenge once again.

The on-site associate went with me to have a meeting with the committee of tribes running (sort of) the country from Hailie Selassee's gilded conference room. We all sat there with our feet up on the beautiful conference room table I suppose in a form of rebellion or dominance, and maybe camaraderie, as I discussed with them the proposal of setting up a legitimate government recognized by the international community and told them that if we could get it organized and arranged for a specific day and time, the U.S. would send out a powerful representative to lend credence and resources from our country to help them gain stability. This was the first meeting only and it met with some affirmative nods and other stares of suspicion. The leader, who had remained the leader now for several weeks, advised us that we would need to make contact with all the other tribal factions not represented in the room and convince them as well. What the hell, I thought this band of merry men were the tribal leaders. After all, there was a conference room filled with them. Over the next couple of weeks, we made numerous trips to other tribal leaders, going back and forth with the main group to report our successes. I also kept my HQ informed of our successes and struggles.

When I had "down time" from tribal discussions, I met with the Security Chief and only member of the security forces for the UN operation. Here was a man glad to see me. He had been trying to maintain security at this huge building all on his lonesome and honestly, and admittedly, did not know what he was doing. I had him give me an entire tour of the security monster including every nook, cranny, and crawl space under the seats of the UN member's main semi-circular conference area, where the regional meeting would take place. Then, I had him do it again the next day with my two Delta Force elements who were anxious for some diversion from the perimeter security that now was self-supportive. I assigned one to obtain and train a guard force for the building and I assigned the other to work with the UN man in obtaining police support on the streets and outer perimeter. Then I sat down and designed the overall security plan for the UN operations in Addis Ababa for the upcoming world-televised conference. I wanted to get out of there and move onto another assignment and my boss had told me I couldn't leave until Ambassador Cohen was safely in-country and the conference was underway. I was trying to be desperately quick and efficient. The few Officers at the Embassy meanwhile were working all the political channels and reporting back on the success we were having to the Department of State. Things were actually beginning to gel. As it all turned out, Ambassador Cohen came, the conference was a success and I was allowed to leave. My two-man Delta team left a few days before me having done what they could, exceptionally well.

My departure wouldn't be complete without the final episode. My "Ethiopian sons" learned I was to leave and were a little more than slightly upset. We had gone through some real character building experiences together and I had sat outside the Embassy walls at night around their fire and laughed with them and given them food and shared conversation that was only probably about 10% understood. It didn't matter. I was that father again to them sitting with them at night like they remembered when they were younger out in the distant parts of the country. The day came and as I was about to take an Embassy car to the airport and wave goodbye to them, the slightly older leader of my 30 young boys with machine guns stepped in and said that they were all taking me to the airport. I trusted them and said yes. I even rode in the front of the cattle truck with all 30 stuffed in the back, diligently watching to make sure no one bothered us on our trip. We arrived at the airport and I was going to say goodbye and walk through the front of the tiny terminal and wait for the flight. They had other ideas. They drove to the tarmac gate and a group of them jumped out and at suggested gunpoint, told the airport guards that they were driving me out to the plane. There didn't seem to be any discussion. We drove out onto the tarmac and directly over to the plane I was scheduled for. All 30 young gun-wielding boys jumped out and surrounded the area like they were protecting me as a "VIP". The airline officials made no attempt to interfere. The young leader held his little broken-English ceremony, handed me a knife they had apparently made, and hugged me voicing his thanks for everything. Then, in turn, each and every one of them hugged me and said goodbye. Three of the top guys walked me up the steps onto the plane and said their final goodbye. No one on the plane commented on my knife. Eventually, the plane loaded and the door closed but the entire truck load of them waited until the plane was wheels-up before they departed. I will never forget the feeling I got from my war strife-generated farm-boy family created in Addis Ababa, Ethiopia.

Chapter Nine
MSD - Gulf War One – The Lead Up - Amman, Damascus, Israel and Kuwait

Amman, Jordan - During the early days of the first Gulf War buildup, my Mobile Security Division team was tasked with going to Amman, Jordan, to protect the American Ambassador. His position in relation to Kuwait and Iraq made his situation precarious and threats were being received against his life and our job was to be with him at all times and to ensure that no one was able to get to him to commit any acts of harm, while supplementing the physical security efforts of the RSO at the Embassy. Every day we traveled to each venue the Ambassador had to attend, whether official or personal. There has never been any shortage of weird and entertaining activities in protection in this part of the world.

While the Ambassador conducted work in his office at the Embassy, the Team would be a bit at loose ends on things to keep us busy so we would volunteer to help the RSO when he needed it. One afternoon, the RSO approached me with a slight but suspicious grin on his face and told me that an American woman had come in to see a security officer to report a problem and he had no one who could take the interview. He asked if I would mind escorting her into a conference room and taking down the facts of the complaint. I was happy to be engaged in work and got my pen and paper. The woman was quite attractive, about 30 years old and seemed to keep herself well dressed and groomed, but was also wearing a local Shalwar-Camise suit, which linked her to being some time in the country where she might have gone a bit "indigenous". An investigator makes a number of assumptions from the outward appearance and body reactions and language of an individual when they first meet them and from watching them for a couple of minutes before going up to them, and then works from that point through the questions and responses. By looking at this attractive and well-kept woman, I was guessing it might be a mixed Muslim-American culture marriage that had become too complicated or violent and she wanted assistance getting out of Jordan and back to the U.S. This is more common than you might think.

I walked up to Ms. X and introduced myself. She reciprocated in an educated, pleasant and appreciative way. I asked her to come with me to a room where we could talk privately and she joined me in one of the small conference rooms near the Embassy entry where "walk-ins" can give their stories without having to go deep into the building past a lot of people. We sat and I told her that I was there to help and whatever she told me would be kept in confidence to serve her best interests. Ms. X smiled, thanked me, and then turned into a total psychotic.

Ms. X got "big eyes", gripped the table to a white knuckle level and began talking at a hyper rate. Right off, without preamble, she said the CIA had planted cameras in her eyeballs and now they saw everything that she saw. She said she was tired of not having any privacy to her life and wanted the cameras removed and the CIA punished for what they had done. Once I regained my several lost seconds of composure, I closed my mouth and began trying to ask questions that might make some sense of what I had just been told. Obviously that didn't work. She stated she had no idea how the CIA did it without her knowing or when they did it but that now, they were watching everything she looked at. When one comes across a truly disturbed and badly in-need-of-help person like this or the ones who limit outside alien communication interception by wearing tin foil hats, it only takes a couple of minutes to verify that they need professional and clinical intervention. I asked her to wait while I consulted with my boss and I went to talk to the RSO. As I walked into his office and found him laughing at my situation, I knew I had been set up with "a regular". I told him what she had said and that pretty much turned the humorous situation to a sober one. He stated that she regularly came in with wacky stories but that this one exceeded the "safe zone" and we would need to arrange for her to return to the U.S. for professional help with family oversight. Ms. X was on a plane that evening back to her parents and help. We never found out if it was too much sun, a chemical abuse situation or whatever other options, but I have never forgotten how first impressions can be completely wrong. Perhaps she just had cameras in her eyeballs?

Damascus, Syria - The American Ambassador to Jordan said he needed a few days of quiet time and wanted to be driven to Damascus, Syria, to spend a few days with his friend, the Ambassador there. The Jordanian bodyguards and I planned the trip and we left. The Jordanian bodyguards were big and well-trained local police officers with very pleasant dispositions and a good sense of humor. They left me with an impression that sticks today that the Jordanians are some of the nicest people in the Mideast. We drove the Ambassador through what was mostly barren and apparently uninhabited desert terrain and after some hours, arrived in Damascus. We took the Ambassador to the Embassy where the other Ambassador's home was situated and he told us he would be staying on the grounds for four days and to come back for him then. Before returning to Amman, the Bodyguards told me that Damascus had some of the best food and they wanted to take me to an authentic restaurant and show me what great food was. I asked what kind of food and they said "meat". I am not big on red meat and basically try to avoid it but I had a cultural dilemma on my hands. We arrived at the restaurant and were seated and they ordered, obviously in a language that passed me right by. A huge tray of unrecognizable meats arrived and they would point to one and say, "try that one, you will like it". I would try it, not like it very much but would stay calm and ask what it was. They would say lamb liver or some other awful animal component and I would pause and breathe deep. About the fourth piece, they pointed and told me it was the best and I obligingly took it and ate it. It was awful and I again, maybe not really wanting to know, asked what it was (so I'd never eat it again). They said it was sheep balls. Worse, they said it with smiles on their faces and they began to laugh knowing how an American would respond. I didn't let them down. I am sure the expression on my face made it clear because they laughed even harder. That was the end of my meal. The Bodyguards and I had become good friends and truly liked each other so the joke was an acceptable one and after we all stopped enjoying my discomfort, they finished up and we drove back to Amman to three days of "down time" to relax. Actually, those three days ended up being some of the best time in Jordan because I met some of the Swedish Flight Attendants who worked the Jordanian President's plane.

Tel Aviv and Jerusalem, Israel – The first Gulf War was on and Saddam had just begun launching his SCUD missiles into Israel as part of his insane campaign. I was told to pick a team and get to Tel Aviv ASAP to keep our people safe and to report accountability of our Americans after each SCUD fell into the city. When we arrived at the airport, the Israelis issued each of us a gas mask and told us it was law to carry it at all times and if we were found without it, we would be fined. Nice entry to the country but how could we argue with a country where beautiful young girls walked around at nightclubs in mini-skirts with 9mm Uzis slung over their shoulders like a purse. It seemed so natural and right at the time. There is just something so "gun show exotic" about a girl in a mini skirt with a sub-machine gun.

For the next month, we worked virtually 24 hours a day. The Embassy had been evacuated down to an "essentials only" level and literally we would work until our bodies and minds quit, at which time, we laid down wherever in the Embassy we were and slept a few hours until the batteries recharged enough to get us back up on our feet. We slept in the Embassy hallway; we slept on the Ambassadors office floor; we considered ourselves lucky if we happened to pass out near a couch. The daytime was spent training our Embassy people, roaming around the city looking at the SCUD sites that were devastated, and working with our host-nation counterparts. Almost every night was spent monitoring the SCUD launches, "reacting" everyone working at night into the hardened safe haven rooms, where we put plastic over the doors and taped them sealed in case one of the SCUDs hit us and contained chemical or biological elements. Knowing what I do now about the size of warheads and their destructive power, there was no need to tape and seal the room, the SCUD would have almost destroyed our building. Following each SCUD hit, my team would deploy into the city to the blast site in order to guarantee none of our people were hit so we would have total personnel accountability. Many of the SCUDs hit the city and killed a lot of people but the Israeli's propaganda was to keep promoting how none of them hit the mark so that Saddam would never know which trajectory was valid. He kept trying though. We must have gone through over 100 SCUD missiles. But soon our total exhaustion would be tested even further.

Chapter Ten

THE GULF WAR,
KUWAIT CITY, KUWAIT

The U.S. decided that Saddam had overstepped himself by hitting Israel and invading Kuwait, and even more importantly, the governments of Kuwait and Saudi Arabia got worried about who would be next and Kuwait wanted salvation. They came to the USG and requested military intervention. So, I received the call that our military was about ready to hit the Iraqis hard in Kuwait city and run them out of Kuwait back to their homes. Once the first few days of U.S. Military action clarified to the Iraqis that they had made a gross error, we were going to take Ambassador Skip Gnehm into Kuwait City as the Iraqis began to flee out what became known as "The Highway of Death", and we would set up Embassy operations again, such as they were.

Flying into Kuwait was surrealistic. From above, you could see very little through the black smoke from all the burning oil wells until you came to one of the oil wells itself, which burned like a volcano and you could see the orange fire through the blackout. It was like flying into what one would think hell was like or something from Dante's Inferno description. There were burning oil well volcanoes everywhere. The Iraqis had apparently torched them all and then headed north.

We landed at the Kuwait City airport on a runway that was so pock-marked from rocket and missile hits that our helicopter had to search to find a flat space. Once down, the military escort vehicles picked us up and worked their way through the destruction. As we exited the airport, the first bad omen of what we were to find in this tortured city was a Kuwaiti woman who had been nailed to a telephone pole and disemboweled. She had also been pregnant and that horror needs no description. I don't think that scene will ever leave my memory but it also reminded me that we were as they say, "game on" for our readiness status and I needed to focus on the mission at hand. The Iraqi soldiers were obviously heartless and had no respect for civilian life in any condition. There was some daylight to see things around us but the sky was filling with a solid black smoke that progressively was overtaking the natural light. Within two days more, the midday sun was virtually gone and the days were all like night and the nights were so unnaturally black that I literally could not see my hand in front of my face. We suffered many minor injuries over the next month from trying to move around at night and walking into structures or stepping off ledges or steps. It was a complete blackout.

We arrived at the Embassy compound and found that the only place to sleep was a concrete floor in one of the rooms next to the pool and that what we had carried in was what we had available to use. The meals were our cold MREs (military "meals ready to eat") and cans of tuna. The pool was filled with black water from all the oil droppings that had contaminated that now unusable water supply. I have to give a lot of credit to the prior Ambassador who had initially stayed behind and stuck it out during the Iraqi assault on Kuwait City. The Iraqis didn't attack the Embassy but they cut-off the water and power and supply line in order to encourage the Americans to abandon the Embassy and leave. As counter-propaganda, the Ambassador let the word out that they were all fine and well-supplied and that the pool was a huge fresh water supply for themselves. This discouraged the Iraqis but it was complete nonsense. The pool was poison and food was limited. The Ambassador had apparently solved the water problem by actually digging a well on the property and there was enough fresh water to supply the remaining Americans and to plant a vegetable garden to help feed her people. Kudos to her.

The American Embassy Officers had all left before we came in and before the major assault and now we needed to get ourselves and the Embassy back on a working status. The Ambassador needed to begin to make contact with any Kuwaiti leaders left. The day we landed, the U.S. military was chasing the Iraqis out the Highway of Death and that was the biggest mess I have ever seen. We drove out to scout out the area and found miles of overturned vehicles, bodies, and missile craters everywhere, and literally hundreds of thousands of weapons lying around everywhere, including crate after crate of rockets (RPGs) spilled on the ground, and pouring out of the backs of upended trucks. There were also Mercedes they had stolen and were trying to take home to Iraq. The miles of "spoils of war" were all spoiled and the area was highly dangerous with all the munitions lying around. As we checked out the area, we found unexploded grenades on the ground with the pins missing and that was the final nail. We got out of the area and put it off limits to step off the pavement. But not for the first time in my career, I would learn that good sense and guidance doesn't always override silly human enthusiasm.

We began to patrol through the now destroyed and deserted areas of Kuwait City looking for anything that we needed to be aware of or possibly people that needed help or Iraqis that needed to go home. I put the Ambassador (Skip) on a morning exercise program to keep him fit in that oily air environment and he ran on a treadmill inside the hotel across the street from the Embassy. After that, Skip would begin his work efforts either in his substitute office or after a little while, by traveling around the city meeting with the emerging Kuwaiti government officials either surfacing or returning from exile. We visited so many Iraqis and they were so enthusiastic about the U.S. returning their country to them, the appreciation and quantity of sweet tea we drank was overwhelming. When we were not protecting the Ambassador, we patrolled our city neighborhood and explored outer city areas where some Iraqis had become trapped and occasionally became recognized and firefights would break out until they were eliminated.

The city was literally demolished. The buildings were bombed out, there were burned out cars and furniture and trash everywhere. We were moving cautiously in and out of cleared and protected doorways and from building to building, clearing each. We entered one building that had at one time been an ice skating rink. The smell was overwhelming and clearly recognizable as decaying human flesh. Inside, where there had been ice on the center rink once when the electrical power and equipment worked, was a partially decomposed mass of many bodies. Apparently, after the Iraqis finished torturing and killing the Kuwaitis they found, they would throw them on the ice and as the ice melted, the mass of bodies became intolerable. We witnessed the results of a lot of horribly creative and mind-numbing torture carried out by a very sick group of Iraqis on innocent civilians. Later, we were present for the opening of the Kuwaiti Holocaust Museum and what the evidence and photos showed was even worse than what we had become aware of. Simply put, the Iraqis had been barbaric and inhuman in their search for more terrible ways to inflict pain and death.

With the skies now black at noon, and with the little oil drops that would fall from the sky, all our clothing was speckled with tiny dots of black and would not be going home to America with us. Everything was ruined. It was fine while we were working there but we would travel back with just the clothes on our backs. After about a month, work was beginning to show signs of recovery on the Embassy but the Ambassador's office was still being rebuilt. When the Army's Third Group had entered Kuwait City, they had been told to take and hold the Embassy property. They claim that what they did was to ensure each room was free and clear of Iraqis, but it seems clear that they were looking for war trophies on the U.S. Embassy grounds. They blew up expensive hard-line doors, they broke down doors and windows and when they came to the Ambassador's specially bolted locked office, they wanted inside badly enough that they decided to torch cut the bolt locking it, even though they had been advised the keys were on the way. What they didn't think about was that as they torch-cut the door open to find the goodies inside, the torch set the office on fire and completely destroyed everything inside and ruined the Ambassador's office and all equipment and information that was for his use. The Ambassador was so upset at their actions, he demanded the Army pay for full restoration and they did.

The Al-Sabah family is one of the richest families in the world and they are Kuwaiti. The Ambassador was to visit Mr. Al-Sabah at his palatial home south of the city on the coast overlooking a beautiful sea, so several of us loaded up and headed south to do an advance of the property and meeting site. We drove along the coastal road in the still-artificial dark for about an hour, watching the ever-present burning oil fields off to the side and feeling the sticky oil on the road. We arrived at the Al-Sabah home and were treated very graciously and shown every courtesy and cooperation on doing the necessary advance work. After we had seen what we needed to and knew where the meeting was going to take place, they showed us to a beautiful room with a TV and told us this would be our waiting room while the meeting was on-going. It was the nicest thing we had seen in over a month and my plan was to catch up on some sleep in one of the comfortable chairs. Mr. Al-Sabah himself entered the room and said hello and asked us what we would like to eat the day of our visit while we waited for the Ambassador. One of the team jokingly said McDonalds. We all laughed and I said anything would be very much appreciated.

On our way home, we took a route more directly through the inferno and we spotted what appeared to be two men standing or crouching in the desert where it was black but highlighted by the orange volcano light. We decided we better find out if we had trouble and cautiously hiked our way over to where we found two oil-mummified Iraqi soldiers who had apparently been shot and while trying to crawl and drag themselves to safety, had died in those positions and literally, over very little time, the oil had coated them and they were in a way, mummified. For reporting purposes, we gave them names and over the next couple of months, would pass by the same area taking Congressional Delegations (CODELS) in to the oil fields or a couple of times, the Secretary of State, and we would always see and check on Bob and Frank, still oil-sealed in time.

Five days after conducting the Al-Sabah advance, we brought the Ambassador to the Al-Sabah home and when we walked into our waiting room, it was filled with bags of McDonalds food. Mr. Al-Sabah had sent his private plane to the next nearest country with a McDonalds' and bought enough food for an Army. Our MSD Army. I knew then that it must be "good to be king" and with his wealth, Mr. Al-Sabah might as well have been one.

The biggest challenge during the months in Kuwait was the CODELS coming out for their photo opportunities and who all wanted to go to the Highway of Death and the burning oil fields. The first CODEL that came out was a big one. 125 Senators and Congresspersons and I had to take them to the dangerous live munitions-covered Highway of Death in 2 large buses. Knowing that anyone who might touch or accidentally kick a piece of munitions could get us all blown to kingdom-come, I gave them all a very in-depth briefing before we left on the dangers out there and the strict orders for everyone's personal survival to stay on the cleared road and to NEVER step off into the mined, grenade covered and rocket-strewn desert. I reiterated this again on the buses as we traveled out. Apparently my English had become a foreign tongue while out in the desert because the second the bus doors opened, like a group of school kids who just heard the recess bell, they ran directly into the desert among live munitions, spilled rockets, grenades without pins, AK-47s and land mines in order to see who could find the greatest treasure. I was shocked, stunned and panicked at the thought that I was responsible for all their lives and we were all about to be blown to hell by one foolish act or another. The only way I could get their attention was to fire rounds into the air to shock them back to reality. That stopped them. They turned and I yelled at all of them like they were children being scolded and ordered them back onto the buses. Thank god they obeyed and no one kicked a live grenade. We got the heck out of there but it was only the first of many. Fortunately, shortly thereafter, the military used special munitions-clearing bull dozers to clean up the highway and out-lying areas.

The Highway of Death and surrounding desert was littered with Iraqi bodies that were fleeing our jets as they came in to destroy the convoy as they headed back to Iraq with the treasures of Kuwait. These bodies brought a plague of large, fearless and almost indestructible black flies - tens of millions of them. And, for quite awhile they fed on the bodies and laid their larva to create even larger armies of killer black flies. Then the bodies were finished and they turned their attention to the next food source and center of civilization, Kuwait City. Like a plague right out of the Bible, they came in as a thick cloud that would have covered the horizon if they weren't disguised by the blackness of the day sky anyway. They would land on our faces and unaccustomed to anyone fighting back, we would slap them and they would just sit there unhurt, biting flesh off our faces. It wasn't a small bite like we know from the U.S. flies, it was a bite that left a red bleeding hole on our cheeks. This was war. It was not one we were accustomed to but one that required full dedication and for a month, everyone did their best to eliminate the killer fly population.

We visited the burning oil wells frequently and watched how they "capped" them one by one and eventually, the dense black cloud and smoke began to lessen and the sky became more visible. We visited the Iraqis Bob and Frank a couple more times and then when some sense of "civilization" began to assert itself into daily life, it was time for my team to leave and move onto more adventurous opportunities. But this was one I would never forget and the experiences of this war and its' obvious brutality would prepare me for missions and adventures to come.

Chapter Eleven

MORE MSD MISSIONS

I continued with my 3.5-year MSD Team Leader tour and in all, carried out around 30-plus Missions all over the world. To finish up the MSD portion, which created such a strong base of operational knowledge and "know-how" under highly stressful and critical threat conditions, let me just mention briefly a couple of other locations/Missions of significance in my memory.

MSD – Santiago, Chile – The primary reason I took a Team to Santiago was due to an alleged assassination threat and a bomb that detonated against our Embassy personnel off-hours. It was believed that surveillance had been spotted and reporting had picked up information about a possible upcoming attack against them. There was already active anti-American sentiment and action taking place in Santiago and other Central and South American cities. In Santiago there had been the bombing of McDonalds Restaurants and Mormon Churches and machine gun fire at walking and biking Missionaries, so the attack seemed a likely follow-on scenario. Worst of all though, an attack had already recently taken place against the Embassy softball team. A softball bat had been filled with explosives and nails, turning it into a shape charge device and it was laid on the ground pointing at the U.S. Embassy team dugout with a timing device detonator. The first game was the Embassy team and the second game was to be the MSG Team playing. The Embassy team game ran late and the device detonated. The RSO was playing and took the brunt of the blast losing his right eye from shrapnel but many others were injured. So, here we were, to see what we could do.

Our "people of concern" worked in several shifts and so during those shift changes each day or night, when they would be traveling from home to work and back home, and would be the most exposed and predictable, that was where we would focus our main surveillance detection effort. We would follow them looking for any correlation of movement by strangers. We also knew that as a group they were quite social so it was certain we would be having long days and nights following them. All this had to be done discreetly so that we could accurately determine their susceptibility to future attacks, while trying to spot enemy surveillance doing the same, and if need be, protect them. Our days and nights were spent just focused on their lives, movements, and attention to their own personal safety.

We learned that they lived normal socially active lives like everyone else and were completely unaware that we or anyone else was watching them. They had an Embassy driver who drove them everywhere and what was a factor was that they ignored the regular patterns the driver set to always drive the shortest and most convenient routes, creating a predictability that any "first job terrorist" could recognize. The multiple routes that they were supposed to randomly select to and from work had settled into the same single fastest straight shot in to work and they were either sleeping in the van or joking around and none of them paid any attention to who was watching or following them. It is a natural human response to settle into a certain deniability of danger or sense of invulnerability when nothing happens to you. But that is by definition why no security person can ever let their guard down. The bad guys are out there looking for those human errors and lapses of attention. When in the danger zone, one must simply always be "game on.' They had been taught this but being young and invulnerable supermen, they quickly lapsed into lazy deniability.

After two weeks of following them and noting their patterns, it was time to make our point.- At 0530 hours one morning, because of their lax routine, we were almost certain they would take a specific route and that it would be exactly at 0530 hours, so we set up our cars on both sides of the roadway and waited. We conducted it just like the terrorists would. Two blocks before our attack zone, we had someone standing on the sidewalk to verify they were in the van and he waved at us as the van passed, acknowledging that this was the target we wanted and they were inside. One of them later noted seeing a man waving and wondered why. One-half block before they reached us, we pulled our cars out perpendicular on the roadway blocking the entire road. Normally in an attack, this is where a team would exit the vehicles and kill everyone with automatic weapons. We did not do that but we knew the debrief at the Embassy would be quite adrenalized. Just before the now-panicking van of individuals reached us, we backed off the attack zone, opening the roadway again for them to pass, which they did with ever increasing speed and excitability. Now we would calmly drive to the Embassy to identify ourselves, show our photos, and we would have a chat with the "should-be dead" personnel to set down some training and operational guidelines and requirements.

When we walked in, we found all of them jumping up and down, waving their arms in the air, telling about how they had narrowly escaped death from an attack. Our counterpart, the Regional Security Officer (RSO) joined us for the debrief. I "laid into" those people like a father who just learned that his son smashed up the family Mercedes. We worked with them for the next two weeks and gave them awareness and surveillance detection courses. We also set up a simple random route and variable time system for them to use and select just before walking out the door so no one, including the local driver would be able to prompt any bad guys. We also hung out with them and got to know them, trying to identify if we had "hard cases" or receptive survivors.

During that last two weeks, we also were involved in a series of attacks against Americans and American businesses including two McDonalds Restaurants, one of which was blown up 20 minutes after my team left it. Two more Mormon churches were shot up by machine gun fire during drive-by attacks. In the park across from the Consulate building, a man placed a make-shift rocket aimed at the Consulate and thankfully, it was inert. Another man jumped the Consulate wall, armed with a handgun and was taken down by force. And, President George Bush Senior came into town and a bomb was detonated near his hotel, causing great stress for the Secret Service. The anti-America and Bush demonstrations made it clear what their intent was.

When we finally departed post, as a parting point of emphasis, we again spoke with our "victims" and told them that they could have been killed and the threat was still active so they better wake up and act right. Humans will be human. Only two weeks after our departure, the driver was running the same easiest route. That morning two weeks later on their same predictable route, terrorists hit their van with a rocket propelled grenade (RPG). It detonated as it passed into the van, ripping off the roof, seriously injuring several of them. One lost his hearing permanently. RPGs are lethal and they were lucky to survive. Such is the precarious learning curve of life.

MSD Summary - I wanted to convey the incredible range of activities and responsibilities that the Diplomatic Security Service and the Mobil Security Division get involved in. The diversity, the threat deterrence, the responsibility placed on the shoulders of DS Agents, is phenomenal. But, on the other side of it is the incredible opportunity to conduct Missions of that depth with the autonomy that the Team Leader and the Team has, to resolve life and death issues in the field. Few people have any concept of who DS is and what they are doing out in the world to keep all of you safe. DS is the most unique and capable Federal Law Enforcement Agency in the world.

Chapter Twelve
THE REGIONAL
SECURITY OFFICER

Few people, including some DS Agents fully realize what it means to become a Regional Security Officer (RSO). This position is a life-crux point in ones DS career when you have to accept responsibility on a leadership level that will either scare you off from accepting this role again or it will form you and find the real you inside and turn you into a world participant on the international security field.

It starts as almost everything does, in a learning curve and mentored stage, positioned as an Assistant Regional Security Officer (ARSO), under an RSO who hopefully will take the time and care to train the ARSO into what he or she needs to become successful at the higher levels. That being said, like being a parent to your children, it is not always easy to find the time to provide the right guidance. The security threats, the growing number of Programs and responsibilities that an RSO must oversee and control, keeps him literally running from 0600 in the morning until frequently late into the night. Within that time, the numerous meetings, the reports and cables to be written, the 20-something Programs that are on-going every day to keep everyone safe - time has to be found to bring the younger talented and motivated Agents (ARSOs) into the picture and mentor them on the Programs you have assigned them to oversee.

So, what does an RSO/ARSO do? I can tell you about the various Programs by name and brief description, but that will never give you an idea of the minute-by-minute complexity or risk-challenge that faces the RSO, or the back door coordination that must exist between all of them working in synergy, nor the politics that always comes into play to keep them working successfully. Even many RSOs don't get it and thus, never become a functionally skilled Program Manager, Politician, and Diplomat with a gun. But, what are some of the Programs that make up an RSO? Remember that security is designed like the layers of an onion. The RSO is the core or heart of the operation. The Marine Security Guards control entry to the building. The Local Guards control the grounds and the gate access. The local Police control outside our walls. Al-Qaeda is somewhere out in the distance watching for a weakness in our controls. And, our Surveillance Detection Teams are further out watching the Al-Qaeda elements as they watch us. All these layers, with the exception of Al-Qaeda, are run and manipulated by the RSO and when possible, he even moves against the Al-Qaeda elements with coordination of the local police or intelligence when they are discovered such as in Karachi during the Daniel Pearl case, or Madrid following the train bombings. There are numerous RSO resources and complimenting Programs that if run well by an understanding RSO, can quite literally create a defensive army of competent employees.

Senior Law Enforcement Advisor to the Ambassador – The RSO is the key daily operational security advisor to the Ambassador and Deputy Chief of Mission. The Ambassador must trust and have confidence in the RSO or it all fails.

The Local Guard Program – The Local Guards from typically Host-Nation, provide protection at the perimeter wall and oversee all "access control" elements including vehicle and personal access checks, deliveries, residential security access and roving patrol units that respond to emergencies of the official Mission Americans. There are usually around 200 to 1,500 guards depending on the size of the Mission.

The Surveillance Detection Program – One of the most successful Programs ever, these local or third-country nationals "fit" into the local community like Americans cannot watching for the bad guys who are watching us. Sometimes in cars or on foot, or bicycles or motorbikes. A good SD Team will literally be a life-saving tool for the RSO.

The Marine Security Guard Program – The Marine Security Guards are a select group of U.S. Marines who for a few years volunteer and are screened and selected to control the Embassy or Consulate entry control doors and building, protection of the classified documentation, and protection of the Americans and locals inside that building or buildings. They are loyal, dedicated and motivated, best-hearted young men who make us proud of our country.

The Residential Security Program – Outside of the Embassy or Consulate, we still need to protect our Americans when they are in their homes and that includes a residential guard, solid doors with strong locks, high walls, door viewers, lighting, cameras, alarm systems, safehavens in the homes, grills on the windows and a long list of other items.

The Physical Security Program – This Program is an ever-evolving one that seems to always be in the process of upgrades. It includes things like perimeter walls, razor wire, special lighting systems, control gates, Delta Barriers, Jersey Barriers or T-Walls, Guard control booths and watch towers, steel doors weighing 1,000 pounds, safehavens, training classes for the employees and staff, thousands of identity cards and etc...

The Foreign Service National Investigator Program – RSOs cannot walk up and knock on a door in a foreign country to ask questions about someone who wants to be employed. No one would talk to us or in some places, we would be kidnapped and killed. We utilize local personnel who are stringently vetted to be our local national investigators and they are worth their weight in gold. While we come and go every few years, they offer the continuity to much of the operation and especially with police contacts.

The Counter-Terrorism Program – What can I say about this. This is one of our most active and important functions and because DS has federal jurisdiction on Passport and Visa Fraud, we are deep into this function internationally, meaning when terrorists are caught, DS usually has some nexus to it or is involved in the investigative operation.

The Passport and Visa Fraud Program – Many thousands of passports and visas are issued at each Embassy and Consulate and people are always trying to gain entry to the U.S. using false documentation because they shouldn't be approved either for criminal or terrorist reasons or perhaps another reason. This is our realm and we now have one ARSO working full time on this function at almost every Embassy.

Criminal and Suitability Investigations – Strongly supplemented by an ARSO who specializes in this during his ARSO tour, we face passport and visa fraud, breaches in classified information/dissemination, robbery, rape, murder and mayhem, including family violence and inappropriate behavior. When we think we have seen it all, something new comes up.

The Visiting VIP Protective Services Program – We constantly have visiting Senators or Congresspersons coming to visit our Posts and usually at the least workable or convenient time for us but it is the best time for them. It could or should be for political advancement but it could be a photo opportunity prior to upcoming elections, a shopping trip prior to an upcoming holiday, or in some cases, it might also be to actually understand how to help the Mission. They require protection and we provide that function.

The Special Protective Equipment Program – This equipment which we refer to as SPE - guns and all the other items that go along with it like ballistic vests, holsters, ammo, special weapons and special equipment. It is very involving and a key life-safety Program.

There is much more that an RSO is coordinating daily but these Programs will help you to understand how many things must interact and match smoothly just to make a day go properly without too many Snags.

Chapter Thirteen

ARSO BOGOTA, COLOMBIA, 1993 - 1995

Certain assignments are language-designated, meaning that we have to attain a certain minimal level of competence in that foreign language in order to get the assignment. Colombia required I learn to speak, read and write at a comfortable normal daily social level, referred to as a "2" level. I joined DS when I was 36 years old. I was now 42. I had never learned a language before and my mind was already sending out stubborn refusal messages. The classes are 6 months long, five days a week, all day long, in a class with one teacher and 3 or 4 students sitting at a table facing each other struggling to learn with no English permitted from day one. We have home work and our weekends are spent doing nothing but trying to figure out what any of the words meant and how to remember them. Language training at the Foreign Service Institute is a nightmare you can't walk away from. Nonetheless, after 6 months of sheer agony, I attained my level "2" Spanish and was headed for Bogota. It was one of the most useful things I ever did.

During my time with the Mobil Security Division, I had completed a mission in Bogota and so I had a sense of the exotic and fun flavor of the city and country. I also knew that they had some of the most beautiful women in the world. I was there as a beginner ARSO to learn how to become a great RSO and this was a period when the Medellin and Cali Drug Cartels were at their peak of death and destruction and also during the time when Pablo Escobar, the notorious Chief of the Medellin Drug Cartel was finally located and killed by the Colombian Anti-Narcotics Forces on the roof of a building he was hiding in as he ran to escape in his underwear. He had been responsible for the deaths of 20,000 of his own people in his anti-government bombings and executions. His loss was an improvement for the entire world. All U.S. Federal Agents were also on the Cartel's "most wanted" list and when I first arrived in Bogota, the Cartels were offering $100,000 dollars to anyone who killed any U.S. Federal Agent. They were also offering $250,000 to anyone who killed the Ambassador. By the time I left two years later, the reward for any Agent was up to $250,000 and the Ambassador was up to $1,000,000. This kind of money, especially in a country where jobs of any kind were so scarce, and Rebels were so available, made us look over our shoulders at all times and watch everyone including 10-year old boys who might shoot us in the back. But, for the most part, Bogota, and really the entire country of Colombia, is truly beautiful and my experience there was exceptional. Even though I am not inclined to go back again, I have wonderful memories of Colombia. While I was serving my tour in Colombia, we operated with a regular running total of about 12 or 13 private Americans kidnapped and missing at any particular time. Some would be bought back and returned, others would not make the ransom and some we never even received a ransom note for, which meant they probably didn't survive the ordeal of the kidnapping and travel to the remote holding location.

This was the first assignment where I literally packed up my life and moved it to a foreign country. Not just a TDY suitcase assignment, this was a complete normal full-service life in someone else's country, and I was excited about it. The first thing you confront is "what will my housing be like". I had a beautiful apartment with three bedrooms and the living room had full wall windows from floor to ceiling that looked out over the city and a small park. If this was what the Foreign Service offered, I was going to be a happy man. I didn't know how lucky I was and that it would be many years before I would see anything like this again. Because the threat to kill Americans was very real in Bogota due to our involvement in the anti-drug campaigns with the government of Colombia, we would be picked up for work and dropped off again at the end of the day in a fully-armored shuttle van with an armed escort vehicle that our shop, the RSO Shop, oversaw. Frankly, I found it more convenient than trying to drive my little Datsun 280 ZX to work and struggle to find parking. And, if attacked, it allowed me to respond with my weapon instead of worrying about driving and shooting.

When I started my assignment, we had 1 RSO, the Deputy RSO, and 10 Assistant RSOs of which I was one. The RSO Programs were divided up among all of us so that we could learn what they were all about and have a chance at autonomous management. I got lucky and one of my Programs was as the Military Group Liaison (Milgroup Liaison). In Colombia, the U.S. had numerous small military-supported operations involved in the fight against the drug cartels as well as working with the Colombian Forces in combating anti-government rebel operations such as the FARC. I was required (or had the opportunity) to visit these sites all over the entire country, to evaluate the work and get a familiarization of what we were doing. This was the best Program we had because it took me into every corner of Colombia and I saw more than most Colombians ever see in their lifetimes; from the northern ocean coastlines of Cartagena and Baranquilla to the southern Amazon jungles and from the western Pacific to the eastern borders with Venezuela - jungles, mountains, high plains, desert, and beautiful coastlines.

Obviously, my travel was a two-edged sword. I needed to do my job and get out to see the operations, but in the towns, the Cartels would try to have me killed, and in the mountains and jungles, the Rebels were attacking the camps and I could be collateral damage or could be taken as a hostage and ransomed for cash that might never be paid since as a U.S. Government employee, we don't pay ransom. I loved it. This was adventure in its purest form.

When I would travel into remote towns in the north or west where Cartel influence was strong, I couldn't stay in any hotels and survive so the Police (corrupt ones but who wanted to keep me alive so they could survive) would insist that I sleep in their jail cells, which had no bed, only a concrete floor and I remember many nights freezing on those hard cold concrete floors, praying for morning to come. I was a pretty tough and capable guy but if they had wanted to get rid of me, there wouldn't have been much I could have done except take a few with me. I would travel around the countryside riding in the back of crappy pick-up trucks bouncing around on the dirt roads and trails until my bones realigned themselves and then eventually made my way back to the helicopter or fixed wing landing zone to depart.

I will mention names of towns or regions where I visited but cannot actually mention the locations of the working camps for obvious reasons. I also traveled with some of our fine U.S. Military folks and that friendship is worth gold still today.

One night in a northern coastal desert-like town Riohacha, when it seemed to be especially hard and cold concrete, I couldn't sleep and was sitting up against the wall of the open jail cell when a firefight erupted in the street outside and rounds began to penetrate the jail house. A lot of yelling was taking place and counterfire. I was told to stay low and to stay out of it. It turned out that some local rebels learned I was in the jail and insisted that I was worth a ransom that could help their local fiscal situation. The police, thank god, felt that the punishment for failing to do their job and losing their American guest would be worse than resisting the local bad guys and fought back enough to make them rethink their strategy, at least for the night. I was out and gone under escort the next morning.

The Llanos is an area of more or less plains with forest clusters and lots of shrub type fill-in and meadows in between. Near the village San Jose De Guaviare in the central region of Colombia, I was with my Embassy Military Liaison associates discussing the rebel activity with the local Anti-Narcotics/Anti-Rebel Forces personnel. They were camped here and had been experiencing numerous rebel attacks and had lost some of their men. We were discussing what they needed from the U.S. Government to give them a better advantage and to overcome their losses and defeat the Rebels. We were sitting at wooden picnic-type tables drinking hot Colombian coffee. We had flown in on two USG rotary wings (helicopters) an hour earlier and they were waiting in the flat cleared area 250 yards behind us. Before we finished our business, shooting broke out 200 yards away on their field of fire perimeter edge and everyone scrambled including us. Rebels were pouring through the tree line and making a run at the camp. Our business became finished for the moment and it was time for the Colombian forces to go to work. We were armed and contributed to the defense but our objective was to get the helicopters up and into the air away from the battle before they became damaged or destroyed, so our participation was as we were working our way backward to the "birds". We were able to get away without any holes or damage to the USG helicopters or to ourselves. This happened twice to me during my Colombian tour and I suppose that these types of life and death encounters I had been getting in DS were gradually, physically and psychologically, preparing me for the greater challenges to come in my later career years.

One of my favorite places in Colombia, and some of my best memories come from a village on the far southern border that lies on the Amazon River. It is actually one town but the border between Colombia and Brazil cuts right through it so each half has a different name. The Colombian half is called Leticia. The Brazilian side is called Tapatinga. There was a joint operation there and a close cooperation existed between the U.S. and Colombian Anti-Narcotics Forces. During my 2 years in Colombia, I made four trips to this region and I loved it more each time.

Very early in the morning, around 0430 or so, the people who made their living off the Amazon River would canoe into the shore on the Leticia side. I always stayed at the only "sort of" decent and safe hotel, a very rustic but colorful place called The Anaconda Hotel. It was about a 100 yard walk to the river's edge and I would walk down to see the fishermen come in with their catches. I have never seen fish or creatures like they brought in. One fish had the head of a dog and its skin was actually used for shoes because of its thickness. Others can only be described as monsters and river creatures. But damn it was fun to look at the spectacle. It was like witnessing aliens on a foreign planet. The people would see my curiosity and "big eyes" and make a point to show me the especially weird ones. They had names for them they would throw at me but at that time, they meant nothing to me. Every morning, this was my routine until about 0600, when I would go back to the hotel for breakfast with a collection of people that were almost as strange as the fish from the Amazon. Where did these people come from and what on earth were they doing in this remote little river village.

On one trip, the Colombian Army General arranged a "fast boat" river trip for me to see Monkey Island and then further up to see the mysterious Pink Dolphins, hidden up a tributary. The Amazon is a mysterious and magical place. The jungles are double and triple canopy, which makes the ground level seem artificial and strangely shadowed and colored. The animal life is totally different from what we have witnessed in our lives, and the sounds that ring out continuously as if they were relaying notice of our visit up river were intense. We stopped at Monkey Island. It is an Island in the middle of the Amazon River that is filled with monkeys everywhere. It is OK to walk a bit and look at them but not to let them get too close or friendly because of the numbers of them. If they think you have something of interest, they will quickly overwhelm you and without meaning to, cause damage or death. There are many types and many sizes and it is amazing to be so close among so many.

We continued a long distance up the river. This was going to be a long one day trip but without the fast boats, it would take many days, and many days in the Amazon requires a lot more survival preparation than just our weapons and sack lunches. During this trip, we crossed through the Peru and Equador borders as well due to the nature of the river's course. Hours later and many miles deep into the jungle, we cut right into a smaller tributary and 30 minutes later we found ourselves back into a small lake with small rivers feeding it. As we slowly moved around the lake, small dolphins with pointed noses and that were the color of light pink would surface next to the boats to show themselves off and ride the small wave we made. They were beautiful and graceful and unique. They caused me to remember the purplish dolphins of the Ganges River in Bangladesh and I was reminded of how creatures seem to take on the characteristics of their environment. No one is certain why they are pink but one thought is that the reddish sediment in the river over time affected them. Plus, they are fresh water Dolphins and that is also unique. The Amazon is one of the most special places on earth and everyone should witness its magic during their lives at least one time.

On another occasion, the American Ambassador wanted to go to Leticia with his wife and since I already had a familiarity, I was going as his protective Agent. I was put in touch with a special man, a legend in that area. He was called "Tarzan of the Amazon" and was named Kapax. He was born there and roamed the Amazon barefoot and in shorts with a big knife on his side. No other clothes or accessories. This man was the real thing. He lived on the Tapatinga side of the town and his mix of Spanish and Portuguese was almost totally unintelligible to me. Nonetheless, he was the most famous guide in the Amazon and I went down early to meet him and make preparations for the Ambassador and his non-adventurous wife.

Kapax and I liked each other immediately even though our language exchange was comical and mind-boggling to anyone trying to listen in. As I learned, here was a man who swam 1200 kilometers up the Amazon in an attempt to raise money to stop the polluters of his river. This was a man who actually attacked and wrestled large crocodiles and killed them with his 12-inch knife as he hung onto their necks like in the Johnny Weissmuller Tarzan movies. They had made movies about Kapax. Yet, here he was drinking a beer with me saying something I didn't fully understand and smiling big-time and calling me his friend and introducing me to his Tapatinga and Leticia friends. Everyone knew him and showed great respect to this wild man for his abilities and accomplishments. Before the Ambassador arrived three days later, Kapax gave me a cleaned crocodile skull with its teeth glued back in. This skull is 24 inches long and he killed this monster himself with just his knife. It had been endangering the kids playing on the river's edge and they asked him to get rid of it before it ate one of them. So, he did it and he was now presenting me with it as a sign of our friendship. I still have that skull and display it on a coffee table and tell people the story of Kapax, the real Tarzan.

The Ambassador and wife arrived and the next morning early we began the three days of "day trips" up the river. Here was Kapax, practically naked, barefoot with wild uncombed hair, only his shorts and his knife, smiling a huge smile, scaring the Ambassador's wife to death as I introduced him. During the three days, we visited amazing places where possibly only Kapax knew. After going up river again in a fast boat to save cruise time, Kapax took us into the jungle and we hiked for about an hour through seriously mysterious and dark triple canopy terrain. As we went, he would show us things that we didn't notice or know such as at the base of a large tree with giant wedges fanning out. Kapax picked up a large branch and swung it onto one of the wedges and the sound reverberated like a loud speaker system. He explained that this was a system for jungle communication and that now, the village we were traveling to knew we were coming. He would make me do everything he did to ensure the lesson sunk in. He also would stop and pick up plants and nut-type items to show us how they could be used and how one could survive for food in the jungle. Most of it was pretty tasty. Some was bland but filling. All of it was fantastic. A short time later, as we trudged and struggled through the mud and dense jungle brush with our boots on (and Kapax stepped right through it barefoot without a single problem), we entered a village. I later asked Kapax about boots versus barefoot and he told me it was much easier barefoot in the jungle and next time I would also go barefoot. I had a hard time picturing that considering the multitude of snakes, spiders, and rough terrain we had witnessed.

The village was remote, authentic, and most definitely NOT a tourist spot. Who on earth could find this place except Tarzan Kapax. I took a picture of all of us in the village with the topless native women and with the Ambassador's wife scowling and it was my Christmas card photo that year. A real hit except with the strict religious elements in my family. The villagers came out to meet us and had indeed been made aware we were coming by the Kapax tree communication system. The women took my hand and led me over to a downed tree and sat me down and immediately began to paint my face with an orange colored clay substance similar to the designs they were all wearing. Maybe my face was just a little too ghostly white for them or maybe Kapax told them we had become friends but it wasn't an option, they just did it to me but not to the Ambassador and certainly not to the seemingly always upset Ambassador's wife. I was honored for whatever reason it was done.

As a practitioner of the martial arts, I had always been interested in all types of weaponry and I noticed 8-foot long blow guns stacked against a hut and walked over to see them. These were not like my high tech, factory made metal tubular perfect instruments. These were hollowed-out reed-type less-than-light wood devices that weren't all that straight either. When the men noticed my curiosity, it was time for a practice session. They showed me how they did it with long shaft bamboo darts and they were pretty good too. Their accuracy wasn't perfect but neither was the weapon and I could see how with a couple of shots, they could bring down an animal if the dart was tipped with poison. Then they handed the blow gun to me and I tried lifting the long wooden tube and holding it without letting it wobble or weave around. The length alone made it difficult but eventually I figured out how to lock my one arm on my chest to support it. Then I blew the dart out to find it missing the target by a yard. Man, I sucked with the real nature model. I tried several more times if only to reduce the smiles and humor on their faces and eventually hit the tree we were aiming for. By that point, they were nodding their heads and I couldn't hold the damn wooden log up any more so I thanked them and we moved away from that embarrassment.

We left some gifts of bright cloth and clothing and began the trek out. By the time we made it back to the boat it was getting late and as we went back down river in the dark and the noises started to pick up, I realized that survival out here would be an act of luck and the grace of God if it required any overnight time. But I also realized that this was maybe the most beautiful real nature location I had ever seen and it was soothing and relaxing to be part of something so powerful, so real and so natural.

The next day Kapax took us back up the river but along a different arm of it that split into the Peruvian territory and then back again into the outer border of Colombia to a biological diversity study camp. This place was so cool. It was built off the floor of the jungle on wood and rope walkways with stilt-based study buildings and some very rough hard-core rooms for overnight stay for the biologists. The mixed nationalities of people here were all interested in the plant life and the animal life and their intent on discovering new forms of both. While the Ambassador and his wife took the instructional tour, and Kapax went off to visit friends in the jungle, I went out exploring the rooms and subjects that were in bottles and on display. I was standing on a walkway and thought I heard an angry little voice in the distance and I tried to figure out where it was coming from. I kept turning my head trying to get the right direction and then realized it was coming up at me. I looked down not knowing what to expect and there at my feet was a miniature monkey-creature less than three inches tall with a fur band around his neck. My first thought was that something in the air was causing hallucinations. I stared at it and it stared at me and kept yelling at me but it was so little it wasn't very loud. I reached down to keep my hallucination going and it climbed onto the palm of my hand and sat there calmly holding onto part of my thumb. I was so intrigued and loved this little guy so much we just stared at each other for 10 minutes. I brought him up close and he reached to my breast pocket and climbed in. Now I knew I was in need of immediate psychological drug detoxification. There was a 3-inch monkey sticking his head over the top of my shirt pocket looking around and up at me. What the hell? I carefully walked toward where my Amazon anchor Kapax was strolling and stood there looking at him to see if he would respond. He smiled and reached out to take the miniature monkey and it climbed onto his hand. He had a name for it I don't remember but later, others referred to it as a Pygmy

Marmoset. If it hadn't been apparently so sensitive to environmental change, I would have loved to keep it as a house-friend but the experts said it was just too susceptible to change and that those who tried to take them away or bought them illegally in the market places always ended up with them dieing. Looking into those tiny eyes, I could never do that. I have never forgotten that one particular encounter with an animal so unique, special and sensitive. I would give anything to have it happen again.

Colombia is a country of unique diversity and beauty and for a boy who grew up a bit wild on the slopes of the Rocky Mountains as Salt Lake City was developing, chasing lizards and snakes - animal life in its natural habitat was inherent in my appreciation of life. I also played with baby Lynx and an albino Boa Constrictor. Colombia was an excellent first ARSO tour that reinforced my connection and desire to live in exotic cultures.

The second Ambassador I served under in Colombia was Ambassador F and I really liked him and his wife. They were kind and caring and for some reason took a special interest in being my friend. Though we protect everyone the same, always exerting 100% attention to duty and willing to take a bullet to protect the Ambassador, there is a certain extra dedication when you personally like the Ambassador and you worry more about ensuring his comfort and safety. That's just the way it is. It's like the focus you would offer to protect family or friends.

One of the trips I was scheduled to accompany the Ambassador on was again deep into the Amazon to see first-hand a Coca (Cocaine) Lab that had been allegedly seized the night before. We also had a visitor from Washington who was on the funding committee. The Colombian Minister of Defense, Botero, son of the famous artist Botero, had arranged for a large group to go. It would contain the Ambassador, our visitor and me, Botero and some of his staff, some Generals and a load of Press. The itinerary was that we would fly from Leticia in two fixed wing planes (one for Press and the other for us) for more than an hour to a remote landing strip deep into the "unknown" jungles and then we would transfer to three helicopters to go another hour to an isolated site where this coca lab had been seized. One helicopter would contain the young Minister and his cronies, one would contain the Press, and the other would contain the Ambassador, our visitor, me, a General, and the two pilots and two door gunners.

As background to what happened later, you need to know that Minister Botero was apparently corrupt (I know, what a surprise) and it was suggested that he had been diverting funds provided by the U.S. and Colombia for the fight against drug cartels and insurgents into his own foreign bank accounts. He was also now asking the U.S. Government for additional money for more equipment, but knowing about his corruption, and where that money would go, and seeing how ineffective he had been in the fight against the drug cartels, we told him to use the equipment we had already provided, which included the helicopters we were flying in.

When the helicopters finally arrived and were hovering over the coordinates, I noticed that there was only dense triple canopy jungle, a small river and no cleared area anywhere that would allow us to set the helicopters down. We couldn't see any lab or operation, no soldiers, and not one inch of space to land in, only one native in a small hand-carved log canoe on the river who pointed at us and waved. I commented to the Ambassador that there was something wrong and pointed out my observations. He became concerned and talked to the pilot about whether this was the right spot. The pilot stated over the headset that it was the coordinates he was given. I then looked for the other helicopters to raise the question and both the Press helo and Botero's helo were at least 1,500 feet above us, hardly visible, just hovering, and here we were, hovering 30 feet over the tree tops, unable to see anything. When I pointed that out to the Ambassador, he realized what I had realized. This seemed like a set-up.

In the next instant, rifle shots rang out. Nine or ten shots in quick succession were heard and I could see that some were penetrating our helicopter. The door gunners did just what they had been trained to do and leaned their guns out and opened up with a hail storm of rounds as the pilot quickly veered left and away as quickly as he could. My hand gun couldn't do much into blind triple-canopy treetops but I tried to contribute.

An hour later, all three helicopters landed back at the remote landing strip we had started from. Upon inspection of our helicopter, there were seven rounds that penetrated the tin can outer shell of the helicopter and not a single one of them hit any of us. This was beyond luck, it was a miracle. Botero made it a major press event and highlighted to them how this demonstrated how much he needed more funding and equipment from the United States to fight these evil devils. And wouldn't you know, he must have somehow gotten the wrong coordinates. We had been hovering over an active Coca Lab, not the one seized the night before where his soldiers were still waiting and wondering where we were. This was no error. This was a greedy attempt on his part to get his hands on more money for himself at the risk or loss of a U.S. Ambassador, a U.S. VIP, and of course me.

Here, I made an ARSO learning curve mistake. I had checked out the Ambassador and our VIP in the helo and they were not hit and were fine, even calm. Upon landing, I checked out the helo to better understand the shot pattern. But, the Press filed the story and I decided to wait a couple of hours until we got back to Bogota to report it to my boss, the Senior RSO. I didn't have a phone and we were in the jungle at an airstrip. The Press had their own portable means. When we finally got back, I got chewed out because they hadn't heard from me about the Ambassador's safety. I explained there weren't phones in the jungle but it didn't catch on as an acceptable excuse. Our photos at the jungle airstrip were in the papers for weeks and the photo inspecting the bullet holes in the helicopter with the Ambassador and our Washington visitor was the big story.

Minister Botero eventually went to Prison for his corruption. A newspaper tapped his phone line and recorded a conversation between a Cartel leader and he, where they were discussing how much of a monetary contribution they would be making to him to ensure his re-election. This recording was played on the radio for months and became one of the most talked-about humorous national embarrassments. The really funny part was that this concept caught on and another politician was later caught on a recording and played on the air where he was talking with the same cartel demanding equal payoff for his election. The cartel was heard to tell him no and to go away. That one also played for months. He was also removed from office.

When I finished my tour in Bogota, the morning I was leaving, Ambassador F called me and asked if I could come to his home first. Of course I went. In front of his home, with him and his wife both crying small "family tears", he presented me with a special award of appreciation for my time and service to him and hugged me farewell. I treasure that.

I met a Colombian girl shortly before having to leave and became somewhat smitten. I had to go to the U.S. to study Portuguese for six months for my next assignment in Luanda, Angola, where there was a brutal civil war going on. She accompanied me for a few months so we could see if the relationship had lastability. I completed my Portuguese language and tested out at a "3" level, which means a technical language proficiency, and that made me very happy. I packed up and left for Angola, where I would be the only RSO for the Embassy's security operation.

Chapter Fourteen
RSO LUANDA, ANGOLA, 1995 – 1998

My first impression was that the city of Luanda was a disaster. My later impression was that Luanda was a complete disaster with a lot of potential. The 35 year-long civil war had literally demolished the country and capital city and taken limbs from what seemed to be the majority of its citizens. Not a building had all its windows, many buildings were blown up, and there was no life, no soul, no open stores, no restaurants, no food and no potable water, no street lights, and there were destroyed cars and junk lining the streets. It almost looked like similar damage in Kuwait City after the Iraqis got through. Stairwells and elevator shafts and even lifeless elevators themselves, of most of the apartment buildings lining "The Marginal" (beach bay boardwalk) had been turned into toilets and crime was rampant on the streets just so that the remaining locals could survive daily. Gunfire could be heard all through the day and night. It seemed like just my kind of place. This was scheduled to be a two-year tour of duty.

The Embassy was a small, walled-compound on a high hill overlooking downtown Luanda City, the Ilha (small peninsula on the water), and the ocean. At night, if you squinted, you might see how at one time the city on the curved beach bay Marginal might have been a very quaint and beautiful Portuguese settlement where Europeans would come to vacation. The Embassy itself was a Scotsman temporary structure which means it was aluminum siding raised off the ground with a skirting around the bottom. It was small, very temporary, and the inner wall linings were being eaten out by termites that formed large colonies in the rooms overnight, and were then scraped off each day again. My office was an unattached trailer and that meant the termites knew I was in a weak position and they were actually winning the daily structural battle. There were mornings that I would enter around 0500 hours and find a new basketball-sized termite mound on my wall like some mounted elk head. We almost all lived in the tiny compound in 30-year old, Florida Everglades reject trailers where one could practically sit in the living room and open the front door and the refrigerator door without getting out of the chair, which made entertaining easy but something 20 levels below casual. Security for this temporary compound and "lock and leave" loose security Embassy was going to take a lot of attention and creative oversight.

Even though conditions were harsh and Spartan, these types of assignments always seem to engender the closest relationships and the best memories because everyone is suffering and the old adage is true about shared suffering becoming easier to bear. The one thing we did have was a backyard-sized pool. That was the entire amenity package for the Embassy and really the city and it was in the middle of all our raggedy trailers. This gave us a real advantage on meeting people since all the Expatriates and NGOs (Non-Governmental Organizations) wanted to come to the Embassy pool. Our community also included a small group of other Missions including the Germans, the Japanese, the Swiss, the French, the U.N., and the Israelis, as well as a few others. And, of course there was every oil company in the world represented in Angola. All hungry to obtain the richest oil fields discovered possibly on the planet. I was personally more interested in going into the rich diamond fields in the center of the country. Since they were controlled by Jonas Savimbi and his UNITA rebel forces, which had already killed a million people, that was probably not going to happen. I would have to settle for the hematite and malachite stone carvings and bug-filled wood carved masks and local art work that filled the weekend makeshift market place down by the feces-and-broken-glass covered beach area. Always being armed provided me with a certain level of comfort and those individuals from other Missions and NGOs preferred to go where I was going to obtain the same comfort zone.

My local guard force was all Angolan, most of who had served in the military or perhaps even with Savimbi's rebel group. That was alright. They had a job earning money now and we had a shared loyalty to each other for our futures. There was no ARSO or any Marine Security Guards. I was the entire security contingent except for my tribal Portuguese-speaking guards. The civil war was still underway. Mostly, the battles were taking place in the countryside but they were killing people in the city every day and night. Early in the morning, I would go to my large steel King Kong front gate, gather a couple of guards, ask them in Portuguese if they were ready and when they shook their heads, we would quickly open the gate, see if any dead bodies were blocking our drive or along our wall and then take the dead bodies and roll them across the street to where there was a steep hill and push them over the hill, where they would roll down to a dirt street 80 yards below where the police patrol would find them and carry them away for burial. I know it may seem harsh but we had no way to deal with dead bodies and from a sanitation perspective for all my people, I had to get them away from our facility. We would then run back to our steel gate and close it and breathe again, while scrubbing our hands with detergent just in case.

There was virtually no power in the city, maybe a couple of hours a day at best but mainly, any place with power was running generators with fuel shipped in specifically for their/our needs. The sound of generators was constant. The airport also had no power so flights could only land or depart during the day. The baggage was all hand carried and frequently never made it from the plane to the baggage waiting room. One's first view of Angola was the baggage room, which at one time had been an actual arrival area with an electric baggage delivery belt system. Now it was dark and very dirty. People urinated and worse in the corners of the room and along the walls while waiting (not usually the foreigners though) and everyone was cautiously watching everyone else for self-preservation reasons. When a visitor or new American employee came in, it was usually me who went to get them.

Once we either got the luggage or realized it was gone for good (as we watched the quick young boy running across the airport tarmac dodging planes with a familiar looking suitcase), I took my visitor out into the light, pushing past the mob blocking the door, trying to see if their friend came back from Harare yet with their provisions while trying to pick our pockets as we walked by. When we got to my lightly-armored Blazer with oversized tires and reinforced frame, I tightly secured their bags, put the visitor into the seat, and made sure their seatbelt was nice and snug. Then we would have our first "come to god" chat. I told them that there were no stop lights and no police. It was like Mad Max.

The only people we would see on the streets would be trying to stop us to rob us or worse and we would not be complying. I looked them in their eyes and told them that once we left the airport front gate, I would be going full speed and never stopping for anything and that they could close their eyes if they wanted to but not to panic and to try and not scream while I was focusing on my driving. Almost every one of them started off thinking I was just joking. Once I left the front gate, they would go "white knuckle" on me grabbing their seat so tightly and get "big eyes". But to their credit, most did not scream (or have the ability to) and disturb my focus to drive through the attack maze. As we got 2 minutes out from the front gate, I radioed my guards to be ready with the gate and to watch for me and as we raced up to it, the gate would slide open, we would race in, and the gate would secure. At that point, the passenger would try to recover, get his legs to stop shaking, and we would have a bond to share. Some of course loved the drive. Those would either be ones I could count on in a crisis or had to watch to keep them from sneaking out at night for a desperate adventure.

Other than the front wall that looked out to the steep hill and down to the sea, we had no other "set-back" from the streets or houses several stories high that looked down into our compound. One such house, as you would expect from a previous Soviet-influenced country, was a Government of Angola (GOA) Intelligence Agency observation house. They watched us and we watched them watch us. Sometimes a wave would be rewarded with a wave and sometimes it would only serve to piss them off. There were also young attractive Angolan girls who continually walked around our block and I suspect they were trolling to hook an American for possible counterintelligence use by blackmailing him after perhaps filming some less than appropriate act. Unfortunately, sometimes these simple tactics can work. Occasionally, an American Embassy officer would think that for privacy during a sensitive cell phone discussion, they could get out of their office, away from prying ears and go outside into the parking lot where they could see if anyone was nearby, and discuss things they didn't want anyone else to hear. When I discovered this, I caught one and pointed up at the audio reception dish that was now pointed directly at them from the house on the other side of the wall. As we watched, the dish slowly redirected itself back up. Even with that proof, sometimes they would do incredibly naïve stuff.

It is unknown if it was related to the GOA intelligence collection, but one Embassy officer was way over his legal limit on inappropriate acts. One night, my guards came to my trailer and told me that this problematic officer had brought in two 12-year old girls to his trailer. The guards had told him of my legal age requirement policy and he had used his American status to bluff them off – so they came to me. I went to his trailer, dragged him out, took the two girls out to the front gate and sent them home and then read him the riot act. It was not long afterwards that I discovered many other things that led to his being dismissed and returned to the U.S. for disciplinary action.

After about four months, having been thinking about my girlfriend in Colombia, and having a pretty good grasp on the dangers and limitations of the place with regard to keeping her safe, I called her and we decided she should come and join me. She felt that even knowing what I had told her about the place, she would be fine. Little did I know at that time what a spirit of adventure she possessed. I believe she arrived in early to mid-November and she was put through the same "run for our lives" airport shuttle ride. I think she might have actually enjoyed it though. She was a sponge for learning languages and in about one month, with her native Spanish as a starting point, she was speaking Angolan Portuguese like a native. In fact, her language was so good and she is so bright, the Ambassador hired her as his Office Manager.

The Ambassador was one of the nicest guys on the planet and we all became fast friends. He would sometimes after work, walk the 40 feet from his office to our tiny trailer, take off his shoes, lie on the couch, put his feet up against the crappy trailer wall and we would drink a beer and talk about life and basketball. His brother is a famous Sports Agent who they made the Jerry McGuire movie starring Tom Cruise about. He was also mesmerized by my Colombian "fiancé" and I think if I had not already been engaged to her, he would have proposed marriage on the spot. As it was, when we announced we were going to get married in a Portuguese ceremony in Luanda, the Ambassador said his gift to us was the use of his house and he would pay for the marriage reception. The one thing I regret about the Foreign Service is that we all part ways after our tours and it is hard to stay in touch with special people like him. What a guy. The wedding was set for Spring.

The Christmas and New Year holiday period in a war-destroyed city is unique. It's kind of fun but also weird and limited in what you can do and how late you can stay out without risking being killed in a gun battle. In this case, most of the gangs started their killing from 10 p.m. on. Our international community friends were having a Christmas Eve party at one of their little generator-fed apartments on "The Marginal." My fiance was an exceptional "networker" and had established a range of friends in the other foreign missions as well as the NGOs. She had even found the Colombian community and "poof", we had a large group of friends. I told her we could attend but had to be rolling home at 10 p.m. I armed myself as usual and we went. The party was mild and limited by U.S. or Colombian standards but there was dancing and music and great food had been prepared by the mix of community cultures.

Again, under conditions of extreme hardship and danger, the best of friends are made. At 10 pm, I signaled her that it was time to go and everyone in the room picked up on the signal. The music stopped, everyone looked at me and asked if we were leaving. I told them yes, and in a flurry, everyone started grabbing coats and dishes and asked if I would escort them all home first. It was about six carloads that wanted protection to get home. I went out first, looking for trouble, and saw a young man stretched across the hood of my improvised Blazer. I told everyone to wait until I checked it out. The young man seemed at first to be passed out. I assumed it was from the local drug culture. I checked his pulse and he was stone cold dead. My fiance had only been in-country just over a month or so and I didn't want to freak her out so I grabbed the literally dead weight of the boy under his arms and dragged him off the car and over to a wall, where I sat him up against it to give the impression he was alive. I then signaled everyone to come out and get in their cars. When she asked if he was OK, I lied and said that he was just drugged. So, we drove the motorcade to their homes and compounds until they were all safely inside their protective walls and then made it to our little compound and trailer by about 11 pm. The next month, I confessed to her that she had seen her first dead person. She handled it well.

Slowly, signs of life in the city began to emerge. One of the first was that a Pizza restaurant had opened for a few hours each night. The pizza was awful and based mostly on a soda cracker-type crust but it was a place we could sit outside a tiny restaurant at tables and sweat heavily while we ate soda crackers with tomato paste and cheese. The town was still absolutely out of control with a limited police presence and those brave and corrupt souls were primarily in the line of law enforcement to get what they could and then get out quick. In the evenings as we would sit at the Pizza restaurant tables with our German, Israeli, and Colombian friends. We would constantly hear gunfire in the neighborhood. One simply adapts and the personal threat standards adjust. We kept nibbling on the pizza. Occasionally, we would hear gunfire next to us and see young men running by our tables and then police chasing them down the street shooting right past us at the young men for whatever reason. When the bullets flew past our tables, and the cops and robbers ran through our group, the Portuguese restaurant owner would come out and suggest we all go inside until it was over. He didn't want to lose some of his only paying customers. It may seem strange to those of you who are reading this, but there is something actually endearing and wonderful about living this type of life filled with occasional surrealistic events. Nothing in life will be more important than friends, family and memories. Over the next couple of years, the pizza drastically improved but so did eventual competition. We also witnessed fewer dinner entertainment gunfights.

There weren't really many wild animals left in Angola. We only heard of rare sightings. The country had deployed somewhere around 20 million land mines during the civil war and completely against all international agreements, they never marked where they had buried them. Nor did they really seem to care. So, one disastrous result was that any wild animals that weren't eaten to survive over this three-decade long civil war were blown up by land mines that were so indiscriminately placed. The other horrible result was that a large percentage of the population had lost limbs to the land mines while trying to start a life planting crops or just walking to school. Certain villages like Kuito or Bailundo, in the countryside near to where constant fighting took place or was taking place would contain a population where it seemed everyone was missing limbs. Congressional Delegations (CODEL) would come to visit and wanted to see these destroyed villages and peoples. I had to go to protect them every time and it always broke my heart. One particular picture I cannot get out of my mind was at an NGO-sponsored and funded clinic where they tended to assisting the limbless. As I was waiting for the CODEL to come out of a presentation in this ramshackled broken building, I witnessed two people carrying a 20-year old girl who was literally only a torso. She had no arms and no legs. They placed her on a chair and strapped her to it so she could stay erect and see the world that she could no longer participate in. That look in her eyes broke my heart permanently.

One of my all-time favorite people I met through VIP visitations was Madeleine Albright. She came out several times in her capacity as Ambassador to the United Nations. Madeleine is one of those rare individuals who do what she does for others, not for herself. She has always taken her job seriously and put everything she had into doing it the best she could. That is also why later when she became the Secretary of State and thus, our number one "Protectee" for DS, she became the best due to her hard work bringing DS into the main stream of law enforcement and bringing certain benefits to us that her predecessors had deprived us of. She did more for DS than anyone else ever did.

Madeleine was very devoted to the topic of demining and she had a personal commitment to try and rid the world of landmines that not only killed innocent citizens years after a war was over, but destroyed the individual's hope for a future of prosperity, as well as any chance they had of rebuilding their nation. Since Angola was "unmarked land mine central", there were a number of organizations with NGO contracts that were trying to identify mined fields and to de-mine them, allowing that nearby village to begin planting crops to feed themselves. It was anticipated that at the rate they were discovering and removing them, Angola might be free of all but the rogue landmine in 120 years. That didn't bode well for this oil-rich nation's poor. To further complicate matters, the UNITA rebel leader Jonas Savimbi and his killer thugs were re-mining fields after they were cleared. I began a collection of the various types of mines in the ground; U.S., Chinese, Russian, Israeli, and others. The design of a landmine was simple and that made the cost minor. The average cost was about $3.00 each to buy and bury. The cost to de-mine them was about $100 each. As the re-mining took minutes and the de-mining took hours and literally lives, this was a very discouraging venture.

Deminers are crazy people. I mean, how could they not be. Look what they do for a living. They dig up live explosive devices (triggered to go off on any contact) with a knife or other rod that they stick in the ground until they hit something hard. I have great respect for them but they are a breed of their own with a wild-ass view on risk. I realize some people say that about what we do to, but I don't put my hand into the hornets nest to find out if they are home. One particular deminer we had visited with several CODELs already was particularly nuts and seemed to personally thrive on that image and behavior. He was our guide for Madeleine's walk out through a "de-mined" field to the edge of a live mine field where the work was taking place. The de-mining of a field is pretty thorough but very time-consuming inch by inch and there is always the chance that one was missed, so when crossing a de-mined field, you still walk on a narrow path single file. "Crazy man" was leading Madeleine across the "safe field" and I was doing preparation work at the vehicles for our next move. The next thing I heard was my name being yelled by Madeleine and they were standing frozen in the middle of the field. Apparently our risk-taking tour guide had entered the wrong field to cross over to the on-going work and they were now standing in the middle of a "hot" field. There was only one choice. I followed the foot prints one by one out to them and then led Madeleine back the same way. The deminer was embarrassed and sorry and apologetic. We continued on our tour but with Madeleine always within my arms reach. About two years later, that same crazy but brave man was killed demining a field. He was a bit of a wild card but he had spent and lost his life to help people who had no hope in life and his loss is all of our loss.

At the end of the day, when Madeleine was back "safely" in Luanda, we took her to the only hotel that still had some windows in the building at the end of the Marginal called The Presidente. We had the best room for her but it was still barely acceptable. The next challenge was the elevator. One out of every three times, the elevator broke down and people would be stranded for a couple of hours. The elevator was only large enough for two people and that was Madeleine and I, standing body to body in order to fit. Who on earth ever designed it and decided that it made sense for a hotel? Madeleine's head only came up to my chest so we stood touching head to chest and took our chance elevator ride. This time we lost and the elevator broke down. So, for 30 minutes she and I stood in that position and got to know each other. This was one of the luckiest times of my life. I really got to spend quality "face time" with such a famous and charismatic person such as her. I found I liked her very much and this is when she and I became friends.

Madeleine and I would share time in Angola on two other trips and would also share an elevator experience on another occasion as well. Eventually, the stairs became the only safe way but it was a hard climb. Six years later in Madrid, I would be lucky enough to spend time with her again as she launched her book tour in Spain. She made me feel like we had a true friendship. It also reconfirmed my opinion of her strength to listen to her radio and TV interviews where she discussed her life, her struggles in her first marriage, and her rise to leadership. I am both blessed and lucky.

Ever since being taught the art of knife throwing in Botswana by my Sensei Ancho, I had continued to improve my skill and was pretty consistent at this point. I had a large six foot by three foot target made of two-inch thick wood, drew a torso on it and began to practice in Luanda. I placed it next to our little trailer and it was very convenient to practice every day.

The knife throwing took on a life and fame of its own. I began to offer to some other employees and official visitors the opportunity to learn the skill and as this is something only viewed in circuses and movies, many were intrigued and wanted to see if they could do it. I told them that if they stuck with the technique I was using to teach them for one hour, I would get them to the point where they got a knife to stick solidly. Almost everyone who tried with sincerity was rewarded with that photo next to the target with the knife sticking out of it. Soon, almost all visitors were seeking me out asking if I was "the knife throwing guy." I taught (only to a minimum level) many and still today people come up to me and remember that I was the Luanda "knife throwing guy" and thank me for it. Some, who lived on the Embassy compound in other crappy trailers would practice and become almost obsessive about getting a consistent skill level.

Spring in Angola and all thoughts turn to marriage. Well, not really, there was still a war mentality but my thoughts turned to marriage, and my fiancé, who I will call "A" and I had set the date and the venue was the Ambassador's residence. We met with the local Justice of the Peace, a large Angolan lady who reminded "A" and me both instantly of the evil animated character, Ursula, from "The Littlest Mermaid". Our plans were to have the ceremony inside the Ambassador's house but the JP told us that the law required that in order for it to be a legal and valid marriage, it could not be done with a roof over us, thus it had to be done outside. I have never figured that one out but OK, we would do it outside in his yard and then continue the reception in the yard as well. The ceremony was to be in Portuguese only. The Evil Ursula spoke a tribal Portuguese dialect that I could barely understand but "A" could grasp. Prior to the actual ceremony, the JP wanted to know a few things like would I be sharing everything equally with "A"? Yes. Would she be entitled to half of everything I already had? Yes. Would I be paying the JP the extra money to put a good blessing on our successful marriage? What am I going to say? NO? I was hardly in a position to debate her positive voodoo so of course I agreed to the extra fee. Besides, she really was a scary woman, and twice my size. The wedding was great and all our friends turned out and the photos are priceless. No one was prepared for this type of an event so the attire ranged from jeans to dark suits. The Ambassador is family forever for this act of kindness.

I am sorry about this next story. It is absolutely true but will seem absurd and far out of reality. One has to realize that living inside a violent world where the bizarre is reality and normal, we naturally process ourselves to accept the bizarre as standard and we do risky things to entertain ourselves. It is the "fish bowl" syndrome. From the outside, the fish look bigger, more significant. From the inside, what is going on seems normal-sized and within the boundaries of every day life and common sense.

One Embassy Officer, his wife, myself and "A" all wanted to water ski. "A" had never done it before and it met the criteria for new sports to introduce her to. An organization within the Embassy had its own ski-sized boat and the necessary equipment. The only place to do it was on the ocean where there was a small bay with a protective peninsula blocking part of the wave activity. The down side was that for a couple of decades of war, this had been where many dumped dead bodies ended up and it was pretty well filled with "meat-fed" sharks. Hummm. Water-skiing versus shark bait. Normally, that would not be a decision-making process to exceed one second. We, however were inside the fish bowl and unable to see the other perspective from the outside. Of course we were going to water ski. We simply had to devise a strategy for survival. One would water ski, one would drive the boat, one would watch the skier when he fell to make a quick rescue and one was on shark watch. Perfect, and somehow at the time it all made sense. So on our weekends during the summer and other warm months, we became water skiers in an ocean bay on bumpy water with sharks swimming around us. I told you this scenario would bother you and seem out of whack but in truth, at the time, it really did seem controllable and an acceptable risk. It is all a matter of perspective. We did it quite a few times with only a few incidents and close calls and "A" learned to water ski under the most extreme of conditions and truly loved it. Those were great times and the experiences and memories are what make life worth living and the stories worth telling.

"A" and I were the Points of Contact for another of our VIP visitors. They were Ethel Kennedy (Senator Robert Kennedy's wife), Michael Kennedy, Courtney Kennedy Hill, and her husband, Paul Hill, who is the famous Irish IRA convicted terrorist highlighted in the movie "In the Name of the Father", and the now infamous federal prisoner Michael Skakel, who we both liked very much and became close to. They visited several times as part of their responsibilities with their apparently charitable organization called Citizens Energy and I would travel out into the countryside with them to keep them protected and safe.

Michael Skakel had not yet been charged for the murder of a young girl, allegedly committed when he was a young man and was a personable and bigger-than-life friendly and kind man. Michael saw the Spartan living conditions we existed under and would bring gifts to make our lives better. The first time he came, he asked if we liked cigars. I don't but "A" is a cigar smoker for some reason and he offered her a cigar that Fidel Castro had personally and recently given to him and he showed the photos with himself and Fidel to validate his claim. I have no idea how he came to be with the Cuban leader. The value however, of that cigar from Fidel made it an extremely gracious and giving thing to do and we saw a good character in his soul. We liked him. Days later, as he was leaving, he asked if there was anything we needed. "A" said we needed a wisk. Without understanding a wisk, who was I to argue our need for one. The next time he came many months later, he showed up with three varieties of wisks and gave them all to her. He had actually remembered that request and it made "A" very happy. Again, I saw a good character in him, which made me sad when a few years later he was imprisoned for the childhood incident. I still remember him fondly.

Michael Kennedy was a quiet one. It was kind of hard to draw out much conversation but I suppose after the rough family times he had experienced, it was understandable. He was bright and close to his mother Ethel and sort of stayed in the background of the operation, whatever it was that their Citizens Energy school and other activities were striving for. His sensitive personality and kind heart broke ours when we heard he had been killed in a skiing accident later.

Paul and Courtney were a truly interesting pair. Paul didn't talk about his IRA times or his imprisonment but it had not seemed to damper his open sense of humor and he was an immediate hit with all of us, especially "A" and me. Paul was very easy to talk with and related more easily or naturally to us than perhaps the others did, coming from a famous family. Paul had obviously also found a home with the Kennedy's and they seemed to respect and protect him. Courtney was the yin to Paul's yang and not too outspoken or overt but again, very pleasant. We stayed in email communication with them for years but have since lost contact unfortunately.

Ethel Kennedy was the one I really liked though. She was strong in character, smart, very gracious and giving and took a real liking to "A" and me. Ethel would even tease me (I think) by saying to "A" in front of me that she was too good for me and what was she doing with the likes of me. Then she would wink and smile at me and let me recover my ego loss. There was also though, something of a deepness in her demeanor. Even when she was laughing or teasing, there was something in her eyes. It was easy to understand why with the tragedies that had befallen her family and life and she constantly fought it. On one occasion up north, Ethel and her entourage had wanted to go to a demining operation and I was with them for protective oversight. Ethel had a bit of a sensitive behavior to begin with and when the deminers exploded a load of mines they had dug up to show their successes, Ethel panicked, ran to the car and drove down the road a few hundred yards and parked. I suppose she was releasing a bit of stress that surfaced from the detonation. Perhaps it was a cumulative result of many experiences. I left her alone but kept an eye on her and after about 20 minutes she came back down and we finished up and went home. I think I really fell for her seeing that sensitive and bruised side of her. That night, she sponsored a big dinner at the seafood restaurant on the Ilha for her Angolan Minister contact and business associates and other VIPs and she invited "A" and me to join them. It was an honor to be treated as friends by her.

The Ilha was beginning to develop after the end of the first year and a half. A few restaurants were sprouting up and even one or two shops had opened. Not much product was available and it certainly didn't seem like it would be competing with Ft Myers Beach, Florida, any time in the near future but it began to give a misleading semblance of normality. Of course there was still the dangerous level of uncontrolled crime; robbing and killing taking place and you still tried to avoid nighttime but it was a start. Even the Marginal appeared to have work being done slowly and by hand of course around the sidewalk/boardwalk that ran along the bay. Again, it was an appearance only, the stairwells and elevator shafts in the buildings were still excrement and urine depositories and most still had no electricity or windows.

Within the first year it dawned on me that with all the other Missions, the U.N. and even the NGOs all trying to survive in the questionable security environment, they needed a central Source of security guidance and a venue to share concerns and solutions, so I started a regular security manager's meeting. Mostly we met at the Embassy in our conference room but occasionally the UN Security Officer, would like to host it at his facility outside the southern part of the city. The group quickly took off and even the oil companies and the few other companies like Debeers, who had interests in the country, joined, giving us a regular base of about 35 attendees. I would provide a general security update on conditions mostly in the city affecting us all. We would discuss anything we were aware of that concerned us including Jonas Savimbi and his brutal rebel group UNITA, and the UN security officer would provide a wider regional brief on countryside incidents and activities. The concept was a real success and it would become something I would duplicate at other postings later on. Washington, which thrives on cables to keep them informed on world "goings-on", loved anything having to do with our security group and the updates on the Angolan civil war progress. I learned that if you want to be recognized and have good visibility and exposure to those who can influence your career and promotions, you need to do good reporting. Good not only in content but also good writing skills with an interesting and clean style. Those things get noticed along with the name of who was doing the reporting.

On one particular occasion, the Ambassador had to go up to discuss some matter with Savimbi related to trying to end the civil war and get negotiations underway between the President of Angola, Jose Eduardo Dos Santos, and Savimbi. The meeting was in Savimbi's "home village", Bailundo, in the middle of nowhere, and it was hundreds or thousands of the bad guys on their side and me and one pistol on the other. We needed to negotiate from a friendly position. The Savimbi thugs protected their leader with a vicious loyalty. I was invited by Savimbi's assistant into the small room to be with the Ambassador and was there as the introductory and superficial discussions took place. Apparently, the thugs didn't like me being in the room with their leader for whatever reasons and I had gotten myself in a photo with their leader, which I still have and treasure for all the wrong reasons. When the superficial meaningless meeting for the press was ended, Savimbi and our group were moving outside to another room next door to get down to the real business at hand. I was right behind the Ambassador but as I exited the first room, I was grabbed by several thugs, had my arms pinned, mouth covered and was hauled off quickly out of sight until the Ambassador, who had no idea I wasn't there with him was inside the next room. Then the thugs carried me across the street into a heavily treed park of sorts, and with AK-47s pointed at my head, told me if I fought back, they would kill me. There was no reason to doubt their threat and they most certainly would have. So, with a couple of men holding me, and a couple of men pointing their automatic weapons at me, another of those psychos beat on me for what seemed to be about ten minutes (it was probably less) until I was pretty well finished. Then they dropped me on the ground to recover and walked off laughing. OK, sometimes you eat the bear and sometimes the bear eats you. Across the park, a Voice of America (VOA) reporter had seen and filmed part of what happened to me and later when he was safe and away from those maniacs, he put out the story on the VOA network about a US Security Officer being brutally beaten by Savimbi's forces.

As with much in life, occasionally there comes a time for payback and I would wait until those faces I would remember would come down to my town Luanda for something.

After I recovered and had wiped the blood off my face and straightened my clothing and demeanor and checked for cracked ribs, the Ambassador came out and asked where I had gone. He looked at my face and dirty messed-up clothing and I told him I would discuss it with him later. We were in a place where anyone could disappear with no questions asked or at least not expect to get any answers to questions asked. The time did come months later when the thugs came to Luanda, and I did eventually feel like there is a certain balance to life after all. I keep the photo with Savimbi, who is gratefully dead now, to remind me that no one is a badass in someone else's territory or control. Forget the Hollywood movies. Dead is dead and it is instantaneous and irreversible.

My original tour in Angola was supposed to be two years. As the two years approached, I extended for a third year. Yes, it was a hard place to be but the job was exciting and rewarding and "A" and I had developed friends and also, DS and the State Department were having a hard time finding anyone who wanted to come to this type of a hardship post, even though we were receiving food shipments pretty regularly from South Africa and the potable water containerized shipments were always on time and now we even had a series of restaurants to choose from. Yes, we got sick from the food sometimes but things were picking up.

The first RSO who opened up this assignment only stayed two weeks. The next RSO came from a similar but not-as-bad as-signment in Maputo, Mozambique, where he had already gone through much of the same type of transition. After two months, he realized he couldn't do this hardship again, and he curtailed his assignment, thus, DS contacted me in Bogota and asked me to quickly learn Portuguese and get out to replace him. After my first two years, as the formality of an Embassy set-up became more necessary, the fact that I had no other security people to help me became a problem. What I needed was a local indigenous man who spoke the various local dialects and who could work with the police and "townsfolk" to validate the backgrounds of our Angolan employees in order to make sure we weren't hiring killers. We call this position a Foreign Service National Investigator or FSNI. I interviewed quite a few people for this job. A lot of ex-military types, some ex-police, and some ex-rebels, who had done some very bad things. Finally I found a man with grace and poise and some real character. He was ex-military, a good family man, didn't speak a word of English (which we would work on), and seemed very bright but he needed an opportunity to make a good life for himself and his family. I liked him a lot and hired him. We worked well together for the final year of my tour and my Portuguese became even better. He began to learn some English but English is not an easy language. You just don't realize that. It was a brutal struggle for him. We became good friends. Years after I had moved on, an RSO who was working in Luanda told me he and his wife had a son and they named him Randall after me. One never knows the impact we have on other's lives. This information caused some tears to seep out. I was very touched by his gesture and felt guilty about losing touch.

The Angolan government, like many in the world and especially in Africa was pretty much totally corrupt. I couldn't think of a single official who was not "on the take", stealing from their country, robbing the resources, and ignoring the condition of their people entirely, even brutalizing them to maintain their power and control. The only reason to run for office or obtain a police job was to get into a position where you could rob the people and the country and save yourself. It really was every man for himself.

Our local guard company, which provided me with my perimeter and now residential security protection, was a British firm. They hired Angolans and gave them good jobs with a steady income but their middle management were all Nepalese Ghurkas, proven loyal and honest through service in the British military and they were tough. We all loved them and trusted them completely. The Project Manager named Pitam Gurung, watched over the safety of "A" like she was literally his own family. They all loved her and watched out for her wherever she was or went like a sister. In fact, one evening, Pitam, the leader of the Ghurkas, and the rest of their Ghurka Unit, held an adoption ceremony to make "A" one of their official sisters. The ceremony involved a lot of their music and dancing, their famous spicy potato dishes, and a formal presentation and speech where they discussed their affection for "A", decried their loyalty to always protect her, and they presented her with a very fine quality Ghurka Kukri curved knife. She tried to hide it but she had tears on her cheeks. They made her an official Gurung family member and she still feels she is.

About six months later, certain Ministers including the Angolan Minister of Interior had seen that the guard security business was a lucrative opportunity and decided that in their unending greed, all money should be going into their pockets. They wanted our guard contract. They had no experience with this type of business. They couldn't be trusted. They would cut the pay of the guards and demand bribes. They would hire family so that they could gain more control and help their family only, even though they would all be completely untrained. They would make our existence unsafe and violate all that I held to be ethical and proper. The British company was told by the Angolan Minister of Interior to resign the contract and leave the country or they would be arrested. A cause for arrest was not significant. Law was meaningless to those who enforced the law. The company had a responsibility to protect numerous Embassies. They had even protected Princess Diana when she came to visit. They could not close down and just abandon us.

The ruthless Minister decided to arrest all management of the company, including all the Ghurkas and at midnight one night, they raided all their homes, arrested them and put them on a plane and shipped them out in the dark of night. I awoke to find my guards with no management and no company to employ them or pay their wages. We, the American government were obviously paying the company, but the entire managerial and administrative organization was gone. The company was forced to declare "Force Majeure", an inability to fulfill their responsibilities. I was not about to allow this type of illegal and unethical action to benefit the ruthless and corrupt Angolan government officials from our operations at the American Embassy. My only choice now was to hire each guard as a direct employee of the Embassy and handle all management and oversight from within the Embassy. I notified my headquarters in Washington, DC, and they concurred. I assured all my guards, who were worried that they had just lost the only hope for their families and futures, that they were my family and I would take care of them. I held twice-daily meetings with them all to reassure them that they had nothing to worry about, and also to make sure that none abandoned their posts and left my people open to the gangs of thugs and killers who robbed homes and killed all the occupants. The war was still active and some of the hardened soldiers had turned to a more lucrative field where their brutality and skills would pay off. They had no second thoughts about killing people if it enhanced their own personal position in life. Pure Psychotic Socio-paths. Through a rapid and responsive group in Washington, the entire set-up was completed in a week and all the guards continued to get paid, got new uniforms, got a new family with a stronger link to America, and we got a highly loyal and dedicated group of guards. The Angolan government got a bad reputation, no money, and a kick in the pants by the international community. They deserved worse.

The Ambassador was looking for ways to demonstrate how Angola was in the process of recovery and he was always searching for ideas and methods to get that point across to Washington. I presented an idea to him of having the local school children compete to do drawings of how they see Angola improving and that they submit them to a committee we could create. We would select the best 12 color drawings, matrix them all onto a full sized poster and then get the U.S. oil companies to print thousands of copies for sale or distribution and put that money back into the schools. We would also pick the top little artist and take him to Washington to present a poster to the First Lady. He loved the idea and pushed it through quickly. Hundreds of color pictures were sent to us and the selection committee involved teachers, a psychologist, diplomats and business people. The pictures were of wild animals in their nearby villages, houses being built, families in happy scenarios, blue skies and green jungles. Even limbless family members with prosthetic replacements able to walk and work again etc… all inspiring works of little school children and rough and natural in skill level. And, the First Lady, Hillary Clinton was going to receive the winner at the White House. The committee selected the 12 best in their opinions, with strong input from the psychologist. We had an art company lay all 12 onto one poster sized product and print them. It is a beautiful piece of work and a wonderful memory that generated not only good will but many thousands of dollars for school development and each of the 12 winners won backpacks filled with great school stuff. The first place winner however had drawn an unfinished home with bricks in the air around it and as it was explained to the First Lady by the psychologist that this was his idea of the rebuilding of his home in the war-torn country. A simple conceptual rendition of the reconstruction of life and futures. Frankly, some of us couldn't understand why the psychologist selected that one since we thought some others were so much more inspiring and beautiful but the program was a huge success and the boy actually went to Washington and completed his dream. We just assumed the psychologist liked the symbolic deeper meaning. When the eight-year old boy returned, he came to the Embassy and I pulled him aside and had to ask. I asked him in Portuguese what his picture represented. He looked at me and tears came into his eyes and he said it was a picture of when the UNITA Rebels and government of Angola military were fighting and they blew his home up and killed some of his family. Whoops! The bricks were flying out, not in. Although in private I passed on the true meaning of the picture and how wrong the psychologist had gotten it, we never brought this mistake into the light. All the kids benefited and schools got supplied and built and the good will was created. Always get a second opinion when dealing with psychology. I still treasure my poster that I was the creator of.

Even though life in Angola would never be described as normal, we did find things that from within the fish bowl made us feel like it had a semblance of balance. We began to see and shop in new local market places. We found their local music with Spanish,

Portuguese and African influences and it was great to dance to. We discovered Angolan artists and bought some pieces that to us seemed inspired and were displayed on the walls of our home and we even held the first July fourth celebrations at a local "Beach Club" where though nothing was like a "stateside" July 4th to us, it was quite an achievement and felt like a bit of home with volley-ball and hot dogs. We still had shootings going on in the city and when the Ambassador had a reception in the yard of his home, the local shooting remained the signal that the party was over. Even though the termites won the war I fought against them, when we all look back on the experiences we had, and the unique nature of the friendships we developed under those circumstances, it seems like some of the best times of our lives and always brings laughter to our conversations.

Chapter Fifteen
RSO KARACHI, PAKISTAN,
1998 – 2002

Toward the end of the third year in Angola, when it was time to bid on another assignment, I was called by my DS Headquarters people. It was time for me to move on to a different duty station and even though I was due to be recalled back to the U.S. for a tour there, I had bid on overseas locations and was hoping to stay out and remain an operational Agent, an RSO running my own show. Remaining lucky, though some would disagree, my HQ said that they needed someone with my experience to take over a critical threat terrorist post that they were having a hard time getting anyone to volunteer for. It was Karachi, Pakistan, and at that time in history, to say it was volatile would be grossly marginalizing the threat. It was being called the most dangerous city in the world and was only going to get worse in the next few years. I felt like Brere Rabbit being threatened with being thrown into the briar patch where he was born and happily thrived. "Oh no, please don't send me to an assignment I would love". Thankfully, I wouldn't have to learn the Urdu language and "A" seemed OK with the thought of living in another battle-front location, this time with terrorists instead of in a civil war.

I remembered my trips to Pakistan from MSD days and was actually excited about getting back. I had been bitten by the oriental carpet bug and the exotic raw nature of the culture, and I wanted to explore and see what I could find. And I knew Karachi would be on the action front again, if not THE front.

We packed-out our meager belongings from Angola, those that had any value, mostly artesan works, bone carvings, artwork, and malachite stone pieces we had bought while there and sent them on to Karachi. Then it was off to "Home Leave" in the U.S. prior to beginning what would become the most dangerous but career-enhancing posting of my life. "Home Leave" is an obligatory vacation and must be taken in the U.S. between two overseas assignments in order to ensure that the Agent or Officer doesn't forget his American roots and go too foreign or "indigenous". There is some truth to that. Living all the time in foreign cultures, one adapts to the foreign environment and can easily be drawn into the simpler and perhaps more singularly graceful or enticing life style.

"A" and I rented a car and traveled all over the western states seeing the beautiful areas I had grown up around like the Grand Canyon and Moab, Utah regions. We then drove across the U.S. through Florida and up the coast, arriving in time to get our departure briefing. Unfortunately, this briefing would be catastrophic for "A" and I as a couple. Violence was erupting again in Pakistan and the spouses and kids were being evacuated and would not be permitted to go back there until a determination could be made that the threat had been quelled. This was unbelievable. We had flight reservations literally for the next day, and now they were telling us "A" had to stay. She was still a "foreigner" in our country and didn't have anyone to fall back on. Both of us took this hard but we had 24 hours before I had to leave and we needed to find her a place to live with a comfort zone around her. There are times in the Foreign Service when life almost gets "out of hand" difficult and this was definitely on the top of my list. I had to go. I was the one expected to protect the American and Pakistani employees who remained in Karachi during the threat.

I have the best sister in the world. We have always watched out for each other and helped each other through times requiring shared conversation or counseling. I called Barbara. It was a huge favor I can never repay, but I asked her if "A" could stay with her just until she got cleared to join me. Of course being who she is, she gladly agreed but I knew what a sacrifice both of them were making and I crossed my fingers they both would survive the inevitable clash.

My sister Barbara is highly intelligent, a Professor by occupation, and is very giving and sensitive to people and patient to a fault. She must be – look at the Brother she puts up with. The evacuation could be anytime from one month to six months and we were hoping for the least time for everyone's sake. "A" got on a plane with only her travel suitcases, since her life's possessions were on the way to Karachi, and flew to Georgia to my sister and a world she had never experienced before. Barbara picked her up and openly welcomed her into a situation that was highly intrusive but she never said a word or complained. And I flew alone to Karachi and into the brewing firestorm that would soon be identified as the heart and soul of the terrorist world with a nexus to virtually every world terrorist act committed.

I arrived in Karachi, walked off the plane into a furnace of heat and was met by a Consulate Pakistani Expeditor, who took my passport and papers and processed me through quickly and took me out to a waiting fully armored suburban with a Police follow car with a driver and three police with automatic weapons to follow me to the Consulate General to ensure my safe arrival. I was checked into the Karachi Marriott Hotel for the few days it would take to get my home ready after my predecessor left the following day.

In my first week on the job, my Pakistani Foreign Service National Investigator (FSNI) came to me and told me that the prior RSO had told him he could go on vacation but that he had to wait until I arrived and he had even gotten a U.S. visa for his vacation to see the USA. I told him that I would honor my predecessor's promise and he could make plans to go. I had a Security Clerk as well, we will call him "H" for his protection. He was young, very bright, highly motivated to advance, and was a computer wiz, and he and I would hold down the fort until my FSNI came back from his 30-day USA tour. The day before my FSNI was to leave, he came to me with his cell phone, radio, and all accessories and said he wanted to turn in everything to me for accountability reasons before he left. I jokingly asked if he was leaving for good and he showed a slight nervous tick at the corner of his mouth. He poorly bluffed that he would return but just didn't want his equipment to disappear. What am I going to say? "Hey, you're making me too suspicious and I am revoking your vacation"? He left and H and I found that we worked well together and I found that he was capable far beyond the Clerk position he was filling. In fact, he was much better than what I had seen out of the FSNI so far.

The month passed and no FSNI. We waited another week just in case, and because he was married to several wives as permitted being a Muslim and he had only taken one wife with him to the U.S. I sent out H to his home to check on his status. He had not returned and his first wife was still in the home wondering where her husband and his second wife were. Oh crap! His second home where the second wife lived was closed up and dark. The neighbors said he had left not intending to return. I put out the proper notification to Customs and Immigration regarding the FSNI overstaying his visa and issued a "lookout" for him. Then, I had him fired from the job and I advertised for a replacement. Thank heavens for H and his intellect and drive to do well. He was a hard worker who just needed and wanted guidance on how to become more in life. What he wanted was a mentor.

About twenty applications were received for the position of Senior FSNI and I whittled it down to a short list of three. Most of them were ex-military, ex-police, or students trying to find a job. For the interview, I designed scenario questions, telling them a story about a disaster and asking them how they would deal with it. I needed to know what kind of judgment they had. The scenario questions followed an ever-worsening sequence of events. First, an anti-American crowd was gathering at a Mosque with the intention to walk to the Consulate to protest. What would he do? Then, they were at the end of the street and loudly voicing anti-America sentiments. What now? Then the mob was at the wall and throwing rocks over into the compound. What do we do now? And finally, they were climbing over the wall. What was the appropriate response under these conditions? The first two interviewees were strong-minded and disciplined men but were missing a certain natural common sense. One was a Policeman who felt that we should just let the mob vent it all out and then clean up afterwards and arrest the instigators the next day, and then beat them to within an inch of their lives as a message to their friends. Hmmm, not really what I was looking for as a good pro-active response. The next was a retired Pakistan military Colonel. When I asked him what we should do when they were throwing rocks over the wall, his response was to shoot them. I stared at him thinking he was pulling my leg and when he sat stoic and unflinching, I said, "you mean shoot them and kill them"? He said "well, we could just shoot them in the legs if you prefer". I thanked him for his time and prayed for a miracle.

A miracle walked into my office as the third man on my short list. "Z", as we will call him for his protection, was a retired Pakistan Naval Commander, refined, elegant, gentle and respectful and very intelligent. His eyes showed that he was alert and in tune, and his answers were just what I was hoping for. This was the guy and I hired him. That was truly one of my (and the U.S. Government's) luckiest days. Z and H became a Senior and Junior team who worked not just as associates but became brothers and also became my best assets and best friends. No one could have known at that time that we were destined to be involved in some of the most well-known international terrorism cases still today. As a team, we excelled. From here, we began to expand our team into what I would constantly refer to as our Security Family and that "Family" concept would not only serve us well but would keep some of us alive later.

As it neared the end of 1998, DS decided to introduce and launch a new Program called the Surveillance Detection Program. This was one of the best Programs DS ever introduced and I knew it would help me so I went to work immediately on getting it started in Karachi and by the end of 1998, we had the first running SD Team in the world and over the years, they identified terrorists and we caught many people who were in the planning stages of attacking us. Their value simply cannot be over-stated.

The SD Team was made up of a totally diverse group of rough men including Pathans, Punjabis, Sindhis, Baluchis, Hazaras, Waziris, Mehmuds, Afghans, and others, who together made us the most capable and thoroughly prepared team possible. We had every language in all of South Asia covered; Urdu, Farsi, Arabic, Pushtu, Punjabi, Sindhi, Baluch, Hindi, and all the other minor local dialects so that no matter who was encountered paying too much attention to our Consulate, we had someone who could pass by and address them courteously in their own language to derive what their sense of purpose was. Obviously, if they were speaking Arabic or Farsi and sitting watching my building from the park across the street, issuing curses at us under their breath, it was damn good to know that.

The hiring process had to be my key to making a sound team and my FSNIs were involved completely in the scrutiny of all candidates. And, I first needed a strong big brother character for the leader of the SD team members. My approach was again one of "my family." They would all be my sons and we would only survive in this volatile hostility of Karachi if we all watched out for each other as a family does. In South Asia, family is everything and it rang a true chord with those I interviewed and hired. I needed total commitment and perfect loyalty to each other and me. Our lives would literally depend on each other. If we failed to be alert and do our jobs, people would die. I needed to make them understand that those lives rested in our hands. I also told them that this was a job only for "a man." If they could not be a real man and understand the protective responsibilities and duties of a man, they were not the ones I was looking for. Obviously I didn't mean a man versus a woman (although because of discrimination

against women in this Muslim culture they could not have survived well in the Karachi environment), I meant the "Code Of
The West", "A Man's Gotta Do What a Man's Gotta Do" kind of
Cowboy man responsibility. Men took care of their family. That
is their responsibility, and again, we were a family of men. We
depended on each other. This psychological perspective and responsibility image was just the concept that helped me identify
the right guys for this job.

I found my Big Brother SD Leader in a man we will call "J". He
was a big man, always smiling except when he needed to kick
butt, and he was a Pathan from the North West Frontier Province
(NWFP) region in the mountains by the Afghan border area.
This is an area that prides themselves on family and being responsible men. Of course many of the Taliban are from the same tribal
background but J was one of the good guys and now, he could
help us select the bulk of the SD family.

Pretty quickly we had 18 good men and we began training them
while we put them out on learner tasks to begin to get the hang of
the job. I held regular meetings with them and always stuck to the
"family meeting" theme. As much as it might have been a unifica-
tion strategy, it was true. We would live or die based on how we
worked as a family. There were many success stories where their
actions saved the lives of American and Pakistani employees at the
Consulate and those stories could fill a separate book. An example
of what they did and how they did it is shown by one day when J,
who spoke 8 or 10 local languages, was walking on-duty humbly
through the Frere Park across from the Consulate as many pi-
ous Muslim men did, when he came upon a man seated on the
grass facing the Consulate. He was lighting matches and symbolically throwing them at the Consulate as he muttered curses

at the Americans in Arabic. J greeted him in Arabic to confirm it and the man returned the greeting. He continued his meditative walk and then when hidden, discreetly gave the order for a police "convergence" and the man was grabbed by a team of Police who took him into custody. In his small bag was a ticket to Kabul for that afternoon and a diary of information and drawings about the Consulate including motorcade movements and timings. He had done his terrorist attack homework and was returning to Al-Qaida that afternoon with his information. And just like that, a future terrorist attack had been thwarted.

I moved around Karachi very actively and sometimes alone. Whenever I did, I notified my SD guys so they could be watching my back. I took risks that I didn't allow others to take but my purpose was to step into the risk zone to gauge the temperament of the area for our people. SD always protected me like their father. I knew with a certainty, even though it was hard for me to spot my guys most of the time in the crowds on the streets, that they were watching me like I was the keeper of the gold. Occasionally I would see one but of course recognition would never be made in order to maintain their protective anonymity. On numerous occasions, they provided a noise or signal that made me turn to see an unhealthy situation coming my way and I escaped. Later, as things got worse in the city and I began to be identified by Al-Qaida for the successes we had against them, I found it necessary to have machine-gun armed police bodyguards with me in most locations in the city during the day but SD was always my backstop. I had a family of brothers and sons who cared about me and I felt good about it. Z never let me forget though that he disagreed with the risks I took and reminded me of that constantly out of an affection and caring that we had developed for each other and the family.

Networking is so important in Pakistan. It was the same philosophy as the SD family but on a ranking police level. I found the Pakistani police contacts to be some of the nicest people I have ever met and even today, many years later, those men are still my close friends and we maintain contact. Some of it has to do with the life and death experiences we shared together. Some of it has to do with my understanding their culture and the way they needed to do things and not being critical of their methods; but instead, embracing the conditions they had to work under and respecting them for it. Their tactics were frequently outside of our normally-accepted law enforcement parameters but it was necessary under the conditions they faced.

One such contact was the Superintendent of the Pakistani Anti-Terrorist Commando Training College, who I will call Uncle. Uncle came to all our Marine Birthday Balls, parties at the American Club, and maintained a close weekly communication with me. We also used his firing range to maintain our proficiency with weapons. Typical to his origins, he would set up an overhead tent at the rear of the firing range and set up tea and biscuits and when he felt we had fired enough, he would tell us to come have tea with him while his Commandos would put on a show for us riding their motorcycles and shooting at the same time. I am not sure if they hit anything but that wasn't the point. It was a demonstration of brotherhood and the sharing of tea with a background of entertainment. Six years later, Uncle would show up at the front gate of the Embassy in Madrid, Spain, and order my guards to tell me that my Uncle had arrived. The Spaniards were incredulous to see this dark Pakistani man claiming to be my uncle but I was very happy and confirmed it to their disbelief. He arrived with gifts in hand and a huge smile and a 5-minute hug.

Our Consulate in Karachi had quite a scary reputation and had been the cause of many employees quitting unexpectedly due to seeing a ghost in the halls. The ghost was a British soldier dressed from 100 years before who people claimed was seen just walking the halls at night. I would have just ignored it but so many of the people claimed to have seen him. One night, my fearless Marine Security Guard (MSG) said he saw him in the hall, gave him an order to halt and when he began sort of walking/floating toward him, the MSG ran into his ballistic-proof reinforced guard control center and stayed there. He was more than a bit distressed by the event, and I suppose his personal response to it. It became such a problem with employees, we were forced to consult with a local "witch doctor", who came to the Consulate and determined that the only way to calm the spirit was to put water over his burial site and he identified where the emanation was coming from. So, we built a nice fountain over the alleged grave site. Unfortunately, sightings continued including my MSG incident. Even though I wanted to, I never got to meet him.

It was only 1999 and most people in the U.S. general public had still never heard of Usama Bin Ladin, but we were already looking out for him and his Taliban and Al-Qaida associates. Karachi was and is still the center of the world for Jihadi recruitment and fund collection. We began to establish a watch on potential candidates who came into Karachi and then would disappear through the Afghan border, usually through Quetta and Chaman and on into various training camps, preparing for attacks and disasters to come that would change the world as we knew it. I began to generate Sources to keep me better informed on who was coming and going. Some of these Sources were terrific and led to significant success stories.

One success story in particular was a man who had been trained as a hard-core Jihadi and had gotten close to the core of the Al-Qaida operation. He was a metal fabricator and had become a weapons maker for Usama Bin ladin (UBL), working for a famous and dangerous man who was the chief designer. As years passed with this Jihadi (and before I met him), he aged and matured a bit and probably never really was the true psychopath. He met a woman and fell in love with her. His heart began to change regarding the value of life and then she got pregnant and he became a father. As he described it to me, he had never imagined how he would feel about a son and the woman who bore it. He told his boss that he wished to take on a different job so he could be near his family. It was granted and he would still receive a monthly salary and remain in the UBL network. After a year of doing this, he sought me out. He wanted to have a better life for his family. One where they would be safe and he could live a normal existence. We had several successful operations over a couple of years I cannot talk about.

In the very beginning of our relationship, when I demanded that he provide me with some substantive proof to establish his credentials, he told me about some Pakistani Scientists who were sharing the secrets of destruction with Al-Qaida and the Taliban. I was highly dubious. This was just too good and I guess he perceived I doubted him. I told him he had to prove it. A few weeks later he showed up and provided a photo of a group of well-known dangerous men at a table that included UBL, some Pakistani Scientists, and miscellaneous other infamous personalities. My report to Washington created a bit of a stir. He certainly proved his credentials.

On another occasion, my Source told me about a specific oil worn by men called Ood ul Harram (Ud al Harram). He said that it was used by UBL's bodyguards (BGs) and that there were many levels of quality but that the best, and the preference of UBL's bodyguards came from a shop in Karachi, and that when they needed more, several of his BGs would come to Karachi to buy it at this one specific store and also enjoy the city, such as there was for enjoyment by Psycho killers. We watched the shop but things heated up shortly thereafter in Afghanistan and we never saw them. I did however report it and bought some for myself.

This Source continued to email me to keep me informed about his life and family but things never really improved much for him. Times were changing in South Asia and the focus was shifting to other grander scale operations. The Human Intelligence aspects had been and were still being overlooked and that later would be sorely regretted by our intelligence friends.

Backing up a bit, it was at about 6 months into the tour while "A" was less-than-patiently still living with my sister and had found a job with the Habitat for Humanity group who wanted to keep her. We were at that point with the State Department where at the 180 day mark, the Department has to either declare formally that the post will be a "no-dependent-allowed" post or allow the families to go back. Fortunately, they chose to allow the dependents to return. "A" began to make her preparations and arrangements through the Department of State in Washington and my sister and I both took deep breaths but for different reasons.

Our house was in the Frere Hall area, which was a three block area encompassing only U.S. Consulate homes in a heavily treed and gardened area across from the Frere Park and within eyesight of the Consulate. We could see the Consulate, we just couldn't walk to it due to the constant threat to kill us and the park was one of the main surveillance points. Within the three blocks was the Consul General's home, the Marine Security Guard's home and gym, the American Club and six other residences for Americans. My home was a large two-story cavernous high-ceilinged block and concrete home with the standard U.S. Government furniture that we come to know and recognize so well throughout our careers. It had a large yard with huge hundred year-old trees and a Mosque across the street that would wake us up about 0500 a.m. every morning. I had taken to going to work at 0500 a.m. 7 days a week not just due to all the work I had but to avoid first morning prayer, which was put out on a loudspeaker system and I swear they had a speaker somewhere in my home. I employed a Christian housekeeper and Muslim gardener to maintain the place so that I could spend my time on my duties. Fortunately I was able to afford it in Pakistan. The yard was truly beautiful. But part of the reason we could safely enjoy our homes in the Frere Hall area was that I had placed 65 heavily armed Frontier Constabulary Commandos in tents surrounding the three blocks and hooked them up with electricity and water to make them happy and want to stay there to protect our homes. Bad guys don't like to mess with the Frontier Constabulary (FC) guys. They are hard-core and will shoot if they are confronted. They were perfect friends to make and everyone treated them well. We also treated their bosses well and made sure they were at every party we threw. These Commandos from the NorthWest Frontier Province were tough guys who seldom were treated nice and by our doing so, they would have given their lives to protect us.

One such FC Boss was a Hollywood-type tough guy we'll call "H". He was big and handsome in a mean and intimidating way and loved Americans and America. He quickly became my friend and my ARSO's friend. My ARSO at the time was a personable and bright young man. He was raised in a Foreign Service family and by a stroke of luck had learned some Urdu language growing up. He had learned bits of Urdu really and much of it was "kid language" and insults or obscenities. Still, it came in handy. H took to my ARSO like he was his real blood brother. He taught him stronger and more insulting obscenities and they sort of hung out together on occasion. The bottom line is that H had adopted him and that was literally an unbreakable bond.

The local newspapers had no ethics or rules about what they could print and there was no rule that you had to verify a Source or even that the information had to be true. Many times the reporters simply made up items that they thought might be of interest to readers. There was no basis for it, just telling a story to fill space. In the town of Quetta, a family name Kansi had a son captured by DS Agents, and who had been taken back to the States for trial because he had killed some CIA employees in Virginia as they came to work one morning. Certain younger and more radical members of the Kansi family didn't like me at all and regularly would make death threats against me. The basic family was a nice family but a brother and some cousins formed a group based on revenge and I was the target. The less-than-ethical newspapers would actually print their threats to kill me and say something like, "The Kansi family has vowed to come to Karachi this week and intend on killing Randall Bennett, the Security Officer for the American Consulate". So, my name began to become a known item but those Kansi threats never came about, even though after about the tenth time, I told the paper to tell them I was waiting and they printed that too. I am a bit more circumspect now.

These false press reports didn't bother me and in fact were quite entertaining, but for my young and inexperienced ARSO, it was much more serious and personal. On one particular occasion (maybe because the paper found that they couldn't rile me over more threats by the Kansi family), the morning paper "The Dawn", printed an article that said the American Consul General in Karachi had gone on vacation and the Assistant Security Officer, naming him by his name, had moved into the CG Residence and opened a Brothel where western women were prostituting themselves and that he would soon be arrested. Sitting at my desk early in the morning reading this story, I have to say that I actually laughed out loud and couldn't wait until my ARSO saw it. I thought it was a real "keeper" and hilarious. He walked in and with a serious face (as much as it was possible over this), I handed the paper to him and with a straight face asked him to explain what he was doing. He read it and went pale and sickly. He actually began to plead his innocence as if I could have possibly believed it or as if it could have happened without my knowing about it. That was as much as I could take and I began to laugh but he was sure that this would be the end of his career when Washington found out. He would never survive the scandal. I tried telling him how ridiculous it all was and that he didn't have anything to worry about. In fact, I told him he needed to obtain numerous copies and send them to family and keep them for his portfolio. He was worried but beginning to calm down. Enter his big Brother H.

H arrived at our front gate like a brewing storm and we had him escorted into the offices. He was like a ticking time bomb about to go off. He paced the office swearing and yelling about how this reporter had sullied the name of his little brother and now had to die for it. He was angrier than I had ever seen him before and even though I think I can protect myself in a fight pretty well, at this moment, H was formidable and irrational. He said that no one could say that about his brother and he was going to the paper and pull the reporter onto the sidewalk and kill him. When we get upset as Americans, we sometimes say things like "oh, I could just kill him", but we don't mean it. H was on his way to the paper and would without any doubt, pull the reporter out onto the street and shoot him in the head. Also, he probably wouldn't be charged for it as the system worked in Pakistan at the time. It took us 30 minutes to explain to H that if he did that, it would reflect badly on us and my ARSO would have to leave Pakistan. His feelings were appreciated but it would make things worse. He finally calmed down and I imagine that today, my ARSO, who went to work a year later for the U.S. Border Patrol, tells this story with a laugh and a spark in his eye instead of panic in his voice. "A real keeper".

"A" had arrived and after a brief culture shock riding from the airport to the house with an escort of several men with machine guns and through the ninth largest city in the world that reflects some of the worst sheer poverty and human misery ever known. She was beginning to get antsy to go out and see some of the town and meet people. I began taking her to the places I had discovered for carpets, furniture, semi-precious stones, and a multitude of other exotic and fun items we couldn't afford if we were in the States. I had been interested in carpets since my MSD trip to Pakistan back in 1990 and now I was trying to learn as much as I could about them and to recognize what they were and what value they had. We would sometimes take a Sunday and roam the market places looking for those deals that would end up being family heritage pieces for years to come and we were finding some. We always did this with a substantial protective detail or at least a covert oversight by my SD Team. I would occasionally take a Sunday alone and just go sit with my Pathan friend whose entire family was in the carpet export business in the Saddar neighborhood. Mohammad K and I had become true friends and he was interested in understanding Americans and things he had heard and read about. We would talk about life, beer, women, travels, the use of internet, kidney stones and exercise; while he would show me carpets from all over South and Central Asia and teach me what I needed to know. I owe him for the education I now have as a carpet collector.

Mohammad K, his brother Mohammad E, and their father and other family members almost literally adopted me and watched over me for the four years I spent in Karachi and still today, maintain contact with me. I value my brotherhood with this Pathan family above most others. Their hearts are true and loyal without question.

The Taliban was beginning to gain a real foothold in Karachi and with 19 million poor people who couldn't protect themselves, it was quite a pool to draw from and intimidate by fear. In local neighborhoods the local Taliban leader would send around notices telling the folks that on Saturday, everyone was to bring their televisions out onto the streets and destroy them since they were a western tool of destruction to the way of Sharia Law. If they did not bring their TVs out and destroy them, the Taliban would kill the family members. There was no police force capable of controlling the size of problem this created. The western shops of clothing and DVDs were burned down and anything that was associated with America could get you killed in those specific neighborhoods. Karachi had begun to change to an even more dangerous and threatening place.

When March 2000 arrived, we experienced our first Karachi Olympics. The teachers at the American School would every year create a series of tough and complicated but fun games that would be the challenges for our local Olympics. Each of the Consulates would create a team and there were also several Pakistani teams created. In addition to the actual games, there were obligatory events involving doing songs with a theme, acting plays, and other embarrassing events to create the right fun atmosphere minus the testosterone. Each group had to have matching theme T-shirts and also had to provide 4 dozen shirts to the school to sell at the event in order to pay for the expenses. The great thing was we bought each other's T-shirts as mementos and they were very creative.

"A" and I needed to get away from the city and we took a vacation to Nepal for a 10-day hike through the Himalayan Mountains. It was to be about 100 kilometers in 10 days and I had no idea how hard that was going to be, up and down steep mountains, staying in concrete or wood huts at night in tiny 12-person villages at 12,000 foot altitudes, eating only the local foods that could be cooked over a fire. By the end of the third day of going straight up, or coming straight down the slopes, my legs were shaking and about to collapse. I was wondering if our 10 days was overly optimistic but "A" seemed to be doing pretty well (Bogota, Colombia is at a 9,000 foot altitude), so I had this macho thing going that I had to continue. The fourth day I woke up and had crossed over the wall. I was fine and my legs began to turn to stone muscle. I still hated the going up and "A" still hated the going down but we were going to finish it. Every time we would begin to think it was too hard, we would look behind us down the mountain slope and see Nepali Gurungs or Sherpas with full-sized refrigerators roped onto their backs and foreheads, coming up the mountain slope and actually catching us. As they caught up, we would step off the trail and let them pass and shake our heads at how embarrassed we were that a guy with a full-size refrigerator on his back just climbed past us. We had a Gurung Tribe young man to help carry some of our gear and a Sherpa Tribe young man who was actually our guide. They were terrific and fun and watched out for "A" every inch of the way. One of the reasons we had picked Nepal was that we were hoping to find the Gurung Village that Pitam, "A"'s Ghurka "Brother," came from to ask about his status following the "Force Majeure" declaration by the Angolan Government. Some of the Gurung villagers along the way said they knew him but the name was so common I doubt it. Our Guide and Bearer would create instant bridges over rivers for "A" and walk barefoot through the river holding her as she walked the bridge. They were terrific.

One night in a small and freezing and pitch black concrete block cell, huddled in our sleeping bags, I noticed what seemed like a darker spot on the wall and asked "A" if she could see it also. She said yes and we put a flashlight on it. It was a spider the size of a large man's expanded hand. A good 8 inches across. I wasn't about to go to sleep with that alien on the wall, waking up with it fixed over my mouth and planting some alien breeding seed into my body. I took my boot while "A" held the flashlight on it and I hit it. My god, the mess was like I had killed a small dog. The thing was huge and meaty. As preoccupied as it made us feel, we were so tired from the climbing we were asleep within minutes.

On another day, we finished in a little village at sort of a mini guest house and ran into some British hikers who were going on our same trail the next day. Apparently two days before, some Maoist terrorists had murdered by machete a couple of hikers on the same trail. So the Brits asked if they could join us and we agreed. We climbed though the magical high mountain pass the next day and avoided the Maoists but it was nice to have other travelers for the two days they traveled along with us. It is amazing who one runs into in the most isolated and extreme locations.

On our final day, as we were continuing our descent, we came to an area that had just experienced a large avalanche causing the deaths of several hikers. The path ran across this still shifting avalanche and it was the only way out without climbing back up a mountain taking a couple more days. The flow of rocks and soil had mostly stopped with only occasional tumbling boulders and gravel so we decided to make an attempt to avoid being swept away. The Sherpa was to quickly bring "A" behind me and the Gurung once we tested out the slope and made our way safely across. The Gurung and I made the 300 yard wide avalanche only ducking and diving a few times to keep from being hit by rogue rock fall and then the nervous moment, "A" and our experienced Sherpa. They ran for it and also avoided the sliding rock. Not too much later, we learned that the entire mountainside we had just crossed, all slid into the valley below, killing several others. We finally made our way down to a little café on the river's edge where our pick-up point was to be and sat and had a soft drink with our Sherpa guide and Gurung bearer who we had come to trust, respect and like very much. We paid them their money and bonuses for taking such good care of "A" and we were put into a small van and driven down into the Capital city of Katmandu, Nepal, for an exhausted night in a hotel before we flew out the next day. We did find a place to get a massage though and during it, I went right to sleep. It was a trip we will always remember and place into the annals of our greatest adventures.

The situation in Karachi was continuing to get more dicey each month. Bombs were going off near the Consulate that would rattle all our windows. Drive-by shootings were killing police officers on duty around the area and we had suicide vehicle bombers trying to catch our vehicles in the city so they could detonate next to our cars. Our drivers were literally driving for their own and our own lives when they would see a car trying to match their movements or they would receive a call from my surveillance detection team that they had spotted a car correlating movement with ours but trying to catch us. We used vehicle intercept tactics that would place cars between the enemy and our own without them knowing that it was an American effort. It appeared simply that traffic had cut them off. In some cases, it was deemed to be such a critical threat that we had to have the police converge and take out the car or stop it if they could. The choices were stop and deal with the police; don't stop and be shot and killed by the police; or detonate the car. One never knew which they would choose.

One day my SD Team leader came to me and told me that in the city, posted on buildings and walls, were a series of Jihadi recruitment posters including phone numbers to call to join the fight against the infidels. I asked him if I could get a set of them and of course my undercover guys walked into an Al-Qaida recruitment center and got me the entire collectors set, which as you can imagine were framed and I still have them.

One thing an RSO can never forget, just like with a corporation, is that we take a lot from the community and place demands and inconveniences on it so we must look for ways to give back. I was contacted by a local Professor who had taken over responsibility for the renovation of a very old Mughal era King's home in the

Clifton area of Karachi and it was going to become a museum. The Professor was going to be the Curator. It is called The Mohatta Palace. The Curator asked if I would be willing to take a look at the type of security they might need. I was happy to do so as part of my responsibility to my community. At first glance as I drove up, the palace itself was like something out of a movie. The architecture was sort of a Taj Mahal meets the Thatta Mosque look and was hundreds of years old. It needed maintenance and painting but it was astounding. As I walked through the front door, I noticed that the thin glass door was the only door and there was no locking device at all. I continued in and found the curator in a room filled with tall glass cases with ancient firearms in them. Some had special gold inlay work on the rifle stocks. They were mostly from about 100 years ago and magnificent - truly museum pieces. What I was looking at didn't correlate with the door with no lock and I asked her what the value of the pieces was. She estimated them at just over one million dollars. Here were two things I loved – guns and a million dollars. I almost choked and got on the phone immediately to my security team and asked them to bring the obsolete and expendable locking devices. We secured the building and then over the following months, installed alarm systems, perimeter lighting, some cameras for monitoring the grounds and building and numerous other control systems. We did this all with expendable systems that had been replaced in the Consulate by newer state of the art equipment. I also convinced my friend who owned one of the largest local guard companies in the country to donate at no charge, protective guard services for the museum. As time passed, it became one of the most inviting and beautiful tourist venues.

"A"'s Community Liaison Officer leadership was to give us all an experience of a lifetime. She learned of the giant sea turtles which came ashore every year on some of the beaches southwest of Karachi and of a lady called not surprisingly, "The Turtle Lady", who worked with the turtles to preserve their lives and breeding capability. "A" arranged trips for us all out to the beach. We had one precarious spot on the way out as we passed through a congested Taliban village but once through, we were relatively safe at the beach. We also took police with us everywhere we went. At that time, the Consulate had a beach house on French Beach for the Americans to use on weekends. It was rough and had no real conveniences but it was a place to throw your stuff and sit on a beach in relative peace. This was fortunately near the same beach the turtles came up on. We drove out early in the day and had fun with a barbeque on the beach. At about dusk, the Turtle Lady came and got us and took us to her breeding farm. After the turtles laid their eggs, she would dig them up and re-bury them in a fenced and protected site to await their birth, then releasing them into the sea. This night, some of the eggs were hatching and we would get to see it and to help the baby turtles go back to the sea safely. As the baby turtles crawled out of the sand, the 2-inch long babies were flailing their arms and legs as fast as they could toward the bright moon globe in the sky that drew a line to the water. We got to play with them a little bit and hold the little guys but then had to let them make a break for freedom and we ensured no birds or other reptiles took advantage of their freedom run. Then we just relaxed and waited quietly for the arrival of the giants. The turtles would wait until about midnight when the full moon would be strongest and the moon would shine a direct line to the beach that the turtles would follow. If the turtles heard or saw anyone, they would go back into the sea and maybe not come back to this spot. I had a pair of night vision goggles so that even in the dark, I could watch the ocean and see the 5 and 6 foot long turtles coming out of the water. I passed them around and it was amazing to see them struggle to move their huge bulks along the heavy sand. Once they found a spot they liked, they would begin to use their fin-like arms and legs to dig a hole. We had to stay quiet but we could hear the sand being thrown around. After the noise from the digging stopped, along with the Turtle Lady, we would go looking for the turtles. Once the hole was dug, the turtles would begin to lay the large gooey eggs and they would settle into a state of Nirvana and nothing could disturb them. We found many large turtles and could actually walk up to them and put our faces next to theirs for a photo without disturbing them at all. We also watched the egg-laying process and they laid a lot of eggs in one sitting. Then we moved away and allowed them to finish, cover their eggs up with sand and drag themselves back down the beach and into the water. It was a unique lifetime experience. We then drove back to Karachi at about 0200 in the morning in a protective motorcade.

One of the cities in my district of control, which included Sindh and Balochistan Provinces, was Quetta. Quetta was and remains sort of the Dodge City of Pakistan. It is wild-west in nature and is a transit point for Jihadis, smugglers and criminals of all ilk. The route followed by the dangerous men went through Quetta, into Chaman, which sits on the border of Pakistan and Afghanistan, and was heavily Taliban in influence. From there they went to Kandahar or Jalalabad or Khost or another of the smuggler and terrorist safehavens. It was my duty to go to Quetta and make contact with the Inspector General of Police and other law enforcement authorities we needed from time to time to help us.

There are two ruling tribal families who pretty much control everything in the city and region. They are the Marri and Bughti families. These families are huge local mafia operations and smugglers. The Taliban and even Al-Qaida had to patronize them if they wanted safe passage in their territory. There was also constant battling between the two families for control of the wealth that passed through their waystation. When a "gringo" like myself wanted to go to Quetta and safely conduct business in town with the police or even just to be safe on the streets, the wise thing to do was to go to one of their huge guarded compounds and pay proper respect by asking for their approval and permission to be in their city for awhile.

My first trip to Quetta, I made contact with the Inspector General of Police (IGP) and delivered gifts and showed him the respect due a man in his position and he advised me that he had made arrangements for me to meet the war lord family to ask to do business in town. He said for appearance sake he would not go in with me but would drive me to the gate, drop me off and wait for me to finish. We drove a few miles to an enormous walled compound that had to be more than 300 yards on each side and had men with AK-47s standing every 6 feet apart, appearing alert and intimidating. The IGP dropped me at the front gate by a gaggle of armed men who verified who I was, took my weapon to hold for me and then opened the gate to the compound. The first thing that caught my attention was that there were at least 500 men with weapons inside the walled compound, just hanging around talking, and some were kicking a soccer ball while others played Cricket. This would not be a place conducive to an intimate assault. Besides a reasonably large home in the center, there were barracks and soccer and cricket fields to keep his guards happy and fit, and a fleet of vehicles. I walked the distance to the home under escort that was silent but pleasant enough and they took me to the front door where I took off my shoes and entered. I was led to a large room where at least 20 heavily-bearded men sat around in a circle on cushions on the floor with a table in the middle. I don't know why I did it but I sort of bowed my head in respect and greeted them with the standard Muslim greeting. The greeting was returned. No one was smiling. They pointed to the cushion that was open closest to my doorway entry point and I sat down. For the next two hours, they served me hot sweet tea and cookies and asked me questions about my life, my family, my habits and beliefs and the nature of my business in town and in Pakistan in general. They were all very concerned with the fact that I had not yet had any children and strongly suggested that I get to it as quickly as I could. Only two spoke English to me and since there was translating going on, I would assume that most of them were Pathans who spoke Pushtu or Farsi, and I am quite certain that some were Taliban related. AK-47s laid across their laps. At the end of the two hours of sober cordiality, they must have been satisfied that I was not a threat to their 500 armed men or compound and that my business was not to interfere with their smuggling enterprises, and just as uneventfully as my entry, they said I was free to do business in town and said goodbye. I was led out the door by sign language again and out to the gate where I retrieved my hand gun and it appeared that the IGP had patiently waited all this time. He dropped me off at the Serena Hotel and I began my innocuous business. Somehow, I actually felt safer in the town now that I was warlord-approved.

In Karachi, I had been assigned a Senior Superintendent of Police (SSP) known as Captain and a Police Special Branch Intelligence Officer we'll call "D" who were my contacts for whatever I needed security-wise. They were picked well because we all really got along and they were bright enough not to try and fool me into thinking that they weren't reporting everything that the Consulate and my security office was doing, back to their supervisors. Captain, "D" and I became sort of a Three Musketeer gang and I will never forget those times. In addition, the Police number two, the Deputy Inspector General of Police was a daily contact for me and we also became good personal friends. The longer I worked with these men, the more we came to genuinely like each other and trust one another. We would often meet just to have lunch and chat instead of for business, and during those times, they gave me insight to how things really worked within their culturally different police operations. I knew that interrogations were done with more force than in the U.S. but they gave me an understanding of the difficulties that they were forced to work within and I came to realize how truly bad and psychopathic the bad guys were that they had to find and question and I empathized with their need to make things work within their own standards. I also came to know, respect and treasure my friendship with the big boss, the Inspector General of Police (IGP) for Sindh Province, we will call "K". Here was a man of solid character and compassion but who also knew what he faced and had to deal with it forcefully. I watched his balance of intelligence and kindness, which shown in his smile and eyes, in contrast to his toughness that could come out when dealing with terrorists or murderers. I learned from him that a mix like that was possible and it was a growing experience for me. A person could actually have 180 degree opposite Yin and Yang components and survive mentally and emotionally if one dealt with it properly.

These men would be my close friends for over three years and we would have many adventures and close calls, some of which I will discuss when I come to the terrorism cases we worked together. They watched over me and kept me alive. They taught me the necessity of dealing with the really bad guys in an equally tough manner and they showed respect for my skills and experience as well. K would years later as Secretary of the Ministry of Interior in Islamabad, tell a room full of foreign Mission Ambassadors that only once in his memory had a foreigner been permitted to work Pakistan criminal and terrorism investigative cases alongside his officers and that was Randall Bennett. He showed me the ultimate compliment when he said in public that they considered me to be a Pakistani.

I continued to work hard on the physical security of the Consulate, the Consul General's residence and the neighborhoods and homes of our Officers. With all the drive-by shootings, the suicide bombings, and the threats against the Americans, it seemed only a matter of time before we got hit hard or lost someone. My job was to try and prevent that. Fortunately, DS in Washington realized the precarious nature of our threat as well and was providing me with the funding to complete all the physical and technical security projects I requested. I changed the perimeter walls of the Consulate and Consul General's home from open and visible bars to 9-plus foot-high solid concrete and rebar walls. We moved everyone from their offices on the front street-side offices in the building to the back side of the building and prohibited people from having or using the rooms near the street since that is where car bombs would most likely detonate. That gave me an additional 23 feet of set-back if a bomb went off on the street. Late one night when no one was watching, we closed off the public streets on both sides of the Consulate and built large almost unmovable concrete barriers so no one could come at us from the side. I say almost unmovable because we had the only fork lift large enough to move them so that when the Pakistan city authorities told us we had no right to close off their streets, they couldn't move them and after months of complaining, they gave up and I kept my perimeter. I had the Frontier Constabulary Para-military guards set up their tents around our neighborhoods and ran electricity and water to them and gave them heaters for the winter and fans for the summer. We made them feel at home and 65 of them protected our perimeter and shared part of our lives. We all would take them food as well after parties and events. We added concrete police booths around the Consulate and added more guards and police for maximum intimidation. And we added beautiful razor wire to the top of the wall. I did everything I could think of to prepare for whatever was to come. The rule is "Hope for the best, but plan for the worst".

My boss in Islamabad was very supportive of all the security efforts I was putting into the Consulate and he was a terrific mentor, friend, and example of a balanced management style. At that time, publications listed Karachi as the most dangerous city in the world so no one wanted to rock my boat too much as long as I kept it afloat, in fear that they might have to begin to deal with it if they did. But, this seemed to be a job I had a knack for and things were blowing up, but not my people. We so far were escaping the attacks and direct threats. My boss, in conjunction with the Consul General put me in for the top DS Award called DS Employee of the Year for millennium 2000. There were four categories of DS Employees and one person would be selected as the winner for each category. Those four were 1) top Special Agent, 2) top DS Courier, 3) top Security Engineering Officer, and 4) top Civil Service employee. I won the top Special Agent and in competition with the others, won the top DS Employee of the Year 2000. Once again, I learned about the leadership quality of the importance of awarding and recognizing your employees for their hard efforts. I live by that example.

About this time, terrorists were trying to hit any target they could that had a "western" affiliation attached to it and the Sheraton Hotel stood out. One afternoon, I heard and felt a detonation out my window. It was obviously nearby to the Sheraton and out my window, I could see smoke starting to rise. I ran out my door to my car below and headed to the Sheraton to see what it was and to offer my help if needed. What the Police and I found showed that sometimes justice prevails. A terrorist had placed a rocket on a wooden fruit cart with wheels and was dragging it to a field with a school on one side, an empty partially-constructed building on another and caddy-corner was the Sheraton Hotel. We found a man who was burned completely on his front side lying in the field, and a rocket that had for some reason penetrated the empty school classroom on a day it was closed and bounced around inside the room, burning it out completely and destroying most of the desks and other items. As we proceeded to try and understand the events and put together the sequence and intent, we deduced that the man was intending to shoot the rocket at the Sheraton Hotel, but as he rotated the fruit cart around, the rocket fired prematurely as he moved it past the school, sending the rocket into the school, and due to those unforgiving laws of physics, the blast of the rocket torched the man's front side. He was still enough alive to confirm our theory but suffered the pain he intended for innocent people. Thank heavens for incompetent people and frequent luck.

I was still doing a lot of self-drive on weekends and found a trail that allowed me to drive far out into the desert where a dirt camel path-slash-side road would lead me past a camp of wandering Nomad tribespeople. As I continued out further, I passed a large isolated Pakistani power plant and entered into a small range of hills about 1000 feet high; perfect for climbing and exploring. The various climbs they offered were challenging and a good workout and once on top of the ridgeline, the coastline was visible and the sight was very relaxing. This became my place of occasional weekend calm and I would bring food with me and eventually started introducing others to the location. I also discovered some hidden Pakistani military observation points and big gun mounting platforms in the hills but they seemed either abandoned or at least not regularly used. There was a very small fishing village named Mubarek, on the coast that could be seen from the ridge and I started visiting it just to see what it was all about. There were some obvious signs of smuggling going on through their quiet coastal entry point but my interest was in a small Island off the shore about one-half mile. This made me think that perhaps it might be possible to do some scuba diving around the island. I had never heard of any scuba in Pakistan but that was part of the interest. I spoke to a fisherman who had a slow "long boat" and asked if it would be possible to get him to take me out for diving. He was confused that anyone would want to go under the water but agreed for a future date. I put that one on the list of things to work out.

"A" and I decided we needed to get out of Karachi for a break and see another side of Pakistan and we booked a trip up north to the area of "Lost Horizon" or Shangri-La, where stories tell of lost civilizations who lived virtually forever. Up in these high northern Pakistan mountains called the Hindu-Kush and Karakorams, 8 of the world's 14 tallest mountains are located including Nanga Parbat and K-2. We flew into Skardu and took a long scenic trip going north through Gilgit and some of the most rugged and raw scenery we had ever seen. One 12-hour ride was through a narrow, single lane road cut along a mountainside with rock on one side and a 2,000 foot gorge on the other. One small driving mistake and we were dead and would remain undiscovered virtually forever. The driver of the car was a crazed and maniacal Pakistani who somehow had driven this road a hundred times each time too fast and out of his mind on a local chew (Beetlenut) that was narcotic in nature and he had somehow up to now survived. Over the period of a week, we made our way to our intended destination of The Hunza Valley, the place of the eternal-life legend. We had also picked up a guide who although Pakistani, looked Belgian. We can thank Alexander the Great for that since he seems to have bred with most women in the Hunza area. They look nothing like the normally dark Pakistanis and mostly consider themselves to be independent. They are Ismailis by Sect, which basically means they are very moderate and also business-minded and peaceful. The Hunza Valley was a paradise of fruit and vegetable orchards and fields in the middle of high snow-covered mountains. It was a complete contradiction to what we should have seen at this altitude. The Agha Khan Foundation had cut huge canals into the mountainsides that fed water down from the high glaciers into the Hunza Valley and below, allowing these gracious people to be completely self-sufficient. It was a beautiful and inspirational trip into a land that few are lucky enough to see.

The villagers of Hunza, also in contradiction to the Muslim world, make two types of alcoholic-based "wine". Simply, one they call white and the other red. They are not really either but we tried them and found them to be bitter but better than the alternative of nothing so we drank a couple of bottles, suffered the next day headaches and learned not to do it again. I guess it is their version of moonshine. We continued to explore the region and went up to the base of the massive glacier sitting at the feet of mountains that climbed 25,000 feet high. It was truly impressive and humbling.

As my two year tour was coming to an end and I began to look at my next assignment location, DS called me and told me they couldn't find anyone who was willing to come to Karachi to replace me. They asked if I would be willing to stay a third year. I feigned fatigue and accepted the third year. With all the adventures I was having and the great friends we had, and the Security family team working for me, of course I wanted to stay for a third year. So, as the years were becoming more dangerous, I was extending to meet the growing challenge. I was so deep inside the fishbowl, I had no idea how bad it was going to get. Although bad is sometimes an interpretation of good based on the perspective.

Not to make it a big part of the story, but on several occasions, I had been driving my car or in other cases, been a passenger in a Consulate car, when the terrorist enemy had made attempts to get their car (implied to have been filled with explosives) next to mine in order to take me out of the game. With the public threats against me made in the newspapers and the written threats that came into the Consulate and the reporting of threats against all of us, this had become the most real death scenario one can have. These suicide car bombers just wanted to get close so they could detonate. For them, a life-for-a-life swap was acceptable. It wasn't for me when one of them was me. I planned to continue boosting the number of successes on my side for awhile and then get out of town safely when the tour was over. That's always the plan. The enemy continued to get angrier and the attempts against me continued.

Though "A" and I both could begin to feel a certain level of separation between us contributed to by the forced evacuations, and as she began to do more alone with her friends and I continued to be so deeply involved in my daily and dark life and death work, we continued to have vacations away together with new adventures that would create bridging links between us. But my not really being able (or willing) to share with her the ugly and morbid side of my job that came home with me in my head at night, a natural barrier seemed to be unavoidably growing.

In March 2001, we had another Karachi Olympics at the American School out in the KDA Housing area. It was to be the best ever and also the last one held. This one was formatted that each group had to begin their competition with a number set to music that would lead to a synchronized 2-person belly flop into the pool. One day in the Marine Gym, the music to The Full Monty was playing as I worked out and I was dementedly inspired to suggest to "A" later that a five man strip tease to that music at the end of the pool finishing with two of us completing the synchronized belly flop might be a hit. She liked the idea and with her girlfriends, they created Velcro break-away policeman uniform-type clothing, put together the dance and strip steps to the music "You Can Leave Your Hat On", and rehearsed us. Along with myself as punishment for thinking of it, our group included a strong bodybuilder Marine, a bad-dancing out-of-shape Political Officer, a somewhat bulbous-stomached communicator, and a soon to be retired grey-bearded Administrative Officer. The rest of us were just praying that everyone would watch the Marine bodybuilder and spare us the disgrace. This was going to be videotaped so the girls worked hard to get us to perform with some sense of order but we were obviously better at other skills. Nonetheless, the day came and we all, wearing little speedos under our Velcro uniforms did the simulated strip dance and ended it with tearing our pants from our bodies and the fat communicator and I did the synchronized belly flop guarding our family jewels the best one can doing a belly flop, and low and behold, we won the event. The video still exists and is still just as embarrassing, but it's a classic. We carried out many other joking competitive events during the long day of fun and ended it at night with a musical dance number that the girls did with the Marine Detachment Commander. It was a number from a James Bond Movie and we won that too. At the end of the day, we tied for first with the German Consulate. That night, not knowing what was coming in September, we thought that things were pretty good considering we lived in the home nest of world terrorism.

With the summer approaching, so was the end of my extended third year in Karachi and my bids for onward assignments had again been submitted. None of them seemed to be gelling and I should have surmised why, but was so focused on my work, I didn't see what was coming. The call came as it had before. My Diplomatic Security Headquarters called and said that once again, no one wanted to bid on or come to Karachi due to the danger and difficulty of life and living conditions. They asked if I would be willing to stay a fourth year. This was unprecedented in my recollection. I had actually never heard of any fourth year additions. Since this danger-deemed post was a two-year assignment, it would mean I would be doing two entire tours. I took it without any hesitation at all. I loved my work in Karachi. I was having substantive results. Al-Qaida was losing numbers due to our direct efforts and I was actually saving lives and making a difference. You bet I'll stay another year. And, "A" was happy here with all her friends. This was the summer of 2001 and I had no idea what was in-store for me in my final year.

September 11, 2001 came, and with it, a total change of all our lives forever. The day it occurred in the U.S., it was 10 hours later in Pakistan and already nighttime for us and as we saw what was happening on the TV, the word went out to everyone to turn on the TV to witness the worst event any of us could ever have imagined. Knowing that Karachi (and other parts of Pakistan) was always a nexus to almost every terrorist act in the world, there was great concern that the normal constant critical threat to the lives of the Americans might somehow be enhanced and attacks would be coming during the night. We had substantial security forces I had placed around our neighborhoods but let's face it, for those of you who truly understand this point, nothing can stop a rolling car bomb from destroying its mission except another car and driver sacrificing himself by blocking or intercepting its path and dieing in the process. If terrorists wanted to run a car bomb into my neighborhood perimeter, the driver might die from gunfire first, but the car would still hit the perimeter and detonate, opening a huge hole that a second vehicle laden with explosives could run through unhindered and go for any house he wanted. Though we were experiencing this tactic at the time, years later it became known as the Jeddah scenario. It is a standard practical terrorist tactic. To illustrate the type of brotherhood and bonding felt by our Pakistani allies in this war against terrorism and their love for Americans and the things that America stands for, without even asking or making a call, the Inspector General of Police issued orders to his police and they flooded our neighborhoods with a large number of police officers to ensure that no one bothered us during this weakened and sensitive time of grief. Many Pakistanis also died in those twin towers when they collapsed. This was very personal to them. The Deputy Inspector General of Police, the number two police officer for the Province, came to my home and spent the entire night in front of my home to protect me personally. I was very affected by this show of devotion and friendship and perhaps that is why I refer to Pakistan as my second home. How does a person respond to someone who offers to protect your life with their own. This was a complete reversal for me since that was usually my job and I now understand the reason people respond the way they do to me when I watch out for them or pull them out of a dangerous situation.

This critical event became the catalyst for our second mandatory evacuation of all dependents. So, very unhappily, "A" once again packed her bags and this time would spend the next six months of separation in Washington, DC, working in the Family Liaison Office inside the State Department. For me, it meant a revitalized and even greater effort to find and eliminate terrorists in my region. This would begin the most concentrated and death-ridden period of counter-terrorism investigations of my career.

One can see that this job and the hardships and separations that come with it, not to mention the stress that was perhaps at times reflected in my less than attentive attitude at home could take its toll on a normal relationship. I was coming home after dealing with body parts from bombings and dead enemies from shoot-outs and I was a bit preoccupied. And, it was only going to get worse as our time there went on. "A" was gone now and once again, my life focused solely on my work.

Chapter Sixteen
THE KARACHI INVESTIGATIONS

During this period of time, I was experiencing around six "walk-ins" a day. A walk-in is someone who out-of-the-blue walks into your Consulate lobby and announces he wants to provide information to the RSO. The majority are people who say they know where Usama Bin Laden is and promise that if you will fund them and equip them, they will go kill him. Others, are receiving signals in their brains from unknown sources about terrorists and aliens who are going to do something horrible. Others are like the tinfoil hat crowd, who are just really mentally unbalanced and have lined their heads with tinfoil to prevent anyone from reading their thoughts. You get the point. Some though, provide good information. Many investigations came from the "walk-ins" and other work with my Pakistani associates, and some of those were highly successful, but I have picked a few investigations to discuss that might be of interest.

JOSE PADILLA – THE DIRTY BOMBER

One day, the Consular Officer, who was a first tour young lady and still trying to feel comfortable in her suit of responsibilities in a critical threat country, called me and said that a tough looking

American character was in her office and wanted a new passport because he had "lost" his. When she looked up his record, she found that this man, named Jose Padilla, had lost a couple of others as well and all of them in a too-recent time period. That always makes us suspicious about the possibility of selling passports. He also looked like an angry guy who was more akin to being in a biker or gang-banger environment than a normal American citizen overseas. She said she was uncomfortable and would I come down.

I walked in and introduced myself and didn't like him either. There was definitely something wrong with this guy and his profile and history stunk of possible terrorist involvement and he was not being honest about where he had been for the past several months. At this time we were seeing a lot of British citizens and some Americans, crossing into Afghanistan for Jihadi training and that was where I was placing my money on him. I wanted some time to check him out so I told him that since he had lost a couple of other passports, I would require additional ID for validation. He was upset and insulted about my insistence on seeing more ID verification so he stomped out angry and said he would be back.

A few days later, he showed up again and this time to spite me, he had brought what seemed to be every form of ID he had ever possessed; Library card, Blockbuster video rental card, drivers license and about a dozen others as well. Well, I guess he was going to show me that he couldn't be messed with. So, I made copies of every single stupid little form of ID or note and paper he had and created a file on him for possible future use. I could usually tell when someone was going to be a problem long term and this guy fit the mold. We had no notice of anyone looking for him (no wants or warrants) so as an American citizen, we were obligated to issue him another passport.

About a week later, another colleague walked into my office and said he knew I saw a lot of "walk-ins" and so would I keep my eyes and ears open for a guy going by the name of Jose Padilla, who they thought might have intentions to go to the U.S. to enact a "dirty bomb" radioactive bomb scenario. I thought he was kidding but since he didn't kid well, I pulled out my now relatively in-depth file and said, "this Jose Padilla?" He got "bug-eyes" when he saw all the data I had on him and asked if he could make a copy. I told him of course and he ran off like a kid who just dug up some treasure in his backyard. Since he liked that so much and since the dirty-bomb plot seemed serious, I called downstairs to my "inside man". He was the Consular Fraud Investigator but since the first-tour Consular Officer was having a hard time controlling him, he had been given to me to manage. He knew everyone and was very effective. He also had a contact inside the records section at the International Airport it might not have been going through normal or even semi-legitimate administrative processes, and I knew that technically, the information usually is not given to anyone, but, when it comes to saving American lives, there is no greater purpose and sometimes in third world countries, a man has to do what a man has to do, so to speak. I told him to go in the back door of the airport and get with his contact and check all paper files and find me the projected itinerary of Jose Padilla.

Several hours later, he walked into my office smiling with a piece of paper in his hand. The itinerary of Jose Padilla showed him departing Karachi a few days before and arriving in another country, then the itinerary went cold. He was obviously cutting his trail for a reason and the investigator was smart enough to recognize that fact. So, then he handed me another piece of paper with a bigger smile. He and his airport associate had checked all records by hand until they found Jose Padilla resurfacing on a flight out of Zurich. We even had his seat number. And his departure from Zurich to Chicago was in several days.

I walked upstairs to the other colleague's office and trying not to have a smile on my face, asked if they would be interested in knowing where Jose Padilla was going to be in 3 days. If I thought he had "bug-eyes" before, that had only been a test run for the ones now. I gave him the information as he stared at me wondering how I could have obtained this and he quickly passed it to his people, who then passed it to the FBI HQ, as I passed it to my DS HQ. The FBI discretely put someone on the plane in Zurich sitting a couple of rows behind Jose Padilla and the rest is history. When Jose walked off the plane with the FBI man inconspicuously behind him, authorities of all varieties were waiting on the ramp and as he recognized the situation he tried to turn back but the FBI man took control of him and everyone arrested and handcuffed him and took him away. Though there is almost never any public recognition, one day much later in a private conference room, the man I gave the original information to gave me a verbal appreciation from their people and then it was all forgotten. Still, it was one of my success stories I am proud of.

THE TEXAN TALIBAN

One day I received a call from my police friends who advised me that there were several obviously American men and a woman checking into the Metropol Hotel and they were talking loudly in public to each other about their intentions to visit a known Taliban neighborhood on the outskirts of Karachi. They were now sitting in the lobby of the hotel having tea and two of the men were wearing typical Pathan clothing like the Afghan/Pakistan border people are known for (and Taliban are seen in) and even wearing the head wrap. Once again, they were conspicuously talking in the open and loudly enough for anyone to hear about their intentions to go visit this Taliban "village" area. The police wanted to know what I wanted them to do about it.

I didn't realize I had been given such autonomy on decision making with the police but this request for me to give them orders was an interesting twist. I asked if they were violating any law, looking for some justification to have them questioned. The Police SSP said it was not permitted for foreigners to visit the Taliban part of the city. With that as a basis of justification, I asked the police to go question the people to find out who they were and why they were here. Whether they might realize it or not, it was in order to protect them from harm. It never ceases to amaze me how naïve people can be to think that because they mean no harm to an enemy like the Taliban, that no harm will come to them. Many people, including missionaries doing "good works" have disappeared or been killed on this assumption. The expression "God will protect us" is akin to the Muslim "InshAllah", which means "if God wills it, so it will be". Bad people don't give a damn about their target's beliefs and have no respect for the lives of infidels.

The police started out with a calm discussion in the Metropol lobby, which was reported back to me almost verbatim by one of my Sources in the hotel, who said that the police inquired why they were in Karachi. The response was tourism. Not likely, and you don't want to insult the intelligence of Karachi police with blatant lies. The police said they had been overheard talking about going to the Taliban neighborhood and that the area was off-limits. The tallest man, a big Texan according to his paper-work, and in Pathan garb, and with a pretty respectable beard said they were only going out of interest to see if they could understand the Taliban's reasons for their hatred against Americans. They would have disappeared, and for some physically torturous and agonizing time would have found out about the Taliban's hatred first hand. He then surprised the police by breaking into conversation with the police in perfect Pushto, the language of the Afghan border people. The police reported this back to me and said that this man was obvious trouble and they wanted me to convince him to leave or they would throw him out of country. The other four said they were leaving Karachi and returning home the next day.

Since this man apparently has/had some Texas political connections and carried quite a colorful reputation from his past, no names will be discussed. I went to the hotel and met with him. I told him his options; that the police would not permit him to visit the dangerous neighborhood and if he persisted, they would remove him from country under force. He said he was going to just hang around out of trouble for a couple of days and then would leave and that he would comply with the police request. The look in his eye and the arrogance in his voice told me otherwise. I gave him my card and contact numbers and said adios.

The next day, the police intercepted him in a taxi (of all unsafe means), on the way to the Taliban area. They yanked him out and took him back to the hotel and told him he was to pack and get out on the next available flight from their country. I think the only reason that he was not severely beaten for showing such disrespect for the police and the local laws was that they knew I had met with him and they weren't sure if he was protected by my good will. The police filled me in on what he had done and I told them that they were free to throw him out of country if he did not comply. This was becoming a big problem for me in that this American seemed insistent that he was going to get himself killed no matter what anyone said. Speaking Pushto and having a big beard doesn't get you by the tribal controls and tribe recognition. They would view him as a spy and his final hours would be worse than he could imagine in his most horrific nightmares.

Surprisingly, or maybe not surprisingly, I received a call from the police the next morning saying that they had secretly followed our Texan and he had not gone to the airport but had instead gone into the Taliban area and started aggressively talking like a known friend to the Taliban. They felt that he must have some nefarious connection to not have been killed immediately and they wanted to know if it was okay with me if they snatched him and took him out away from the area. For his own safety and because he now had become a suspicious character, I said yes. The police took the Texan Taliban to the police station and questioned him until they were tired. What they understood was that he might have had some U.S. Agency experience with these people years before and he felt he could still relate and fit in with them. He didn't seem to understand that the Taliban were different than Afghan freedom fighters. It was assumed that the U.S. support to the Afghans during the Russian invasion had some strong play here and that he had some "boots on" time in Afghanistan during that period. The police felt he was arrogant, not very savvy, and was never going to obey the laws, so for his own good, they deported him and solved what might have become an ugly problem later of shipping a body back, if we got it back. Months later, I read some press about this man in Texas with political connections who had prior connections to the Afghans and who had visited our lovely city and been removed. Much later, another U.S. Federal Agency asked me what I knew about this man. Ah, the circle of life.

THE DANIEL PEARL INVESTIGATION

The Daniel Pearl case was my case. The book Mariane Pearl wrote called "A Mighty Heart", about her life with Danny and his terrible end, was a love story about them and contained insights to his intellect and wit, his good nature, strong character and the love they shared. It contained little of the actual behind-the-scenes case. The movie by the same title released in summer 2007 had much of the book and a little of the case activities, but not really much could capture the essence and chaos of the city and the environment we worked in, and the facts were not totally accurate and were sorely incomplete. It was a good gist and a good drama and the acting was excellent, but when you have a story that is starring Angelina Jolie, you revise the story around her, instead of the investigative facts and the team who dealt with the case. I like the book and the movie. The book was a good love story but depicted some of us oddly and incorrectly, but apparently how Mariane viewed us. I can live with that because I love Mariane and her son Adam. The movie was a good drama but again, changed what actually happened and even the sequence of events. I can live with that also because it accomplished some good in its awareness to the public about the event and it made Mariane happy to have this as a remembrance for Adam. I even thought that Angelina was brilliant as Mariane, and that Will Patton, who portrayed me in the movie, was unnervingly like me in many ways. He is one of the nicest and most talented people I will ever meet.

But it is time for me to finally tell the sequential facts about this case and even though I might leave out some things that happened in order to protect myself legally and my deep involvement in all aspects of the case, this will be the essence of what happened and how it happened, minus too much operational daily minutiae. This part I dedicate to Mariane and Adam who I will watch over from afar as long as I am still on this earth.

I had some true friends I had been working with throughout my time in Karachi. In order to protect them, I will only call them by the friendship names of "Captain" and "D". Those who know these men know who they are. The Inspector General of Police (IGP), who I have discussed before had designated these men as my primary contacts. Captain was my police criminal investigative contact (CID), and D was my police intelligence bureau contact (IB). We had become more than that. We were and remain friends. The three of us would become the leadership of the investigation into the kidnapping and eventual murder of Danny Pearl. My role was as the only American investigator to actually work the operational end. The FBI would come in after a week to do what they do so well and that is tracking of names and facts, as well as faces and forensics when possible. They would not however, be out on the streets with the Pakistani assault team with me because they do not operate in foreign environments and had no established relationship of trust with the Pakistanis. D would be our Intelligence Source and linked us to essential Pakistani components for information and cooperation. Captain was the leader of the Pakistani side of the investigation and the assault team was his team. I was lucky to be permitted to work within a Pakistani investigation and still remain the only foreigner they have ever allowed to do so. Captain was the host-nation lead on this investigation and he knew what he was doing. He also had some excellent experience that brought him to this point of leadership. Before the Daniel Pearl case, Captain made his mark by capturing a man in Lahore named Javed Iqbal. This sick, demented psychopath had over a period of some years, kidnapped, sexually molested, then strangled and cut up into pieces over 100 children, then placed the pieces into 50 gallon drums of acid. The capture of Javed Iqbal and the ridding Lahore of this plague was a national moment of joy. Captain earned his bars. And so the story goes. . . .

On the day of 22 January, 2002, I had an appointment with a Wall Street Journal Reporter named Daniel Pearl. He wanted some background on the area and also wanted a security briefing on what and where was or was not safe to do or go in Karachi. We met at 1400 hours and during the one-hour conversation, I gave him my standard security briefing and then he asked me about a religious leader named Sheikh Gillani, who was the alleged spiritual head of a group or religious sect called Al-Fuqra. Danny said that his investigation verified that Richard Reid, the idiot Shoe Bomber, had stayed with the Sheikh in Lahore at his religious retreat/home for one week prior to his failed airline shoe bombing incident. I was disturbed that I had never heard of the organization nor the man. After this many years here, I was sort of the local expert on terrorist groups and leaders and to have never heard of this one was surprising. I told Danny that I had never heard of them and asked why he was interested. Danny said he was to meet at 1900 hours that evening with Sheikh Gillani to interview him about Richard Reid. Danny wanted to know if I thought that was a safe thing to do. I told him that I was bothered by my unfamiliarity with the organization and that he should be careful. I said if he was going to meet him, it should be at a very public place with lots of people. Danny said the venue was the Village Restaurant that was connected to the Metropol

Hotel. I felt better about this location because it was controlled and public and told him so. Danny then said that it was possible Sheikh Gillani might want to take him to his Madrassah (religious school) to show him around and I adamantly said no. I advised Danny that Madrassahs (plural is actually Madaris) were "no go" places because once inside, you could disappear forever and no one would ever be able to find you or help you. Danny said he understood and that it shouldn't be a problem since the interview was at the Village Restaurant. I liked Danny. He had an honest smile, intelligent eyes, was smart and quick with humor and mentioned his wife Mariane and that they were going to have a baby. We discussed introducing our wives at some point if mine got back to Karachi and at 1500 hours I walked him next door to the Marriott Hotel, where I watched him catch a cab back to the Zam Zama neighborhood where he and Mariane were staying with a Wall Street Journal associate named Asra Nomani. Then I sat down at a table in the hotel lobby's Nadia Coffee Shop with the Korean Consul General, where I had promised to meet him for a discussion on security issues. That was the last time I saw Danny alive.

I always arrived early for work, usually between 0500 and 0530. That allowed me to get my 14 hour day started by clearing the official emails and cable traffic from Washington from the night before and perhaps even get a cable written or a report done prior to the onslaught of problems that kept me running full speed all day long. It also allowed me to avoid being awakened by the mosque with the loudspeaker system 60 feet from my residence back door. Being awakened by a blaring prayer at 0500 is not a pacific thing for a security officer trying to maintain his "center" amid daily life and death crises. On January 23, 2002, it was no different. I was up by 0400 and at my desk by 0500. So, at

0710, when I received a phone call from Asra Nomani, telling me that Danny had never come home last night, I was already at full speed and able to initiate procedures I had put in place a couple of years before to deal with prior and potential kidnappings.

Coincidentally, in the week prior to Danny's disappearance, I had dealt with three different cases of Americans going missing and our coordinated efforts had found all three. Each of them had been recovered within 24 hours from their disappearance. But, the process and ensuing operation was based on immediate or rapid notification and by the time I got the call, it appeared Danny could have been taken up to 12 hours before.

I initiated our procedure which included calling our Deputy Inspector General of Police (DIG) who immediately put the entire police force on alert and they cordoned off the major roads leading in and out of Karachi. I then contacted my friend and the boss of the Citizen Police Liaison Committee (CPLC), a highly-effective voluntary organization specializing in kidnap negotiating and with eyes and ears all over the city, and he put his people to work on the streets, as well as utilizing his city-wide GPS "tracker" operation. This consisted of numerous roving patrols of armed men who were constantly moving throughout the city waiting to hear that one of the cars they had electronically "registered" with a tracking device had been stolen or was in trouble. They began looking for any vehicle that might contain Danny and also began questioning contacts and Sources in neighborhoods. They also matched up with the police at the roadblocks. I also put my 18-man team of Surveillance Detection Specialists (SD) on alert and they circulated looking for any sign of Danny. They knew the town well and knew the areas where criminals might take someone to hide out. Our problems were the 12 hours of lost time, dealing with the ninth largest city in the world containing up to about 19 million people, and daylight in the Al-Qaida neighborhoods, which could get our people killed just by going into them. It was like the proverbial needle in the haystack search but after the windstorm had blown the haystack around for a few hours. This meant we would have to take a more traditional and extremely difficult path of methodically investigating the disappearance in a city where everyone distrusted and hated the police and all the bad guys wanted to kill me. But, that is what we do and I now took Danny's loss personally. I fully intended to insert myself into the investigation no matter what rules the Pakistanis had against foreigner interference, and my goal was to return him smiling to his wife Mariane. Fortunately, the Pakistani investigative team selected were my friends, and I was accepted as family, and the Inspector General of Police, K, trusted me. Even the then Sindh Province Governor, Mohammedmian Soomro got personally involved, and the infamous Pakistan CIA equivalent, InterServices Intelligence Division (ISID) assigned a Colonel to provide shadowy oversight and occasional assistance.

Through the early morning, I continued to get updates from the police, CPLC, and my SD Team. It didn't appear that we would get lucky as with our three cases the week before. We held what is called an Emergency Action Committee Meeting of the key Consulate Officers to discuss the incident and we notified the Department of State and Diplomatic Security Command Centers. I made contact with Captain and D and filled them in on the details, which had already been given to them by police headquarters. I told them I would see them at the residence in Zam Zama and by 1000 am, it was time I went to the home of Asra Nomani where Danny and Mariane were staying and introduced myself and tried to collect any information that might help us locate

Sheikh Gillani and Danny. The investigation had to commence immediately. I grabbed my Senior Pakistani Investigator, Z, and we went to get whatever information we could.

Z and I arrived at the home in Zam Zama and introduced ourselves. The first impressions from Mariane and Asra were of fear, panic, and distrust of us. I felt a real resistance initially as to who and what we were but realized that as reporters, that was probably a natural response to Federal Law Enforcement Officers. I felt the same thing toward reporters. As we began to talk about the night before and Danny's plans, police vehicles pulled up out front and Captain and D arrived and entered the home. We greeted each other with the traditional cultural hug of close friends and then I introduced them to Mariane and Asra. For the next hour or two, we went through all the details that could be provided, identified the gaps of information we had to fill, and went through Danny's notes and the laptop to see what we could find. Danny had his own "short hand", as it appears most reporters do, in order to maintain secrecy of their working notes and the deciphering was going to be the first hurdle to overcome. We needed to know everyone involved in the chain that led him to the appointment last night. All along, we kept hoping that Danny would pull up out front. When we left the house to get back to work, Mariane and Asra were to try and derive whatever they could from the scribblings and laptop. The next almost five weeks would become the most difficult, interesting, challenging and eventually heartbreaking investigation I have ever conducted.

Obviously, I cannot take you through everything done in the five week investigation. That would be 300 pages alone. But, I will try to provide the highlights as my notes and memory can pull them together. Those familiar with the book and movie titled "A

Mighty Heart" will see some differences in information and perhaps perspective, and of course other details not known before, but that is how humans are. Our memories always have a tint of self-perception and our minds make adjustments over time to fit what we feel most comfortable with. Mariane's loss was awful and her book is a love story. No one can relate her love and life with Danny except her. When the limited outside facts about us and our actions came into life and memory in the book and moreso to a greater degree in the movie, she naturally remembered things in a slightly and sometimes completely different way. Even the Director, who met with me to learn of the nightly actions, altered his movie to fit what the movie needed or Angelina Jolie wanted. That is life folks. I don't object to anything Mariane said or does. It is her story. But, as with portraying me in the book with long hair to my shoulders (it was of course not true), it is an acceptable memory interpretation and fine with me. On a daily basis, usually in the early morning hours or at sun-up after we finished our raids or other nightly investigative work, I would write down the entire day and night's events and that is what I will relate. So, it doesn't matter if some of the facts are slightly different. The story is the same and so is the unfortunate outcome. For example, neither the book nor the movie discuss that months later I supervised the excavation of Danny's body in the desert on the far outskirts of Karachi in a small, 12-home, dirt-street Al-Qaida neighborhood. It pretty much never went further than the Pakistani press.

We put all our people on the street showing photos of Danny and canvassing the restaurants and shops in the area of the Metropol Hotel and The Village Restaurant. We interviewed every employee. We also identified the Al-Fuqra Headquarters in Lahore and worked to get a local Al-Fuqra (AF) Madrassah contact. The options we were faced with at the time were of course first and the worst that he had been kidnapped by terrorists, or second, that Danny had been picked up by ISID, IB, or local Police for questioning, as that did occasionally happen when they wanted to know what someone was doing in their precarious neighborhoods. All Services denied having Danny. We still hoped it would be like the Pakistani reporter for Time magazine named Ghulam Hasnain, who had disappeared on January 22 while investigating the dangerous Indian criminal mafia boss Ibrahim Dawood. He was returned coincidentally on January 24 to his home after being interrogated by the ISI for two days. He had a controversial reputation and Ibrahim Dawood had a lot of power in the region. We also had several points of concern we had to realistically take into account. Karachi was the center of the terrorist recruitment and funding world; Danny lived in India and Pakistan distrusted everything Indian; he was an aggressive American reporter; and he was Jewish in a Muslim country. We decided that this last point needed to stay very "close-hold" just in case.

Even though the actual Joint Investigative Team (JIT) was Captain of CID, D of IB, and myself, we also had the Inspector General and all his resources, the ISI elements (but we would never know what they were doing), and even the CIA was keeping their eyes and ears open for information. We even began to hear that the FBI wanted to join in on the investigation.

By January 25, Asra and Mariane had compiled an excellent detailed summary of all computer and hard copy notes from Danny's records. At this time, the "Player" of interest was Sheikh Mubarak Ali Gilani, the leader of Jamaat-ul-Fuqra, who Danny was supposed to have met with the fateful night. An article published in the Boston Globe on January 06, had sparked Danny's interest when it claimed that the crazy "shoe bomber" Richard

Reid had ties with Sheikh Gilani. The chain of contacts we had to work with included an Asif Farruqi, a journalist for a Japanese press organization called G.G. Press. Asif had been paid $100. per day to assist Danny with arranging the meeting with Gilani. Asif then introduced Danny to Zafar Malik, a reporter for the Urdu language newspaper JANG. Zafar then introduced Danny to a dangerous man known only by the first name of Arif, who was known to belong to the terrorist organization called Harakut-ul-Mujahideen, which had close ties to Al-Qaida. Arif introduced Danny to Chaudry Bashir, supposedly a disciple of Gilani. Bashir then introduced Danny to a man named Imtiaz Siddique, who allegedly set up the meeting with Gilani for that night. First, our concern was sparking because of the lengthy list of introductions including some very dangerous people. Second, Arif, Bashir, and Siddique were completely out of phone contact. They had dropped off the grid and that was a very bad indicator.

A brief rundown of the contacts and meetings leading up to the kidnapping follow but I will try to be succinct. I realize all too well how confusing this long list of difficult names can be.

January 09 – Danny and Asif travel to the Pindhora area of Rawalpindi and meet Arif at the offices of the Harakut-ul-Mujahideen terrorist group to try to get to Gilani.

January 11 – Danny and Asif hire a taxi at the Marriott hotel in Islamabad and travel again to Pindhora and are picked up by Arif at a crossroads leading to Rawalpindi. Danny, Asif and Arif proceed to a cheap hotel called the Akbar International Hotel, where they go to a room on the fourth floor for a meeting with Chaudray Bashir (later to be identified as the planner of the kidnapping Sheikh Umer). It was shortly after this meeting that Asif found out that Arif was connected to Al-Qaida.

The next week – a number of basically irrelevant meetings were arranged and cancelled or sometimes held that led to nothing. This was all part of the bait and switch approach to "hook" Danny.

January 16 – Bashir (Umer) emailed Danny and told him that he and Gilani had read some of his articles and enjoyed his work. Bashir stated that the meeting with Gilani was going to happen soon.

January 19 – Bashir (Umer) sent another email to Danny stating Gilani had agreed to meet with him but it would be in Karachi in a few days when he returned there.

January 20 – Bashir (Umer) sent another email confirming that the meeting would be either the 22nd or 23rd in Karachi. Apparently the player Imtiaz Siddique was involved in setting up the meeting. He was actually the "cut-out" for Bashir/Umer.

January 21 – Danny and Mariane had been in Islamabad and flew to Karachi and stayed with Danny's Wall Street Journal friend and associate Asra Nomani, in the Zam Zama neighborhood.

January 22 – 1130, Danny met with the Federal Investigative Agency (FIA) Chief, - 1200 to 1315, he met with the Director of the Civil Aviation Authority, - 1400 to 1500, Danny met with me at the American Consulate, 1530 to 1630, Danny then spent time at the home in Zam Zama with Mariane. Danny then took a taxi to the Cyber Internet Services for a brief time, and from 1750 to 1825, Danny spent the time with the Chief of the Citizen Police Liaison Committee, where he reported that Danny received a call during which he stated, "yes, I'll be there at 1900 hours for the meeting" (this was the Village Restaurant meeting). At 1826 hours, Danny called Asra Nomani and told her he was on his way to the appointment but would be home for dinner. At 1830 hours, Danny received an incoming call on his cell phone from Imtiaz Siddique and heads for the nearby Village Restaurant. Cell phone records also showed that Danny received a call at 1911 hours which lasted until 1916 hours. Following this call, Danny dismissed his hired car and driver and was not heard from again.

January 23 – At 0710 hours, I was sitting in my office and I received the call from Asra Nomani. And the investigation began.

Back to the investigation - On January 25, a contact of mine told me they heard that Sheikh Gilani was leaving Karachi on his way back to his home and headquarters in Lahore. "D" found a Gilani departing on a flight and he was detained briefly but turned out to be the wrong person. Other rumors circulated but were later determined to be planted to divert our interests from the true course to give the enemy more time to establish themselves. Police Officers were dispatched to Lahore to interview Gilani but he had been missing for a few days so they waited and watched. It was also learned that the son of Gilani had a car dealership in Albany, New York, and that there were entire communities made up of mostly African Americans in the U.S. who still followed Gilani and sent him money to support his religious objectives. It appeared that much of that money then re-circulated to New York perhaps into business interests. It was also reported that the mystical Bareilvi Al-Fuqra group may have changed their name to either Tanzeem-ul-Fuqra or Tehrik-ul-Fuqra.

January 25, a reporter for the newspaper JANG, reported that one of his Sources remembers 3 men walking out of the Village Restaurant with Daniel Pearl. We had no credibility rating for this reporter nor the Source and all local reporters were smelling money from the pockets of the Wall Street Journal (WSJ) so we had to be very careful about what and who we believed. The JANG reporter was interviewed but the facts were weak. The Director of Security for Dow Jones and Company made contact with me. He is ex-FBI and he asked if we needed FBI assistance. Since the FBI works mostly from door to door and Karachi can only be worked through local Pakistani Police, I explained to him that they were welcome but would be pretty much restricted to the inside of the Consulate. They would not be permitted on the streets of the city. He said he concurred but then messages about FBI assistance started coming in to the Consulate and from the Embassy in Islamabad.

January 26, The WSJ contacted me and asked about the capability of the local police to carry out the investigation. I advised him that they were capable and really the only option in this Al-Qaida filled city. I also told them that their best people were heading the investigation. We discussed the disadvantages like a 12-hour head start and they understood but commented on the stress build-up in the WSJ headquarters, I advised them that both Mariane and Asra were still very stable and in control and not yet showing outward signs of constricting-stress. I spoke to the DIG of Police about the JANG Source and mentioned that I had heard that the police had "misplaced" Gilani three months before and he admitted that it was true and that they had been seeking his whereabouts. He stated that because of his "cult-like" followers in the U.S. they were keeping an eye on him. Unfortunately, this increased our suspicions and focus on Gilani, which diverted us from what might have been a more successful direction.

The Akbar International Hotel was visited on this morning and the entire neighborhood was canvassed for any sightings or information that might point us to an identity of Bashir, Arif, or Siddique. I reported back to my headquarters that my money at this time was placed on the Bashir connection. Phones were tapped in the hopes of catching a call for ransom. Normally after 2 or 3 days, a call would be placed if it was a kidnap for ransom scenario and we were all actually hoping that was the case. Since we had not received any call yet, we still thought it was possibly a kidnap for ransom but with the entire country looking for Danny, they would have to be more cautious. We also found the connection between the Al-Fuqra group to a group in the U.S. called "Muslims of America". We also found a phone listing for Al-Fuqra with an address at the Metropol Hotel, which is next door to the Village Restaurant. Again, a solid lead but a diversion in the end. Asra Nomani called me to tell me that a Source of Arif named Zafar Malik, had just called Arif to tell him he was going to Muzzafarabad (3 hours outside Islamabad) to look for Bashir but did not say why. The police moved on the cell phone to try and locate it. During all this, my Senior Consulate Pakistani Investigator, Z, was trying to trace the IP address of four emails on Danny's computer in an attempt to locate Bashir or Siddique. He had identified a list of users on the system at the same time Danny was on and one name was Chaudray Bashir. We began to dig deeper into the electronic tracking.

NOTE: Sheikh Sayyid Mubarik Gilani al-Hashimi, the founder of Jamaat-ul-Fuqra (Community of the Poor) in 1980, was on the U.S. Department of State's designated list of terrorist organizations and reported as such from 1996 to 1999 and was dropped from the list in 2000. Their principal period of activity was in the mid 1980s, when they were involved in several bombing incidents in the United States and there were several convictions for murder and arson. The group is virtually unknown in Pakistan and unlike other groups who like to emblazon themselves with flags and signs, Al-Fuqra maintains a low profile. Sheikh Gilani was the custodian of a well-known shrine called Hazrat Mian Mir in Lahore but frequently traveled in and out of the U.S. for extended periods. The Muslims of America (MOA) is a reclusive organization that maintains communities in Ohio, New York, Virginia, South Carolina, Colorado, California and Canada. It was run from a 67-acre compound in Delaware County, Ohio. They seemed to be advocates of Kashmiri independence.

January 27, I met with a Wall Street Journal contact and the Chief of CPLC to discuss setting up a meeting with the Federal Minister of Interior (MOI), Haider, to solicit technical support from the ISI (Pakistan's CIA) since our mysterious ISI Colonel seemed to have dropped from sight after the first day and we needed ISI's support. The police "lookout" at all bus stations has failed. The checks at the Akbar Hotel in Rawalpindi led to Muzafir Hussain as the man who rented the room for the meeting between Danny and Bashir. Muzafir turned out to be a 60-year old man who had no idea about anything and did not fit the profile and description. Bashir was clever enough to use local names of people to cover his trail, which indicated a structured plan at least reaching back to two weeks prior to the kidnapping. This made it seem more terrorism than criminal. Other name leads in Rawalpindi turned out the same. Just older men who had no clue of the operation.

At 1100 hours, the WSJ (Mariane and Asra) advised me that a Honolulu-based FBI Agent had contacted them and advised them that there were FBI Agents coming to assist. The FBI had not contacted me and that was improper. At 1300 hours, we had the meeting with MOI Minister Haider and it was very unsatisfactory, resulting in Haider essentially blaming Danny, accusing him of interfering in national matters and alleging that Asra Nomani, of Indian origin, was a spy in Pakistan. We all left depressed and upset.

An email was received by Mariane and Asra from Bashir. It casually asked how Danny's meeting with Gilani had gone. He said he was on business in Lahore and would go see Gilani to ask his impressions and was signed "stay in touch". Records show that he had previously read Mariane's email to him telling him that Danny was missing and asking for his contact and help. So, it was clear deception on his part and an amateurish slip-up pointing us now more strongly toward him. Mariane played the game and responded with an email to Bashir, telling him again of Danny's disappearance and asking him to telephone her since he was a "caring friend" of Danny's. All the news media were starting to highlight stories on Danny's disappearance.

We were still looking for Gilani and we had discovered that his brother-in-law was Khalid Kowaja, a retired Pakistani Air Force officer who worked for ISI, but at the end of his career, grew a big beard and became a radical Muslim. It was reported that following 9/11, he brought four Black-American Muslim women to the home of Gilani for religious training. Following this, it is reported that there was a flow of Black American Muslims spending time in Gilani's home from the "Muslims of America" group.

The January 27 morning JANG newspaper printed an article stating Danny was CIA with possible connections to the Mossad and the Indian Intel Agency RAW and that he had been staying in the home of another Indian woman named Asra Nomani.

The destructive article came from the same JANG Source we had talked to and was probably in retribution for being questioned. JANG was known to be very anti-American.

At 1150 hours, the first email of Danny was received by the WSJ in the U.S. showing a facial of Danny with a gun pointed at this head. It was sent by the "National Movement for the Restoration of Pakistani Sovereignty" and stated that if America wants Danny back, the prisoners in Cuba must be returned to Pakistan. The email was forwarded to Mariane and Asra and given to us but we needed the original to obtain the senders IP address and track it down. I voiced my concern to Mariane and Asra about their health and welfare, essentially food and sleep, and especially since Mariane was pregnant. I was beginning to respect and personally like these two strong women. I went to their home, where they had not gone outside for a week and told them I was getting them out for a breath of fresh air. I knew just a change of focus and scenery would do them good. Z and I took them to a secured in-door mall called "The Point", and we walked around looking and acting almost normal in the middle of this absolute horror and chaos of the kidnapping. I then took them to the McDonald's restaurant in the mall thinking this would be a positive reality shock. Mariane said she had never eaten in a McDonalds before and Asra got big eyes because she loved them. They both ordered and we ate with a semblance of normaility. After, we walked a bit more and then I took them back home. I thought they just needed a complete cleansing of a week's worth of stress.

We placed Z and a police computer expert inside their home to work full time on the task of tracking the email header of the first demand. Z worked all that night and discovered the header had an original email address at the DAWN newspaper. The FBI

Team arrived and I took them to the Zam Zama home that evening from 1700 until 2100 hours for their introduction and to see what they could offer on the cyber tracking.

January 28, the majority of the day was spent trying to specifically track the IP header of the email. It was found that a man named Mansoor Ejaz, a Banker and known Kashmiri activist living in the U.S. had received the original email on a site entitled "kidnapperguy.com" and had forwarded it to the WSJ. He was interviewed and he admitted that he had given Danny the contact number of Khalid Khowaja, the brother-in-Law of Gilani and the beginning of the series of contacts. Khowaja was also a reported associate of Usama Bin Laden and was an outspoken critic of U.S. vulnerabilities for attack. It was Asra Nomani who months before had interviewed Khowaja at his palacial home in Lahore and witnessed the four black-American women. Ejaz became a high interest person and also became uncooperative and threatened to use his high-level contacts to back us off.

In our Joint Working Group daily brief, which now involved the FBI as well, we discussed offering a reward in order to turn the kidnappers against each other. The suggestion was passed to the WSJ for their fiscal consideration.

The FBI Team that had arrived had little to no overseas experience with the exception of the initial and temporary Team Leader, a woman serving in the Islamabad Legal Attache Office. She organized her people and tried to find the right avenue to pursue. The problem the FBI Team faced was that they only had experience in the U.S. This was Karachi and it would kill an inexperienced or unsuspecting foreigner in a heart beat. The concept the Agents had arrived with was that they would go door to door in Karachi like in the U.S. and ask questions until they got workable leads. I advised them that this was the most dangerous city in the world and also the 9th largest city in the world, 95% of which was totally off-limits due to Taliban and Al-Qaida control and that they would be staying in the office suite I provided them and only traveling to the Zam Zama house and back and only in fully armored cars with armed follow cars loaded with guys with machine guns. I made it clear that if they did not follow that guidance, they would be on the list of people we were searching for or the "dead list". They understood and came to stronger comprehension the longer they were there. I would be the only one going out at night on raids with my police contacts and the assault team.

On January 28 and 29, in order to slow down our investigation with false leads, several threats were made to divert our attention and resources, including to our Consulates in Karachi, Lahore, and Islamabad and the Karachi airport and the Marriott Hotel. All calls were placed from Imtiaz Siddique's phone.

January 29, we had one minor success. Our Surveillance Detection Team in Lahore had heard from one of their Sources that a particular house might belong to Sheikh Gilani and had staked it out with their Source for possible identification need. As they watched it, two cars pulled up to the house, Gillani and two bearded men got out, went inside the house and came back with Gillani's wife and son and departed. This led to his capture the following day and our beginning of his interrogations.

January 30 was a low point for us. Newspapers all over Karachi had been given information from a police officer that discussed the technical tracing methods we were using to find the kidnappers through cell phones and emails. This "leak" seriously damaged our efforts and some of those we were tracing went cold and disappeared.

We believed we had identified Arif, the alleged Harakat-ul-Mujahideen/Al-Qaida "person of interest", as a Muhammad Hashim, whose father was a Maulana at a Madrassah in the town of Bahawalpur and which had a connection to the Jaish Muhammad Jihadi group. Arif/Hashim and his three brothers were now all being sought.

The Wall Street Journal (WSJ) had sent back a plea to the "kidnapperguy.com" website, telling them that Danny was just a regular good guy with a pregnant wife and not trying to affect foreign policy, and asking that they let him go. This plea got wide coverage and went into many other media sources but had no effect.

At 1420 hours, the second demand email arrived at the WSJ Offices in New York. The WSJ did not pass this second email to those of us doing the investigating in Pakistan for five hours. This email was different in content and nature and there were misspellings.

At 2230 hours, police raided the home of Arif, now known as Muhammad Hashim, and found it deserted. Arif had quite a criminal record including one murder charge he was not convicted for in 1999. When we spoke to the family of Arif, they said they had been informed that Arif had been killed in a shootout in Afghanistan fighting his Jihad against the Americans on January 25 and that the family had held a memorial service for him. What we discovered though was that Arif had spoken with his family on January 26 and convinced them to play this role to mislead the police.

January 31, we conducted a two-hour interview with Gilani and the FBI was allowed to participate. Gilani was not completely honest and changed his answers occasionally. He claimed he had never even heard of Danny Pearl until he read about him in the papers and was surprised to hear that he allegedly had been meeting with him. One problem was that he also denied ever hearing about any group called Jamaat-ul-Fuqra and we knew for a fact that was a lie. He gave up his driver "Haji" as a literate man who could have done the emails and speculated that maybe he was Bashir. Gilani was an old and simple man who only had enough motivation to con Americans into sending him money for religious purposes but not enough to pull off this kidnapping. We all felt he was not likely involved but since he had also told us deliberate lies and not fully cooperated, he would remain as a guest of the police for awhile longer. We convinced Gilani that if he was innocent, he should put out a press statement that he was cooperating with the police and that the kidnapping was against the world of Islam and the Holy Koran and that Danny should be released unharmed. But, after consideration, we felt it was better to allow the true villains to continue believing that Gilani was on the hot seat so they wouldn't panic and do something rash or disappear.

We obtained a photo of Arif (Muhammad Hashim) at a wedding six years before and showed it to Zafar Malik who identified him as the man we wanted but said he had no beard now and was older looking. A definite hit on Arif pulled things a bit tighter. We continued working our electronic searches with some success.

At 1910 hours, a third kidnap demand email was received. This was very different from the first two and made poetic flair and religious references to Allah for the first time. The writer said they were untouchable like the air, the seas, and mentioned the graveyards. He wrote like a juvenile and we thought was maybe a "copycat" effort.

At 2030 hours, I received a call from Asra that Mariane was experiencing bad stomach pains and they needed an OB/GYN. This was certainly the first time I had dealt with this type of emergency. I had a local Pakistani friend who was even more pregnant than Mariane and I called her and asked if her baby doctor would help. She was very sympathetic about the case and immediately called her 80-year old doctor who was asleep. She said he was an old and afraid man and would only go if she came, so I grabbed a large fully-armored Suburban and driver and bodyguards with machine guns in another car and we went and picked her up. She was a petite girl so I kind of picked her up and placed her inside the tall Suburban and we went on to the Doctors house. I lifted her down and we went to the Doctor's door. He was a very sweet little old man who was a bit afraid of all my men and guns but my friend had been right to come along. He felt comforted by her. So, I lifted the Doctor into the Suburban, went around and lifted my friend back into the Suburban and we headed for the house in Zam Zama. After lifting them both down, the doctor met privately with Mariane, where he diagnosed the problem as stress-induced stomach pains with too little sleep and improper nourishment and gave her something for it and she was able to sleep. I had money for the doctor but he said he knew about the case and was ashamed that his people had done such a thing to guests in his country and he would not take money for the night visit. I took the two out to the Suburban and reversed the process to get them both home safely. They were both back in their beds by 2230 hours.

This had also been the day our larger FBI Team with computer specialists arrived and many of them would stay until the case concluded. Others would rotate out as needed.

February 01, at 0930, I met with the Inspector General of Police to discuss an action against one of the internet providers who seemed to be originating some of the kidnap emails. Throughout the day we prepared for a nighttime raid to seize the equipment and people involved, and hoped that would lead to the recovery of Danny.

I personally contacted the parents of Danny to assure them that we were doing everything possible to get their son back. Though I couldn't tell them any of the specifics of an on-going international terrorism investigation, I felt it would help them to hear a voice of someone on the ground working to get Danny back. They seemed to appreciate it.

We had traced the emails to an apartment building email server. Unfortunately the server serviced over 70 apartments and we would need to wait until we saw the same email IP address come through the server to identify the exact apartment. We placed a savvy undercover police officer in the internet café overwatching the server and when the IP address popped up, he noted it and we now knew where to go. By 1700 hours, our Assault Team of myself, Captain, D, and Captain's tough Assault specialists were prepared for the raid, seizure and hopeful rescue. The FBI would not be allowed to go. Now we just waited for dark and the lateness of the early morning when everyone would be asleep. The neighborhood we would raid had numerous bad elements and we knew the specific apartment would be in dangerous territory.

February 02, at 0030 hours, the apartment resident arrived home and the raid took place. The police seized everything including the computer, which apparently the owner, thinking himself to be a real wiz at computers, told us he had wiped the harddrive. Never underestimate the technical capabilities of an FBI computer specialist. Back at the Assault Team headquarters, the computer was given to the FBI and they went off to begin their work. We began to question the first solid lead we had obtained in the CID Tactical Operations Center.

Note – Originally there were multiple apartments that seemed to be involved in the emails. One containing a young man named Fahad, the other containing a young man named Ubaid. During the questioning of Ubaid, he 'gave up" a computer hacker specialist named Waqar, who allegedly did aircraft repair work. In a follow-on raid of the apartment of Waqar, we found diagrams of the A-300 Airbus and this raised a big red flag from the recent past twin tower attack. The evidence and Waqar were turned over to the appropriate U.S. authorities for needed follow-up but he wasn't our boy.

At 0230 hours, the police felt that additional questioning of Fahad was going to be needed and I went back to my office which was just next door to the Central Investigative Division Offices, to do my own reporting while they continued with their questioning. At this point, I called and woke up Z and asked him to join the CID Team and help with email technical questions and Urdu translation.

We had now received six kidnapper emails regarding Danny, the last stating he had been killed and his body dumped in a graveyard. During the previous night, we searched every graveyard and found some unburied dead bodies but none were Danny. At 0600 hours we began the search again in daylight. Still no body.

In the follow-up interviews with Fahad and Ubaid, we discovered that the cyber cafe server had the same password for all 70 units attached to it. The password was "password" and anyone could sign on to any unit with the same access. This complicated things dramatically. So, we grabbed all 70 computers from every apartment and began to search through them all. All 70 apartment renters were also interviewed to try and get a "short list" of computers to check.

At 2200 hours we met with my friend from CPLC and he laid out an excellent chart for phone tracking that his organization had put together from all the numbers acquired thus far. It linked all the critical numbers and suspects and showed who had called who and how many times over the past weeks. The chart seemed to highlight two main characters who had communication with all the suspects. We requested that ISID and IB set up phone intercepts on the entire list of numbers in an attempt to hear what was now being said. It was agreed upon.

Everyone was getting very fatigued. The days were spent developing more leads and conducting the business we needed to in order to keep our other Consulate operations functional. The nights were spent running down the leads, conducting raids, interviewing possible suspects and miscellaneous other actions. Our adrenaline was getting pretty well used-up and we were averaging about 1 or 2 hours of sleep per day, sometimes only when we passed out on our desk or on our computer keyboards while trying to write up the daily report to feed the Washington information monster. We continued to push hard but it was all just our motivation to help Mariane, and our need to kick in one more door and find Danny safely huddled in a corner and see the smile on Mariane's face when we took him home. Sometimes bodies and minds can operate on very little sustenance when an objective is so critical.

February 03, at 0030 hours, a lead obtained by FSNI Z, who had been working on the computer IP headers at Mariane's home, identified Aslam Haaris as the producer of what the Team had named "the Seas, Oceans, Wind, and Grave, and apology" emails. These included emails numbered 3, 7, and 9. Aslam turned out to be a 16-year old young man. He was immediately brought to Karachi from Lahore and we met with him at 1400 hours. Aslam related how he did the first email as a "bad prank" and then felt sorry for it and began to send apology emails. He knew he was in trouble and showed serious signs of fear. He said he learned of the kidnapping like everyone else, from the newspapers and accessed the CNN and BBC web pages to get every detail he could to make his email renditions seem more realistic. He said he thought he could fool the world and then came to realize the significance of what he had done. All this energy had been spent again in pursuing a false lead. Aslam's father was brought in on what his son had done and he was released into his father's custody.

As we were conducting the interview with Aslam, we were also coordinating a plan for another raid on a cyber café in Peshawar, where some of the phone and email connections had led us. It would take place on the coming Monday when it reopened.

At this time, it appeared to our Team that we had four possible groups of emails and email senders. According to our Team's numbering, they broke down as;

A. Aslam Haaris represented emails 3, 7, and 9.
B. Emails 1 and 2 with accompanying photos (our best leads).
C. Emails numbered 6 and 8 – the graveyard emails
D. Emails 4 and 5 regarding ransoms.

The one obvious thing was that there was a serious degradation of writing skills and intellectual rhetoric as well as focused organizational thought in all the emails following the first two. This is what led us to believe we had "copy cats" and "pranksters" like Aslam, screwing up our already-difficult work.

At 1930 hours on February 03, we received email number 10, which used the screen name "kidnapperguy" and mimicked the first one but was similar to email number 6, which claimed Danny had been killed and dumped in the graveyard, and 8, which reaffirmed Danny was dead but stated Danny's body would never be found, and disowned another email asking for the $2 million dollar ransom. This email number 8 compared Danny's missing body to those bodies that would never be recovered in Afghanistan. It also stated that they did not kill Danny because he was a journalist but because he was an American and that they had no personal enmity toward him. He was like the Afghans, just collateral damage. The writer also wanted the readers to know that the Americans and British will never feel safe traveling anywhere in the world. The only emails we all agreed we could be sure were from the kidnappers were numbers 1 and 2.

February 04, at 0030 hours, the Captain called me to tell me that police officers had found a body and they were quite certain it was Danny. I was to come to their local Morgue to identify him. When I arrived, I was escorted into a back room where a body of a man about Danny's length and general stature was lying on a table. This man had been shot in the right temple, execution style. Immediately, I noticed some inconsistencies that made me begin to doubt that the hunt was over. Starting head to toe, his hair was too short, and the hairline was too receded. The nose was not quite right and the arms didn't have much muscle tone like the person had not done much physical work and the hands were a bit effeminate and small. I remembered Danny's hands as having shown vessels and signs of having done real work. The final thing that caught my attention was the upper lip. It seemed to push out from underneath. I asked the examiner to lift the upper lip and when he did, the victim had braces on his upper teeth. This was not Danny Pearl. The Wall Street Journal Desk Officer, John Bussey, was now in town and I called him to tell him it was definitely not Danny. I described the body but John said he still wanted to verify it himself. I told him it was not necessary but for some reason, he felt he needed to see this body. I told him that he couldn't take taxis at night so I sent my armored vehicle to pick him up and brought him to the Morgue. I am still confused why, but he walked in, said it wasn't Danny and walked out. All that effort for nothing. We felt we needed to get a grip and relax a bit so I took Bussey, and we picked up another WSJ reporter and friend of Danny named Steven Levine, and we called the Consul General and we all met at my home at 0230 to take a deep breath, have a glass of wine, and be grateful it was not Danny and that we still had a chance to get him back.

February 04, 2000 hours, I was called by Captain. He had great news that Z, the FBI computer guys, and the police computer tracers, had identified the sender of the first two emails, which included the photos of Danny. He said that because of our long-standing relationship, and with the authority of the Inspector General of Police, I was also to go along on this all-important raid. We would be rounding up several suspects and it would be in dangerous neighborhoods controlled by Al-Qaida. This demonstrated and reaffirmed that they considered me as part of their family. I had accompanied them on other "raids" and investigative interrogations but this one would be of a nature with an exceptional level of risk. It would be a series of grabs, escapes, interrogations, and runs to grab the next one. It was bound to involve armed resistance and my Pakistani friends wanted to make sure that nothing happened to me. They had captured the first link who was now in custody and I was to come right over for the interrogation and to prepare for a long night of raids.

I asked if I could bring an FBI Agent on the raid to represent their interests. They refused. I told them that I would take full responsibility for his actions and control. We'll call him "Tom". There was strong resistance since there was no long term relationship of trust between them but Captain finally told me if I took full control of his actions, I could bring one FBI Agent but I had to keep him out of the way. It was also sort of agreed that we would not be part of the initial entry assault, but would enter seconds after his guys entered and gained control. They were still very protective of my welfare and I respected their position. But I alone would always be part of the interrogation team. The group identified as being behind the kidnapping, and the subject of the raids we were about to make, was the Jaish Muhammad Group.

For reasons of necessary propriety, the following details about the raids have been sanitized. Sometimes there are things that just should not be portrayed or presented. This will convey the essence of the night's activities while protecting certain facts and actions that would only serve to be detrimental.

I arrived with "Tom" at Captain's investigative cell to find the man who had been the sender of the emails #1 and #2, sitting bound and naked on the floor. It was Fahad. He confessed to being given the photos and wording and being responsible for putting them together and sending them out. He was one of our 70 IP addresses from the apartment building. He was also told to burn the photos and claimed he had done so. Fahad confessed to being given the notes and photos by a man named Salman. We wanted him.

Our car included Captain, D (IB), myself and Tom. Salman lived in a very dangerous neighborhood controlled by vicious thugs and killers attached to the "political" party called Muttahida Qaumi Movement, or (MQM). He was a killer who lived in a small apartment off a narrow alley with limited access and worse yet, limited one-way egress.

The Team advance element went into the neighborhood and got quietly situated. It was now about 0100 hours in the morning and we were hoping most were asleep to give us the best opportunity to get in, grab him, round up any evidence and get out alive, back down that narrow alley. The signal was given and the Team went in. It is never possible to break in quietly, so there was a limited time inside before there would be no safe exit. Salman was immediately grabbed, as were all cell phones, papers and anything else that seemed possibly useful. Running out the front door, there were windows lighting up, dogs were barking, people were yelling, guns began to fire, bullets hitting the sides of the alleyway, and at the end of the alley, there was a car now blocking the way and it was being lit on fire. The run with Salman continued under fire and past the burning car to our vehicles, which had come racing up to pick up the team and then we were gone, miraculously without an injury, racing off to the nearest police stronghold, where we could interrogate Salman, and force him to give us the next name in the line of kidnappers.

The interrogation was "typically Pakistani". A bit psychologically and physically rough and intimidating so we knew he would talk before long. The FBI Agent always stayed out of any direct action and removed himself from any interrogations. Our problem was that once we started this series of raids, we had to complete them by morning first prayer when they all gathered at the Mosque. The word would be out that we had captured involved sources and the bad guys would go-to-ground and possibly disappear. We only had until morning light to hopefully get Danny back using these Sources. Within a reasonable period of time, Salman told us that a man named Adeel or Adil had given him the materials, which he passed on to Fahad.

Adeel was a Jaish Muhammad Jihadi, who was known to be total hard-core and it was rumored that he had fought against the Americans in Afghanistan and had been wounded several times, including losing part of a hip. Strangest of all was that Adeel was also a Police Constable for Special Branch (IB), the same group that D worked for. He had taken time off to go fight the Americans and to train as a Jihadi.

We now had Fahad and Salman with us as we went to raid the home of Adeel. Adeel lived in the outskirts of Karachi in a strict Al-Qaida/Taliban, little dirt-street neighborhood. At about 0300 hours, we raided the home of Adeel. The Assault Team went in through every window, balcony entry, door and rough opening at the same time and within seconds, Adeel was snatched from his bed, several cell phones were grabbed and we looked around for papers. Before we finished, outside, other homes came to life, people were yelling, the team was telling everyone to get moving and it seemed like everyone began shooting. Everyone was now running down the dirt road toward the stashed cars as the gun fire fully erupted and with us was Adeel in his underwear and bare-feet. Everyone made it to the cars and we drove literally for our lives. We were very unhappy about not finding Danny in Adeel's home.

We drove to the nearest and safest, as well as strongest police station to question Adeel. Again, with only me and the Assault Team in the room, Adeel was questioned rigorously. It was obvious that Adeel had been given professional "resistance" training by the games he would play to get out of answering. He would pretend to be tired or to "pass out". On one occasion, he acted like he had passed out and one of the biggest men on the Team looked at me, winked, and then clasped his hand over Adeel's nose and mouth. Adeel was instantly up and alert and the big man smiled at me. I have often wondered about the degrees of resistance for every man, including myself. Watching these men, professionals, all big and tough, hardened men, I felt a true appreciation for being on this side of the action. I was honestly grateful that they were on the side of the goodguys.

Adeel eventually told us he had received the photos and materials that he gave to Salman at the Sabil Wali Mosque from an unknown Source who delivered it for Sheikh Umer Saeed, a man known for the hijacking of the Indian airliner and his subsequent release along with Jaish Muhammad leader Masood Azhar. Sheikh Umer was also identified as the man at the hotel meeting in Rawalpindi with Danny named Chaudray Bashir. Fahad, Salman, and Adeel also all stated that they had known Umer and had meetings at an

Umer family residence in the Karachi KDA neighborhood.

Our entire Team next went to the Sabil Wali Mosque, regularly attended by Umer, in the hopes that Danny might be held inside. We met with failure at the Mosque so we proceeded to the family home in KDA. We tracked it by a cell phone call placed earlier. Sheikh Umer was not there, but we found his three Cousins and his Aunt. These four family members were taken into protective custody. We asked the Aunt if Umer was here and she replied no but she could contact him. Captain asked her to dial the number on the cell phone of Adeel, knowing that Umer would answer a call from Adeel. As a shock to us all, Umer answered and Captain said "Sheikh Umer, this is Captain with CID Police. We know everything and have Fahad, Salman, and Adeel in custody. We also have your Aunt and 3 cousins. Turn yourself in to save your family any further embarrassment." Umer paused and then hung up. In this culture, it is unacceptable that ones actions should bring disgrace upon your family so the Aunt and Cousins being in custody was serious to Umer. To further solidify the chances that Daniel would remain unharmed and would be released soon, Umer's father was called and was taken into custody. We encouraged Umer's Father to call his son and implore him to release Danny. We found that the Aunt was too old to remain at the jail and one of the Cousins had asthma, so we took them both home to their own comforts. The point had been made. We didn't need to cause discomfort to any innocents. It was found out though that the final kidnapping meeting was held at the Aunt's home in the front yard, where they all decided the final details of the action. The youngest boy Cousin had sat and listened to the plan as well.

In further researching the background of Sheikh Umer, it was found that he was a proclaimed member of Al-Qaida and considered to be a favorite "son" of Usama Bin Ladin. He also allegedly made a $100,000 payment to Muhammad Atta of the World Trade Center bombing infamy. The case was tying together and Umer was definitely the one we wanted.

Upon returning from a long night's work that was successful but not successful like we had hoped, myself and the FBI Agent met at the Consul General's home to call the Ambassador and give her a complete update of the night's efforts. We asked that she call President Musharraf, requesting he call the persons holding Masood Azhar, who was under house arrest, and convince him to ask the kidnappers of Danny to let him go. By expediting this request, the members of Jaish Muhammad would learn of it at morning prayers, only 30 minutes from now (0530), and additional pressure could be applied to release Danny. The Ambassador did meet with Musharraf and made that request. Unfortunately, Sheikh Umer went silent and disappeared. For the next day or two, everyone studied the Bio of Sheikh Umer to understand his motives and future actions.

Through our continuing interrogations of Umer's cousins, as well as the kidnappers we had captured, we found out several more pieces of the puzzle. Salman had been the one who purchased the Polaroid camera that took the now-infamous photos of Danny, used in the emails. He had provided it to an unknown man described as "ugly man like Adeel but with large black lips". We felt Salman was still holding back on the information he knew, selfishly giving out bits and pieces as he was forced to come up with more. The middle cousin named Haroon, told us he had seen Salman and the ugly man together at the house and assisted the police with making a sketch of him. Since we had not found the ugly man yet, we thought he might be one of the ones actually holding Danny in isolation. The police took the sketch of ugly man and began a sweep of the Jaish Muhammad neighborhoods, showing it around and asking for recognition. It was confessed that the training and final walk-through of the kidnapping had been done in the front yard of the Aunt's home and the cousins described the meeting in detail. Allegedly, besides the spectator cousin boys, present were Umer, Fahad, Salman, Adeel, and ugly man. There was always some suspicion though that ugly man was actually Adeel.

An interesting note was that the oldest cousin had advised the Aunt that he did not approve of allowing Umer to have his meeting at their home but the Aunt had replied that he was family and they had no choice. At the time of the raid at their home and the seizure of the Aunt and cousins, the oldest cousin had spoken to his Aunt in Punjabi thinking no one would understand and not knowing that Captain spoke Punjabi, saying "I told you no good would come of allowing Umer to come into this house". Apparently, the family understood Umer was a bad seed. A review of the phone calls made from the home identified that the middle cousin had made numerous phone calls to Umer. He was impressed with Umer and the calls also showed that the middle cousin was being used as an intermediary around the time of the kidnapping between Umer and a man named Rizwan Fayaz. We took Rizwan into custody and began questioning him. Haroon was the middle cousin and we began re-questioning him about his previous statements now from the perspective of being a hostile witness.

February 06, 2002, we finally found an ID with a photo of Sheikh Umer and the ID was using the name of Chaudary Bashir. The final confirmation was linked.

We learned that the police did not detain Umer's father. The father had placed a call to the police saying that he would turn himself in but he wanted a chance to convince his son to turn himself in first. The family home was in Lahore and while the family was comfortably detained under "house arrest", the police found a photo of Umer's wedding. In the photo were many people, some of whom were identified as well-known and wanted Al-Qaida personalities. Our hopes for getting Danny back now rested on the fact that Umer's family was detained and the few other facts that were known. To take Danny's life now would only dramatically harm Umer's entire family. This thought actually gave us a breath of hope and we were praying it was true. We had also made contact with influential Muslim religious leaders like the infamous Mufti Shamzai of the Mosque and Madrassah in Binori town and he was making a plea for Danny's return. His Madrassah was however, thought to be a recruitment and funding center for Al-Qaida Jihadi recruits. Mufti Shamzai was also quick to state that Umer was not Jaish Muhammad, but actually Lashkar-e-Taiba, a more radical and dangerous sect known for killings. What was actually appearing was that Umer had the reputation and charisma to easily move between several different radical groups, being accepted by all of them.

The three emails that had a similar reference to the graveyards and dumping the body were traced to Peshawar. Two came from a cyber café and the third was traced to a residential address. Because of the similar connection in language and content, this was a slip up for them and a break for us. In coordination with my friend, the RSO in Peshawar, the Peshawar police raided the residence and seized two men and one computer. That loose end was cut.

Because we were all still concerned for the health and welfare of

Mariane and her coming baby, The Consul General, sent his personal residence cook to go work full time in Mariane and Asra's home. This would ensure that they stayed in better health.

Pressure on the middle cousin Haroon, revealed that he knew Umer had shaved his beard off and he admitted that he was traveling under the fake Pakistan National ID of Bashir. The cousin said he last saw Umer on January 22, when he came to the house for the meeting with Fahad, Adeel, ugly man and Salman, now being spelled Suleman. Haroon also stated that Umer had been in Karachi on January 24 and 25 because he called him to discuss a family "money collection" matter.

We also discovered another man named Majid who had been making calls to Umer and he was detained. The two earlier reporter "fixer" contacts of Danny, Asif and Zafar, were brought back to Karachi for new questioning to see if we missed anything. Asif had never mentioned that Zafar had been the link between himself and Arif (the Al-Qaida terrorist) until after the kidnapping and that made it a bit suspicious. Also, we found that Asif had previously been a writer for a Jihadi publication and his brother-in-law still was. We had new leads and we would follow them. Danny's final day taxi driver also became a follow-up interview. Even the shopkeeper who sold the polaroid camera was interviewed. Jaish Muhammad leader Azhar Masood had tried three phone numbers he had for Umer but all phone numbers were now disabled. I found it interesting that Masood had three numbers for a man he claimed was not Jaish Muhammad but rather Lashkar-e-Taiba.

February 09, 2002, we traced two charges on Danny's WSJ American Express card that appeared after his kidnapping but both had normal explanations. Our Special Branch (IB) contact had identified that someone had booked a reservation on a PIA flight Sunday morning under the name of Sheikh Umer Saeed from Karachi to Manchester and on to the United States. We contacted the FBI in Islamabad to advise them, but the name was a fake submission, perhaps again to distract us.

We re-interviewed Asif and Zafar for four hours regarding the links in the chain leading to Danny's kidnapping and though nothing helpful came up, we were able to obtain the list of Jihadi associates and phone numbers from the JANG newspaper crime reporter Zafar. We used them for cross-referencing in our case data-base and as part of our bigger picture general terrorism investigations, which were already now heading to over 1,000 possible connections and leads.

It was discovered in a late night interrogation with Suleiman that he had been holding back information and he was in fact the first cousin of Arif (the third link in Danny's chain) and that Arif was known by his real name of Muhammad Hashim. This established a stronger involvement in the overall kidnapping operation by Suleiman than just email passing.

Fahad had been bragging about how he had "wiped" the harddrive clean and that there was nothing on it to connect him but the FBI specialist had pulled the first photo of Danny off his computer with the gun to Danny's head.

February 10, 2002, from midnight on until 0700 hours in the morning, we continued conducting our rigorous interrogations of the three Jaish Muhammad kidnappers we had in custody. During the long night, several revelations were made. As these revelations came about, the assault team and I would go out and conduct raids following up on the information. It was critical we acted as quickly as we got the data. We were conducting raids about every two hours and they were getting even more precarious as our profile heightened. But, we had no choice. Each day that passed lessened the chances of Danny's safe release and we had to deny any doubt while picking up our tempo, if working all day and night without sleep for weeks could have an increased tempo.

The revelation that led to the first raid this night was when Suleiman revealed that he had been part of planning the kidnapping and he provided names and addresses of residences of interest that might lead us to other residences and persons that hopefully would lead to Danny. I went out on the raids with the assault team.

After returning, it was Adeel's turn for a revelation. He identified a Jihadi who acted as an intermediary for weapons and suggested that he might have assisted the team that conducted the actual physical kidnapping. This time we took Adeel with us to the location. A man by the name of Abdul Majeed was seized and brought back to our CID headquarters for questioning. It turned out that he had nothing to do with our case but he was identified as a weapons and logistics facilitator for terrorists and had previously led Umer and another man to the house of "Mansoor". Mansoor was one of the Indian Airline Hijackers in 1999, from Umer's earlier actions that got him imprisoned and then later released with Azhar Masood in negotiations that resulted in his release in Afghanistan. Mansoor however had been recently killed in another battle somewhere. The other man at Mansoor's house with Umer was identified as Kasim, another of the Indian Airlines

Hijackers. During Adil's interview, Adil also casually stated that Umer had been "adopted" as one of Usama Bin Laden's favored sons, directly linking Umer to Al-Qaida. To us, it also meant that if Al-Qaida was somehow involved in this kidnapping, it might be only the first in a series of westerner kidnappings.

One of Captains men had been delegated to run down one of the fake two million dollar ransom emails and he got his man this night in Rawalpindi at a public call station. We could now officially cross off that line-item.

February 11, 2002, the harddrive taken from the raid in Peshawar made its way to our offices and the FBI computer specialist began to break it down for details. This was the computer that generated the "graveyard" diversionary emails. They stated that although it was the actual source of the emails, they had been generated from another cyber café. But, the most interesting thing was that it contained curious Arabic and Iranian information that would go into immediate study and evaluation.

Looking at the phone and email cross-referencing index that has been established from this case, with now a thousand possible terrorist connections, we realized that following this case and the hopeful recovery of Danny, the police and FBI would have an incredible "terrorist pursuit" data base to work for years to come.

Captain flew to Islamabad in the hopes of capturing Umer. From an arrest in Islamabad by Captain pertaining to Danny's case, the suspect alleged that the organization behind the kidnapping and now associated with Umer, was the lesser-known Harakat-e-Jihadi Islami. He also claimed that one of their associates named Jameel Ahmed (known as Hassan), was the man who passed the photos taken of Danny to Adeel. This would then probably make Jameel Ahmed "ugly man" and might possibly link him directly to the independent cell holding Danny.

February 12, we arrested a man at the Karachi International Airport who was a friend of Majeed, who we had arrested previously. There was a possible connection to our case and this man had previously sold weapons to Suleiman. It was a good connection. We now felt we had a profile of the actual kidnap team that consisted of:

Kasim – from Sukkor. He was involved in the Katmandu plane hijacking and was known as Asim.

Abdul Salam – Assumed to be one of the plane hijackers as well.

Shaikh Mohammad Adil – This was our Adeel and was also now identified as one of the plane hijackers.

Jameel Ahmed – Known as Hassan and in reports as "ugly man". It was suspected that he might also be the one physically holding Danny.

I realize that the details of this case, the names and code names, and war names, and brotherhood names, and terrorist warrior names of each of these people is almost impossible to keep straight. We had to do this throughout the case in order to run down the leads and sometimes after spending many days on a name, it only tracked back to someone we already had, but under a different name. This is part of the chaos we faced in this type of an investigation in a Muslim nation where the first name of the father becomes the last name of the son and the first name of the son (and last name of the father) becomes the last name of the son's wife, and where everyone makes up several names for themselves known only to that special group they want to know it. Now think about our Consulates in these countries who have to do name checks before issuing out visas to America.

Captain called me from Islamabad and told me he had Umer in custody and was bringing him to Karachi on a 1900 hours flight, would be in by 2100 hours and to be at the CID headquarters at 2200 hours to interrogate him for Danny's location. This was one of our happiest moments and re-injected me with adrenaline.

Quickly, the press had the information and we began putting out mis-information that Umer would stay in Lahore and be questioned there. We needed to get Captain safely back and Umer into our custody for questioning. The FBI Agent now overseeing his group (and a man I was really beginning to like and respect), we will call "Father John". He and I would be at the CID headquarters for the interrogation and we placed additional security at the WSJ house to keep them safe from press. I had weeks before had their entire street blocked off with police and guard posts at both ends to keep the vulture-like press away. It also allowed Mariane to go walking undisturbed but with a bodyguard on her street to help her health and pregnancy. She was under tremendous stress and we needed to keep her and the baby healthy.

February 13, 2002, throughout the late night and into the early morning hours we interrogated Umer. He changed his story several times - that Danny was fine and being held, to Danny was fine but out of his control with another cell of his organization that he had lost control of, to Danny being dead. One firm point Umer made was that he had been the organizer of the kidnapping and had created compartmentalized cells of people who performed only one role of the kidnapping and never knew the people in the other cells in order to protect his operation, and in the hope obviously of keeping himself from getting caught. That part had failed. Umer stated that he had at one point spoken with one of his "collaborators" and had sought the release of Danny. His associate did not release Danny and later told him that Danny was dead. In further interrogation, Umer stated that he himself had actually been in the hands of the Government of Pakistan, in Lahore, since turning himself in on February 5th. We now had a missing week in custody and ISI (the Pakistani CIA) stated that Umer was not detained until February 12th. Umer coincidentally has an Uncle in Lahore, where he was detained, who is a retired ISI Colonel and apparently kept Umer with him at his home. The ISI was questioned about the difference between Umer's story and theirs and their Commanding General said he would look into it but that Umer had been discovered hiding in a mud hut in a Lahore slum. That was not really Umer's style and Umer remained adamant that he had been in "house arrest" detention for a week at his Uncle's place before turning himself in.

When Umer was found and during the questioning, Umer was kept in leg irons but was in good health and had no marks on him. What struck me as odd was that the police were behaving differently with him than with the other kidnappers. There was a sense of reverence almost like they respected him for being who he was and having been as close to the top Al-Qaida man as he was. Umer was clean, had short hair, no beard except a one-day growth of hair. Not what I would anticipate from a man hunkering in a Lahore slum. He was arrogant, confident in his position and openly admitted to planning the kidnapping. He also admitted to being Chaudray Bashir. He made several statements to us about hating America and said he welcomed opportunities to kill non-combatants (innocent women and children) in reciprocation for killing the people of Afghanistan and for the bad treatment of those being held in Guantanamo.

I had agreed to work with the FBI Agent "Father John" and we agreed that I would be the bad guy and he could be the good guy. For about 10 minutes, I insulted Umer, raved about his killing of innocent civilians and how it contradicted the Holy Koran, and basically challenged his pride and manhood. I used every bit of bad language on him in my insults that I had ever learned in my life. I even gave him a challenge to take a swing at me to really go overboard since he prided himself on a false reputation of being a martial artist and I had 20 years of teaching it. Umer was totally dedicated to his Jihad and hated America and Americans. He showed sparks of intelligence in his ability to plan long range events but couldn't maintain his focus on a linear debate. He met the true profile of a Sociopath/Psychopath. Even though part of the reason locals respected him was that he had an education, his school records showed that he couldn't concentrate and he never graduated. He found his place in a high chair among the uneducated. And let's face it – he gets caught for every act he commits. After I finished being a maniac, "Father John" played his compassionate role for awhile.

During our long night of interrogation, Umer stated that he wished to help find Danny now because of Daniel's pregnant wife and had told Hussain to release him. Then he said that he was pretty sure Danny was dead. He said that perhaps Danny had seen the kidnappers faces and they were forced to kill him. Our team was going to remain optimistic until we had absolute proof that Danny was dead or until hopefully, we kicked in one last door and found Danny there.

Umer stated that he planned the kidnapping but "contracted out" the job including the "grab", the hiding place, and the detention personnel. He said Hussain had arranged it for him and that Hussain had "served" him in Afghanistan and could be trusted. He also admitted that Suleiman was the one who made all the weird threat phone calls to throw off our investigative team and made a lot of calls to India to make us think it was an Indian conspiracy. There were many lines of questioning followed that night. We had so many questions we wanted answers for and hoped that we could get some truth from this Maniac. Umer said he would call other Jihadis and ask if they knew where Danny was but would only do it with a new and clean phone. We figured that this was to give them a pre-established signal and we couldn't be sure it wasn't the death order signal so we asked for the numbers he would call and first researched them and listened to them.

Umer also made some other interesting comments. He stated that only the first two emails were from his original plan and that the others were derived from other people. He also said that he had never given money to Muhammad Atta but admitted giving money to Jihadis in Afghanistan to wage war and kill Americans.

During this long evening of ping-pong responses from Umer, the creative Captain worked to become pals with Umer by spending alone time with him and confessing his "respect" for him. The sleep deprivation must have been taking effect because Umer responded to Captain and asked for the opportunity to do his ablutions, say his prayers and hold and read a Holy Koran. After Captain allowed Umer to do this, Umer began to open up a bit and confessed some useful information. He told Captain that he had created a "cut-out" man who was to take over command if anything happened to Umer. The cut-out went by the name of Farooqi but his real name was Amjad. Umer confessed that after the three email associates were arrested, he contacted Farooqi and told him to pass on to Hussain to release Danny. When Danny was not released, Umer assumed that Hussain must have killed Danny due to a recognition mistake. Umer called Farooqi back and asked to talk to Hussain and find out what had happened. Three days before Umer surrendered on February 5th, Farooqi came to visit Umer and told him that Hussain told him that Baji (Danny's code name meaning elder sister) had died of a heart attack and that they had cut up the body and buried it in various scattered locations. Umer told Farooqi to tell Hussain to release photos of Danny being dead at a location that would bring a quick response to the burial scenes. Umer told Captain that at that moment he believed Danny was dead but had come to think that there might be a separate plan underway and that Hussain had organized his own operation for personal gain. Umer told Captain that Hussain was Lashkar-e-Taiba, which was an organization of hardcore professional terrorist/criminals and killers.

Captain, the ISI Colonel, and the rest of us believed that there was a chance that Danny was not dead because of the Lashkar-e-Taiba connection and the switch to a possible "hostage for ransom" interest. We also believed that they might wait until things cooled down a bit before they began their ransom operation. There was currently no body, no new photos, and no demand for ransom.

At 0500 hours February 14, the interrogation ended. While Captain had been bonding with Umer, I had gone with the Assault Team, which had split up and we raided Jamaat-e-Islami and Harakut-e-Jihadi Islami offices and Mosques and eight Jihadis were captured and brought in for interrogation. We hoped that they would have a connection to Umer and Hussain. We returned about the same time Captain finished up.

On one night like many similar to this one, when I returned to my office around 0600 hours and had been up for 30 or 40 hours without sleep, I sat at my desk to write up my notes for the day and night's activity into a cable for Washington. While poised over my keyboard, my physical system shut down and I fell asleep sitting with my fingers on the keyboard. At some point, I was awakened by a phone call and was several steps beyond groggy. The caller said "where is your day's report?" I mumbled "who is this?", and he said "this is the White House Command Center". I didn't understand and said "what command center?", and he responded with "the White House". I said "what White House?" and he said "the President likes to read your Daniel Pearl case cable first thing every morning, where is your report from last night?" You need to understand that I was very tired and had been jerked out of practically-speaking, a "coma state of being", so I said "what President?" Yeah, I know. The caller said "The President of the United States". Well, I was awake then and he repeated that the President liked to read my nightly update first thing when he got up so they needed it soon for his morning reports package. Needless to say I finished the report pronto but this was a real eye-opener for me to find out that something which was so singularly-focused for me in my little corner of the world could be having such an impact that the President of the United States was monitoring it.

February 15, 2002, finally the newly arrived Polygraph Examiners got their chance to work on Umer. They began at 1930 hours and finished at 0100 hours February 16. Five questions were the key items put within the series. They were:

- Were you held in detention on February 05? The results were inconclusive.
- Do you know the house that Daniel Pearl is being held in? The results said he was being intentionally deceptive and took countermeasures to compromise the results.
- Do you know where Daniel Pearl is being held? The results were the same deception as before.
- Do you have a means of contacting Daniel's captors right now? Same deception.
- Do you know of other planned acts of terrorism or violence? Same deception.

All that work to use the Examiners and the best we could get was an"inconclusive.

At 0100 hours, a lead came in by a contact who said he knew a man named Syed Sohail Akhtar. The lead claimed that Syed and another man named Riaz were holding Danny in a local Madrassah and he said that Danny was alive as of two days before. A meeting was arranged for the following morning between the Source of the information and Syed. If it took place, the Assault Team would take him into custody and find out what he knew. Though the lead sounded good, by this time, we had gone through dozens just the same without much success. I remained positive though and we ran on every lead we got. The most interesting part of this lead was that Riaz was identified as the financial manager for the legendary Indian Mafia figure, Daud Ibrahim. The "Mumbai Mafia" figure head is alleged to be in Karachi hiding-out but protected by Pakistani Police, who were being paid handsomely no doubt.

February 16, 2002, our attempt to grab the financial manager Riaz was set back when he failed to show up at his shop the next morning. Our suspicion grew regarding leaks in the police force. Three other addresses for Riaz and Syed were obtained and we decided to watch them for our most viable location and time.

February 17, 2002, I went over to see Mariane and Asra with Captain and "D" to assure them that we were doing everything we could. Mariane said she felt comforted when she saw the team daily. We had really grown to love these people and all of us felt very protective of them. We are taught and trained not to get personally involved in our cases but this had gone far beyond that. We were all taking it very personally and running ourselves into the ground to get Danny back to Mariane. They had become our own.

Captain, D, and I sat down and discussed what raids we thought would be best for the night. A "Syed" lead had several kinks. We would try to set up raids for tonight but if they didn't work out, we would be forced to try other directions in the morning. We were not sure now if this Syed was the same Syed we wanted. He had three addresses listed and we checked them all.

In addition, we planned to pick up Riaz at his business in the morning at 1100 hours. If he failed to show up at work again, the "Union Leader" of the Money Changers would be "coerced" into calling him down to his office on some pretense. If Riaz really was the Financial Manager for Daud Ibrahim, we could all end up in pieces for disturbing his business and I could see the concern even in the eyes of our Assault Team. The Mumbai Mafia leader was infamous in this part of the world and no one could escape his reach.

Our complaints about the Polygraph Examiners leaving after examining Umer only, made an apparent impact on Washington and they turned them around and sent them back to polygraph the other kidnappers. The Polygraph Examiners arrived on a night flight and began to prepare to polygraph Adeel, Suleiman and perhaps Majeed the terrorist facilitator. I felt that if I were a Polygrapher, I would certainly want to interrogate and question on a lie-detector anyone who was a facilitator for terrorists.

February 18, 2002, Captain attempted to pick up Syed at an Institute at 0900 hours but there were so many students, identification couldn't be made without alerting him and possibly losing him in the crowd. The Captain picked up Syed's boss and took him back to the Institute to identify Syed Sohail but the crowd had gone. Captain asked his boss to call him and a woman answered and said Syed had left town until after the upcoming Eid holiday. We were all suspicious so we staked out the Mosque he attends. If he failed to show up there, we would raid his home. If all else failed, he was scheduled to come to his office the next day, but we would see.

The shop of Riaz the money man, was visited by the Team and we found it had been "closed" for the past year. Since our Source said he met with Riaz there just days before, we staked it out. We obtained the utility bill for the shop and it showed payment was being made by an address on the other side of the city so that lead was being followed up as well.

This night, the Polygraph Examiner intended to examine Adeel. My Pakistani Senior Investigator would participate as translator and observer of cultural innuendo.

In the middle of all this 24-hour-a-day stress and anguish, my wife "A" returned from her second "ordered departure". She was very happy to get back to Karachi and all her friends and personal belongings. I had been working 15 hour days before the Daniel Pearl case and during the search for Danny, I had been working 24 hours a day and only slept when my body and mind crashed, literally. Mostly, it was sleep spent with my head on my desk at the office. Carolina had been following the case in the news and understood what it was about but of course had no conception of the depth of involvement for me. I could only hope she understood that what I was doing meant trying to save someone's life.

February 19, 2002, we continued receiving leads that we had to follow. Most were bad leads and some, intentionally so. We investigated every one. We also visited Mariane and Asra every day to keep them informed. It was almost four weeks now and the stress was thick like a cloud in Mariane and Asra's house. Throughout it, I remained positive in my messages to Mariane, refusing to believe we weren't going to get Danny back. That was the only course to take. If we were going to "saddle up" every night to go out after very dangerous people whose goal in life was to kill us, and perhaps me especially being the American working the investigation, we had to have a positive, high energy outlook to continue and to stay alert and focused.

Adeel was Polygraphed and it indicated he was not being deceptive. He was so hard core though, he didn't mind telling the truth about how he wanted to do the kidnapping and how he wanted to kill Americans. To him, this was a truth he rejoiced in. Suleiman was also polygraphed but he was still playing his odds and it was inconclusive and showed deception.

But finally a high note in our efforts. Riaz was captured and we had a chance to question him. There is that one large hurdle we face though - that he is the financial manager for the Mumbai Mafia boss Daud Ibrahim, who can actually make people disappear quite easily and the police want to handle this with great care. He could reach into any home of any police officer in Pakistan or India or the rest of the region. We would do this questioning with a sense of respect or our assault team could all be dead in 48 hours.

I asked my Special Branch Police friend "D" how Daud could move about Karachi so fluidly when he was such a well-known wanted criminal. He raised his hands to the sky and with a wink stated that it was all up to Allah.

Captain asked Riaz (now correctly spelled as Riyaz) if he would cooperatively lead them to Syed Sohail and Riyaz complied. They took Riyaz with them and picked up Syed Sohail. When the Assault Team with Captain and D returned to the CID headquarters, they called me to come over for the interviews. I grabbed Z and the two of us walked over and into the CID interrogation rooms. Immediately we recognized Syed Sohail as a man who by another name had been a regular "walk-in" at the Karachi Consulate General following the 9/11 attack. He would come in and say he had information and we would follow it up but nothing he had ever said "panned-out". We had felt that he was possibly "probing" us to see what he could find out about our operation rather than actually trying to give us any valid information.

Riyaz was a big man with a very calm and controled, almost meditative sort of spiritual character. I was intrigued by him. Throughout the next hours, we were able to determine that both

Riyaz and Syed Sohail were not part of our case and had just been connected peripherally. One interesting thing came out when I asked Riyaz if he had committed murder. He paused, and then calmly in his "Buddha state" said yes, he had killed men a few years back. I thought this was curious that he had killed someone, and that he would without concern tell us he did. I asked him the details and he said that two men had raped the young daughter of his neighbor and Riyaz had learned of it, so he took the only proper action and killed them both. I just really couldn't argue with that one. The interview was over and he was free to go.

February 20, 2002, information was received in my office that a Pakistani reporter who acted as a "stringer" for a U.S. news service had been contacted by two men who claimed to have a videotape of the death of Daniel Pearl. We weren't over-reactive having had numerous claims of this before and having searched every graveyard in the entire city. We would follow this claim with proper procedure. Initially, the stringer was to come to the office of the reporter he worked for, to show the tape. I had sur-veillance posted to watch for any ambushes or "set-ups." I also hoped they could follow the reporter and the two possessors of the alleged videotape to whatever location they went back to so I could follow-up later as needed. We were also trying to insure that this reporter didn't end up missing as well. Up until midnight, the two "criminals" continued to call and cancel and reschedule the meeting. After several false meetings, we heard that the criminals had met with the reporter but when they got together, no one had a way to play the videotape. It seemed like another typical false lead that might fall apart. The reporter said the two men went to get the appropriate equipment. Local surveillance advised me that the reporter showed up, got into a vehicle that matched the one we were looking for and drove to a residence. The reporter received another call that night from the two men saying that they would try again the next day.

This was an RSO operation and we were keeping the DS and FBI Headquarters informed of the lead. We had not involved the police in it because we needed subtlety on this one and didn't want the police to scare away the two men. I wanted them and the tape they had. The FBI "Father John" was working with us still and everything would be coordinated properly.

On another side of the investigation, three phone calls were made around 1330 hours from the missing cell phone of Daniel Pearl. One call was made to the Chief of Captain's Assault Team. The caller told him to release everyone or his wife would become a widow. He received more death threats than anyone I had ever met. He received more than I got. It was routine for him so he took it in stride. Then his wife called and told him she had received two calls advising her to counsel her husband to release everyone or they would kill him. I spoke with Captain about my concern for this and he told me it wasn't a problem. Since we had "experts" monitoring Danny's cell phone number, I went to those people and asked them to tell me where the calls came from. Their response was a suspicious "oh sorry, our equipment went down for two hours right around that time and we didn't get it". I couldn't trust anyone now except Captain and my IB friend D. Even cell phone numbers we had obtained risking our lives to get, and that seemed to have direct links to terrorist operations and Danny's kidnapping specifically, had been given to the FBI to trace through the phone company's data base and the FBI kept telling us that they needed more time. When another U.S. Federal Law Enforcement Agency came through Karachi, they said they would get me the answers within 24 hours. The next day they told me the FBI had contacted them and told them to back off. The FBI was handling it. We never did get the answers to our cell phone trackings from our raids and the FBI just left us hanging. I was very embarrassed having to tell Captain that we didn't have his answers.

Those of us who made up the Assault Team were upset and unsatisfied. We also felt we wanted to re-interview Riyaz so we brought him back in. Again, Riyaz was a cooperative gentleman and even admitted to participating in a bombing incident that seemed to have been quietly and quickly dismissed. This man truly felt he had a protective shell over him because of his connection to Daud Ibrahim. Again, he seemed not to be involved in this case but I wanted to try something with him. I pulled him aside and respectfully asked him as a personal favor, as a man of honor who would kill men who raped a young girl (so as a man of character), if he would please approach his powerful employer and ask him to use his connections to find Danny and let us bring him home. He said very gently that he would speak to Daud but that he usually did not involve himself in these types of matters. It was as much as I could hope for from the Mafia King.

February 21, 2002, on this morning Fahad, the transmitter of the emails and photos of Danny with the gun pointed at his head, was taken into court for his initial hearing and plead guilty and identified the other participants as his co-conspirators, including Sheikh Umer, helping to tighten the prosecutor's case.

In the middle of all this, which was actually normal for our workdays, my Special Branch Police connection informed me that a car with Americans in it and with a protective follow car behind it was being targeted for attack in the Muhammed Ali Society (KDA) residential area. This is where the American School was located and also where Umer's Aunt's house was, only two blocks away from the school. As the RSO, I have a Congressional Directive to be responsible for security oversight of the American School. So only weeks before, I had met with the school and suggested they begin using an armed follow car to protect their teachers when moving about. The Special Branch (IB) friend told me that the enemy had made an initial plan to attack the car but called it off because there was now a follow car protecting them. He also said they were in the process of revising their plan of attack to take into account the follow car. I advised the school leaders and teachers and a lock-down on movements went into effect. Also, the Consulate drivers, Officers, and my Surveillance Detection Team were all placed on alert. We also put out two additional Roving Patrols to watch for the enemy and to provide a physical and psychological deterrent.

At 2130 hours, we received notice that the alleged video of the Death of Daniel Pearl was going to be delivered to us in the lobby of the Sheraton Hotel. I contacted my friend, who was the General Manager of the Sheraton and asked him if we could use his audio/visual conference room for a purpose that night. He didn't pry, he simply said he would make it happen. That is what friends are all about. It would be just the FBI and me once they delivered the tape. I wanted to be able to go after them later if necessary. I did not like loose ends or unanswered questions so I wanted their location just in case they turned out to be involved other than as conduits of a tape. "Father John" would receive the tape. The rest of us would be there as back-up to prevent anything from happening and to protect "Father John".

About midnight, a big man in a Shalwar Camise walked into the lobby. He handed the package to "Father John", told him the WSJ had agreed to pay him $200,000 and walked out. We took the package up to the Sheraton's A/V room and very carefully began to un-wrap the package, which seemed to have numerous layers of paper around it. Every move was photographed. Every layer was carefully preserved. When we finally got down to the last layer, we discovered it wasn't a tape, it was a video camera with a micro-tape inside it. The A/V room had no equipment to deal with this and we needed to verify the camera was not an explosive device activated to the tape release button so we took it to my Consulate guard post x-ray machine and looked at it. It was only a camera with a tape.

At that point I told them we could take it to my house and connect it to my TV/Video system to verify. My wife "A" was at a late-night function with her Pakistani friends and it would go until the sun came up so we had privacy. I then called Captain and told him to meet us at my house and that we had received a tape that was allegedly the death of Danny.

We arrived at my home. There were about 8 of us. Then the police came and we were 20. To preserve the camera and any possible prints on it, we carefully removed the tape cassette and put it into my own camera and connected it to my VCR and into the TV directly.

The tape was crushing and broke every one of our hearts. The video showed Daniel Pearl talking about being Jewish with "Zionist" parents and he made references to the treatment of the captives currently in Cuba, as well as obviously reading a prepared script about the improper policies of the U.S. Government. This part of the message lasted about two minutes and it was obvious he was under extreme duress. The next one minute and fifteen seconds showed Danny, with barbaric acts of mutilation being committed against him. He was, as everyone now knows, beheaded as he was tied to a chair. It was clearly Danny. I don't think any one of us even took a breath for that almost four-minute period. Then, no one could move or make a comment. We were stunned.

The Consul General and the high-ranking police officials were called to my home to verify the video and discuss our next action. I requested our local doctor be on hand to go with us when we had to go tell Mariane the horrible news. It was now about 0200 hours on the morning of February 22nd. For the next two hours, my home was used as a planning and command post. I now had about 50 persons, mostly police wandering around my home and seated in various rooms planning and orchestrating the next move.

I called the Wall Street Journal Regional Chief John Bussey, and told him what we had. He was at Mariane's home and left suspiciously for my house with WSJ reporter Steve Levine, not telling Mariane or Asra anything and leaving them very upset and suspicious. Once Bussey had also verified it was Danny, we all cleared out of my home around 0400 hours. The multitude of police went off to set up the next operation, including one team getting to the Source who provided the tape to thoroughly interview him. Now, Captain, D, myself, "Father John", the Consul General, the doctor, and a couple of others went to do the hardest thing we had ever done in our lives. We had to tell Mariane that her Danny was dead. We had failed. Asra called me on my cell phone and asked what was up. I told her we were on our way over.

We arrived at Mariane and Asra's home and with the way Bussey left, I can only imagine the stress Mariane was feeling when we all rolled up in our vehicles. We walked in and Mariane was staring at us silently. John Bussey, who was Danny's boss, told her that he was sorry, Danny was dead. She asked how we knew for sure and he told her there was a video of his death. Mariane paused just for a couple of seconds and then turned and walked to her bedroom and for the first time in this entire horrific event, Mariane let her emotions go and slammed the door and screamed and cried for what seemed an eternity. My heart has never been broken so badly. I had let her down and now she and her soon-to-come baby boy Adam were without a husband and father. I don't think there was a single hardened law enforcement officer in the room that didn't have water leaking from their eyes. All the effort, all the brutality, all the hopes were now devastated. The Doctor checked on her to make sure she was physically alright, if that could possibly be said at this moment. We left to allow her some privacy, to return the next day to help her to get home to her family for support.

A few days later, Mariane, being the courageous woman she is, threw a dinner for the group of us that had worked this case with every ounce of energy we had. We all entered feeling like we were now strangers in a home of someone we had offended gravely. We were tentative about every word and action. Mariane walked over to me and put her arms around my neck and told me I was a hero, that she understood, and that what we had done was incredible. She repeated that I was a hero to her and I had to walk away because I had water leaking heavily from my eyes again. How could a person who had been through so many shootings, bombings, interrogations, devastation and picking up of body parts, be crying in front of this woman. And how could she call me a hero when I felt that I had failed her in the worst possible way. I had allowed her husband to be beheaded. I would never feel alright about this again in my life.

We had the dinner and Mariane made a speech to all of us show-ing us what true strength was. She told us all we had become heroes and should not look at this as a failure. What we had done was miraculous and incredible and she would love us forever for our efforts. Mariane's brother had flown in from Paris and joined us for dinner. At the end, we all sat on the couch and a photo was taken; a photo that I cherish. It is the entire investigative group minus the actual assault team, and one can see it all in our eyes - the entire story.

A day later, we took Mariane to the airport and said goodbye. I stayed in contact with her and with Adam but not as often as I would have liked because of the job I have. We remain friends and I would do anything for her and Adam. I continued on the investigation even after the FBI left and eventually we captured one of the men who killed Danny. This case was still one of my main focuses until the day I was forced to leave Pakistan July 22nd, and many interrogations and a few raids still occurred. At this point, I just wanted some serious justice, and perhaps as a means to moderate or justify to a degree what had been my first direct serious failure resulting in the loss of an innocent non-combatant life.

One evening, I was sitting on the bed with "A" and she looked at me and asked why I was crying. I didn't even know I was but there was water on my cheeks. On the television was a news story about Danny being dead and I suppose my system just responded. A few days later, "A" was evacuated again for a third time, this time to her home in Bogota, and she would not return to Pakistan or to her friends.

A few days after that, the FBI were leaving and I had kept them pretty much locked inside the Consulate so I took them to a TGI Fridays restaurant to thank them for the help and friendship. I excused myself to go wash my hands and on the stairs going up, I received a call from the Director of Diplomatic Security. He was known for his understanding and insight into people. He told me that I had done an incredible job on the Pearl case and he knew how hard it could hit a person when they put so much into a case. He offered me a free vacation back in the U.S. to get my head straight if I needed it. I thanked him very much and told him how much it meant to me that he would recognize the effort and make a call to me. I told him I still had some murderers to capture and wanted to stay on it. I was touched at what a great organization I worked for and again, the theme of my life, how lucky I am. I washed up and returned to the table with the FBI guys. I described the phone call I just had and said what a great group I worked for. They then commented that they had also received a phone call earlier from their offices but they were told they had screwed up and would be dealt with when they returned. THAT is what makes the difference with the Diplomatic Security Service.

I testified against Umer, Fahad, Suleiman, and Adeel in a Pakistani court and Umer was sentenced to death but remains in a prison cell today, and the other three received life sentences.

To finish this case, in May 2002, I received a call from the ISI (covert intelligence agency) Colonel who had been our contact and he stated that the one we captured as one of the killers of Danny had identified the location of his detention and murder. He had told everyone to secure the site and not touch anything until I arrived. The Colonel was picking me up in five minutes.

We drove almost 60 minutes to the furthest outskirts of Karachi, to a small 12-home neighborhood of Al-Qaida supporters and one radical Mosque. The small cinder block walled compound had police troops surrounding it and the press was already there. I walked inside and looked into the first small cinder block room on the right. There I saw the truck seat Danny had been sitting on in the photos and the backdrop was on the floor. There was also a blood stain on the concrete floor. I walked out and looked at the quarter acre compound filled with grape vines and small citrus trees. There was also an outdoor shower and a toilet in the ground. I took note that even if Danny had run and escaped from this compound, he had miles of desert and would not have had any idea where he was.

I walked over to where two men with shovels waited for me. The Colonel asked if they could begin and I said yes. It was a spot near the far wall. As soon as the first shovel full of dirt came up, the smell of a dead body permeated up from the earth. They continued and without going into too much detail, we found Danny's remains in the hole, cut into 10 pieces and still with the sweat suit from the email photos covering the body parts. This was another very hard day for me but I photographed the excavation as I was supposed to for evidentiary purposes and then I departed the small compound where Danny had spent his last days, never wanting to see it again.

During the interrogation of the killer who led us to Danny's grave, he stated that Danny had been killed approximately at the end of the first week though we had not known that and continued on for almost another month.

This case took on a life of its own afterwards with books and a movie being made about parts of the investigation. My recounting is to provide the parts that were not ever discussed or revealed. The amount of effort by me, the FBI Agents assigned to the case, and especially by the Pakistani government demonstrates how hard they tried to save Danny. Pakistan can be a great ally of the United States. It might not always seem so on the political level but on the real daily level we will hopefully always be friends and allies. And, I will never forget the lessons I learned from this case and about myself. It added a substantial part to the development of me as Special Agent Randall Bennett.

AL-QAIDA'S ATTACK ON THE FRENCH SUBMARINE ENGINEERS:

As usual, I had arrived at work at about 0500 hours on May 08, 2002. At 0715 hours, I sat working at my desk on a typically clear, dry Karachi day that was already over 100 degrees. I felt and then heard an explosion that literally made my body pitch forward onto my desk top. I automatically knew it had to be close and turned to my window to look out. From two blocks away over the tops of some Government of Pakistan buildings, I saw smoke billowing from the Sheraton Hotel. Without pause, I ran armed out my office door down to the parking lot and jumped into my car and raced for the hotel via a short-cut out the back entrance, which would get me to the site quick. In the 60 seconds it took me to reach the corner of the intersection that the Sheraton sat on, I had called my surveillance detection team and Z and asked them to meet me at the scene ASAP.

I arrived at the corner and the first thing that I saw was an arm and shoulder laying in the intersection, palm up and weirdly pointing toward the hotel entrance, as if guiding me. I looked right and saw the smoke, broken metal parts everywhere, and body parts and people lying all over the road and sidewalks as far as I could see. I parked my car on the intersection corner and ran to the point of detonation, making note of the details of the carnage as I moved.

It was easy to determine the impact location. A full size bus was bent in half, burned, windowless and twisted and halfway onto the sidewalk and the road. It was folded as if it had been a child's toy. There were some pieces of what had been a car wedged into the folded middle of the bus. The car was obviously the weapon; a large suicide vehicle bomb that had pulled up to the bus as it sat loading passengers and detonated.

Within the two minutes that had passed since I was thrown forward onto my desk, citizens were already trying to get any survivors off the bus. There were no sounds of anyone alive but I joined in the effort by climbing through a broken bus window to see if anyone could be helped. As I straightened up in the now bent bus and focused on the disaster inside, it was enough to make even me feel sick. What I found were limbs, half torsos, heads, and masses of pink tissue everywhere and in no order or sense. The scene literally stunned me for 20 or 30 seconds. I was standing in the middle of at least a dozen disassembled people. I refocused and began to work. The smell was overpowering. The worst smells a person makes while alive don't even begin to compare with open and exposed bodies. And, it is a sickly-sweet putrid smell. It hits the gag reflex like a karate ulna strike to the throat and few can withstand immediate vomiting. I am sure I went pale for a minute but recovered by attempting to focus and ignore what was surrounding me and under my feet. It was also mixed with a smell of post-blast explosive residue.

I started organizing the few Pakistanis who had entered the bus and who seemed capable of dealing with such a horrific scene but who probably had the same expression that I must have had on my face. First we checked quickly for any signs of life, climbing literally through mounds of indeterminate piles of tissue and miscellaneous limbs. We found a few persons making noises but most were missing some parts and a lot of blood. Trying to carry them outside to now waiting small EDHI ambulances parked in the explosion site mess was complicated, and we were faced with the difficulty of maneuvering through the jackknifed bus and over slippery territory. After we carried out the third temporarily alive person, I spotted my security staff guys and told them to begin photographing the entire scene, to document it for evidence and the inevitable follow-up investigation. I had already noticed that by-standers had begun to pick up evidence and remove it from the scene and saw some with sheets of flat cardboard, scooping up mounds of pink tissue and pushing it to the curb. This crime scene was deteriorating quickly but the potential lives came first. The next best thing was to quickly and exactly document everything for future reference through photos. I specifically remember a hand from the wrist down, lying palm up in the middle of the road about 20 feet from the bus. It was photographed but never found again later for collection. Someone had actually taken the hand as a sick curiosity I suppose.

After removing the few bodies of those who showed some signs of life and sending them off in the mini-ambulances, we began taking out the body parts. We carried out half torsos and limbs and after I carried out a few of those, I climbed out and began my overall walk-around and post bomb-blast investigation analysis, to the degree I could under completely uncontrolled conditions. It was about this time that the police arrived and I began giving them directions to seal the crime scene area. They kindly but somewhat ineptly complied. With the police in place and surveillance detection taking the photos, I moved into the blown-open Sheraton Hotel. The blast had taken out most windows on every floor and the main blast gutted the restaurant used for breakfast. The General Manager and Assistant Manager of the Sheraton were both my goods friends and remain so and I needed to see how they were doing. I simply walked through the now blasted-open restaurant wall and window area and into what had been a beautiful place for breakfast. Inside the restaurant, standing in all the rubble were Thomas and Edmund looking at the devastation. They saw me walking toward them over the dust-filled piles of broken glass, roof tiles and structural bracings and even though at the moment, it all seemed so futile, it seemed almost like they were glad I was there. We all shared a moment of mutual condolence and understanding. It was a bonding that keeps us friends today. We will always be friends.

As I continued the investigation, it became obvious how Al-Qaida had been able to so perfectly time this horrific act. The bus had been filled with French submarine engineers and Pakistani engineers. Eleven French Engineers and two Pakistanis died in the blast. Many more people were wounded and maimed. The French had sold submarines to the Pakistanis and part of the multi-year deal was assistance on assembly and preparation. They were currently working in the Port of Karachi on the second of the submarines. The French had been highly predictable in their movements. The bus picked them up curbside at the Sheraton where they all stayed, at the same spot and at the same time every day. Their predictability was 100%. Their ease of targeting was perfect. Anyone could have done a little homework and set up this attack.

For the next few days I continued working the investigation and compiling information including interviews, the security staff photos, and all evidence I could obtain to help put this investigation together. The Pakistani police had of course taken over the investigation but they had arrived long after the blast and after much of the evidence was stolen, moved or altered. Thanks to my security staff, I actually had the best and most comprehensive data on the attack, which I shared with the police due to our outstanding working relationship and their ability to canvass the streets and run down the usual suspects. Because it was the hotel my friend Thomas ran, I wanted to get the guys who did it and the Pakistanis had the ways and means to find them in a crazy and dangerous city like Karachi.

The French had no investigative Agents on the ground so a few days after the blast I was called by the French Consulate with a request to meet with some investigators who had flown into town from Paris. Of course I agreed. We met and I presented all the information that had been collected so far. They were a little arrogant considering the position they were in but expressed their appreciation and asked if I would continue to be sort of a defacto investigator for them. I told them I would be working the case for a variety of reason and would keep them informed. They had just taken a huge loss of life and it was important that the planners and living perpetrators received what was coming to them. At least one was dead, the suicide volunteer. Eventually, the French would have a team of analysts in town to work the case.

The streets that ran alongside the Sheraton Hotel had been shut down to all traffic and though the body parts had been picked up off the streets and out of the tree tops and scraped off sides of the surrounding buildings, a lot of metal pieces and the folded bus itself and the remaining shell of the bomb car were still sitting and scattered all over the road for the next two weeks. There was also glass everywhere since every window in the entire Sheraton hotel and the Pearl Continental Hotel across the street had been blown out.

While I waited for the Police to do their usual roundup and interrogation process to come up with a short list of candidates, I worked with the Sheraton Hotel on establishing tighter security standards for their access and customer security policies and procedures. The Hotel's Pakistani security officer, who had been my recommendation for hiring, worked with me to close off all hotel underground parking and to set up vehicle inspection control points. All luggage would also be checked outside the hotel and then brought in after it was cleared. The shops in front were a weak link and they began a transition to either total cooperation or elimination by becoming a vacancy. Bollards were placed around the Hotel property perimeter to prevent close-vicinity vehicles from charging to the hotel, and the sidewalks were given a protective railing to add to the set-back distance to the hotel. No chances for a follow-up attack could be permitted and we didn't want to overlook any weak points to the hotel security plan.

The General Manager of the Sheraton is one savvy and balanced man. Almost nothing ever bothered him to the point of a loss of focus. Because of all the bombings and killings we all had experienced and survived, he set up a weekly free food and drink event for a group of people who were within his circle of friends and contacts. It became known as "The Karachi Survivors Club". Nothing could get him down. He would turn a disaster into a bonding experience and a public relations and positive attitude event. Honestly, these gatherings helped all of us to keep our spirits lifted during the worst and most dangerous time in Karachi's history. He even created T-shirts for the Survivor's Club.

The investigation lasted for about four weeks during which time, the police and I interviewed and interrogated many suspects and sources. Eventually, from tracing the car pieces to a recent used car sale and then tracking the men who purchased it for cash, the two Al-Qaeda associated men who put it all together were caught. They are currently still in prison in Karachi and are not supposed to ever get out.

This case wrapped up about the same time as the ISI Colonel who had worked the Daniel Pearl case with us, came to me and took me out to excavate Danny's body. There was seldom if ever a slow day in Karachi during this period, but I learned a lot and experienced more than a person maybe should in the areas of life and death. Ten years later, in March of 2012, a French Superior Court Judge flew to Chandler, Arizona, to interview and debrief me on this case again in an attempt to find some closure on what was still a political controversy in France.

THE KARACHI U.S. CONSULATE SUICIDE VEHICLE BOMBING:

I had been relatively successful at bringing to justice quite a number of Al-Qaeda operatives and there were others that I will not be discussing in any books or articles. Leave it to say that there were many other raids and operations that will remain outside the scope of scrutiny. This nonetheless had put my name in the local Urdu newspapers almost every day for awhile and not in a good way, and even though I had been given an unofficial local jesting title of "Mayor of Karachi" due to all my contacts and local activity, there was a rising level of anger toward me by the radical elements who felt that I might not deserve to continue my occupation after damaging theirs to such a degree. I, of course felt they were wrong and intended to continue doing my darndest to put them out of business. But, apparently local Al-Qaeda elements began to hatch a plan to retire me the hard way.

Friday, June 14, 2002, was technically speaking, a freaking hot day. It was a clear day outside and the temperature in the morning was already well over 100 degrees. On Fridays at 1100 hours, I would regularly hold an RSO Section all-hands meeting in my office. My office was located at the end of the building closest to the Marriott Hotel and on the corner of the building closest to the main road in front called Abdullah Haroon. Remembering that I had removed everyone from all offices on the front side of the building, made mine the very closest office to the road.

We had been having military visitors for about two weeks and they hung out in the extra office that had once been where I put the FBI Agents working the Pearl case with me. Their mission was to evaluate our security from the perspective of a possible future need to rescue and evacuate us to the ship if things went horribly wrong in Karachi. Were they kidding? We lived our lives in Karachi in the middle of things going horribly wrong daily. They were very nice guys and their objective was to make our lives even safer so we were happy to have them there.

One of the enlisted men kept going into the off-limits office across the hall from my office and doing some communication equipment checking work in there. He would finish and then leave the door open so that I was exposed to the side of the building I had ordered everyone to stay out of and away from. The closing of all doors was critical in the event a bomb detonated and that had been our fear for almost four years now since I took over this assignment. I kept telling him to do his business quickly and get out and to CLOSE THAT DOOR.

As I was preparing for my Friday morning all-hands meeting at 1100 hours, the enlisted Marine was working in the room across from my office and he had the door open. At 1030 hours, The Marine Major who was in charge of this group came into my office and asked if I had a little time to go look at some items we had been talking about for the past week or so. The site was about 1.5 miles away. I told him I had the 1100 meeting but he said this was about his only available time and so I postponed my team meeting until the afternoon. As we departed, I told the Marine across the hall he had been exposed long enough and to close up and get out of the room. He concurred and began to close down his equipment checks.

At 1050, the Marine Major and I left out the back door of the Consulate and we arrived at our destination 10 minutes later. What I didn't know was that Al-Qaeda somehow knew about my Friday 1100 meeting and knew where my office was situated in the building, closest to the road and the corner of the building. They expected me to be sitting there at my desk in that office at 1100 hours.

The Major and I had begun doing our business, and at 1110 hours, we were rocked by a loud explosion that seemed to be dangerously close and in the direction of the Consulate. We departed and raced back to the Consulate where we could see smoke rising into the air. The Consulate had been hit and it was easily viewed to be right in front of my office as ground zero. As we neared the far side of Frere Park across the street from the Consulate, the chaos made it clear that it was going to take too many minutes to get around the park so I jumped out of the car and raced across the park through body parts, again, piles of pink oozing tissue, and people screaming and crying. The Major had followed me and I asked him to go inside to begin accountability. As I reached the smoldering crater, I tried to contact my Assistant RSO inside and then my FSNIs but the systems were down. Then I heard a radio call from the Marine on Post One and I knew that they were taking personnel accountability and moving everyone out the back just like we had practiced in our almost weekly drills. The people were responding perfectly and getting to the safe area at the rear of the building. Everyone inside the building was safe with only five minor injuries reported from flying glass. Had they been in the streetside offices, we would have had casualties.

This was the moment when the four years of reinforcing the physical security at the Consulate General and all the other measures we took to proactively prepare for a very large vehicle bomb, paid back all the money we had spent on the upgrades in saved lives.

I began my work at the bomb site, trying to lock down the crime scene and moving all the curiosity seekers away. I was yelling at everyone and trying to prevent what I had seen at the Sheraton Hotel from happening to my scene. I needed everything left alone to have our best chance at catching the perpetrators of this obvious terrorist attack. It only took a second to see that it had been a very large vehicle bomb suicide attack. The location of the crater, pieces of vehicles scattered all around, even the leaves from trees were starting to fall down like rain after being blown sky-high and the road was beginning to be covered by a layer of green leaves. Police were arriving and I began to get them to set up a cordon around as much of the bomb site as possible to keep people away. I could already see people out in the park, carrying a sheet and scooping up piles of tissue onto it for god knows what purpose. I could only imagine they were trying to help clean up but they were screwing around with an evidence scene. In order to catch and retain as much as possible in a chaotic scene like this, I had my security staff begin to get photos of everything again. This seemed a bit like Deja Vu and it wasn't a good thing. I looked up and saw some body parts hanging in the trees above the road. This was going to be complicated.

I was missing 14 feet of my concrete wall, two 4 feet by 4 feet by 9 feet concrete planters that acted as protective bollards, a concrete police outpost had vaporized as did the police officer inside it, and a large limb of a 200 year old tree in the Consulate's front yard was blown off, taking part of the the blast and protecting some of the front of the building near the communication equipment office across from mine. Every window in the building had been blown out but because of the Mylar we put on the windows to prevent shattering (something we learned from the Nairobi bombing), most were lying more or less intact in the front yard. I could see that holes had been punched through the outer wall by my office and through the window grilling into my corner area. If the Marine had been in that office working still, he would be dead. As it turned out, he had left and remembered to close the door. At the opposite end of my front Consulate wall from where the one police officer and post had been vaporized, we had another police officer on duty. On checking him, I found him almost cut in half at the waist but still alive. A piece of metal from a car had traveled 150 yards in a split second and sliced through his middle. He mercifully died on the way to the hospital. It had been a miracle that he was alive from the injury at all even for a moment. All in all, there were 14 people dead.

I verified that all our people were secure in the Consulate and found that my ARSO and the Acting Detachment Commander had reacted perfectly, just like we practiced hundreds of times. When the explosion went off, the Acting Detachment Commander initiated the Duck and Cover alarm and then moments later went to the evacuation alarm. All the employees had picked themselves up off the floor, dusted off the glass and rubble and immediately began to move down the stairs and out back in an orderly fashion. The ARSO and Marines began their floor-by-floor and room-by-room check for injured and possible dead. Everyone had done very well and because of four years of diligent physical security upgrades, we had all lived and only five persons had minor cuts from flying material. This had been a huge and horrible attack but a textbook success from a security preparation perspective. This goes to show what can be done when headquarters is intelligent enough to support their Field Agents and my HQ had been providing me with unquestioned maximum support my entire tour. In the midst of this death and destruction, there was some silver lining

I continued back out to my crime scene and began my modus operandi evaluation. The sweetly rancid smell of exposed human flesh scattered everywhere was overpowering. The high heat was acting as a catalyst to speed up the process of deterioration and some of those trying to help with the un-requested clean-up were beginning to get sick and throw-up on my crime scene. This was at least beginning to discourage some of them from continuing their "help". Also, like a Biblical plague, the large black flies had already caught wind of the opportunity and had moved in. They didn't care if it was dead tissue or alive. They were biting all of us making this disaster complete.

Initial quick review showed the crater to be about 4 meters across and 1.5 meters deep, through the hardest macadam and solid rock that could be under a road surface. The bomb had evidently been substantial. Best immediate speculation showed that it was a vehicle that had come rolling down Abdullah Haroon road and as it got to the closest point to the building (being my office), it had detonated. Besides our damage, the Marriott, next door had suffered great damage to their storefront operations and every window in their hotel. There were a lot of people being sent out in ambulances with bad glass cuts all over their faces and bodies from the Marriott Hotel. They had not put Mylar on their windows and the people took the full force of all the flying glass. We would later find out that the size of the bomb was about 160 kilos (350 lbs) of high explosives that had been packed into the suicide vehicle. The size of the explosive package clearly demonstrated that they wanted to maximize death and destruction. There were 14 dead - all innocent people on the outside of the Consulate. They had killed their own people in their attempt to kill Americans, and probably me specifically. A suicide bomber is not using much self-judgment when he is rolling to his moment of death. His mission is simple and straightforward with no alterations. Any room for self-injected judgment may lead to his changing his mind. So, even if no Americans are apparent, the bomb will be activated.

The police and I continued to secure the perimeter of the blast scene but it had been so large that huge and heavy chunks of steel were being located almost a half mile away. One vehicle axel was located a quarter mile away on the roof of the Consul General's home. It had traveled high over a four-story museum before plowing into the roof top. An apartment building a half-mile away had every window blown out.

Inside the Consulate, every window in the entire building was blown out. All the drop ceilings were now like loose floor tiles. Some doors were blown off their hinges and mine had flown across the room at my desk. Small slivers of glass residue covered everything in the entire building including the computer keyboards, which later even after cleaning would penetrate our fingertips as we typed cables on the progress of the investigation. Chunks of concrete from the wall and the vehicle barriers and police booth about the size of footballs had penetrated through the window grills into some offices and into the outer walls of the Consulate. A piece about the size and shape of a larger rugby football was lying in the office across from my office where the communication equipment had been stored. It had come through the grill and bounced around the room smashing everything it came into contact with, eventually coming to rest. I picked it up later when I re-entered the building and took it to the window grill to see where it could have fit through. It was about one-third too large to get through any opening in the grill, yet it had. Apparently it had been traveling so fast and with so much force, the shape in travel was more oblong as it found its way through a grill opening and as it slowed down, it took its normal size and shape. Sort of a "Concord Jetliner" type of effect where the Concord in flight was longer than when it was stationary. The physics of explosions are mind-boggeling and very scary.

As I walked the front grounds of the Consulate inside my violated perimeter wall in order to validate that our total accountability hadn't forgotten a gardener or other work person, I came across a sight I will never forget. On the grass, sitting "or standing" perfectly side by side and three inches apart, were two bare feet from the ankles down. They were the same size and both were pointed in the same direction and lined up even with each other in position. It was as if someone from the ankles up had simply been taken away, leaving his feet in place where he had been standing. At first, I was certain that we must have had an employee working or walking in the front yard area. I insisted on a further verification of all people. Once again, every single person was accounted for. It was also impossible for someone to have escaped past the security controls to find themselves walking the grounds. The only conclusion was again one of those physics mysteries that come from large explosions. Someone outside the walls had been killed in the explosion, blown apart at the ankles or worse, but the two feet had traveled through the air, landing exactly side by side inside my compound in that bizarre positioning. That is a hard picture to get out of one's head.

The investigation began with the crater. And once again, the FBI was invited to come work the investigation scene since it involved an attack against Americans. Their forensic skills would be useful and their evidence collection would be thorough but the actual investigating would still need to be done by the Pakistani police and that meant I would be involved in the actual search and interviews. We would have the FBI around for awhile, while they collected, itemized and packed-out their crates of evidence for shipment back to Washington, D.C.

As we collected vehicle parts and license plates and engine block VIN numbers we found sifting through the rubble, our first lead was that a driver education car with four or five young girls learning to drive had been right on ground zero. The normal assumption would be that if a car was on ground zero it must be the car bomb, but this profile just seemed impossible. Young girls with enough hope in life to want to learn to drive was strike one. Girls at all were also not the normal suicide bomber profile. And, one never wastes resources like 4 or 5 willing suicide bombers in one blast. So, we put that aside assuming they must have been exactly next to the actual vehicle bomb and continued digging in the crater. The FBI insisted on doing the digging and residue sifting so I let them. I knew that there would come a time when they would pack up and leave with their crates and I would finish the investigation with my Pakistani friends. I just needed to make sure I knew of all evidence so I could use it in our later search for the criminals. As we got deeper into the crater, we found a VIN (vehicle identification number) about six feet down. This allowed us to trace the car to a license number and then to an owner. As one would expect though, with a vehicle that is going to be used in a crime, the owner had just sold his car to a man who paid him cash for the old junker and never discussed names and no one seems to have titles or official transfers unless it is a new expensive car. The owner was thrilled to get more money for the piece of junk than he ever thought he would.

Over a couple of weeks, the FBI finished their sifting and I finished getting all the limbs and organs out of trees and rounding up all the evidence we could find over a half-mile radius. I also still had the street in front, Abdullah Haroon, sealed off and was keeping all press away from the site to preserve whatever we could of the evidence and work being done. The Pakistanis were being unusually patient and highly cooperative about allowing us to cut off this main traffic thoroughfare, considering that the FBI was not allowing them to participate and not sharing. Eventually it all would come down to the Pakistanis catching the perpetrators and they were already in their "usual suspect roundup" mode and were working with me on it. Where would we be without understanding our cultural brothers from the country we live in? The FBI packed up their valuable spoils of evidence in crates and left town, certain that once they had all this crap back at their headquarters 8,000 miles away, the crime would be solved in their labs. We never heard from them again.

In the days following the bombing, the Pakistani employees, who I had become like family with, surprised me further by coming up to me in the halls and hugging me and expressing to me that they felt I had saved their lives. They stated that every time I made them do a practice drill for a bomb, they thought it was just crazy American stuff again but that those drills are what saved them and all the efforts we put into the physical security had made it possible for all of them to survive. They had tears in their eyes when they hugged me and it brought moisture to mine as well. I hadn't thought about that aspect but they were very sentimental about their sense that it was me who had saved their lives that day when they were thrown to the floor, though I wrote up my ARSO and the Acting Detachment Commander for Meritorious Honor Awards for their actions immediately following the blast. The truth is it comes down to everyone involved when you have a success like this including DS headquarters who kept giving me the money to enhance the security.

I worked the case with my Pakistani police friends and the assault squad and several weeks later, we identified the organizers of the attack. Obviously, the bomber had already gone on to meet his maker and to discover that he really didn't have a legion of virgins waiting for him for his murderous actions. What a surprise that must have been. The organization behind it was clearly identified as Al-Qaeda and the police and intelligence Special Branch felt that it was a direct attempt to kill me for the successes I had against the Al-Qaida organization. Just one more lucky moment in my life. If I had been in my office having the Friday morning meeting, it is likely that I and some of my brothers would have been killed. I am sure that their failure to get me once again and the fact that I even worked the case and discovered that it was them, must have further infuriated them. Well, they can at least feel satisfied that for the rest of my tour in Karachi, I had to work without glass in my windows in 120 degree heat and with pigeons flying around my office and the hallways, and their perpetual cooing. I am not a fan of pigeons now. I guess I should have also realized that Al-Qaida would not stop at this attempt to get rid of me.

My DS Headquarters was getting very concerned at the number of attempts, attacks, incidents and escapes that were racking up on my tally. Our Director called me and said that they wanted to bring me home early, immediately, before anything could happen to me after going through so much. Well, I truly appreciated his concern and personal oversight of me but my replacement had not come yet and I just could not leave all my friends without protection and go home before things were finished and someone was in my place to continue the fight. So I politely declined/insisted and stated I would finish my tour. I did not like to leave things unfinished. At least for all the troubles and personal threats, and for the inconveniences my wife had gone through, they had offered us Madrid, Spain, next and in fact, I honestly thought I was looking forward to Madrid and a bit of quiet normal time.

I received a phone call from my good friend, the Inspector General of Police, K. He invited me over to his offices at the Provincial Police Headquarters for a lunch. I assumed it would be with himself, the DIG, and the few Officers I had become close to. The lunch was just K and I. I was really touched by this. He had taken his valuable time to have a one-hour private lunch for just the two of us. I had never heard of this before. This man's time was very limited and an hour was a lifetime he was offering to me. We talked about our adventures we had shared in the past years together and there were actual tears forming in both of our eyes as we reflected on the many cases, deaths and tragedies as well as the brotherly bonding that had formed between us. It is one of the most precious moments of my life and career. K also told me that I was the only foreigner the police had ever allowed to be involved in Pakistani terrorist or criminal cases in his entire recollection. He said that the reason he permitted it was that I understood the Pakistanis and the way they had to carry out their investigations and I had never criticized their methods or actions and had always lent a hand and my expertise to the advancing of the investigations. He then paid me the ultimate compliment and said that he felt that I was a Pakistani somewhere in my soul. That has stuck with me all these years. He then gave me a prayer rug and a Plaque from the Sindh Police, we hugged and said goodbye and I left feeling like I was running away from home.

My replacement arrived two weeks before my transfer time and for those two weeks I tried to give him four years of experience. Much of the time, we either get no transition time or at best a day or two. This was unusual to get two weeks but showed the understanding and focus that DS had about the severity of the threat in Karachi. But, DS made some changes to the Pakistan tours. Because of all the bad things that had been happening in Pakistan, it was decided that it would be termed a Critical Threat Terrorism Post and all tours would now only be for one year. That was a significant change and made some sense, but the Pakistani police would never make the effort to befriend or cooperate with an American Security Officer the way they had with me if he was just going to come for a year and then turnover again. I did the best I could and told my replacement that he needed to rely on our exceptional FSNIs K and H since they would be the continuity from year to year. Then the day came when I turned it over to him and I went to my house to wait for my shuttle to the airport two days later.

AL-QAIDA'S FINAL ATTEMPT AGAINST ME

I was scheduled to leave on Sunday July 23, 2002, on a flight out of Karachi International Airport. That meant that after leaving my replacement in total control at the end of the day, Friday, July 21, I had a Saturday to relax and prepare for the Sunday departure. I planned on just a nice relaxing, coffee-drinking Saturday morning without a concern in the world so to speak. My two suitcases were packed and sitting upstairs ready to go so I was as ready as a person could be.

I sat there Saturday morning alone in my Karachi home of four wonderful and eventful years, thinking of my wife waiting in Bogota, Colombia, and feeling guilty that with so much that had happened over the final several months, I had been unable to communicate with her very much. Also, the things I had seen and done had sort of put me into a dark place where I didn't feel good about calling her too often to discuss how I was. It was 0900 hours on that Saturday morning, I was in a t-shirt and jeans with big holes in the knees, and a knock came to my door.

I was pleasantly surprised to see my friends. The "Captain", "D" the IB Officer, and even the ISI Colonel were at my door and wanted to talk. I assumed that it was a final farewell between friends but the three of them together sort of felt intense.

The ISI Colonel advised me that the ISI had individuals undercover in the Karachi Al-Qaida operation and that those covert operatives had advised the ISI that Al-Qaida knew I was departing Karachi on Sunday and knew the flight and time and was committing serious resources to make sure I did not get out safely. You have to give them points for dedication to cause. There is really only one logical route to the airport so all they had to do was put enough people and resources into place and I wouldn't make it through the choke point. If they were serious, they would get me. After all I had been through in the last four years, I had no problem accepting what they said. Captain said that they wanted to take me out to the departing flight today and had already made arrangements. There was a large 10-vehicle police escort waiting to take me to the airport now.

I went upstairs and changed my clothes. I had already showered and was ready to go in 15 minutes. I grabbed the two suitcases, called my replacement to advise him I was leaving and went out the door thinking to myself that I felt satisfied with the work I had done here. It had been substantive and I had accomplished a lot and had many successes. I also remember thinking to myself that I had seen and done things that others only see in movies or read about in fictional novels, and foolishly, I remember thinking that I had become sort of "the real thing" and survived. I felt content and happy at that moment with who I was and what I had become. I had honestly contributed to the safety and security of the planet and what could be better than that. People's lives had been saved by my work. I also remember acknowledging to myself that I had failed Mariane Pearl and that Danny was dead and I would have to carry that with me forever. But all in all, the balance of justice was tilted favorably at this moment in time. Plus, I was definitely one lucky son-of-a-gun.

The police escort included Police SUVs with up-mounted machine guns, motorcycles as route clearers, and other armed vehicles to protect the sides of my Consulate Fully Armored Vehicle. This was quite a serious motorcade put in place to get me safely out of Pakistan. I was touched by the concern my Pakistani friends were showing me.

We arrived at the airport and pulled up to the departure curb. At first I didn't understand why there was such a crowd at the airport drop-off point and then I realized that I recognized the 50 persons standing there waiting. The Police had contacted my police friends from all over the Province, as well as Z and H, and told them I was leaving today. Standing here in front of the airport were all my closest police and other friends from the past four years of hard work. They were actually "The real Thing". These important men had come from all over the Province just to be at the airport to say goodbye. This would never happen in my own culture. Here were people who had become actual new family to me. For an hour, I smiled, hugged and reminisced with all of them and then it was time to say goodbye and go inside. That was one of the hardest moments of my life. I looked back at that group and froze that picture in my head. That incredible group of tough guys who lived a hard life in a difficult third-world country, standing there with smiles on their faces waving goodbye to some jerk American Special Agent who only spent four years with them. It was amazing and life-concept changing.

The IGP had given his men very clear instructions on my

protection. Three Officers were to stay with me every moment in the airport and were to walk me onto the plane and stay in the walk-way until the plane pulled away. No one was to bother me and no checks were to be done on my paperwork or passport as I processed out and through the airport. He didn't want anyone knowing I was in the airport or leaving early. And he must have been serious about it. The Officers walked me through all customs and departing check points without allowing anyone to look at my ticket or papers. The luggage had been checked-in by the Consulate expeditor and we went straight through and to the Business class lounge. The three Police sat with me and watched everyone in the lounge with suspicion and one posted himself at the door. I am sure that to the others I must have appeared to be a prisoner who was being escorted out of country. I told the young Police Officers that I was fine and they didn't need to stay with me and were free to go. Their eyes got big and they looked like they had just been sentenced to death. Perhaps that is what it would have been if they had not done their duty and stayed with me because they made it clear that they were under strict orders to make sure I was on the plane and the door was closed the plane had wheels-up. OK, I guess I was going to have to make pleasant small talk for awhile longer.

When it was time to board, they formed a protective diamond around me and walked me onto the plane. Then two of them backed onto the walk-way ramp and stood there scrutinizing everyone who walked onto the plane while the third stayed with me. Once the plane was loaded, the Police Officer with me said goodbye, did the usual hug and hand-shaking and walked off and joined his two comrades. I saw out the window that the three of them were still standing there as the plane began to be backed off and I imagine they even reported back to police headquarters when we had wheels up.

I really felt like I was leaving a home where I had become closer to fitting-in than anywhere else I had ever been. I was leaving my family behind. I also felt like I was leaving the action that I loved and going off to a calm normality that I no longer understood and didn't think I fit into anymore. The thought about life in the United States seemed disconnected and not my life anymore. The people there took life for granted and had no concept of what was really going on in the world of bad people who wanted to destroy the U.S. I knew that I had also become a different person, more pensive and observant and perhaps a bit less outgoing and inter-active. The attacks and life and death I had just lived through had changed me and it was a different man leaving Karachi in July of 2002 than the one who arrived here in 1998 with no idea of what was ahead of him. I would never be the same again and now I had to face a wife I had neglected, who had been evacuated from Karachi three times for 6 months each time and who now was waiting in Bogota for me to come and get her and was prob-ably angry with me for my lack of communication and with no understanding of what I had gone through and with no chance of my being able to explain it to her. This was probably not going to go well. I was exhausted from the years and fell asleep and slept most of the way to Washington D.C., where I would conduct my out-briefing with the International Operations Desk and our DS Director. After that, I would fly home to Arizona, where I would drop off my luggage and then go to Bogota to get "A".

When I arrived in Washington, D.C., I felt as usual, very out of place in such a passive and comfortable safe environment. The people were hustling and hurrying around on the streets and seemed so oblivious to who and what was going on around them.

Even loud noises didn't seem to make anyone jump. My intention was to do the out-brief and get back on a plane. I never really wanted to spend time working in the home office. I was definitely an overseas operations man all the way. I knew that I would never attain the highest levels of our organization without headquarters time but that was OK with me. I had already obtained my "ONE", which is the highest rank without being promoted into the Senior Foreign Service and that was higher than most of us thought we would ever get. I was ahead of the promotion curve with my peers so I was content never seeking the Director's desk and instead taking the fight to the enemy overseas.

I quietly and inconspicuously slunk into the DS/IP/NEA/SA (South Asia Desk) offices and introduced myself to the receptionist as having an appointment with the Director. She called and talked a bit louder than I had, announcing my name. All of a sudden, I saw people standing up at their cubicles, looking over the space dividers at me. I wasn't aware that it was me they were staring at but no one was behind me. Then, they all began walking toward me and broke out in applause. I think I almost panicked. They all came up to me and shook my hand and congratulated me for my successes against Al-Qaida and the Daniel Pearl case specifically and what they called "my brilliant reporting". They all said that they followed my daily reports and it had been the highlight of their days to follow the story. The pats on the back and handshaking and supportive praise, in the somewhat weakened condition I was in, honestly stunned me into silence. One does not want to cry when being congratulated for being a tough guy. It is bad manners and terrible for the reputation. One female DS Agent, who I have had respect for since the day I started, when she was my Class Advisor, told me it was the best reporting she had ever read and she thanked me for my sacrifice. Perhaps that meant more to me than anything. I felt lost and unable to properly respond to them. I seem to remember sort of shyly mumbling thanks and quickly heading toward the Director's office. A moment of "glory basking" missed but I will never forget what they did that day.

Chapter Seventeen
TRANSITIONING FROM TERROR TO HOME

After a confusing day in Arizona, I flew to Bogota, Colombia, feeling more tenuous than anytime I had entered a terrorist safehouse knowing that a firefight was going to ensue. I was very uneasy and realized that I had not yet transitioned from terrorism to caring husband mode and I felt almost introverted and sullen. I had thought I should take a week to try and adjust before flying to see "A" and possibly ruining any chance of making things right, but she was absolute about my need to come immediately and here I was, a stranger in a strange land, still having sleeping and awake nightmares and jumping at loud noises or fast movements around me.

"A" picked me up at the airport and was cold and distant and hardly had a word to say to me and didn't even kiss me so I knew that I was further from resolution than I had thought. Out in front of the airport, her family was waiting. I wondered if they were there to welcome me or attack me. Man, I was really in a confused state. I knew that I couldn't possibly explain to her what had brought me to this present condition and yet without that, how would I ever reconcile my actions. This was the damned rock and a hard place scenario and I would have to hope that the days we would spend in Bogota would somehow allow me to normalize and would allow her to soften toward me and what I had endured. But as adversarial as she was to me with her silent treatment and her private phone calls, her family seemed to like me.

We went to various restaurants trying to open up our communication and spent time just trying to get to know each other again but I came to realize that we were facing more than just the Pakistan separation. We were also facing a 22-year age difference and at this age, it had become a generational and cultural blockage. I wasn't sure that this was solvable but I was going to try. She was cold to me and very unforgiving and just wouldn't seem to give it a try. I took solitary walks in her neighborhood to seek retrospection.

The most normal I felt besides her family's attempts to welcome me, was at three restaurants we visited when FARC terrorist bombs went off nearby either before, after, or during our meals. I actually felt more comfortable with that scenario and it brought a smile to my face and a bit of humor to think that no matter where I went, things blew up. That was funny. There had been no violence in the city for quite awhile and when I arrived, the national terrorists blew up stuff to welcome me. As usual though, the bombs always just missed us and my luck held out.

We finished our time in Bogota and left for the United States to spend some time on our Congressionally-mandated "Home Leave" to assimilate back into the American culture before we would go to Madrid, Spain. Our government has a policy for those of us in the Foreign Service. They want to ensure we don't go completely indigenous and forget our own culture and in this case, that was a good idea.

We flew to Arizona so that "A" could meet my family again and they would have a chance to reacquaint with her. It was a stilted and difficult period and most of my family asked me why she was so stand-offish. So, we cut that part short and decided to tour the western states, just enjoying the scenery and searching for places we had not seen and wanted to visit. Then we left for our next assignment of four years in Madrid, Spain.

Chapter Eighteen
RSO Spain and Andorra:
September 2002–March 2006

The reason I was lucky enough to be the Senior Regional Security Officer for all of Spain and the small country on the northern Spanish border called Andorra, was that my threat profile with Al-Qaeda was crackling hot and my DS leadership wanted me to find a place where not much happens and I could cool off. It was selected by me because "A" deserved a nice place and Spain is sort of like the motherland for Colombians. She was thrilled and back in a country where her primary language was the mother tongue. I really hoped this might work out and turn things around on the relationship front. We arrived in Madrid in September.

We were given a top floor apartment in a building on the corner of Hermosilla and Serrano, just six blocks from the Embassy. I could walk back and forth every day to work and for years, we had not been able to walk anywhere without being a target. Serrano is like the Rodeo Drive of Madrid. All the major name shops are on Serrano. It was not a place that I could afford to do any shopping but as a locale to live, we were in the heart of it all and very happy about it.

The apartment was filled with all the beautiful furniture I had designed and had made out of Rosewood in Karachi while living there, as well as the carpets and other handicrafts we had collected. Our apartment was beautiful and stylish. It had real entertainment capability. We threw a lot of parties and people loved coming to this apartment to be among friends and see the items collected from around the world. It was comfortable and cool. It seemed that life might just take a turn for the normal.

I worked long hours at the Embassy to improve the RSO Programs and was very concerned about the physical security of the Embassy building. I had just been blown up in Karachi and I didn't like the fact that this Embassy sat virtually right on the sidewalk. I remembered that while working in Karachi, I had monitored returning Jihadis from Afghanistan get on planes and fly to Madrid, where we figured out they were receiving their plans and money for operations or going into "sleeper cell" mode. Now, here I was and I knew we were vulnerable.

I launched a few new physical security upgrades but obtaining money from Washington was a problem since we weren't considered a high threat terrorist post. The point they missed sitting at their desks was that if you are making all your traditionally high threat posts strong, then in fact, the "soft targets" like us became the high risk targets and we were in fact, now very high risk. I pushed as hard as I could and we put in bollards on the street-sidewalk edge, new and heavier-duty Mylar on the windows, and even got approval to begin a new outer perimeter upgrade including the guard's access control booth. And, we set policies about people being exposed at the end of the building closest to the street. I revised the surveillance detection program and emphasized discreet coverage of the building and personnel. Everyone in Embassy management knew my background and what I had been through and they were afraid I would try to turn their comfortable life in Spain into a fort-mentality operation. I tried to balance the two. We did the best we could to get new security implemented in the first six-months of this scheduled four-year tour and fortunately, I had an Ambassador who was one of the best guys I have ever known and he and I got along very well. And, I had a very experienced and professional Spanish security team. This was Madrid and we all expected a quiet and wonderful cultural experience but I had to do what I knew needed to be done just in case.

Then, less than six months into the tour, on March 11, 2003, what I had been anticipating and trying to prepare for occurred. But fortunately and by the grace of god, it occurred away from our building. A series of bomb detonations went off during morning train-commuter rush traffic and 191 people were killed and two thousand were injured. The detonation sites were unbelievable. The carnage was massive. Though Spain's internal Basque-country-based terrorists ETA are always the first thought for bombings, and in fact the explosive used was the standard ETA explosive, contrary to normal ETA scenarios, this bombing was designed to maximize death and injury, and that was not ETA's modus operandi. Also, no advance warning was given and ETA always called an hour ahead to get the innocent people cleared out of the explosion site. Within 24 hours, Al-Qaeda was identified as the culprit and I was back into the hunt for Al-Qaeda. Our quiet Spain tour would forever be changed.

The first thing I did was to identify all of our surveillance detection reports of un-verified personnel, and to gather all of the photos taken of previously unidentified suspicious individuals, searching for any clue or sign of early-stage surveillance that might have been done on our facilities. I told my team to go back two years and find every unanswered report and photo for review. The SD Team was thorough and accurate. As we went through the thousands of reports and photos, we came across one report with photos of a man almost exactly one year before the train bombings, standing across the street from the Embassy near his motor-scooter and conducting what appeared to be discreet surveillance on us. His face was clear in the photo as was the license plate on his scooter. The train bombers had placed backpacks filled with explosives on the trains and then exited, leaving the innocent Spaniards to die. The faces of the nine men with backpacks entering the train stations had now been identified and our photo was one of them named Sayed Barraj.

So it appeared that almost exactly one year before they executed their hateful plan on the trains, this terrorist had been conducting surveillance on our Embassy as a possible target. It became obvious that their terrorist team had deemed our Embassy to be too hard a target and had chosen something else less threatening. As with all terrorists, they are bullies and cowards. Even the young vehicle suicide bombers have been lied to by their manipulating evil Mullahs in order to get them to carry out the act that the Mullah preaches about but is too much a coward to do himself. Many times they even use a back-up man who can detonate it remotely in case the young man changes his mind at the last minute and decides to live.

Since Sayed Barraj was now identified by the Spanish police, we decided to work our only other clue, the license plate of the motor-scooter, and the fact that the scooter had the markings on it of a well-known package delivery service. Over a brief time, we traced the delivery routings Sayed had made during the same period of time that the surveillance was being done on our Embassy. We were looking at the only period of time that we knew for a certainty that he was actively doing that work. Having the flexibility to be out delivering packages, and the cover of the company itself, gave him the freedom and opportunity to conduct his surveillance under what we refer to as a "cover for action". That means a logical reason for being where he was and doing what he was doing, instead of standing on a corner and writing down license numbers of cars leaving the Embassy gate. His job was a perfect cover and included mobility.

As we traced his routes and deliveries, as well as the receiving logs of the places he made deliveries to, we found one that bothered us a lot. Sayed had delivered a box to a Spanish Ministry and the receptionist had been busy, so he had walked in with what had been a medium-large box, set it down without verification or recording, and walked out un-checked. We had two responsibilities now. The first was to provide all the data we had including the photos of Sayed Barraj to the police working the terrorist case. The second was to talk with the Ministry about their lax security procedures. We did both and got a startled response from both parties. The police were grateful and the Ministry went into shock. We worked with the Ministry to fortify their access control procedures. The Spaniards were not used to this form of terrorism meant to maximize the carnage and they were stunned as well as a bit defensive at allowing us to help them. I believe it was their pride and Socialist independence but we did what we could.

This bombing was so significant and so well-timed, with the national elections just 48 hours away, it became crystal clear that there was a strategy to change the course of the election, which was assumed to be an easy win for incumbent President Aznar. But with this disaster and the claim that it was because of Spain's support to the Iraq coalition, the entire country turned to the only alternative there was and that was Zapatero, the Socialist Party candidate who had never really had any true job except being the Socialist candidate who never won. Now, he was the new President of Spain and had to figure out what to do with that responsibility. Literally, Al-Qaeda altered the outcome of a national election.

The police continued their pursuit of the nine terrorists. We assisted to the degree they would permit, such as with the use of our Ion Itemiser, which told them what the explosive material was that had been used. But we really had to act and investigate from the sidelines because of the same pride problem. Finally, the police had identified that the terrorist cell was hiding in a particular apartment building in a section of Madrid and a covert action was put into place, to follow thorough late night surveillance, in order to ensure that they would get the entire cell and not endanger the other occupants. But, while waiting and watching, another special police group learned of this location and decided to beat the first group to the glory of capture. While the first group was staged and hiding and conducting their surveillance, they witnessed the second group sneaking up to the building entrance with no backup and no knowledge of who was inside or missing. This turned it into a sprint for who could get there first and as one would guess, all the movement before things were in proper alignment was noticed from the window by one of the terrorists. Eight of the nine terrorists were in the apartment and the ninth was walking down the sidewalk toward the apartment. When the ninth, who happened to be Sayed Barraj, saw what was happening, he fled. The police had sacrificed all their planning and control, which included the element of surprise, because of jealous competitive zeal. The police charged up the stairs to the second floor apartment and as they almost reached the door, the door flew open. Standing in the doorway were several of the terrorists, all wearing suicide bomb vests. Apparently, each cell member wore their vests or at least had them ready to put on in case something like this happened. They swore their allegiance to Allah and detonated. The blast killed the first police officer instantly, and seriously wounded several others and literally destroyed the second floor of the apartment building and ruined the rest of the building for habitation. Eight of the nine train bombers were now dead and no interviews would be conducted regarding the planning or organizational personnel involved. Interestingly, only the terrorist we had caught in a photo evaluating our Embassy as a target remained on the loose. We continued to search for him over the next couple of years but he probably fled as fast and as far as he could go.

Even though eight of the nine train bombers were dead, what this meant to me was that the terrorist sleeper cells in Spain had been awakened and now, the lives of all my people were in jeopardy. Our focus for security would now change to a much higher threat level.

Besides the work and viable cases we had in Spain, there were a lot of wonderful cultural experiences. My responsibility for this Mission included Madrid, the Consulate in Barcelona, and the other small consular assistance operations in Vallencia, Malaga, Sevilla, La Coruna, the Island of Mallorca off the eastern coast of Spain, and Grand Canaria in the Canary Islands. Plus, the Mission included a small country on the northern border of Spain, called Andorra. It was a tiny mountainous place with friendly people and beautiful scenery. It was also a duty-free zone so shopping and skiing were its sources of income. Being able to travel to all these locations for work purposes may have been the highlight of the Spain assignment.

What I also discovered by accident was that on a tiny island in the chain of Canary Islands, lived Ambassador Melissa Wells. Melissa was the Ambassador who I wrote about from the Kinshasa, Zaire, adventures earlier. Once we found each other again, we began to have reunions in Madrid, which included dinner, lots of red wine, and loads of laughter as we relived and re-told the stories about the crazy times in Zaire with President Mobutu. She is such a unique and bright woman. Even as she has aged, her energy and focus exceeds most people I know. I never made it to spend time on her quiet island with her and her husband but that may be for future travels. We still email.

About this time, the Daniel Pearl case was re-surfacing in the form of two things. A Documentary was in the works called, "The Jihadi and the Journalist", for which my input was being requested, and the FBI Director, Robert Mueller, was inviting me at the FBI's expense, to come to Washington, D.C., to receive a special award called "The FBI Director's Award for Excellence", in the field of international terrorism investigations.

The Documentary was being produced and directed by two men, a Pakistani and an Indian, which is unusual in itself. They lived in London and were very committed to Mariane Pearl and the project so I would help them in any way I could. They had been working on this project for about a year when they began to ask me to review the material and make comments. I discussed with them the information that I could without violating anything still classified. This allowed me to provide a good deal of insight on Sheikh Umer, the case investigation activities with the police (up to a point), the trial, and they were some of the first I told about being the one to excavate Danny's body. These two young men were independents and they needed to sell this project to a reputable news organization in order to get wide distribution and recoup their expenses and hopefully make it a profitable endeavor. Coincidentally, they were in New York visiting Mariane at the same time I was passing through on my way to Washington D.C. I wanted to see Mariane in New York and make sure she was OK and the Producers arranged an authentic Chicken Tika dinner at Mariane's home that they were preparing and cooking themselves. I flew in and spent the day with Mariane talking about her life and transition and of course her son Adam who had been born a few months after she left Karachi. He was the cutest little guy with his naturally curly hair and big smile. I thought the dinner would be small with just the four of us but Mariane had invited some of her journalist friends. As the crowd began to arrive, they all seemed to know my story within the Pearl case and their attention and appreciation paid to me made me feel embarrassed and guilty. I still wasn't over the fact that I had failed Mariane and lost Danny. I didn't feel that I deserved people being nice to me. A tall woman with a dynamic smile walked in and walked straight to me and said I must be Randall. She began to let tears go and hugged me to her tightly. This was Sarah Crichton, the daughter of Michael Crichton and one of the sweetest people I have ever met. She had been the editor and friend of Mariane on the release of her book, "A Mighty Heart." I took an instant liking to Sarah and could easily see that this was a person with a good heart and solid character. The dinner went well but was a bit stiff for me because I felt like I was being evaluated for my past performance and as I said, I felt I had failed. I may have drunk too much wine to compensate. Reporters from various large and well-known news agencies were there and the personal questions kept coming. They did respect my need for confidentiality on certain aspects of the case though. The dinner ended, I said goodbye to all of them, hugged Mariane and went back to my hotel to refocus my perspective. This had all been a bit too much attention for a field operative.

The other link to the Daniel Pearl case was the FBI awards ceremony I was invited to months later. The FBI was giving me one of their highest awards, directly from their Director, Robert Mueller, and they were even footing the bill. They also said I could invite family to attend. It isn't often people get into the bowels of the FBI headquarters in Washington, D.C. so I invited my family and my brother Allan, who was living in Connecticut, and my sister Barbara, who was living in North Carolina. Both said they would come. DS arranged an Agent to be my driver and escort around the city, which really helped to ease things. The day came and our DS Agent picked up myself and family and took us to the FBI HQ. We were escorted into their auditorium and I was seated in the front rows. The FBI had also invited Mariane to be there to hand out the awards for the case to myself and their FBI Agents and that made it all the more wonderful. The time came and they called me up. On stage was Director Mueller, one of the soberest persons I have ever met, and Mariane, standing on the far side of him with a smile on her face that beamed like a million candle power. As I approached Director Mueller, and he had his right hand out to shake and the award in his other, in preparation for the photo to come, Mariane stepped around him and threw her arms around my neck and hugged me for what seemed like minutes. Nothing meant more to me than that. However, poor Director Mueller showed a complete lack of comfort and had a shocked and dislocated look on his face as if he couldn't figure out what to do. Then, she let go, still smiling and we finished the handoff and Director Mueller could re-establish his composure. The photo with Mueller and Mariane is priceless. I am also so glad that my family was there that day to see me and support me. After the ceremony, we got together for group investigation team photos and our personal photo time. Asra Nomani was also there with her little son, Shibli, who had been born a couple of months after Adam. It was an excellent reunion. Then, it was back to Madrid and more preparations to keep Al-Qaeda at bay.

This FBI Director's Award became one of the nicest awards I have ever received. I had received the DS Employee of the Year award in 2000, and 3 Superior Honor Awards and 5 Meritorious Honor Awards, but this was unique because the FBI seldom gave one outside their own FBI family. Since then, FBI Agents who have come into my office and seen it, haven't been able to believe that I have something they have coveted more than anything. I thank the Karachi Pearl case FBI Agents, especially "Father John", for what were undoubtedly their efforts to get me this award.

Within the first few months of the tour, the personable and brilliant American Ambassador to Spain had gotten his new Executive Assistant, a former Assistant Secretary of State from California, and his very sweet pregnant wife. They were to become best friends and I consider them still to be. I believe it was a few months after arrival, the wife went into labor and even though I really didn't know them well yet, I drove to the hospital to be there for them. They didn't speak Spanish and I was fluent and they hadn't settled into the culture yet so I wanted to just be a comfort zone coordinator for them. She had her baby, a beautiful little girl and I was there a few hours later. They didn't quite understand why a semi-stranger would care to be there to support them but they did appreciate it. I liked these two. They were just very aware and special people and that seemed obvious to me. I decided I would watch over them and their new baby. I may be a pathological demon of a man when it comes to my enemies but I am a true and loyal friend to my friends and will do anything to keep them safe.

We had a number of celebrities come to visit Madrid. Partly they came because our Ambassador is such an influential man and partly because Madrid is a hub in the European region. Tom Cruise came out because of our Ambassador and while there, he showed what a good-hearted guy he is by walking around the Embassy, having his picture taken with all the girls. Every desk you walked by in the Embassy seemed to have a picture of that female employee with Tom Cruise. He really made an impression. Antonio Banderas came in as well for a visa and he also showed great heart by posing for photos with the girls. He seemed like a very genuine and caring person. Of course the Spanish girls swooned and we practically needed the medical section to go on overdrive. While at the Reebok gym one day, all the trainers were whispering that Arnold Schwartzeneggar was coming to the gym because he had a preview of his Terminator 3 movie in town and wanted to get in a workout. I really respect what Arnold did as a leader for youth fitness programs and I like his national loyalty and strong character and I had sworn that if I ever had the chance, I would tell him that he had been a source of inspiration to me in my current occupation. Well, as I was working out, the gym got quiet and I saw all the trainers moving away to the walls in awe of "The Man". I continued working out but then I just couldn't stand it so I walked over to him and introduced myself and told him how he had been an inspiration to me. I was surprised to see that we were nose-to-nose the same height (5 foot 10 inches) but he was considerably more bulked that I was. He thanked me and said I was looking fit and then, I guess thinking I might be a crazed stalker, said he wanted to introduce me to his friend, who obviously was his bodyguard. This man was about 6 foot, 8 inches tall and huge. I got the picture and told him I understood and walked away and left him alone. Oh well, I had done what I promised I would.

In my Angola tour, I had spent time on several occasions with Madeleine Albright in her capacity as Ambassador to the United Nations and then again as Secretary of State and we had become friends. She currently had a book out in the United States called something like "The Most Powerful Woman in America". But she was now a civilian and I was advised that she was coming to Spain to promote her book. So, I decided that since I wanted to provide her protection, I would take a few days and put myself at her service along with some Spanish Police Bodyguards. I was really pleased to find that Madeleine remembered me and was happy to see me. The protective detail became more of a friendly escort and we enjoyed our discussions and meals talking about the experiences in Angola, her recent change from politics and the reasons behind her book. I was actually fascinated to listen to Madeleine talk on Spanish radio about her life before the State Department and the husband she had gotten divorced from. As her story was revealed, I came to understand the true depth of her strength. This was a woman who was the Grand Canyon of character. She had become who and what she was through her grit and personal drive. I have immense respect for her. Our casual dinners with great Spanish wines were a highlight for me and there was a lot of laughter and humor involved. I still clearly picture the Madrid nights at outdoor restaurants with the lights highlighting the trees down by the Park across from the old Palace and our sitting there enjoying ourselves with the Police Bodyguards comfortably protecting our perimeter. Before departing, Madeleine signed a copy of her book to me with meaningful comments and I treasure that book.

The Spanish Publisher for Madeleine's book was with us most of the time and she was terrific and very attractive. She was actually an American citizen who had married a Spaniard years before and remained in Madrid. I spoke good Spanish but I envied her complete mastery of the language. Even after Madeleine departed we remained in occasional contact and she was probably one of the final clinchers for my starting this memoir. Having learned about the Daniel Pearl case and my involvement, and then the other cases, she insisted I tell her tales of an Agent's life and from that and her strong encouragement to write, this book began to take conceptual form.

I am convinced that men who go through "hardening" life and death experiences, and who deal with the ugly and jaded side of life must compensate in order to emotionally and psychologically survive, by becoming more sensitive to the relationship side of life, and that they come to feel a greater warmth to the beautiful things like children and people-sharing happiness. It is a yin and yang thing. We balance out the very bad by becoming more sensitive and caring. Thus, some of you have probably seen very tough men who do hard jobs, generate tears at an emotional television advertisement involving family or some sense of national loyalty or sacrifice. Man, that'll get you every time. Just like a soldier who comes back from war. Show him a TV commercial about honor, loyalty and sacrifice to a combat unit or children and tears will come. Perhaps that is one of the explanations as to why men accept unhappy situations for so long and still remain loyal even without any hope of personal comfort for them.

Not very often does someone in my position in life and occupation get the opportunity to meet someone of such impacting significance, that no matter what I might have done or accomplished, it seems dwarfed by the impressive accomplishments of that person. Such was the case with our Ambassador in Spain. I have only met one person in my life who is in his category, and I remain today, wholly impressed, in awe, envious, and awkward in his presence. He is the best man I have ever met. He was a Presidential Appointee to the Ambassadorship in Spain for his skill and support to the Republican Party. He started in life from scratch as a boy and today is a huge success in the southern California business world. The rarity and uniqueness of achieving what he did is unimaginable and one would think that a person who attains that stature would have to become a bit of a starched shirt and perhaps stand-offish to the little folk like me. He is an anomaly. And as he goes, so does his wonderful wife. I had just come from Karachi where survival depended on me and my guidance, and within the world of people I protected, people looked to me to take care of them. A lesson I had learned in life is that seldom did important people care about the plain folk. I looked out for them and sometimes they looked out for each other but they didn't look out for me. I was sort of on the outside of that circle. The Ambassador seemed to take a liking to me for some reason and actually sort of looked out for me. It was a new and interesting concept, and a bit unnerving, but great. And within his circle were the couple who had come from California to assist him. His Executive Assistant kept his life organized; in Spain and to some degree linked with California. I realize that most of you live in towns or neighborhoods where you have your circle of friends and you have probably been friends with them for many years. For me, roaming the world for almost 20 years, and before that never living in one place for more than a couple of years, I had no tight circle of American friends. It was more like a loose passing association of friends. Being accepted by the Ambassador and wife and this special couple became my first "circle of American friends" in a very long time and I liked it.

The Ambassador was generous from his pocket and his heart. His Executive Assistant and I wanted to make sure he never felt like our friendship with him, and our true pleasure at being with him and his fun spirit and character, ever seemed like it was because he had deep pockets so we typically insisted on paying for the dinners and movies and left his pockets out of the deal. They were the type of friends, with sharp wit, kind hearts, political savvy, and a dry sense of humor that made me want to spend time with them. We would all plan nights when we snuck The Ambassador and his wife out for a normal night without police bodyguards and we would take him to a movie and dinner to give him a semblance of real life again. Plus we selfishly loved the personal time joking around with him. And he would joke with the best. Many times he would look at me, look at beautiful "A", who drew everyone's eyes in a room, and tell me that I had married above myself. I thought he was kidding at the time, but I would admit to knowing I had "married up".

And as I said, for some unknown reason he liked me. He had an idea of where I had come from, the attacks I had fought my way through and basically what I had done, although I have never told anyone even including up to today, everything I had done to protect my people in Karachi. I was concerned they would not understand that in order to beat evil men, you have to use evil against them. The Ambassador accepted me for who I was and didn't worry that I might turn the Madrid Embassy into an anti-terrorism protective zone. I appreciated that. And he sort of marketed me to others. I didn't understand exactly why, I guess I still don't. But I loved the guy for it. I remember one time South of Valencia at a meeting of Spain's top businessmen who wanted to pick the brain of one of the world's most successful American businessmen. I went along with him as his protection and was as usual keeping a low profile so as not to interfere in his important matters. The Ambassador insisted I sit at the table with all of them and eat lunch together and I was happy to do so but remained quiet. I listened to their business smarts for about an hour trying to absorb some knowledge that might enhance my own financial advancement and the Ambassador offered suggestions on how to invest in Spain and achieve greater profits. Eventually, I guess he had about enough and was a bit bored, as his focus was always searching for new information and inspiration. All of a sudden he said to all the businessmen, pointing at me, "Do you know who this man is? This is Randall Bennett. He is the best Security Officer in the world and the one who captured the kidnappers of Daniel Pearl. He is a true hero". I was flabbergasted. Then he went on about how great he thought I was and I frankly had no idea how to respond. So, I kept my mouth shut, but I will never forget how I felt, that a man I respect so much for his accomplishments and true depth of character would praise me in front of all these important people. It wasn't the last time he did that either. He would catch me off guard when he did it and I was always stunned and knocked over. Forget his deep pockets, The Ambassador has a deep heart.

During my last year in Madrid, the Promotion Board met in Washington, D.C., and to my total surprise, I was promoted into the Senior Foreign Service. This is equivalent to being promoted to a one-star General. I had never really expected to make it to the top of the promotion strata, but I had and I suspect that the bombings and shootings and successful investigations of notoriety I had been involved in had pushed me into that rank. To step over the barrier into the Senior Foreign Service was far beyond what I had thought or hoped to achieve. It was like the old corporate "key to the executive lounge" in its own way. Being a servant of our government, it only meant a few hundred dollars a year more in income but the status and image seemed significant.

A friend of mine in DS was working in our Headquarters and he was what we refer to as our Desk Officer. Essentially that means he watches over our needs from afar and acts as our advocate when we need a battle fought in HQ for funding, manpower or support. He is the Chief over a region of the world. His name was Mike and he was a great guy, about my same age, very easy-going and very likable. Occasionally the Desk Officers would come out to a post to conduct a "Program Review" to make sure the RSO was running his Programs the way DS wanted them to be run. Mike knew my programs were fine but it was a great chance for him to get out of the office and to come to Madrid and sample some great Spanish red wines with me and catch up on our friendship while we talked business.

Mike was much loved by everyone in DS. He arrived on Sunday and we spent several days actually talking over the Programs, taking easy light lunches and having Vino and Tapas for dinner. Thursday morning, Mike felt some pains and tightness in his chest and was taken from his hotel to the hospital. I raced to the hospital to find him in a bed in a private room and hardly able to focus or talk. The doctors said they thought he had a blockage of a main heart valve and they would have to run the inflatable device to open it up. It was going to be touchy but doable. By noon, Mike was worse, less coherent, and they called for a second opinion and more tests. By mid-afternoon, Mike was talking with me but it was obvious something was terribly wrong. The new tests revealed that the main valve connection to his heart was torn and it was in a place that could not be repaired. The prognosis given to me was that he would die, and soon. I spent the next hours sitting with Mike and he had been given some drugs that allowed him a greater level of coherency. He asked me to help him take off his ring, his watch, and a special medallion he wore on a gold chain around his neck that had been given to him by his Foreign Service Nationals in an Eastern European country he had been RSO in. Those employees who worked for him had meant a lot to him and obviously it was reciprocal. They gave this to him and he never took it off. Mike told me to give the items to his sister who was flying in the next morning. I told him he could give them to her and he told me he knew he would not be alive by morning. I was a bit stunned that he realized the gravity of the situation and was dealing with it with such courage and control. I was holding Mike's arm and head for most of the past hour and trying to make him laugh and remember the great times. They were some golden hours and I felt privileged that I got to be with this great guy at his end. About midnight, I let go of Mike's arm and shoulder and had to leave the hospital. We said goodbye for what we knew would be the last time. I took his jewelry for his sister and walked out and shortly after, Mike passed away. I always thought to myself afterwards that I would hope to have as much grace, dignity and courage as he did if I found myself in the same position. The way we arrive is not nearly as important as the way we go out.

As I tell these brief stories and segment of my life in Spain, first, they are but a small bit of what occurred, but second, I am leaving out all the investigations we continued to pursue on a daily basis. Our bread and butter were the investigations but I wanted to trail away from that for a tour to link back to a bit of my life and why it took me in a particular direction. In this case, it wasn't the investigations that altered my path, or changed me as a person, it was the life issues and choices.

In the Embassy, we had an excellent relationship with the Spanish Police, mostly due to the Senior Investigator Juan Luis. He had come up through the police ranks earlier in his life before going civilian with the U.S. Government and he now knew all the top Police Chiefs. So, I had easy access into their offices and he was always with me. Our relationship took on an actual "Brother" sense. The Spaniards are big on rank and respect so we always went to their offices to demonstrate that we knew who was running things, and occasionally we met in a restaurant and ate dinner and drank too much red wine. That was a good bonding experience. So, knowing that, we were shocked and caught off guard when one day the Senior Police Chief for the entire country asked if he could come to my office to talk. We had no idea what this meant but it just wasn't done. We welcomed him as graciously as we could and I will never forget how he sat across from me and poured his heart out, asking for my help. What it must have taken for him to ask for our help is unimaginable in this culture. He told me that he had 12 police officers in Baghdad and because the new President of Spain, Zapatero, had removed Spain from the coalition, the police officers now had no access into the Green Zone. They were not only living in the more dangerous Red Zone, but they couldn't retreat into the safe Green Zone even under attack because they had no coalition member access badges. He was pleading for my help to save his men and he literally meant "save them". A threat by Insurgents to kill his men had surfaced and he didn't know what else to do. When death was coming your way in Iraq, it came quickly and with force. For me to see how much he cared for the lives of his men that he would reduce his own "face" and come to me asking for help almost hurt. I told him I would resolve it and quickly. He left almost "hat in hand" but we tried to make him understand we were all close friends and the same in purpose.

One of my ARSOs in Madrid, and one of the best I have ever worked with, had left our post early to go to Baghdad and was there now. I contacted him and explained the problem and that we needed to issue access IDs to these Spanish Police, coalition members or not. It wasn't their fault that Zapatero acted foolishly. They shouldn't have to pay for his error with their lives. He understood as did his current RSO boss there. With negotiation and favors, the IDs were issued quickly and the Spanish Police were able to "fall back" into the safety of the Green Zone and even access food and supplies at the Army Exchange again. There were few places to even get food in the city and these Spanish Police were getting hungry as well as scared. Within a short period, we had things arranged and the Senior Police Chief was not only surprised by our efficiency and capability, but he was overjoyed that his men had been literally saved. The Senior Police Chief believed so strongly that the lives of his Officers had been saved that he had the Government of Spain, Ministry of Interior, issue medals to my previous ARSO and me. I was presented the medal in a police ceremony and we mailed his to his home in the U.S. It was "The Medal of the White Cross of Merit".

I guess all things "life and love" must seek their own level. I was a field operative in need of an active field to work in and "A" and

I decided our non-compatibility was not going to work. We decided to stick together to allow her to finish the Masters Degree and I got the call from DS Headquarters, asking me to take the Senior RSO position in Iraq. There seemed to be a certain balance to the two things coming at the same time. It had a bit of that same romantic flavor as the broken-hearted French man joining the French Foreign Legion and being sent to a deserted posting in Africa to get over his broken heart. The biggest romantics in the world are men who have to fight away from family and friends. It is yin and yang, balancing the warrior with the aesthetic side.

My tour in Spain was to be completed in August but DS needed me in Iraq to take over what had become our largest responsibility in the world, by the beginning of June. And, in order to go to Iraq, I would have to complete the very difficult 7 week military/ Agent-type special training program called "High Threat Tactical Course". I would have to begin this in March. The tour in Iraq was just one year but it would be a busy and dangerous one, and hopefully gratifying. I knew it would give me that chance to get over the divorce with my necessity for singular focus on keeping our people in Iraq alive. It would also pay me extra money called "danger pay" and that would help to make up for the large cash settlement of the divorce.

Following our divorce, "A" left for the Washington D.C., area about a week before I did with her household effects and a new life's hope and then I left after putting my effects, with the exception of a single suitcase on wheels, into storage in a USG warehouse in Germany. I have to admit that with my life now taking on a singular focus of this training and then fighting a war and commanding essentially the third largest Army in Iraq, and with my entire life being carried in a single suitcase for the next year,

I felt a sense of relief. My concerns now and for about a year and a half to come would be simply life-safety in nature, with the thousands of lives I would be responsible for, but all the other minutiae that can pick at you and make one's life sometimes unbearable, would be gone. I was about to live the life of a minimalist and I felt relieved and uplifted like I hadn't felt in years. Pressures I wasn't aware I had been carrying fell off me and I smiled and felt like me again after so long. I liked me. I was happy with who I was and what I had become and accomplished. This had been a good thing for both of us.

Chapter Nineteen
HIGH THREAT TACTICAL TRAINING, MARCH – MAY 2006

At almost 56 years old, and having begun to move more into the senior management status for the past couple of years, I knew this training was going to test me completely. No one my age had gone through the course before and HQ was curious and a bit concerned that it might be too much. But what they didn't fully realize was that I was different. Besides my continued strict physical discipline throughout my life (I only weighed 10 pounds more than when I was in High School), I was a person who refused to give up or quit, and of course I had my luck "thing" going for me. I had done some reading on my kind of luck at always just missing being blown up or shot, and being able to recognize or sense danger as it approached me, or when someone bad entered a room and I would be drawn to look at them. Someone had done a study on this sense and it was called "Proximity Sense". I was hoping it would remain active on this next tour. This High Threat Tactical (HTT) Course was harder than Army basic training for 19-year old soldiers. That was fine with me right now. I wanted to re-create that focus in myself and this sounded like it was a challenge that would do that. I also knew that many of the young men in the class with me and even a couple of women, would be working for me in Iraq and it was important that I showed them I am able to fulfill the requirements of the course just as they must and what leadership by example means, and to begin to guide and mentor them not just through the course but to also set them on the correct path through DS. I have always believed that those who work hard for me have a life-long open ticket to call upon me for anything they need in their lives or career and I take it very seriously.

I had worked out regularly in Madrid and was in pretty good shape. That is one thing that will never change in my personal discipline. Staying in good physical condition is an imperative and relates to all other aspect of enjoying life. It was unfortunately also true that I was carrying a lot of long-term injuries with me and past broken parts that never quite healed completely and even an artificial knee and permanently broken ankle with a bone that pushes out the side and prevents complete rotation. All my physical activity was just a bit more difficult and painful for me than for others but I had adapted to accept that in my life and that would not deter me. I knew there would be substantial daily pain in the HTT course, but I was inspired to test myself against these younger men. I love this stuff. Of course, I didn't actually know how hard it was going to be or I might have balked a bit, but I also didn't know how much fun some of it would be. At 55 years old, I was getting to do adventurous things most young men only dream of having the opportunity to learn and do. It would be my new start on life and I was determined to come out of the Iraq tour alive and safe and that goal went for every one of the men and women I was responsible for.

We arrived in the classroom at the DS Training Center our first day and we were to immediately participate in a physical fitness test to see where we stood on conditioning at the beginning of the HTT. It would only involve push-ups, sit-ups, and a 1.5 mile run. The first two wouldn't be so bad but the age thing had taken a toll on my wind and running, not to mention the knee and ankle problem for sustained running pain. To max-out the sit-ups, we needed 60 in one minute. No problem and I hit 60. For push-ups, we also needed 60 in a minute and I did the 60. I could see the young guys were surprised that their new boss was doing more than they were in some cases and they didn't know what to think of it. I had their attention. The run was a different matter though. I needed to save or pace myself on pain and injuries for the knee over the next seven weeks so I would not be sprinting the 1.5 miles. I needed to still have a functional knee at the end of the course seven weeks from now. To hit 85% of my perfect goal on the run, I needed to finish in under 12 minutes and that seemed fine. I would pace it out to do just that. One young man in the class was definitely a world class runner and when we started, he was gone and out of sight in no time. As I approached the half way mark, he was heading for home already. I had about one-third left and I saw the same young man running back toward me as if he was going a second time. As he reached me, he turned and started running with me, encouraging me to pick up the speed. This young man was out here for my inspirational benefit. Well, it did have that effect and I didn't want to let him down or embarrass myself by having this new son run it twice. I was still beating some of the younger men who were behind me but I needed to show him that his effort meant something so I began to run harder and finished in 11 minutes and 10 seconds. Not great, but not bad. This young man's efforts with me were to be a true indicator of the heart and courage I was to witness over and over again by my people in Iraq.

Obviously I won't go through the entire training course but I will tell you about some of the unique and more interesting aspects that were included.

We went through equipment issue which meant the full "kit". The Predator ballistic vest, helmet, handgun and drop-holster, machine gun and 14 magazines, gloves, knee and elbow pads, water "camel pack", and all the other miscellaneous items that one would need to have a chance at surviving in a war-level firefight. When all the gear was on and the magazines were all loaded, we were adding about 65 pounds additional carry-weight. When you see the soldiers running and it seems like they should sprint faster with bullets flying over their heads, try sprinting carrying 65 extra pounds and in boots. Our training would be done most of the time with all this gear on to get us used to what we would endure. The other factor, Iraq gets up to 140 degrees beating down on all this heavy gear.

Our course however, would be done as the freezing weather was ending and the humid and warm weather would be starting up. I hate the cold but in this gear, I hated the heat as well. No complaining. Just do it and be enthusiastic. Some days started at 0400 hours and finished at midnight, starting over again the next morning at 0500 hours. There was almost no time to eat. I was living in a hotel with my one suitcase and my only hope for taking a lunch with me to the woods or the firing range the next day was if the Subway Sandwich across the street stayed open late and I made it back by midnight to get a sandwich to take the next day. I lost the 10 pounds from post-high school and trimmed down like I had not seen myself in 35 years. That part was great, the lack of sleep and swollen knee and freezing weather was the down side. The classroom sessions at various other Agencies was a nice break for us occasionally.

We trained in chemical-biological weapon attacks and decontamination. We learned to assemble and use all the tactical communication gear that would allow us to link up with the military when we needed a rescue or were under attack. We spent a lot of time on the use and value of map reading and Land Navigation as well as incorporating a GPS into the land-nav as back-up for those who didn't read the natural terrain as well. Fortunately, I was raised in the mountains and woods and land navigation just came natural to me. I had also developed some tracking skills.

We also re-learned personal protective tactics but more closely designed for the type of war combat we would be involved in. Whether it was walking and protecting or driving under conditions of roadside bomb attacks like Improvised Explosive Devices (IEDs), or Explosively Formed Projectiles (EFPs), also known as shape charges, it was all now designed for combat survival, not attacks on the streets of Washington, DC.

Helicopters were going to play a big part in our daily operations and in fact, I would have my own RSO Air Wing to manage that included initially 10 helicopters, which were flown and maintained under contract to Blackwater employees, who were some of the most talented, courageous and dedicated men and women I have ever known. So, we spent time learning everything about dealing with the Blackhawk helicopters from communications, getting on and off quickly, where not to walk if we wanted to stay alive and in one piece, and emergency medical response, which was something we anticipated needing.

We spent a lot of time with weapons; all kinds of weapons that constantly hung around my neck and my hand gun that was always in its drop-holster on my thigh, to larger crew-served machine guns like the M249, and even the M-203 grenade launcher, with which I qualified as a Grenadier. It also meant learning to use our optical sites and our night vision gear for shooting and driving to become competent no matter the environment or time of day and night. We had to qualify and re-qualify on all these weapons until we were almost sick of them and that is hard to do with an Agent. We love the skill time with weapons. We loved it a little less in all the gear but we understood the necessity. We fired in rain storms, snow storms, and sleet storms. I remember one day when it snowed on us three separate times just during the morning as we lay in the freezing mud and snow shooting downrange. We ran and shot, we shot and ran, we dive-rolled and shot and ran, we drove, rolled, shot and ran. We fired in the dark, in the light, in woods, in fields, from cars and into cars, and we began our "close quarter battle drills (CQB)" and "room clearing" tactics for going into dangerous buildings to purge snipers or insurgents. This was also done during the day and the night when we went in using our night vision capabilities and special optics to rapidly pinpoint the shot to the enemy. We did every maneuver that could be imagined so that we incorporated all those experiences into our personal skill set. And we just kept doing it over and over 12 to 15 hours a day, mixing it in with all the other training we needed. Each new skill we incorporated was adding to the package that would be required as we advanced through the course. Ex-Army, Marine, and Navy Special Forces personnel were our instructors and they were tough but good. They knew what we would be going into and they wanted all of us to have the best chance of succeeding possible. And at the end of each long day, all the weapons got broken down and cleaned. Then on the way back to my hotel I would hope to find a place to buy food to carry in my pack for the next day before trying to get a few hours sleep and start all over again.

We spent a weekend at a gym on one of the local Army bases for the purpose of practicing fighting and defensive tactics – in full gear. This included grappling or wrestling as you might think of it, and in the gear, until we got the hang of leveraging our gear weight into the process, we were sort of like turtles stuck on our backs. Some very experienced and talented people taught us how to maneuver into choke holds and out of them twisting and balancing ourselves around. At the end of each day we were totally exhausted and the vest and equipment had cut our bodies up and left us bruised everywhere but it was fascinating and rewarding and this sort of activity was really trimming any excess weight off me. The artificial knee was always swollen now and most parts hurt day and night, but thank you Ibuprofen.

One of the really unique experiences in training was held at a training facility in West Virginia. This was meant to enhance our driving skills and that has always been a special expertise of a DS Agent since we protect world leaders. We have to be able to drive bumper to bumper in a formation at 100 miles an hour and anticipate each other's moves. This was different. We were going to learn to drive at midnight with no lights and with one eye using the night vision goggle (NVG) and the other blind in the pitch-black. It took awhile to get the balance and perception and the NVG gives a limited view and sometimes you miss spotting holes or objects but by the time we finished the training, were doing high-speed driving and off-road driving through dense woods with a relative professionalism. In Iraq at night, in the desert, this skill would come in very handy. While it was true that I would be the boss of my 2,350 person armed security team, and would spend most of my time in Saddam's Palace doing work that would keep my team alive or giving orders to rescue people, I needed to understand completely, what circumstances and limitations my people would be working under. At the time, I didn't know that the enemy would bring the action to the Palace consistently.

The other intriguing and fun part of this training was the true off-road training we received. I do not mean like the off-road driving that civilians do in the U.S. This was unlike anything I had ever conceived or heard of. We learned how to set and maintain the RPMs at a forceful level with one foot and regulate our movement and speed with only mitigating the brake. This maximized the control and power to go over any terrain.

We simply drove through woods, plowing down trees and running over anything we wanted to in order to get to where the instructor said to go. I was impressed and stunned at what these jeeps could do. We didn't go fast, we just went anywhere and everywhere. We learned to navigate through thick wet deep mud puddles, over rocks and huge boulders where we leveraged one tire on one boulder at a time with the rest of the team filling in large gaps as the driver negotiated one wheel and then waited while we made it possible to go over the next. This was done on a steep 45 degree angle going up and then down. I would have bet that this sort of thing was impossible before actually doing it. In Iraq, we were experiencing numerous IEDs disabling our vehicles after being hit and part of our training was learning how to hook up a tow strap in seconds and pull the car and the injured men to safety. If the car was destroyed, we also practiced cross-loading our injured to another vehicle while providing cover fire against the enemy. There was forever the weapons practice.

I will always remember with a sense of excitement and laughter, when one time driving through the woods, or really, over the woods, the instructor took the wheel and drove to a quarry and stopped. We all got out and looked down at the virtual straight down dead-drop embankment that reached the bottom 20 feet below. It was cool and we thought it was a break until the instructor asked us if we thought we could go over the edge of the "cliff" and survive. We laughed as we thought it was a joke until he said "get in, let's try it" and I said to him that I thought it was physically impossible to go over a cliff without ending up crashed on our roof top. He smiled and we got in and tightened our seat belts as tight as we could. None of us were going to back out of this training exercise even if he was insane. He lined the car up at a 90 degree angle to the cliff edge and we began to edge toward the lip of the cliff literally one inch at a time. As the front tires began to go over the edge, he kept control of the car, still allowing only fractions of movement and very controlled. We found ourselves with the front tires hanging over the edge, not making contact with earth and the back tires continued an inch at a time, nudging us forward. As the back tires reached the edge, the front grill and all of us in the car were looking straight down at the bottom of the cliff. We were literally hanging over the edge by the back tires. I seem to remember my only final preparation was a phrase that slipped out automatically when I looked at the ground straight below and I said "holy shit". So much for any final words of wisdom. Hanging from the back tires, he slowly allowed the brake to release a bit more and the tires reached that point of leverage where the jeep released and we went head first, straight down, hitting the earth but staying erect and leaning against the cliff, and not rolling over onto our roof. At that point, I heard similar words of wisdom from each member of the team in the car. But quickly, the instructor gave the tires some power and the jeep nudged our front grill out of the dirt and up and the vehicle righted itself and we drove off into the quarry. Wow, that was great. Then we came to the realization that we were stuck in a quarry. How were we going to get out? Certainly not the same way. I knew I could safely bet my money on that. He pointed to a softer dirt portion but it was a steep 60 degree angle if it was a minute and also didn't seem possible. Nonetheless, this was a learning day and sure enough, he raced for it and up we went, spinning and swerving our way to the top. Another miracle. We got back up to the cliff where we started and all got out to once again look over the edge to reconcile what we had just done. It still looked impossible and dangerous. Then after taking several deep breaths, the instructor said, "who's next"? So, not wanting to admit that we couldn't do anything any other person could do and had done, we each took our turn driving over the cliff and then fighting our way back up, sometimes taking several attempts to get back up. It was terrific and changed my entire perspective on what off-roading actually can be. Fortunately, he didn't make us do it in the dark using NVGs.

We continued doing things that were creative with Hummvees and Jeeps and sedans and took them onto a race track for speed drills as well and of course practiced shooting as we drove. The instructors set off pyrotechnics on the track to similate IEDs and EFPs and we had to properly respond to survive. It was all a great learning experience. On one such exercise, we were told to do the entire 3 mile race track course at high speed but backwards and I don't mean the opposite direction. We drove backing up at high speed including through the explosions and serpentine barriers until it almost felt normal. Obviously part of the reason for this type of exercises is to instill confidence and a sense that there is nothing you can't do and no emergency that doesn't have a solution. It worked.

We practiced our skills at mapping our way through woods and using the terrain formations to find our way to various specific spots deep in the woods and then on to another mapped spot. Being born and raised a mountain boy, I never felt better than when I was free-walking through the woods. I can look at a map with the terrain lines marked and look out into the woods and know just where I need to go to find the spot on the map. We paired up and my partner was a big friendly Bulgarian/American young man who was expert with his GPS. Since I didn't trust the GPS method, we were able to double check each other. I got him quickly to the approximate point on the map and then he used the GPS to fix the spot within a yard and we always found our hidden marker. We certified on the course so fast that we were the first ones to return and after two hours of waiting at the finish, we were still the only ones home so the Instructor asked us if we would like to run another course. It was hot and we were in full gear but being in the woods gave me a sense of freedom and my partner liked it too so we mapped out our routes and set off on a second course. An hour and a half later we returned from a perfect trail, hitting each mark and there were still four groups out on their first run. Three came in shortly thereafter but one was still missing. This worried a few of us so we began to devise a plan to grid search for them. It only took 30 minutes and we located them and brought them back, tired and worn out but not harmed.

We worked intensely also on our advanced tactics for close quarter drill or "room clearing." We became very proficient with clearing a building and precisely killing all targets at a running speed, from room to room. Silent but fast and precise. The confidence was surging. This team I was working with was going to make me proud in Iraq and I vowed to bring them all back alive. They were now my family and no one was going to take my family away.

We practiced our trauma medical treatment and re-learned the techniques for bullet wounds, sucking chest wounds, and of course the usual and varied head wounds that were affecting so many of our folks in Iraq now. We would work our way through thick woods, up and down mountains in full 65 pound kit and then stop to practice techniques before returning to where we had come from but from a different direction. It was all coming together.

We began our instructional time on the Blackhawk helicopters and incorporated their capabilities into our maneuvers. Now we ran while shooting, treated one another, carried some on stretchers we made on the spot, found vehicles and drove a distance, abandoned the car as broken, then pursued a course through woods, searching for the magic helicopter landing zone (HLZ), while being barraged by grenades and chased by snipers. Eventually, many hours later, we came to the HLZ, loaded our casualties and flew home to base to begin the skill refinement again the next day with new challenges and new twists thrown in. And I still hoped to be home before Subway closed so I would have food the next day.

Week seven came after about ten years of hard work in varying days of freezing cold and heat and humidity and we were all hoping the final exercise would go well and that none of us would embarrass ourselves. We "final-rehearsed" all our combined skills through what was called comprehensive skills days and then the final day came. The event would be all day and would encompass all the various new skill sets we had acquired as well as introduce us to some surprises to test our natural judgment.

We gathered in the early morning in a constructed Iraqi city in the middle of a densely wooded area of an immense military base far away from the normal world and it was very realistic. My day started on a personal high point. Several Secret Service SWAT Team members had come to watch our final test day. They had tried similar training in their organization but theirs had not worked and ours was gaining a reputation. The much younger SWAT leader introduced himself to me and stared at me. I was trim in the waist and broad at the shoulders and in tough shape. I am 5 feet 10 inches tall and had begun the course at 171 pounds and was now 157pounds lean and was in full kit. He knew how hard this course was supposed to be even on the young men and he asked me how old I was. I looked him direct in the eyes with a small smirk and told him 55, and he continued to stare. Then he made it all worthwhile when he shook his head and said, "when I get your age, I want to be just like you." OK, now I was ready to take on the final exercise.

The final day would begin realistically as much of our actual high threat time did in Iraq – protecting someone and moving through dangerous country where the enemy wants to kill you while you attempted to get to point "A", where your "Protectee" needed to go. We were driving fully armored Suburbans and felt we were totally equipped to handle whatever was thrown at us. The route specified led us to drive out on a road running through meadows, fields and wooded areas. After we had driven about 20 minutes away from Little Iraq City through what continued to look like perfect attack sites, we were given orders to reverse course and take our Protectee back to an appointment in Little Iraq City. As we approached the town, now there were people everywhere, walking through the town as if this was actually a town in Iraq or at least a sector of Baghdad. There was also Arabic music playing and activity everywhere. All sense of order vanished and the town's activity and our unfamiliarity with the nature and business of this town threw everything into a sense of seat-of-the-pants chaos. We were going to have to do this the hard way. We had no advance person to give us a situational report (sitrep) and we needed to take our Protectee into the town and to an office we had no control over and no insight into the layout. Months later in Saddar City, we would see that this is how every day is; a constant gamble with lives.

Since we did not have guidance that these people were the enemy, we were prohibited from pointing weapons at them or being rough with them. We were to diplomatically negotiate our way through the city streets on foot, paying very close observation to every window, door, face and movement. Though we were not loaded with live lethal ammunition, we were loaded with Simunitions rounds that fired just the same, hurt a lot, leaving a wound, and making a mark on you indicating you had been hit. These stung like crazy and could blind someone not in gear and would even embed itself into your skin.

As we moved tactically and with a coordination enabling a 360 degree observation and protection of our "package", the amount of movement and action around us made us feel very vulnerable. We ordered our vehicles to go around the block since they couldn't pass through the narrow road and they were waiting for us at the opposite end. As we neared the appointment building, shots rang out, people ran, guns came up and we all were pointed at different windows and doors while those protecting the Protectee had moved him inside a doorway and covered him with their bodies.

HIGH THREAT TACTICAL TRAINING | 309

Someone yelled "gun, second floor 12 o'clock" and "the game" was on. We fired at the enemy and they tried to get clear shots at us as we ran for the vehicles trying to maintain a complete circle of coverage. We radioed ahead that we were taking fire, continuing to run and told them to be ready to move. They were radioed in and listening to us and were waiting to go with the cars lined up to race away, offering us an armored box to protect ourselves in. We ran from doorway to window and side alley, always looking for the enemy to stick a barrel out of a window or show himself and when he did, we took him out. These rounds hurt them as well.

Once in the cars, we raced for the outskirts of the city to get some distance between ourselves and an enemy with unknown capabilities. Our Protectee was unhurt and showed no marks. As we flew down our advance-planned road of escape, we had only gone about 250 yards when one of the cars was directed to be disabled by a rocket. We immediately pulled the other two cars up to the sides of the dead car and cross-loaded the passengers and what was now a designated wounded Agent into the two remaining vehicles and fled.

We reached about two miles from the town when the next action event occurred. A roadside bomb destroyed one of the two remaining cars. We couldn't all fit into the remaining car and were best suited for survival by keeping our resources together. The protective vest and gear was taken off the wounded Agent and put on the Protectee. This allowed us to cut the weight down on carrying a wounded guy on a soft stretcher, which got very tiring very quickly, running with him and your 65 pounds of gear and weapons. We quickly constructed the carrying stretcher and placed the wounded Agent on it as we started taking incoming mortar rounds from the enemy who had followed us from the town. They might have been semi-non-lethal mortars but when they hit, they knocked us down and you knew absolutely that a hit would be a real termination. Plus, they took our sense of hearing away and we were reduced in our own personal sensory capabilities. We grabbed the stretcher and began to fire back at the enemy as we all moved quickly in a spread-out formation into the woods ahead of us and in the compass direction of a known and mapped helicopter landing zone about 6 miles away. Moving with heavy wounded and equipment, as well as the protectee, with an enemy chasing for six miles would take hours to reach it if nothing else happened. Figure the odds.

We were providing a buffer distance for the group carrying the wounded and running the Protectee. We needed them to get ahead of us and the enemy since they were moving slower so we fought back to stop the enemy from gaining on us. They were lobbing mortars and grenades, which staggered us when they hit close. We did hit a few of them and they realized that they needed to change their chasing tactic. We began to move quickly away to catch up to the rest of our unit and after about another mile, I was declared wounded. The remaining team members now had to make a quick stretcher under fire and get me on it. I hated being designated wounded. I wanted to fight back. I did what I could to assist anyway and gave guidance but had to stop once that was realized. The objective was to remove the leadership and see how the team cooperates and continues on in an organized fashion. With me being silent, they did exactly what they were trained to do and did it professionally. I was going to love having these talented guys working for me in Iraq.

Working the compass and terrain maps, corroborating with the

GPS, continuing to run and fire carrying a stretcher that required changing position so that the arms didn't get too fatigued, and trying to lose the enemy and get to the Helicopter Landing Zone (HLZ) was quite a task and we had been going for hours, not to mention all the adrenaline we had spent from the first attack in Little Iraq City. Everyone was under constant hydration to compensate for the hottest day so far and running on fumes for energy.

Hours passed and we were united with our other team element and approaching what seemed to be the correct coordinates for our helicopter extraction. It was an open field with wooded areas surrounding it. This was a perfect place for the enemy to conduct their final surprise. They could wait until we ran into the open to mark the field and then once the helo landed, we would have to move into the open to load up.

The radio announced I was no longer wounded and I recovered in a flash and started to look for options, but we still had one wounded Agent and a Protectee to deal with. I sent two-man teams in each direction around through the woods to clear the entire perimeter of enemy and meet on the other side so we would know we were safe when we ran. They would remain on the other side and come out when we started to move. This improved our odds substantially since we now had a large part of the perimeter under observation.

The HLZ was marked and we called the "birds" in to extract us. Within minutes we heard the rotors and then saw the familiar, and by now greatly welcome, Blackhawks coming our way. They touched down and we went as fast as our tired bodies would allow, but with those not carrying or supporting someone, maintaining a 360 degree cover fire if needed. We didn't need the cover fire and soon we were buckled in and flying away to debrief.

Once we were back to our base, the debriefing was concluded and we were all happy with the results. This team had worked like we had been trained and there was respect and confidence, as well as a realistic humility at what it would be like for real, having made an impact on us all.

That night, I slept for 12 hours. The first night I had slept more than 3 or 4 hours in a long time. My entire body was in pain, was covered in bruises that I had kept throughout the entire seven weeks, and my plastic right knee was swollen badly, but I felt like I had really accomplished something significant. I believe I slept with a smile on my face. I can't say enough positive about the retired Special Forces guys who had brought us to this point of expertise in only seven weeks (and I think had been our enemy during the final exercise). This had been harder than my pre-Viet Nam Army Basic Training had been when I was 19 years old and I had come out of it a lot better prepared than I was back then. Their training would keep many of our guys alive and even more of those we had to protect. This would be my fourth war of varied types – Viet Nam, The First Gulf War, the War in Angola, and this Second Gulf (Iraq) War. I knew my responsibilities would be greater in this one, commanding my own "Army", but I felt more prepared and more aware of what to expect than I ever had before.

Two days later, we had a chance to be together as an entire class again and we said our goodbyes and for some, our "see you laters" since they would be joining me in Iraq soon. Gear and weapons were cleaned, checked, and turned in. Our equipment and weapons would be waiting for us in Iraq when we arrived. For those of us going to Iraq, we were told we could only take one bag that we could run with once we hit the tarmac in Baghdad. Anything more would slow us down and make us sniper fodder. We all took them at their word.

From here, I had two weeks to see my family out west and then would fly on to my one-year tour and adventures perhaps like none I had ever had before. During the latter half of the training, we had been given a weekend of "down time" due to training changes and my sister Barbara had driven up to see me. I would not have a chance to see her again for a year and she is very special to me. I feel like we are the most similar of all our family and we have always had a different communication than with the rest. I was grateful for the time. She has always been my strongest supporter. Now, with this being my fourth war, I hoped I was prepared for the adventure.

Chapter Twenty

THE CALM BEFORE THE STORM

I flew from Washington, DC to Phoenix Sky Harbor Airport and rented a car and drove to Tempe, where my family home front is located. Since I had no actual home of my own, my U.S. government home address is my Mother's address. Having lived overseas for about 14 years consecutively now, it worked well because it allowed me to go back to where the family is to check on them ever year or three. I thought I might look for a home to invest in and maybe return to at a later date for retirement. It was summer 2006, could I have picked any worse time to put my money into a home just as the home market was beginning to crash.

I spent a number of days with the family, catching up on whose babies were having babies and all the new names I couldn't associate with yet but it was always fun. My family all love kids. I must have 100 nieces and nephews and when I spend time seeing them all, it is great to see the new little faces and see those innocent children and to be reminded why I do what I do for a living. It really isn't for me although I have been fortunate to find a job I love. I do it for those kids.

Well, after a few days of the actual goo goo ga ga, I was played out and though happy to see children again, I got in the car and started driving. I headed up through northern Arizona and went east into New Mexico. I have made a few trips in and out of Santa Fe and Taos, New Mexico, and had always thought they might be nice places for a guy with my background to settle down one day and be innocuous with some land to isolate myself and just find my niche. I had been Googling real estate in New Mexico and made contact with a realtor in each location.

I drove to Santa Fe and made contact with the realtor there. She took me to a home she said was outside my price parameters by some distance but that it was so unique she just had to show me. Damn, I should have been hip to that psychological approach. It was adobe, sitting on 5.5 acres of land on a hill backing against a mountain with bear and cougar, overlooking Santa Fe, just a short 6 miles into town. The home had an indoor and an outdoor fountain with small pools and it was just so cool. OK, so now let's go look at what I can afford. Crap. Everything else I looked at just didn't seem to make an impression after that first one. I went back to the first house several times and it was beginning to get its roots into me. It was way past my financial limits, especially after the divorce, but I knew I would make extra money while in Iraq and hey, wasn't it a good investment and tax assist. Where were the people saying "buddy, here comes a housing crash and a serious period of economic destruction. Hey, I was a warrior at this point and pretty much out of tune with the U.S. movements and culture. I missed the key notes and told the realtor I was interested. Dammit.

While working on the purchase package including financing and negotiations etc…, I received a phone call at my hotel from a man named Michael Winterbottom. He is a Hollywood Movie

Director and he said he was the one who was going to direct the movie of the same name as the book, "A Mighty Heart" about the kidnapping and murder by Al-Qaeda of the Wall Street Journalist Daniel Pearl. He knew of my involvement and stated I was one of the seven main characters in the movie. He said whereas the book was a love story, he wanted to include some of the action in the movie and would like a chance to meet with me to talk about what we did on the case. This was pretty interesting and I told him I was in Santa Fe and would be heading for Iraq in about a week. He said he was in New York City and heading for Los Angeles and would stop in Santa Fe and buy me dinner so we could talk about the action sequences. It was fine with me. He also got my interest when he told me Mariane would be played by Angelina Jolie and Brad Pitt was a Co-Producer.

Michael arrived the next afternoon and had reserved a hotel room at the same classic hotel I was staying in and we arranged to meet at a specific time for dinner. At the designated time, I knocked on his door and we walked down to the plaza to find a restaurant. Michael is a very personable man and I liked him. I hadn't been sure I would. I know nothing of his world or industry except the bizarre things we see in the tabloids about the craziness. We walked around Santa Fe's beautiful little tree-filled plaza where free concerts are given at night and the grown up hippies of yesterday have settled into their pleasant liberal lives and it was quite the Yin to the Yang of my life. I loved it.

We found a restaurant and sat and ordered the first of two bottles of wine and dinner. Michael wasn't high pressure or pushy in any way. He just wanted to know from my perspective what we had done to try and get Danny back. I was very honest with him but also told him when certain things could not be used or presented.

He was agreeable. He seemed to only be looking for a way to "represent" our nightly raids and shootouts to give the idea about what we went through and to bring some action into the film. For that reason, I gave him a thorough perspective for a "big picture" understanding but told him his parameters for use, including mandatory clearance by the U.S. State Department. I liked him. I felt comfortable with him. He seemed a normal guy and could listen well and was obviously bright. I get bored quickly with people who aren't fast thinkers and Michael is definitely a sharp man. After quite a few hours of discussion, and two full bottles of wine, Michael asked me who I thought could play me in the movie. I thought about it for awhile but the question was so preposterous to me from the basic concept of someone playing me in a movie, my response certainly couldn't be a serious one, so I said "George Castanza", meaning the short bald character from the Seinfeld TV series. Michael stared at me for a couple of minutes not sure if I was serious and then I let him off the hook and said I was joking and had no idea. He said they had a few prospects, one being Will Patton, who is such an exceptional Actor. I was thrilled and impressed. Michael and I walked back to the hotel, said goodbye, and that we would keep in touch, and for some reason, that brief connection to the world of glamour and glitz made me feel like maybe my adventures weren't quite as exciting as I thought. That wore off quickly as I refocused on closing on my home and preparing for battle in Iraq. We would see if anything came from this movie concept but right now, there were other "real and tangible" things I had to deal with. I drove to Tempe, Arizona, to say goodbye to my family and headed off to my next big adventure.

Chapter Twenty-One
RSO Iraq, June 2006 - July 2007

I had covered a lot of ground and done many things in the 18 years my career had covered up to now. I had made changes in the job and the job had greatly changed me. I wasn't the same person I was when I started out in 1987. That is normal for all of us no matter what we do but I had been through things that other Agents had not and I could feel the differences. On the positive side I could feel a sense of calm and confidence that comes with experience, and especially from multiple times living through the experience of death and destruction. But, I could also feel a darkness that I kept to myself. My feelings about the enemy no longer fell easily into the categories that Federal Law Enforcement Officers were supposed to uphold. I had learned that in order to beat the enemy, you had to think like them, and to at least a degree, a degree that would not be acceptable to our law enforcement standards, you had to act and be like them. They had to fear you and you had to behave with them in a manner that they understood. They laughed at our weakness and knew that if they just waited, we would eventually feel sorry for them and release them back to their acts of terror again, but with a great deal more knowledge about us and how to terrorize us better. We needed to be an equal evil but for good.

The journey to Iraq was just like it should have been to maintain my history. We had a transit in Paris and while there, we were all evacuated from the airport for a bomb threat and we were delayed an additional 2.5 hours. It was handled in a totally unprofessional and chaotic way. The French seemed to have no experience at all with this sort of response. Some people wandered back to the gate where the bomb technicians were, to watch them work at "ground zero". Others left the airport and came back in later to our hallway past the security unchecked. Those of us who just wanted to continue on our flight were told to wait, sitting on the stone floor in a direct-line hallway 100 yards from where they thought the bomb might be. If it had gone off, or if there was one at all, the detonation would have followed a fast direct-effect line to us and depending on the size, at least some of us would have died. It was a half-hearted and half-witted wasted exercise. They finally decided it was nothing and we continued on to Amman, Jordan, where the Embassy had a special section that just dealt with those going into Iraq. They were exceptional and very compassionate. We were treated almost royally, sort of like it was our last meal. I was exhausted from the 26 hours I had already been traveling without rest. As I exited the airport customs area in Amman, I saw a man holding a sign with my name on it. He saw I had only the usual prescribed one bag and didn't try to take it from me but said he was from the Embassy's Iraq operation and he would take me to the hotel for the night and we would be coming back the next day to depart for Iraq. I had been in Amman years before and it was nice to see the growth and modernization it had gone through. When we pulled up to a beautiful five-star hotel, I was impressed and elated. I checked-in speaking jibberish from my fatigue but they were prepared for me and for my jibberish and soon I was in a fabulous bed (the last one for a long time), and sleeping soundly – also the last sound sleep for years.

The next morning after I had a chance to eat a great breakfast, I checked out and was again picked up efficiently and taken to the airport. I loved this Amman operation. What I was not yet aware of was that we didn't allow our people to fly into Baghdad on commercial air due to the threat from the Saddarist/Bathist party terrorists. Getting into or out of Iraq is the most difficult and complicated part of the whole trip. You are not supposed to land on the commercial side of the airport in Baghdad because the Insurgents will shoot you down out of the sky or mortar the plane when it lands, so you can only come in at night and you tightly circle in for a landing on the better-controlled military side. That meant you had to deal with the military which flew us in on basic model C-130s, - hot, very uncomfortable nylon strap seats, and you needed ear plugs or you would be deaf when you landed. For some reason, someone had made a mistake and put me on a Royal Jordanian flight and I followed my guide. Three hours in the waiting lounge between 200 people all smoking and we finally departed. Within 2 hours, we were landing at BIAP (Baghdad International Airport) and here began my new understanding of what it meant to be the Commander of the third largest Army in Iraq with my own helicopter wing and 2,350 armed professionals to back up my orders.

As I walked off the plane, to the side on the tarmac were two dark blue helicopters and a dozen heavily armed men in what looked like my type of equipment and gear. A young man in similar gear approached me and called me by name. Others surrounded me and walked me over in a protective diamond to the helicopters and made sure I got properly strapped in. These were two of our "little birds" that flew fast and acrobatically. They held two pilots in front, one door gunner on the right rear and either another door gunner on the left rear or in my case, one passenger. The pilots were really the acrobatic controls and they were the best in the world. They were the same actual men who survived the "Blackhawk Down" incident and were now retired Special Forces contractors working for me under the Blackwater contract. When I say I strapped myself in, that is not quite correct. The doors don't exist and you sit on the edge of where the door would be with your feet and legs and part of your torso outside the helicopter, standing on two metal pegs. A nylon strap is wrapped around you to keep you from falling out when the Pilots bank left and you are literally looking straight down at the earth. The birds were already rotating and ready to go. They were given orders to make sure they got "the boss" safely to Saddam's Palace and they intended to do so no matter how radically they had to fly back. There were also two large Blackhawks that had been arranged to act as attack cover and to be the insurance policy that the new Commander didn't have a short and disappointing tour. The flight was only about 20 minutes but the pilots flew anything but a normal straight pattern. I think they might have been testing the new Chief to see if I would throw-up, but the flight was fast, and with a lot of turns and radical left and right banks, which meant I was a "hanging angel" outside the bird much of the time. I couldn't let them know, but I loved it. They probably thought I was a "desk jockey" but this sort of thing perfectly met my adrenaline need. Nonetheless, we did fly into the Green zone and land across the street from the PX and the huge Embassy compound known as "The Palace". This was my new territory of control. Waiting for me were a number of my key Agents and some of our armored vehicles to take me inside the Embassy controlled zone and to my new home.

My home was a "container", or small 10 foot by 15 foot trailer. There were two containers connected in the middle by a shared bathroom. The room contained a (smaller than) single bed with a mattress that was like concrete, a small table with one chair, one air conditioning unit, a small hanging closet, one TV, one VCR, and one small refrigerator. Perfect. It contained the basics for life and considering I would only be in the room for about 4 hours a night, it would be fine. My entire focus for the year would be work and more work, a simple Spartan existence with minimal possessions. The meals were all provided as was the laundry service. Everything was designed to allow a single purpose to every moment with no distractions or concerns, except staying alive of course. And my focus was to keep everyone here alive. That was THE job.

Though it was only June, the first three days we had an early "heat flash" and it was 124 degrees. People kept saying "yeah, but it is a dry heat, which being from Phoenix has always really annoyed me. It is just a matter of baking or broiling. On the plane or during my travel, I had caught a bad bug and during my first two nights, I was violently ill all night long and became desperately dehydrated. I tried to catch up with the dehydration but was just too low and finally took myself to the medical unit in the Palace/Embassy. They pumped two liters of fluid into my veins in just 40 minutes. I plumped up like the Pillsbury dough-boy and had to pee every 10 minutes for the next several hours but it did the trick and I was back on the mark.

I didn't understand the true significance of my position here for the first week as I sorted things out. The RSO in other Embassies is certainly a strong position but I had no idea of the impact here. I first started to get the idea when I was standing in the food line and the military person standing next to me asked what Section or Agency I worked in. I said I was the new RSO and the place went quiet and everyone in the line turned to look at me. I thought I had just violated a cardinal rule of revealing myself or was showing obvious signs of the Ebola virus. Then everyone began to whisper while staring. I could hear them saying, "hey that's the RSO". What the hell did this all mean? I would soon learn that the thousands of persons in and out of the Palace and my grounds all knew their safety and security rested in the hands of the RSO Section and that we were the ones who rescued civilians and military when they got attacked and blown up. This reaction, which continued my entire tour was a bit unnerving but I eventually became accustomed to people pointing at me and saying "hey, that's the RSO". It certainly worked well when I needed people to run or clear an area quickly, which happened way too frequently. But also unfortunately, it meant that I was always under total scrutiny and there could be no mistakes, and my personal life was zero and I couldn't have any involvement even if a woman threw herself at me (OK, I threw that line in just for the humor, considering that there were thousands of young, fit, good looking guys for them to choose from) because it would be all over the camp within minutes, and the image, respect and credibility would be out the window. Literally, I would have to be the image that they had created of my position. Yin and Yang again. It always comes down to the good with the bad.

The DFAC (cafeteria) was incredible. There was way too much food and it was all excellent. Whoever gave the contract to KBR for the food should be our next President. The variety of choices at every meal was unbelievable. Breakfast was eggs, Belgian waffles, every type of breakfast meats, fruits of all varieties, every cereal, pasties to kill for, grits, oatmeal, etc… Lunch was six different main choices or cold cuts, sandwiches, fruit, 10 different salads and on and on. But dinner was the killer. Every night would be a half dozen main choices from lobster, shrimp, prime rib, meat loaf, macaroni, etc... and all the dozens of side choices and desserts by the truck load. You simply took what you wanted. There was no limit and no restriction. This was a major problem. We watched people put on 10 pounds in their first two weeks from the "big eyes" syndrome. It was a two-edge sword. On the one hand, the only "comfort" we had was the food. There simply was nothing else that was our positive distraction. On the other hand, I couldn't have my men and women getting out of condition. And there were four meals a day in case you worked the midnight shift or just wanted to eat again.

It became part of my briefing to all Agents that they had to watch their food intake and exercise regularly. There was no choice. I checked on them regarding their workouts and watched them for bodily inflation. Our job was too critical to have them slowing down in a life or death crisis. Everyone depended on us to take care of them and that might include running to them, throwing them over our shoulder or dragging them at a full run to safety. The worst part, there was unlimited Hagen-Das ice cream just for the asking. A person might just as well pour it down their pants because it was surely going to end up on their ass anyway. Even I had to set up an eating discipline. I required a period of "comfort zone" too, so I would watch my fried shrimp in-take and only allow myself ice cream once a month. Nice job though KBR. You made life and death bearable.

The gym was a state-of-the-art operation and the equipment was the best. My regimen became a workout from 0430 until 0600, a shower and catch a quick cereal breakfast and be in my office by 0700 hours working. There were early morning attacks that obviously had me in earlier or all night but this worked out pretty well. I would allow myself Friday morning off from the gym as a psychological high point since Friday was their Saturday and I would sleep an extra hour and still be in the office by 0630 or 0700 hours. I had to set some positive psychological markers for myself as an internal morale control and this and monitoring the "pie-chart" tour countdown was the other.

To start off understanding the scope of our operation, the RSO controlled hundreds of armored vehicles, as well as helicopters, John Deere "gators" (high speed stronger golf carts), and military-type assault and protection special vehicles like Saxons, Mambas, Grisslies, Strikers, and of course numerous Hummvees. The Gators were like ATVs on steroids and I also used them to jet to the PX or around the Green Zone for a change of air.

I quickly toured the entire Green Zone (now called the International Zone or IZ) in order to understand what we had to deal with and that included the bombed out buildings, Saddam's cross swords on his parade grounds, the various torn down statues of Saddam and his large "Busts" lying in fields. The Palace itself was about 300 plus yards long and was divided into what we called the North Wing where my offices were located, the Center Section where the main entrances were and also numerous offices and conference rooms and a lot of military operations, and the South Wing, where the mini-DFAC was located for lighter meals and the Medical Center as well as hundreds of other offices. The South Wing also contained the Green Bean Café where you could actually spend money to buy "Starbucks" like coffees and muffins. It was also one of the mental health and welfare centers with books, open internets and places to sit and be normal until the next rocket came through the roof. It would take 10 minutes to walk from one end of the Palace to the other and there were numerous ways one could select to vary the route for entertainment purposes. The bathrooms were the size of a private home and in the beginning had gold fixtures. Those were taken out to protect them. The entire Palace was cavernous and had 50 foot ceilings.

Beyond all this other description, life was a serious matter and the environment made it clear that this is a war zone. We were reminded of that in every way and by everything we saw. Every trailer was "walled-in" by stacks of sandbags intended to catch the lethal shrapnel when a rocket hit near your trailer. Sandbags also line every walkway and every area we hung out in. There were also concrete bomb bunkers positioned all over the compound. If you heard the whistling of a large rocket overhead coming down, it would be best if you were in a bunker instead of your tin-walled "trailer". The buildings showed the obvious signs of prior attacks and various compounds and buildings were named for those who were killed previously. There were also U.S. military uniformed people everywhere as you would expect and more Colonels and Generals than I have ever seen in one place. There were literally full-bird Colonels by the hundreds and they seemed to be the staff in Baghdad, rather than the leaders.

The humor was dark here and everything seemed a bit surrealistic but I have been through all this before and I felt comfortable and almost at home. Even in this heat, I never saw too many people in the large Olympic sized pool but I did see people running for exercise in the blast-furnace air. I liked being here. It was the place to be at the most important time to be here.

Saddam's trial had begun a few blocks away from our Palace and within the first week I was in Baghdad, the infamous terrorist

Al-Zarqawi was finally killed and the world got just a little bit better. The work hours got established for my regimen as Sunday through Thursday (the regular work week) from 0700 to 2200 hours and Friday and Saturday (our weekend) from 0800 until 2000 hours for a break. Of course, with the regularity of the attacks, we worked whenever the rockets fell and the Insurgents loved to launch around 0200 in the morning. Fortunately the Green Bean coffee shop is open 24 hours a day and busy almost all the time.

This was the initial perspective on my new assignment and it was all within the first week of my tour so it was inevitable that it would change in some ways. All in all, I felt good being here and it was obvious that the assignment was bigger than I ever could have imagined it to be. The level of responsibility was huge and involved the entire country. Our main operational centers where I had other RSOs stationed included Basrah in the south, Al-Hillah in the South-central, Kirkuk in the north-central, Irbil in the north, and Mosul had just been closed down as a diplomatic operation and was military only. We received total support from our DS associates in Washington and as our number one oversight manager and supporter used to say – "All Iraq, All the Time." He created that slogan for himself and us and he lived it and practiced it. Many times, he was a lifesaver for us. My entire team in and those out of Iraq were terrific.

I decided that the adventures in Iraq would probably be noteworthy and began a diary. I turned the monthly diary notes of events, tragedies and incidents into a monthly family letter to let them know some of what was going on. I obviously cut parts out that a typical protected and naïve religious American family would not deal with well and with so many young nieces and nephews who would be in on the reading, I had to watch the gore and cruelty. There was obviously going to be a fair amount of that.

JUNE 02 THROUGH JUNE 21, 2006:

There was never a dull moment in Iraq. Baghdad was the center of the activity and we never had a time when we could just sit back and take a deep breath and put our feet up to talk about what had transpired and where we would go next. We just had to keep running as fast as we could and hope things didn't get past us. In the first week of this reporting period, Al-Zarqawi was identified through some excellent on-the-ground intelligence and verified through those brilliant predators. The Hellfire rockets were launched and his reign of terror was ended. This same week, maybe coincidentally, maybe not, President Bush decided to make a surprise visit to the Palace and express his gratitude for everyone's efforts. The Secret Service decided they would come in under the cover of another Agency so no one would wonder who they were or ask what they were doing. Of course all RSO staff noticed these people who were out of place in our backyard. My DS Agents were the smartest, most alert and observant people in-country. Immediately, we all noticed that there was a new team of guys on our campus stating they were something else but dressed and acting like they were Secret Service. It was that obvious to us all. Some Agents came to me and voiced concern that we were not in the loop and it seemed clear to all of us that one of three persons must be coming to town; The President, the Vice President, or the Secretary of State, and we immediately eliminated the Secretary because she was our primary Protectee and we would have been advised. That left two. The Vice President was having heart problems and it would be foolish or suicidal for our government to send him at this time. To all of us, that meant the

President was coming. So that I could begin my security preparations, I went up to the Deputy Chief of Mission's (DCM) office and laid out our view on who and why we knew the President was coming and told him we recognized the Secret Service guys and that it was naïve to not bring the Chief Security Officer for all Iraq into the planning. To his credit, the DCM, who is one of the smartest people I have ever met, immediately recognized the truth of the situation and he walked me down toAmbassador Zal Khalilzad's office and told him we had figured it out (like it took more than a first tour RSO to guess) and they told me what was happening. That made 6 of us who now knew about the visit (officially) and my intelligent DS Agents who figured it out on their own without too much trouble. I called my Section Chiefs in to my office and we planned our strategy and logistics for use of our protective resources and helicopters to keep the President safe. We worked all the details out so that at the last minute when the front office decided to tell everyone (the moment the plane touched down at BIAP) we wouldn't have the President in any danger of political or "intelligence agency" lack of coordination and protection. Sometimes an RSO has to be proactive to keep people alive in spite of it all. Our Motto had become – "The RSO Section, keeping people safe in spite of themselves." I thank God though for the astute perception of our DCM. Time and time again, his wisdom would work things out.

With all our resources in play, the trip went without a flaw. I had several hundred armed men working to help the Secret Service protect him, 50 armored and heavily armed vehicles, all our helicopters, the Army's Blackhawk and Apache helicopters, and a tight control on his movements. All his meetings were in the Palace to minimize his exposure. Knowing that the moment his plane was spotted coming in, and the first time an Iraqi official was advised that the President wanted to meet with him in the Palace, the terrorists would know and would begin their strategy to rocket the Palace. The military put forces into play to shut down Saddar City. It worked.

Following all the meetings, the dozen key Officers of the Mission including myself were lined up in the Rotunda and the President went down the line shaking our hands and saying hello. He was very personable and I wanted to say more to him like "thanks for all your support on the Daniel Pearl case", but decided that it would seem commercial and instead just opted for a quiet hand-shake. I did however, tactically place my Marine Detachment Commander and Assistant Commander in the hall where the President would pass, knowing that the President would never pass up a chance to shake their hands so they got their moment as well, and of course the most important photo opportunity. I was impressed that the President had the courage to come to this dangerous place. I learned a lot from this experience about how I was going to have to do what was right whether some others thought it was or not. I would also strongly rely on the DCM as an intelligent and insightful ally.

The running joke with all 7,000 people at the Palace was that this place was like the movie "Groundhog Day", because every day was exactly the same with the exception of when they at-tacked, how hard they attacked and who got hurt or killed. The sameness was that we worked 7 days a week, no weekends, no holidays. Every Wednesday, we had a special shrimp dinner and Karioke at night. Sundays were Lobster and Prime Rib night. The events planned by the military health and welfare folks repeated exactly the same week after week and it seemed like waking up each morning was an exact duplicate of the day before.

While exploring my territory in the IZ, I went to the Al-Rashid Hotel and met an Iraqi man named Ali who ran the little carpet shop in this blown up and dirty, disorganized hotel under renovation. He was a very nice man but had nothing of real value in his shop and didn't really know much about carpets either. I felt sorry for him trying to start a business in this disaster zone at a time when the Insurgents would kill anyone (and their entire family) who worked with or near the Americans. He was good hearted and courageous and also mentioned he had 15 children. I paid him too much money for a carpet for my office floor and I started having regular conversations with him and would bring over people who wanted to also buy a carpet in Iraq. Slowly, his business, his store and his supply of carpets got better. It was fun to watch this little corner of rejuvenation take place and to be a catalyst for it.

There was virtually no animal life in the entire city. One never saw any dogs or cats. They had all been eradicated for sanitary reasons if they had survived the original war attacks. That was true for the Palace grounds as well. KBR had been given orders for safety, medical and sanitary reasons to keep all animals away form the compound. Most of us wanted cats and dogs around and when we saw a stealthy surviving cat carefully moving from trailer to trailer, we were encouraged and it became a topic of conversation and morale. There were also some small grey desert foxes that would make a run across the compound about 0400 hours in the morning looking for anything to eat. They were small with big ears and must have been smart to have survived.

The heat was intense and no one ever went or walked anywhere without bottles of water in their pockets or a camelpack on their backs if they were going on a mission. I had never drunk so much water. Everything involved drinking water. At every meeting, everyone had their bottle of water. Walking to and from your trailer, you always had your bottle of water, and every 50 to 100 yards were huge stacks of cases of bottled water for everyone to take to their trailers or to pick up as you were walking. Our military obviously had gone through this before. Water, water, everywhere.

It was time for me to take the "city tour". I needed to get an overhead perspective of the city, the routes our vehicles were taking, and where the key ministries and buildings were in the Red zone. I arranged for my "little birds" to take me up. One would have two gunners to run cover fire and mine would have me with my M-4 and another gunner with a larger caliber weapon. I had been forewarned that my "tough-guy" Blackwater guys liked to test out their new boss by giving him the roughest and wildest ride they could to force him to throw-up. And those pilots allegedly could pull full loops with their helicopters and I am not sure that physics-wise, it was supposed to even be possible. I would again be sitting on the edge of the door frame hanging out and since I actually loved this stuff, I felt quite certain I would be fine. In fact, I felt I would probably be practically giggling from the joy ride. I had no idea what 130 degree weather in "full kit" and two hours of loops and vicious left and right banks could do to a system but it was very informative at this early stage of my tour to understand the layout of the city from overhead and to see the chokepoints and traps on the streets and alleyways that we had to drive down. I would be giving orders for my teams to go into these areas and I had to know what that meant when I approved or denied a requested move to a venue. These pilots were amazing. I loved it. One second hanging out in a free fall position, held in by that strap and the next looking up or backwards.

By the second hour, my focus on the venues was shrinking and my focus on not throwing up in this heat in full gear was becoming more primary. I made the entire two hours without barfing but I have to admit that it was a close call. The pilots were grinning when we landed but I had made the grade. Apparently, most had thrown up before. They had even stretched the tour longer to try and force me to but victory had been mine – by about 10 seconds. We also had not been hit by any rounds being fired at us from the ground and that was impressive and a very good thing. We got hit every once in awhile which is why they fly the way they do but today had been a win.

I turned 56 years old on June 19th and worked 15 hours so it passed without much notice. But, I closed on my house in Santa Fe, New Mexico, on my birthday and that made it a memorable day. We were also providing protective details for three Governors from South Carolina, South Dakota, and Alaska, and things were going pretty well. So far, I was enjoying the adventure and happy with my work.

JUNE 22 TO JULY 08, 2006:

The heat had a life to it. Breathing too deeply felt like it seared your windpipe and lungs as it went in. A person learned that if you jogged outside in this intensity, not only would it hurt your lungs and make you feel weak for a period afterwards, but also the stomping on the soil step after step, apparently raised particles or atoms of residual explosive matter, not to mention the other historically Iraqi non-hygienic matter and that would make some feel like they had a bronchial infection for awhile. When you tried to breathe through your nose, it felt like it was burning the inside of your nose. Eventually, most people ended up in the gym. And it wasn't just the temperature, the sun was so strong that it created a blinding light effect. It seemed to put a halo on everything, similar to a bright aura.

We, the RSO Section, had one of the only facilities that served alcohol in a war zone. The military was completely prohibited from consuming any alcohol and that made good sense. The RSOs and Security Engineers created a bar called "The Lock and Load Bar". Yes, of course that's what it was called. What else would Agents in a war zone call a bar? The bar was run and maintained by the Security Engineering Officers because the location was in the little courtyard next to their offices outside at the end of the Palace grounds and they were the best equipped to install fans, water spritzers, light systems etc…and it was a highly desirable place to get into. We had originally designed it just for the RSOs to chill out and bond and to hold occasional meetings and celebrations in, but found that it was needed by a wider crowd of good people. So, it grew and became famous and the t-shirts were made and it became a legend talked about by all USG travelers in and out of Iraq. We initially had a few problems with people who overindulged and had too much uncontrollable adrenaline, so I had to put some rules in place as all new creations of civilization seem to necessitate. I don't know why people just can't control themselves. I put a midnight shutdown on it for alcohol consumption and all non-RSOs had to depart. It was by invitation only so that we wouldn't have a group of uncontrollable folks enter resulting in a necessary use of force to correct it, and there were no weapons permitted in the bar area. I also set a rule for my RSOs – they were NEVER permitted to drink to the point that they were not able to respond in an emergency and perform properly and professionally. We were the ones who were there to save people's lives and run out to rescue them so we had to be able to perform

24-hours a day. That pretty much meant never having more than a drink or two for the entire night. My guys were very good about it except once or twice, which required minor intervention.

The time was flying. We were so busy all the time, responding to rockets and mortars and vehicle motorcades that got hit by Improvised Explosive Devices (IEDs) and Explosively Formed Projectiles (EFPs), it seemed before we could sit down, another week had passed, It is an odd fact that the more one crams into a week, the faster it goes. The week itself would be physically exhausting and mentally bashing but then it would be Friday again and you could hardly believe it.

It was in the midst of this almost surreal daily environment, an even stranger event took place. People from Plan B Productions, Brad Pitt's Production Company, called me in Baghdad. Man, did that seem out of place. They told me that the movie about the kidnapping and murder of Daniel Pearl was going forward and that they had selected the Actor to play me. His name is Will Patton. I was staggered not just by the fact that I was going to be a character in a movie but that an incredibly talented Actor like Will Patton would be portraying me. This might as well have been a dream because it just didn't fit in with my current daily perspective. They asked if it was possible for me to get approval to travel to Kuwait City for three days to meet with him and let him do a character study of me. How do you correlate your makeshift plywood office in Saddam Hussein's Palace with your predator vest and your weapons with Hollywood? I felt that if I didn't take part in Danny's story, and having met with the Director in Santa Fe, I would be making a lifelong mistake so I requested authorization of my headquarters in Washington and they saw potential promotional gold in this and said OK. What do you know? Now, what to wear from my vast selection of 3 pairs of pants and four shirts and two pairs of desert combat boots. I guess he would have to take me as I was, sweaty and in para-military garb. They would now begin to set the date that worked for everyone and I went back to my primary focus of keeping everyone alive, which was getting harder to do.

We were beginning to have more rocket and mortar attacks, as well as attacks on our motorcades than ever before since the inception of the war effort. This had become the worst year for deaths and attacks since the Iraq incursion began. I was glad it was me here watching over these people instead of someone who hadn't faced this before. I had to create more restrictions and tighter security packages as the attacks became more frequent. I even had to eliminate some venues or change the way we went to them. We began to use helicopter drops with our cars staged at the venues as backup plans in case things "went south" as the road ambushes became more frequent and much more aggressive and violent, as well as better equipped by the enemy.

Fortunately, the 122 mm rockets being lobbed at us from Saddar City (12 kms away) were proving to be old stock, which meant they were not as consistently reliable to project and the launching systems were mostly homemade "V" shaped slides which further reduced the accuracy, but they could always land them somewhere on the IZ, maybe just not on the Palace consistently. The U.S. Military wouldn't listen to my pleas to counter-attack. They had a rule about no collateral damage to civilians and the enemy knew it so they launched from school yards, mosques, neighborhoods, and that meant they could continue to do it without the fear of us killing them. The military would send out a road patrol to the launching site but by the time they got there, if they didn't get attacked on the way requiring my guys to go rescue them, the enemy was long gone. This was not making any sense. We were pretty sure that there were Saddarists in the IZ and as a rocket would fall on the IZ, they would be on the cell phone advising the enemy to adjust fire to bring it closer to the Palace, because the enemy began to "walk the rounds in" on us and by the third rocket, it was usually right on top of us.

Between life and death comes entertainment. Our military Health and Welfare (MWR) folks created a "Baghdad Idol" competition similar to the show that was apparently such a hit in the U.S. Every Wednesday night was Karaoke night unless rockets fell and it was quite popular. I never quite understood the Karaoke need in people but the "Idol" show seemed like much needed entertainment and all the Karaoke participants were drooling for this chance. The competition was held over several weeks at night by the pool where a stage was built. Tables and chairs were always there for outdoor eating at night if a desert breeze came through and for the events that MWR had. Groups brought coolers of beer (except the military) and extra chairs and everyone set up their little camps to enjoy the show. We all sat there sweating uncontrollably in the stagnant, windless nighttime air, but it was what we did most of the time and we just accepted it. I had decided that I needed a change of view so I left my office and also attended. I avoided most of the poolside events so that my guys could feel comfortable not having their boss always scrutinizing their moments of relaxation. But it turned out it was actually funny and some of the contestants were very good. The most important thing was that it was another bonding event in the midst of this war and terrorism and everyone needed that psychological break. Even FOX TV was permitted to come and cover the event on the "finals" night.

Even in Baghdad we tried to celebrate the Fourth of July but like at most Embassies in the world, it would be turned into a representational event for the foreign leaders instead of an event for the Americans to celebrate. Ambassador Khalilzad wanted this opportunity to further patronize the stubborn Iraqi leaders. For me, it meant that every Agent worked, every Blackwater contractor worked, snipers were placed on every roof top, our helicopters were all in the air running cover or staged to rescue, the IZ was placed on high alert and more troops and tanks were deployed to the International Zone Points of entry (IZPs), the Combat Surgical Hospital (CSH) was put on alert, and we anticipated being rocketed by Muhqtada al-Saddar and his militant terrorists. We did have a couple of rockets hit within the IZ but they were about a mile away and just did some building damage so I guess their trajectory planning wasn't up to snuff today and our chanting for good luck paid off.

My RSO operation was made up of various Sections, led by my more senior RSOs and each of them performed critical functions, many times independently of each other but never without my overall coordination. One Section, which we affectionately called "the Bull Pen", included my 10 contracted Intelligence Analysts, my DS Investigations Section, and my Counter-Intelligence Section. It was an enclosed and secure big open room carved out of some of the north wing. The Palace has 50 foot-high ceilings so we built the Bull Pen with a normal roof to create decent work space, but on the walls, hanging on hooks, were weapons we had collected from various places and people and incidents. There must have been 50 weapons of varied makes, models and nationalities hanging there. Once the others in the Palace learned of our "exhibit", they asked if they could come into our secure space for a photo opportunity and it also became a favorite photo for all the

Senators and Congressmen who came out. Included on the walls were the famous shotgun Saddam Hussein is always pictured with and the gold-plated AK-47 that his son Uday would carry to look cool as a psychopath as he tortured adults and children, and even girlfriends he tired of, for pleasure. The room made one heck of a photo background but of course we had to put sheets over all our terrorist tracking charts and operational plans when we allowed those VIP Photo Ops.

I had hoped that with all the open area I might be able to set up a knife throwing course as a personal distraction again so I had shipped my throwing knives to Baghdad. The big spaces, sand dunes, and controlled areas were perfect. I asked the woodworking guys of KBR to make a wood platform for standing up according to a drawing I provided them. Within 2 weeks it was done. I packed it on a Gator (the golf cart on steroids) and went out to a corner of the compound where no one was housed and nothing was happening and stood it up. I had a wide tip magic marker and drew out a silhouette on it and gave it a try. The skills were rusty but it only took about 20 minutes to get my distance and form back. Now, I could teach knife throwing lessons again. During the year, I taught many Marines and Agents and even some civilian women who wanted to know if they had the capacity to do it. I can teach anyone to have some success within an hour but only a few will actually become skilled at it. Nonetheless, when they got their first successful "sticking", we took the required photo of them next to the silhouette with the knife sticking out. There were many proud moments and a lot of sweating out on the knife-throwing range.

The increased frequency of rocket and mortar attacks continued. Crowds of people diminished at the pool and passing across the compound now became a matter of "fastest way from point A to point B", staying inside the hardened buildings as much as possible. But, even the buildings weren't safe. One rocket had gone through the central Palace dome and caused a lot of injuries and destruction. When we would get multiple sequential days of rockets coming in, I ordered everyone to wear their ballistic vests and helmets even to cross from their trailers to the DFAC (food hall). Anytime they were outside, it was in a helmet and predator vest. Then, if we went several days without a rocketing, we allowed them to chill-out with optional vest and helmet wearing to allow them to have a sense of normalcy for their morale again. It is most difficult making security decisions, taking into account that the people here were mostly non-combatants and they had fragile psyches that I was constantly juggling to keep them mentally stable and content, but yet controllably safe. The obligatory opportunities for leadership and managerial development were abundant here. There were things we had to consider that no one and no place else in the world had to take into account.

This place and this tour, and my job, were immensely challenging, but so gratifying and intoxicating in its scope. In a single hour, I had been lifted in joy by rescuing three soldiers who were shot-up by the enemy and then had my heart broken when a nice young 23 year old man in the next moment was blown up by a random rocket that hit his trailer while he was changing his sweaty clothes. How do you explain this kind of thing.

JULY 09 TO AUGUST 05, 2006:

Every day I thought I had experienced the maximum heat possible we scored a new temperature high. In my little shared shower, there were cold and hot water taps. No one ever touched the hot.

With just the cold water faucet on, the water coming through the Hades-like earth got heated to an unbearable temperature. We took a temperature reading on the grounds of the new Embassy Compound and the air read 143 degrees. The heat outside sucked the air right out of ones lungs like it was trying to cool itself down with what you have inside. A person breathed shallow and carefully so as not to scorch the windpipe and lungs. A cloth across the face seemed to help and I guess that answered why the Arabs in desert movies wore a cloth across their faces.

In the first two weeks of this period, we were hit with 46 rockets. They fell almost every day and two persons had been killed and thirteen had been wounded. There was talk of additional U.S. troops being brought down from the north to be inserted into Saddar City, in Baghdad, in hopes of getting some order and control back. Our military still insisted that they couldn't bomb the sites in Saddar City that were launching these killer rockets and mortars because of the possibility of killing innocents. The expression "sitting duck" was derived from just such a scenario. Though I was glad to hear of the extra troops coming down to assist, I was also sorry for the young men and women. They were scheduled to go home in one month, and as much as some of them obviously looked forward to the additional action, many had already begun dreaming of seeing their families. But, we had a real problem. People were dieing and we needed to get it under control or at least convince the enemy that their losses were not justifiable for their attempts to kill us. They needed to be wiped out for the betterment of the Iraqis who cowered in their homes, afraid of the violence and so that we could get all our people home.

I began to receive phone calls from the actor Will Patton, just wanting to talk to hear how I spoke and the way I used language.

He was terrific and every time a call came in, the office went wild, whispering that "its him". We were discussing the possibility of my meeting him in Dubai or Kuwait City for a couple of days but I honestly didn't think DS would allow me to get away from this job and I wasn't sure that I could in all good conscience leave my people here. It was certainly fun talking with him though.

Celebratory fire had become a real topic. When any ceremony of joy or anger took place, all the Iraqis went outside and fire bullets into the air. They never thought of them coming back down and sometimes people randomly died from a bullet to the brain as it droped back down to earth. They just accepted it as the will of Allah. It's a pretty irresponsible way to shirk blame. Many of us had come home to our little trailer box at the end of a long day and found a stray bullet lying on the floor under a new hole punched through the roof. In my first case of this phenomenon, I awoke with rain dripping on my face and pillow. I moved the bed to put a bucket under the rain trickle and when I moved it, I found the bullet that had put a hole in my roof. Later, I came home to find one lying on the floor, but I never considered these as close calls. When they hit the tin roofs, they lost enough of their force to prevent them from being fatal. They could still embed themselves in your body or head, but not likely kill you. The uninterrupted bullets would not be so forgiving. The concept of firing bullets in the air and not knowing where they will come down seemed so primitive to all of us. It was difficult to understand their way of thinking in this culture.

The call came from my headquarters in Washington that I was to go to Kuwait City for three days and allow Will Patton to do a character study of me for the movie. DS had realized that they could do well with this positive promotion and publicity, having a DS Agent in a movie portraying some of what we do overseas for the U.S. government and its citizens. I grabbed a small back pack, threw in one extra shirt and extra underwear and socks and a book to read. My helicopters picked me up and flew me to BIAP, where I had to wait at Camp Sully (named after our brave Agent who lost his life saving an American Foreign Service Officer) overnight to catch a C-130 out the next morning. It was just never easy getting in or out of Baghdad. It always took at least one entire day sitting in the heat to get a military flight any-where. Being the equivalent rank of a Brigadier General, I got on the morning flight and landed in Kuwait. I could not believe it. It was actually hotter than Baghdad. How could that be pos-sible? But the good part was that I was checked into a room at the Hilton Hotel on the beach. The bed was a King size and the sheets were cool. I didn't miss my little concrete-mattress single bed at all. Will Patton was to arrive later in the day so I went to downtown Kuwait City. The last time I had been here was during the first Gulf War and we had been cleaning up dead bodies and being shot at by abandoned Iraqi soldiers who got left behind the line when their buddies fled. Isn't that ironic. I now was living in Baghdad and back in Kuwait City for entertainment of sorts. Life is just plain unusual. The city was rebuilt and had grown sub-stantially but I still recognized certain areas where we had gone through some bad experiences years before. Where there had been a hundred Kuwaiti bodies piled in a defunct ice-skating rink that had melted, there was now a shopping center and a great restau-rant that I ate in. I also took time to go into a theater to watch the new Superman movie that had just come out. It was undoubt-edly an out-of-body experience to be away from the rockets and in a movie theater like nothing was going on in Iraq. For a short while, I would savor it and try to assimilate into normalcy.

Later in the day, I waited seated in the hotel lobby where Will and I were to meet. I looked down the hallway and saw a man walking toward me smiling and I swear, he could have been one of the Bennett brothers. It was Will Patton. They had done a great job picking someone with a resemblance and I kept looking at him and seeing my brother Steve in his eyes and face. Not only the resemblance, but Will also had the temperament of a Bennett boy. He was just a nice guy and somewhat shy and even a bit reserved. OK, I am not the shy or reserved one in the family but I recognize family when I see it. I immediately liked him and felt comfortable around him. We sat and talked for hours and then ate our meals together and I could see him watching me with Bennett-like never flinching eyes. He was studying every move I made and every idiosyncratic habit I had. I guess that is why he is such a terrific actor. He knows his business and how to become the character. He even began to speak back to me with the same voice inflection I had. It was a bit unnerving and I began to feel conspicuous with the ways I used my hands to talk and the expressions I used. But I have to say that he made me feel relaxed and casual and it truly was like having a brother with me. I knew this guy was going on my special Christmas list. Will said they would be filming in India in October and asked if I would come and join them (and Angelina Jolie) . The two problems I saw were that the Director probably wouldn't want someone there saying "hey, that's not how it happened", and I was going to need a break so badly in October, going to "work" in India probably would mean I would be a wreck when I returned to Iraq. I told him I would think about it. I knew that every day in Iraq was so totally exhausting, if I didn't get my 2 weeks off in a completely calming place where I could sleep and relax, I might not make the year. That meant mostly being alone. True, Angelina Jolie would be quite an inspiration and I would love to spend more time with my new brother, but we would have to see. My responsibility to my people came first. I said goodbye to Will Patton, hoping we would meet again.

I flew back to Baghdad in the super-heated C-130 military aircraft sweating all the way and landed at BIAP, where my helicopters and my protective team were waiting to pick me up. I liked this part. It was efficient and smart. I would be at work in 20 minutes. My "15 minutes of fame" was over and it was time to get serious again. Lives were at stake and people were counting on everything we did. I hoped the movie wouldn't make me look too foolish or cowboyish.

CODELS were still rolling in by the plane load and Secretary of Defense Rumsfield came to see us too. We spent some quality time with him and I found him to be a straight-shooting and honest-intended man. We all liked him a lot. It took a lot of our resources as well as the military's though and was very energy draining with his being one of the top targets for our enemy to try and take out.

Coming from Arizona and having been in the Middle-East many times before, I have seen my share of sand storms. But what we saw rolling across the desert at us was very different and besides being awe-inspiring in its own way, it also generated a deep genetic fear to see nature take on this kind of power. The sky turned pink and that was a clear indication to me of a coming sand storm. Then, just enough rain fell to wet the place and we saw it. It was rolling in like a thousand-foot high wall of solid sand. It almost looked like a tidal wave but of pinkish-tan substance. It reminded me of the special effects used in the movie, "The Mummy". In the movie, it is staggering and impacting. In real life, it truly is something to see, to stare at, to marvel at, then run like hell for cover before it completely encapsulates you and buries you in the psunami of sand. Even the trailers, which seemed to be pretty well sealed, ended up with a light coating of sand covering everything inside and small piles at the doors and window cracks. It was amazing and I wouldn't want to face one out in the desert. You would wake up under five feet of sand.

After only two months here, and having witnessed so many atrocities already, I began to be discouraged by our attempts to change the culture of a people who had been sectarian-killing each other for 1400 years. Hey, get over it. Move on. Try to go forward. This was the longest Hatfield and McCoys revenge war on the planet but was called the Shia versus Sunni war. Another thing that really stood out to me was the holidays that they celebrate. In the U.S., we base almost all holidays around things that make us happy or make us think about the good things in life. The Muslims holidays seemed to highlight the negative emotional and sorrowful events. Their holidays or memorials like Muharram included whipping and cutting yourself to re-live the pain of a past tragic experience, or remembering and mourning the death of the grandson of Muhammad and on and on. I don't think we fully realized how totally different our perspectives on life, the world and respecting each others lives and freedoms were. Maybe I was just beginning to get worn down a bit but there was certainly a lot of torture, maiming and killing going on among their own people just on the other side of the river every day. It was Iraqi against Iraqi and it was absolutely brutal and horrific with the daily decapitations and dismemberings. The hundreds of bodies showing signs of being tortured and then thrown in the Tigris river to be picked up further down when they floated by our military posts or patrol boats. I remembered 15 years before going to the opening of the Holocaust Museum in Kuwait City, seeing all the tools and Iraqi methods of torture and I thought back to all the atrocities I personally witnessed in the city at the end of the first Gulf War. There seemed to be a clear pattern with these people. If you were the wrong sect, or the wrong cast, or out of favor, or in the wrong place at the wrong time, your life could be forfeit in the most gruesome way they could creatively concoct. I didn't understand this thought process but began to wonder if Democracy wasn't the wrong form of governance for a people who acted this way when no one was putting fear into them to behave. They didn't seem to be helping themselves. Maybe free will didn't work with them.

Our helicopters traveled in pairs in case one was damaged and we needed to leave it or destroy it to keep it away from the enemy. We would cross-load the people from the damaged one into the other and scramble for home. This day, we traveled to one of my outposts called Al-Hillah. Its other name locally was Babil and yes, it was the location of the Tower of Babil. In fact, on a day without enemy attacks, one could risk a quick trip to the original location of the Tower, which now was just a mound with rubble and not even that big in circumference. Everything is a matter of perspective and in this case, our stories over the years and the movies and the images of a huge towering structure reaching to the sky like the Sears Tower might not be true. It must have been the principle of the thing, rather than the threat to God's kingdom. It just couldn't have been that big a deal as we would see it today.

But Al-Hillah had been taking some rocket attacks and I needed to have a first-hand understanding of their perimeter and defenses and their facility and its ability to withstand hits and protect our people. It was only about a 1 hour and 15 minute helicopter Flight from Baghdad to Al-Hillah. But whenever we went anywhere, it was in full gear. Predator vests, helmets, machine gun, hand gun in a drop-down holster and lots of magazines of ammo for each weapon. You just couldn't risk not being prepared for trouble. Many think that a person is safe in a helicopter but in order for them to fly, they have to be as light as possible and that means the skin of the bird is like a tin can. Bullets go right through. So, the enemy liked to take shots at us as we flew by. It was somewhat frequently that we took rounds through our helicopters and we had to do repair work on them all the time. Most of the time we were pretty lucky and sometimes, people were wounded. As in my entire career, I was a very lucky man and that was still holding true. Hillah took two rounds of 122 mm rockets while we were there and the pilots wanted to move the helos from the small landing zone, assuming that the enemy was trying to hit them and take them out of operation. So, I authorized them to stage further over on a U.S. Base and we continued our Consulate status review.

My RSO in Al-Hillah had established a "Home Guard" cadre of Iraqis in the area surrounding our Consulate. They got paid a monthly stipend and in return, they watched for Insurgents setting up rocket launchers to hit the Consulate. Most of the time, the launching of the rocket brought awareness to the Home Guard of a problem, who then gave us the coordinates of the enemy and we would zero in on them if they didn't flee too quickly. It was working pretty well and the Home Guard were people who just wanted to be successful farmers and they wanted peace in their area, so the level of loyalty, which was a hard commodity to get here, was as good as we could hope for. All in all, the morale of my people in Al-Hillah was good, the protection was respectable, and things were going as well as they could in the middle of a war zone. We flew back at the end of the day and as always, the pilots flew low to the ground, about 30 to 50 feet above the ground, and as fast as we could, zigging and zagging their route, running serpentine courses to keep anyone spotting us on the ground from having an easy or straight-line shot at us. The closeness to the ground meant that we came upon anyone on the ground before they even knew we were coming and that usually prevented them from getting a shot off. Not always though. When we arrived back at the helo field across from the commissary, we inspected the birds and found that two rounds had made contact but fortunately not with any individual. We could see the pattern of shooting at our helicopters picking up momentum and that began to worry me and even moreso, it worried the extremely talented Blackwater pilots who flew every day. Personally, I was still enjoying the thrill of low, fast and somewhat risky helo flights. That would wear off before long. Every day, I came to more closely recognize the inevitability of death as we dealt with more and more of it on a personal level.

Then, as our world of the surreal would have it, it was Sunday night and dinner was Prime Rib and Lobster Tail. I didn't eat either not being a red meat eater and the lobster was too rich for someone trying to maintain a "young man's conditioning" but here we were, stepping from being shot at to eating like kings. It sort of held that "every day is your last meal" kind of concept or approach.

AUGUST 06 TO SEPTEMBER 01, 2006:

It seemed that with 60-plus Special Agents working for me that there was always a group out on one of our allotted vacations to remain sane and we were constantly filling gaps in the missing jobs. My Deputy, who had been here before me and was about to finish up his tour, was now out on his final "leave". That meant that I handled everything managerial and decision-making, and as always it kept me busy 17 hours a day and at night as well. It turned out to be a blessing to learn how to run things myself because this Deputy RSO left for his onward tour a month later to Bangkok at the International Law Enforcement Academy and my new DRSO arrived at Post with only a brief turnover with the outgoing one. He seemed very talented and able and I was thrilled that I was going to be able to turn over some of the daily Programs operational control to him. I had been here running 100 mph, 24 hours a day, 7 days a week for almost 4 months now and I wanted to get the new Deputy up to speed quickly so I could get out on my first mini-vacation. I could feel my brain burning out and my energy was tapped. I was really looking forward to some quiet time in Thailand, maybe a little diving, and certainly a lot of sleep.

It was also time to think about my follow-on assignment after Baghdad and we were told that in reward for volunteering, we would be given preferential treatment on our bids. So, where did I want to go that was available? I didn't have much time to think about it. I received a call from my DS headquarters and they told me that Pakistan was looking like it was becoming more violent and active and they needed an experienced senior RSO to take the assignment. The four years in Karachi and the temporary duty assignments years before in Pakistan had certainly been interesting ones. They had taken a toll on me, especially that final year in Karachi, but I would already understand more about the culture than probably any other American there and I would have an opportunity to see all my friends in-country again, and maybe even have some Rosewood furniture made to replace the pieces

I had lost in the divorce. You should know something about me by now, so yes, of course I agreed to take the Pakistan assignment following Iraq. But, Pakistan also had a 3rd place favoritism status on bidding out for onward assignments following Iraq and Afghanistan so I realized after taking these two critical threat postings, I should be able to get a sweet assignment and I just happened to remember that the RSO in Bangkok, Thailand, was leaving in the summer of 2008, which would time perfectly for me to take his spot. I negotiated with the Director of DS and the DS Assistant Secretary to get a guarantee that if I took Islamabad, Pakistan, after Baghdad, I would be assured of being assigned to the peaceful and beautiful Thailand for my next, and maybe final, assignment. I had been doing these hardship assignments most of my career and had more experience with death and destruction than perhaps any other Special Agent in the U.S. government, and I was thinking it was getting near time that I considered trying to assimilate into some form of normal life with people who lived typical lives with homes and garages, if that would be possible for a person like me, who now had been to the dark side too many times. Bangkok would be the starting point at my assimilation. DS authorities agreed and I kept their email that told me I would be assigned to Bangkok in case I needed it later for documentation. But for now, I had a new Deputy RSO to break in so I could go visit my future new home.

We were feeling queasy about being in a five-day quiet spell without a single rocket falling on us. After being hit almost every day, that span of time made me think that something big was being planned and we doubled all the external control points on the Green Zone (IZ) and placed tanks there to do serious damage if the force was big. We had experienced the usual snipers from across the river landing rounds in the Palace grounds but not a single trailer had been blown up and not a palm tree had been decimated by a blast. I still wasn't finishing work until 2300 hours on many nights but at least we weren't running for our concrete bunkers.

Down south in Basrah, it never got better. We had a Consulate there and I had my strongest RSO and an ARSO there watching over a group of Americans who were trying to bring Democracy to a bunch of terrorists, thieves and bastards who were constantly bombing, rocketing, and mortaring our compound, which was shared with the Brits. They had begun sleeping inside their office building to eliminate having to get out of bed three times a night to run to the hardened building to survive the incoming rockets. It was just too tiring so they set up cots in their offices and moved in. Their trailers were still being bombed and we lost food storage trailers or generators or personal trailers almost every day. The Americans would pick what they hoped was the quietest time of the day and would run to their trailers to shower and change clothes and then run back to the limited protection of the building. Unfortunately no one could predict random fate.

A nice young man was our communications technician in Basrah and he had not been back to spend more than 5 minutes in his trailer in about a month. On a particular day, he missed his rock-hard single bed in his tiny personality-less trailer and told our RSO he was going to go to the trailer at noon, the quietest time, and take a nap on his bed. At 1220, as he slept, a 122 mm rocket found its way through that big sky, with so many possible trajectories and thousands of variables to alter its course, directly onto and into his trailer, detonating and instantly killing him and totally destroying the trailer. It was the only rocket launched in that sortie and it could have hit anywhere within miles, but it chose that exact spot as a man slept for the first time in a month on that 3 foot by 6 foot mattress. We planned a memorial service in Basrah and I flew down in a C-130 and then helicoptered over for the ceremony. It was somber and tearful. He had been loved by everyone and had even been doing some volunteer work for the community teaching them about computers. He was a generous and kind young man who was going to be very missed by all.

There was only 1 Iraqi Consulate employee left alive in Basrah and much to my surprise considering the risk to her, she attended the memorial service. The majority of the Iraqi employees had been murdered by the terrorists/Insurgents once they were discovered working for Americans and sometimes it was even their own family who told on them. On occasion, it was their own family who killed them. Frankly, I was wondering how this woman had survived and why she continued working for us with the past horrible record of failures.

The Health, Welfare and Recreation arm of the military was once again sponsoring an event for entertainment. It was a bodybuilding competition. In this environment where there were 100-plus men for every 1 woman, this event just had a real comical sense to it. At least from the RSO perspective it did. There were some military guys and a few gals who took this confusingly serious though. Well, my RSOs were an enthusiastic group, always looking for a way to boost their own morale so they decided to enter someone, a very funny and friendly ARSO, who was almost the opposite of a bodybuilder, just for the humor of it. He was 135 pounds skinny but had a flare for entertainment and was such a friendly guy, everyone knew him in the Palace and liked him. So, much to my teary-eyed laughter that night at our open-air stage area by the pool, the other instigating RSOs and ARSOs had convinced him that he needed to shave his body, heavily baby oil himself, and then worked with him on poses that might have at one time seemed serious, but with his inability to carry them out properly, just left him looking like he was posing for a specialized men's magazine. My god, I thought I would have a stroke I was laughing so hard. There he was though, with his famous big smile trying to move and pose to music. The crowd went wild with laughter and it was so funny that they wanted to give him the award on the sympathy vote alone, but that would have defeated the basis for the event with the serious bodybuilders, so they gave everyone an award but our ARSO was the highlight of the event and a terrific stress break for everyone.

One of our medical staff was in the habit of going out into the parking lot in front of the Palace to take smoke breaks. We kept telling him smoking would kill him but he was just one of those relentless smokers. There weren't that many people who smoked anymore but he was one of them. This particular day, he was just standing outside the main entrance of the Palace, smoking with his "break buddies" when a bullet fell out of the sky and went right into his stomach fat about 2 inches deep. Lucky for him he had what is technically called a "belly tire" but when it happened, he was knocked down. He then picked himself up, looked at the wound and walked back into the medical unit and had the Doctors remove it and stitch him up. He was fine but had a large gash and a great scar for a unique story. And he kept smoking.

In Baghdad, the kidnapping and killing of our Iraqi employees was becoming a problem similar to the serious level of Basrah. In fact, we couldn't hire them and "clear" them fast enough to replace the ones that were being killed and disappearing. The moral issue here is disturbing. Did we continue hiring them knowing that we might be sentencing them to death and that a good percentage of them might be killed because of our ethical desire to "help" the Iraqis find jobs? We were down to about 10 percent of the employees remaining. In order for them to come to work at the Palace or even to reach and enter the International Zone (IZ), they had to take several different taxis to misleading locations, then mix that with buses that go the wrong directions, and then change their clothes and disguises several times. They did this every single day just to try and make it to the Embassy Palace alive and then home again. That should reveal to you just how desperate people were to get some money and have the hope of being given U.S. citizenship and to get the hell out of this nightmare of a country. On the other hand, and complicating things further, the only way we can hire new Iraqis is by running them though my polygraph examinations since we can't go out to do door-to-door investigations, or ask their schools or previous employers for references without sentencing them and their families to death, and of course getting ourselves killed doing it. What we were finding was that a large percent of those applying for jobs failed the polygraph and we had to deny them employment. We literally had terrorists asking to come to work for us in the Palace and that was a very disturbing concept. At least we were catching them, but getting Iraqis to work inside the IZ was not going to work very well.

Our season was finally beginning to cool down. The days were only around 110 degrees and it was a nice change. My Deputy RSO was doing a fine job and I had my eye on that vacation in a couple of weeks. The Iraq Study Group, led by ex-Secretary of State James Baker came out and I felt bad about what I had to do, but I prohibited them from going out into the Red Zone for their own safety. Fortunately, former Secretary of State James Baker supported my decision and the group also included other impressive former leaders like Lee Hamilton, Edwin Meese, Robert Gates, Leon Panetta, former Senator Robb and William Perry. It was an honor to get to meet them and brief them on the local conditions. I just wanted them to finish and get home safely. Retired Senator Robb wanted to go into an active combat situation on the streets of Fallujah but I couldn't allow it even though he was a former Marine.

SEPTEMBER 02 THROUGH OCTOBER 01, 2006:

I had done a number of lengthy interviews a year or two ago and they had been edited and were part of an HBO Documentary called "The Jihadi and the Journalist". It was the story about Daniel Pearl and the kidnapper Sheikh Umer who was responsible for getting Danny killed. I asked my family members to see if they could record a copy of it for me. My sweet little Mother wrote back in a letter to me that she would try to get a copy of "The Jedi and the Journalist" for me and that gave me more joy than anything to see her interpretation so many miles away from any concept of a Jihadi. It made me feel she was safe from all this. Of course she would be worried about the Jedi Knights I suppose. One has to take humor where they can find it in a war zone.

The Supervisor of my Tactical Operations Center (TOC) where all communication was handled, and where we monitored on-screen all the movements and activities of our teams out on the road or in the air, came running into my office and told me they had just intercepted a distress call from a female Air Force Major and that the military rescue was quite a distance out. Besides her location, which was for some reason out in the Red Zone, all we knew was that she had screamed that she was alone, unarmed, and had taken fire and was stopped now with a large group of armed Iraqis surrounding her car and demanding that she get out. There were several components here that made no sense. Why was she in the Red Zone? Why was she alone? Why was she unarmed? And, was she totally insane or incredibly stupid?

Within seconds we had the fully-armed, small, fast little birds ready to fly and we were on the way to her location, which was only a moment away by air, about two miles deep into the Red Zone. The brand new-to-Iraq Air Force Major had taken a car alone and gone out unarmed to drive around the Green Zone to see what it was like. When she reached our External Control Point that divides the International Zone (IZ) from the Red Zone, she had just been oblivious to it and passed on into enemy territory, not seeing the soldiers waving at her to pull over or the tank protecting the entry or any of the other indicators that this was a crucial dividing point. She had driven several miles and realized the environment had taken on a dramatically "Dodge City" look and turned around to go back, realizing that she didn't know the route she had taken with all her turns and detours. At that moment, a sniper on a rooftop opened fire on her car, shattering the window and splattering glass into her face. She got a breath and at least had a number to call out for help, which was picked up by my TOC controllers. As our little birds came up on her position, which took us a bit to locate specifically in that disaster zone, the sniper was spotted on a roof top with his weapon. As he was turning his attention to the helicopter, one of the Blackwater Door Gunners killed him. We then saw that the Major's car was surrounded by Iraqis with AK-47s, pounding on her car and shaking it yelling at the woman, apparently to get out of the car. At least they hadn't shot her yet. We circled over the mob to get their attention and then slowly, deliberately, and as menacingly as possible with all our state-of-the-art weapons and firepower pointed at them, settled down on the ground next to the crowd. The violence momentarily abated and they began to back off in fear of the rotating blades and the fierce "wash", as well as our aggressiveness. We got to her car and pulled out the mis-directional Major and brought her to the helicopter and got out of there quickly as her car was being torched and burned, which had probably been their intent but with her in it. We flew her directly to the Combat Surgical Hospital (CSH) for treatment on her glass injuries to her face and hands from the sniper's windshield blast, and then we went home to wait for the next emergency. All in all, I was once again very impressed with the operational capability and the professionalism and courage of this Blackwater organization.

Two days later, we had our next opportunity to demonstrate our skills and capabilities to an organization that was not one of our own but was an ally. If we were available and not in demand to rescue our own people, I had a policy that we would use our resources to rescue allied forces and personnel if they were trapped, under fire, or injured, and if there were not already substantial appropriate military forces on the way. In this case, the Protective Detail of an NGO (non-governmental organization) called on the airwaves that they were under attack and fortunately for them, they were intercepted again by my incredible TOC personnel. They had been taking heavy fire and were now barricaded inside a building. Their reporting said that they were under fire by both Iraqi military and police. This might seem strange and unusual at first but believe me when I say it is not.

We reacted again with our armed helicopters. We took a combination of little birds for fast maneuverability and firepower, and medium-lifts for passenger carry capability. We flew over the building and sure enough, down below were about 40 Iraqi military and police, united in a battle and firing everything they had at the building like it contained George Bush himself. The "enemy" numbers were too great to go at in a frontal assault so we would have to be intelligent and sneaky. The little birds distracted the Iraqis in the front, slowly settling down to "see what was going on", allowing our guys to run in the back to evacuate the NGO folks. The team in the front walked up to talk with the police and military (fully and heavily armed of course and much better shooters than they were) and we asked them what was happening. An Iraqi military officer who easily could have been a Saddam Hussein look-alike, said that the NGO PSD (Protective Services Detail) had in an unprovoked act, opened fire on the Iraqi police as they were driving down the road and the Iraqi military had come to help their brothers against these (let's use dogs here instead of their explicative) cowardly dogs. We said that we would take charge of the NGO and would investigate the action. Weapons began to come up on both sides and that meant it was about time to say goodbye. The radio had signaled that the NGO personnel were out and gone so we said that the Iraqis were in charge as we backed our way to our little birds, with the other medium-lift hovering overhead with two crew-served machine guns trained on the enemy. That is serious firepower that makes everyone think about being cautious. As we flew away, we looked back at the building where the NGO vehicles were still scattered and parked in front. They were being turned into scrap iron and the building was being peppered with holes by the intensely focused Iraqis. I have no idea how long they continued to shoot up the place but I hope they were feeling less aggression after wasting all that ammunition. This was no way to have to do business.

It was currently Ramadan and normally that means in the world of Islam that things are supposed to be peaceful, while they all go about fasting from food and water during the day and then break their fast at sundown and eat, drink and party until late. They are usually too tired and hungry to fight and create trouble. That has not been the case since terrorism has become the radical Muslim past time. They use the "Jihadi" excuse to not fast so that they can have the strength to fight and wreak havoc. We were witnessing an actual increase in attacks during this Ramadan season and three of our motorcades had been seriously attacked in the first three weeks of the Ramadan 40 day period. The attacks followed the now-routine scenario of the motorcade being hit by roadside IEDs or EFPs and then being followed up by the use of small arms fire (rifles and machine guns) to try and kill as many as possible. Only luck or "Manifest Destiny" as some might say had prevented us from experiencing any loss of life. We had minor injuries but that has to be expected when you get hit by an IED or a shape-charge blast EFP. The Insurgents were busy trying to kill as many of our people as possible and knew that with a majority of Iraqis being off the road celebrating the period of peace, it reduced their associated collateral damage during attacks. But they didn't really care if they killed their own.

My first "Rest and Recreation" (R&R) break had been scheduled for October 12th to 30th and after 4.5 months without a day or even a minute off and no more than a maximum of 3 hours sleep per night, I was desperately in need of it. My new Deputy RSO had been learning the routines and seemed to be a very smart guy. I prayed that he would stay consistently engaged to allow me to go on leave for 2 weeks. Exhaustion can really take a toll on the mind and body. Fortunately I had a terrific team. What could possibly come up that would require me to further delay my R&R?

I was sitting at lunch eating soup in the little DFAC, watching my personally allocated 15 minutes per day of sports on the TV mounted on the wall, when a man walked by me and both our sets of eyes fixed on each other, trying to calculate why we seemed familiar. He recollected first and even called me by name. Then it hit me. In 1991, when I was on a MSD mission in Zaire (related in a prior chapter) evacuating personnel and protecting the remaining Americans at the Embassy and Ambassador Melissa Wells, as well as meeting with that psycho President Mobutu, I met a unique man with the U.S. Department of Defense, Defense Intelligence Agency who we will call Bill for preservation of anonymity. Bill and his partner worked gathering information on the tenuous daily situation in Zaire and passed it back to everyone in their chain to keep them informed on the situation in case we might need additional support for the remaining Americans (us). That seemed like a good idea to me and I liked knowing they could do it. Bill and I had worked for a couple of months together including on some nighttime reconnaissance for the possible evasion and escape means and methods if things went to hell and our capabilities were superceded by an enemy, being Mobutu's reckless and unpredictable Presidential Troops. Once this Zaire crisis was over, Bill went somewhere else and I went across the river to deal with another coup, this time in the Congo. Bill told me that he had seen that the name of the RSO was Bennett and had wondered if the world was actually small enough that it might be me. After about 15 years, it seemed a shot in the dark but those of us in this unique field of endeavor are constantly amazed at how our world continually brings us back together. Not all of us survive to share the reunions but when we do, it is a precious and bonding moment. We shared some lunches and dinners together to catch up on lost and living personnel and friends for the short period he was there and it was just another of those wonderful but surrealistic small world moments.

In another case we encountered, an Iraqi lady working in one of our State Department Sections allegedly had been kidnapped. A note was delivered to the Embassy demanding $200,000 dollars or she would be returned to her family in pieces. The money was paid by various groups but that was actually the first thing that made me suspicious. "They" connected the Embassy/US Government and her family in a single statement. It was a death sentence for the employee if the family knew as well and they wouldn't even care if she came back in pieces if she was an American collaborator. In fact, probably the entire family would be executed publicly for the transgression of the employee. The demand made me suspicious. It was just intuition on this one and it comes from doing hundreds of investigations involving the greed and weaknesses of humans, and of course has made me horribly jaded after all these years. I kept that to myself and to my investigative team since all the other Embassy Officers were sobbing at the possible loss of their friend. I put out a BOLO (Be On the Look-Out) on her with all our U.S. military units who monitored the highways and by-ways and within 2 days, she was nabbed by a U.S. military unit, alone and driving her car on the highway down south trying to cross the border through Basrah into Kuwait. Captured with her was the $200,000 and her personal luggage. Though she was alone with the ransom money and her luggage, freely driving south, she claimed she was still kidnapped and stuck to that story. Talk about red-handed. But, she refused to change her story. The money was returned to those who paid it for her safe return and we had her clearance and access to the Green (International) Zone revoked. It seemed that every day brought about new bizarre training opportunities for my young Special Agents.

On September 19th, 2006, we held the one year memorial gathering for DS Special Agent Stephen Sullivan and three Blackwater brothers; Kenneth Webb, Peter Tocci, and David Shepard, who all lost their lives exactly one year prior in Mosul, Iraq, when they diverted their follow car directly at the charging suicide vehicle in order to save their Principal who was the target of the terrorist suicide car bomb. Even though we only permitted DS and Blackwater to attend, easily 300 people came to pay their respects. We were there that day to honor their service and respect their bravery and sacrifice.

Three terrorist-insurgents pulled up in a Red Crescent Ambulance in front of the Combat Surgical Hospital (CSH) in the International Zone. They were all shot up from an obvious battle with our guys but were somehow driving and riding in a "neutral" ambulance and very unnervingly, inside our alleged safe and "controlled" International zone. They demanded medical treatment and true to our American form, we treated them and healed their wounds. My people and our military colleagues conducted a thorough investigation on who, when, what, and how they got to our front door. I also didn't like the fact they were using our Ambulances to get around. It signified a serious breach in the perimeter control and even worse, that the Iraqi government and NGOs were assisting the insurgents with resources we provided to them.

OCTOBER 02 THROUGH OCTOBER 31, 2006:

Every day was a 17-hour long roller-coaster and at the end of each one, I hardly had the strength to walk the 200 yards back to my little "container" and cautiously sleep for a couple of hours before what was becoming a more regular nighttime activity, and that was the incoming rocket attacks. I was sleeping partially dressed, and I would quickly finish and run for my Tactical Operations Center or race to the rocket detonation site to see if anyone was injured and needed emergency medical attention. Though the "ground hog" days and "enemy-disrupted" nights were running on as one continuous experience, this was the best assignment I had ever worked. We all were so engaged in such life and death activities from one minute to the next, and actually physically rescuing people who were under conditions of death threat, that to be able to contribute so substantially to a mission and cause, it just made everyone feel more relevant than they ever had before in their lives. We were like functioning competent Zombies from the fatigue, but we were focused and unified like no other experience life could offer.

One of our most northern constituent postings where I had an RSO manning the shop was a town called Erbil, situated in the more peaceful Kurdish region. I needed to get up there to take a look at the compound they lived and worked in. The descriptions of their living and working conditions made me very uneasy and there were apparently Iraqi private citizens living in homes in the middle of our improvised compound. This would not meet standards and made me wonder why we hadn't been hit by Insurgents already in such a target-rich environment with so little control.

I arranged for two of my medium-lift helicopters (Bell 412s) to fly me up to Erbil for an overnight visit so I could see for myself. On the way up, we would refuel in our Regional Embassy Office (REO) in Kirkuk, where I had another RSO and ARSO posted in a bigger outpost but more safely positioned in a compound with an adequate level of protection, everything being relative to the level and proficiency of attack of course. Anyone can be hit by a successful attack if the planning and scope are right.

This was the sandstorm season so we would have to watch for 200 foot-high walls of sand moving toward us at a high rate of speed. We would not want to be in the air when the engines and rotors got plugged with sand and we were all blinded. After about two hours into the flight, flying fast at 30 feet above the ground to prevent any waiting enemy from knowing we were coming until we were right on top of him, then we could either shoot him or speed past him before he could get his bearings and aim, we saw the inevitable. . .a large sandstorm bearing down on us. The pilot spotted a Wadi (dry ravine) up ahead and we landed the birds in it quickly and tied the blades down to keep it all intact, just barely before we were overtaken. We waited the storm out for hours and finally it lessened enough that we made a run for Kirkuk and the U.S. military base nearby. We radioed ahead and my excellent and reliable Kirkuk RSO was there with our armored cars to take us to the Kirkuk REO since it was apparent we would not make the further flight on to Erbil this time. The helicopters would clean up and refuel on the USG base and then fly to the REO, pick us up and fly us back to Baghdad. We would have to try the Erbil REO run another time. At least I was able to get another look at one of my constituent posts and see the good work my RSO had done, and that he was reasonably safe and protected. Kirkuk is the center of the big northern Iraqi oil fields and that meant that most likely at some point, there would be a civil war between the Sunnis, the Shias, and the Kurds for control and share divisions of the oil profits. Kirkuk has real potential for volatility. With sand in our boots, hair, and underwear, and looking like raccoons from the sandstorm and our goggles, we were picked up at the REO and made our way low and fast back to Baghdad for the night and made it just before sundown. That greatly reduced our threat potential although it meant we were back in time for the nightly rocket volleys into the compound, for which our military still were not returning fire.

I was now in a situation where I had been about five months without a single day off. When my first Deputy rotated out to his next assignment after 2 months with me, the first replacement Deputy was cancelled due to having a heart attack during our High Threat Tactical Training course. He had his assignment frozen until his health could be stabilized for his own safety. Fortunately, within my leadership ranks, my Section Chiefs were stellar. Nonetheless, with more than a dozen meetings a day and more administrative work than can be imagined, not to mention the daily personnel fires and conflicts that inevitably come up - the military screw ups and conflicts with the civilian population, and our nightly forays into the rocket fire - I needed a break. DS had actually sent me that DRSO that I mentioned before, and for 5 weeks, I had worked even harder and longer hours with him to bring him up to a level where he could hold things together while I took 2 weeks off in Thailand just sleeping and remembering the joys of life and freedom. But with one week to go before my time off, my very competent DRSO (and he was), developed personal issues that required him to return to Washington before I could take my first break.

My 110 hour work weeks with even more late night hours made me a walking zombie and my two Office Management Specialist (OMS), who were the best I have ever encountered in my career, became my mothers and sisters, watching out for my health and welfare, screening away any appointments that were not necessary and occasionally finding me slumped over my computer, briefly unconscious from a sleep deprivation shutdown. My batteries were drained and the limited hours of sleep per night were not recharging them. I was literally running on empty. Thankfully and insightfully, DS arranged for two men to come out from Washington to fill-in for me while I took my R&R. I departed Baghdad and 2 days later arrived in Bangkok where I slept, ate, worked in the gym, went to see movies, and just walked around enjoying the freedom and peaceful environment. The night I arrived in Bangkok, I went to bed in that nice, cool, clean sheeted, king-size deluxe hotel bed and went into paralysis until I tried to open my eyes 13 hours later.

General Casey was the Commanding General during this time and he seemed to be on top of things. However, the International Zone, which he was also responsible for the protection of, had become a porous haven for terrorists, illegal and unaccounted for weapons and large quantities of explosives. How could we all feel safe and how could I protect the Embassy (Saddam's Palace) and all the 7,000 people I was overseeing there if the IZ was now infected. They could drive a suicide vehicle bomb right up to my gate and kill hundreds. I began a campaign along with my military counterparts in the IZ to clean it up. General Casey caught on and began what he called a "Tiger Team" to "retake the IZ". He specifically asked me to be on it and that made things much easier for me to maintain a level of control on what might be rolling down the road toward my gates. It also made it clear to his Colonels and Generals that they needed to pay attention to the RSO operation. Our working relationship was excellent and we coordinated well.

Iraq had reached the most violent levels of the entire U.S. incursion and everyone was under the constant night rocketings and suicide bombings all over the country. Things were at their worst ever. DS was now talking to me about going from here to Islamabad, Pakistan, and I had been watching the reporting and insurgent movements. I predicted to DS that the next couple of years in Pakistan were going to be the worst and most violent ever. When I arrived there and things went to hell, I didn't want them blaming me again for the rise in terrorism. It is a reputation that has its good and bad points.

I was standing next to a wall surrounding Saddam's big pool by the DFAC, talking to a visiting Congressman as he was preparing to depart back out of the country. We still had a constant flow of Congressional Delegations and the RSO Section had to keep them safe while in Iraq. We call on assistance from "Big Army" when we need bigger guns or more equipment but so far, we had not lost one of them. I said goodbye to the Congressman, put him in the armored car, closed the door, and waved to the Agent to take him away. As I turned my head a bullet whizzed by my face and embedded itself in the wall. It literally was an inch or two from my face as it passed. The bullet was a random attempt to hit someone, fired from across the river, and once again, it confirmed that I was a blessed and lucky person, hopefully with a mission to complete. I picked it out and kept it. It was from an AK-47 and was a 7.62 mm that would have demolished my brain had it hit me. From this point on, I walked to the DFAC closer to the protective wall so the random angle from across the river was reduced.

The Secretary of State, Condoleeza Rice, was going to make a low profile visit to Baghdad. Initially, only a few of us were to know and I had been trying to turn it off because of the upsurge in violence and the fact that we had lost control of the entire civilian side of the airport to the Bathist radicals. That meant that when she tried to land her plane on the military runway, which ran parallel to the civilian runway, the insurgents, some who worked in the control tower, would have preparation and warning time to launch rockets and mortars at her approaching plane and could have a reasonably good chance of even hitting the motorcade we would send out to the plane, and the helicopters we would use to bring her to the IZ and the Palace for her meetings. The Bathists had also forced everyone living around the airport to move out so that they could have their own radical elements living in the approach patterns in order to shoot at planes landing and taking off. They simply threatened to kill them if they did not move and that gave them a control and positioning that was as dangerous as it gets. The enemy held every airport position and had distributed, as close as we could estimate, hundreds of keys to their people to access the tarmac-to-airport doors so that they could come and go without any checks or scrutiny and we knew they had brought large supplies of weapons and munitions to the airport and stored them in warehouses they controlled on the airport perimeter fringe areas.

I discussed my concerns about the limitations on security control of the airport and therefore the precarious nature of the airplane landings with the Secretary of State's Staff and our own Front Office. Her DS Protective Detail was concerned and wanted to alter the schedule but we were not allowed to vary the arrangements. As the Secretary's plane was coming in on final approach, sure enough the terrorists fired two mortars that landed on the runway ahead of her plane and the pilots diverted and circled around for a pause while they considered the next action. The Secretary's plane circled over a nearby U.S. Airbase and did finally land and she conducted her business and then got back out safely but every resource I had was put into play as well as the Big Army elements.

A couple of days later I awoke to repeated loud explosions that were shaking my trailer and I heard whistling overhead, which meant that rockets were close. My trailer was literally rocking on its foundation or whatever it was resting on. I stepped out to see if I could identify the direction. South of the IZ, there was a small FOB (forward operating base) for our U.S. military and it was where they stashed a large dump of ammunition and explosives. It was the primary one for our region. Somehow, the Iraqis got lucky enough to hit one of the bunkers with a mortar and it set off a series of sympathetic detonations at the other bunkers that literally kept blowing up for about 6 hours until god only knows how many thousands of tons of explosives, rockets and mortars were expended. The whistling overhead was the sound of some of our own munitions traveling miles from the blast site. It was October but it was the biggest Fourth of July I ever witnessed.

Strangely, but with a $1 Billion dollar a year RSO budget, I didn't have any money for discretional representational use. It was hard to believe that people are still so penny wise and pound fool-ish but I needed a source of money for creating and producing plaques for my Agents who served me for their year, to com-memorate their tour and to let them know they were appreciated. They all needed something for their "I love me" wall when they moved on. Being an ex-businessman, I designed a polo shirt with our exceptional RSO Iraq "Crossed Swords" logo on it and we decided on the slogan "Resistance Is Futile". It seemed appro-priate for the RSO to voice our sentiments about resisting our policies on our T-shirts. I contracted with a company in Texas and the shirts became an extremely high demand item. We made them in polos, dress shirts, jackets, casual work shirts and t-shirts, and we sold thousands. All funds were meticulously tracked and there was no profit. All funds were donated to the RSO farewell plaques and charity causes in Iraq. We also gave a lot of them away as goodwill and representational gestures. Every TDYer and VIP wanted the shirts and on the Secretary of State's visit, a Washington Post reporter saw them being worn and wrote an article in the Post calling them "the Hottest Item in the Green Zone". We were pleased to bring some joy into this war zone and every Agent, Office Manager, and Security Engineer would leave with a beautiful plaque.

It was about this time that the HBO Documentary called "The Journalist and the Jihadi" was released. This was the one that I had contributed interviews to regarding the Daniel Pearl case and had met with the Producers in New York at Mariane Pearl's home for dinner in about 2003. Apparently it was well received and I began to get emails from people who saw it and liked it. We didn't get a lot of HBO in Baghdad so I was anxious to see it. Apparently, Diplomatic Security (DS) had a showing of the Documentary at our World Headquarters in Rosslyn, Virginia, across the river from DC. This was exciting to be a part of something that hopefully would bring about a positive aspect from something so horrible. People need to be educated about the terrors that are going on out in the world all around them, and that DS Agents witness and deal with every day to keep Americans safe.

I have intentionally left out many of the daily rocket attacks and deaths and roadside IED and EFP attacks and firefights that have made our daily operations so precarious, but I wanted to relate this following story about the courage and bravery and heart of my men. It is not my intent in this book to relate every one of the hundreds of incidents that occured but rather to show the life and character development of the DS Agent. This story is only one of many, and I will relate a number as we go along. It demonstrates what we faced and should be a source of pride to all Americans for the capability and loyal devotion of our Americans on the front lines of the global war on terrorism in order to keep it from breaching our U.S. borders. I often tell people who can't understand why I do what I do, that I do my job for the children. For the next generations who may have to face this nightmare. I want to rid their world of as much terror as I can.

Informationally for this next story, "Raven" will be used as the call sign for our numerous protective security details made up of DS Agents and Blackwater Protective Agents who kept our people alive in the Red Zone.

At approximately 1400 hours (2 p.m.) on October 22, 2006, the Raven 7 Agent in Charge (AIC) of his Protective Detail and Protectee came onto the radio being monitored in my Tactical Operations Center (TOC) to advise us that his Team had been requested by the Principal (Protectee) for an extra ten minutes at the venue with the Minister of Public Works. It may not seem like a big deal but if we lost our exact schedule by even a minute, it was time to reach out to see if something bad had happened. We stuck to a rigid guideline as prepared at the beginning of each day. Our Protectees often didn't realize how critical a few extra minutes being exposed in the enemy's territory could be. It was time enough to gather and set up for an attack as we departed. All team members responded with an acknowledgment of the delay. This Protectee was notorious for recklessly overstaying "the plan" so it was not completely unexpected. She was part of the Iraq Reconstruction Management Section and was known to run long meetings. Raven 7 had escorted her many times to venues in dangerous areas and they were highly skilled at keeping people alive.

Several minutes after the original scheduled departure time, a series of explosions rocked the street just outside the venue gate and T-Walls (12 foot high concrete visual and blast deterrent sections). The fourth of the blasts was less than 75 meters from the gate that Raven 7 should have already departed through. We had to consider the possibility that they were timed devices and that the enemy had recognized our approximate limit at a venue. My TOC called me immediately. I raced to the TOC to be there for any command decisions that might involve life or death.

My Section Leader for the High Threat Protective Section had gone on this specific mission as a periodic validation of tactics and operations and was now caught up in the attack with Raven 7. The entire Team knew exactly what to do and it came from extensive training and a cohesive understanding and too much experience.

The Agent in Charge (AIC) went to the Principal and told her they needed to go immediately from the venue before the enemy had more reinforcements arrive. Explosions go off in the city all day long and some are much worse than others. We didn't know if these were rockets, mortars, vehicle bombs, personnel suicide bombers, IEDs or a host of other possibilities, but they each had their own threat and risk and we needed to get out. The Principal's first response, as well as that of the Minister, was that these things happened all the time in the streets of Baghdad and it was fine in the office, there was nothing to worry about. It might be noted that the Minister's office wall facing the street side was lined with sand bags. This insane comment by the Minister and supported by the Protectee, was made just seconds before the fourth explosion blew out the Minister's windows. As the AIC was rapidly and forcefully moving the Protectee down the stairs to evacuate her from the precarious building to the fully-armored motorcade, the rest of the Team was fulfilling their individual tasks according to procedure to provide cover fire for her and the motorcade, and the counter-snipers were searching for a target that needed to be eliminated. The objective was to get our Principal out safely and some of Raven 7 would be staying behind to ensure the safe departure by providing cover-fire. The temporary sacrifice was necessary and it was our job and simply how things had to be done. We would expect to recover these other assets and elements once the focus on the Principal by the enemy dissipated at this venue. The Shift Leader ordered the Tactical Commander to notify Raven Base in the TOC of their situation and requested our RSO helicopters, flown and maintained by exceptional Blackwater pilots, to attempt an air extraction to save the risk of an overland run through unknown enemy assets. Other Team members began to set up a secure protective perimeter around the pre-designated landing zone (HLZ) the helicopter would touch down in. Helicopters have no armoring and thus need to get in and out very quickly before bullets and rockets tear them to pieces. Each venue has a technical security survey done on it in advance to lay out every contingency and response to any emergency so that when something happens, the response is 95% already calculated. The Tactical Commander advised Raven 7 that two Hughes model 530F "little birds" would be on venue within minutes. The two small, fast and highly maneuverable helicopters were almost identical to the AH-6 attack helicopters used by the U.S. Army Special Forces. In fact, virtually every one of the responding pilots working for us was a retired veteran of the Army's elite 160th Special Operations Aviation Regiment, the feared "Night Stalkers", with thousands of hours of experience behind the controls of the versatile aircraft. This unit proved its courage and skill in numerous hazardous and famous conflicts but was perhaps best known for protecting American Army Rangers in the deadly street fighting in the operation in Mogadishu, Somalia. You would remember them from their courageous actions in the movie "Blackhawk Down". These guys are the best. The helicopters only held one passenger (the Protectee) with 2 door gunners and two pilots so it was expected that the rest of the protective detail would stay behind and fight their way out later.

The Raven 7 Team first had to get the Principal to the low visibility armored Mercedes Benz and to get her ballistic vest and helmet on. Never leave home without it. They will save your life. Almost immediately after getting her "geared up" for extraction, the Blackwater helicopter crew radioed that they were on scene and ready for extraction. The perimeter security team went into action and pushed out the perimeter further, risking themselves to obtain more "set-back" protection for the Principal and helicopter crew to have the best chance of excape. Once the Team had maximized their perimeter reach, the little birds, in a flash and with dust and debris flying everywhere, dropped in quickly to the Ministry's back yard to pick the Principal up. The door gunners stepped out with their large crew-served machine guns and assessed the area and roof tops to gain perspective and a certain personal comfort level as the AIC and other members of the "in-close" Raven 7 Protective Team rushed the Principal from the relative safety of the armored sedan to the helicopter, strapped her into a space on the padded floor in the back of the tiny aircraft. With the door gunners back into active positions hanging out of their doors, snapped onto their safety lines and with their weapons ready to bring down hell onto anyone trying to kill them, off they went, all within seconds.

This was only part one of our concern since now we had the

Raven 7 Team to get safely home and we would use multiple assets to assure that happened. For our Raven 23 Tactical Support Team (TST) also known as a Quick Response Force (QRF) as well as our other RSO Blackwater Air assets, the drama never ended and these elements were all called into action to get Raven 7 home safely in case the original explosions, which occurred in reality only moments before, were only the first part of a more complex attack.

RSO Blackwater Air assets A and B were up in the air finishing another mission and redirected themselves on command from the TOC to provide overhead cover and routing direction for Raven 7 and Raven 23, the QRF, which were hopefully all about to link up and join forces to safely fight their way back to the International Zone. Baghdad traffic was always chaotic and confusing and congested, far beyond what anyone has seen in another third-world country. There was no comparison and I have seen the worst of the worst. The atmosphere of war and insurgency eliminated any rules, laws, or moral or ethical or even logical assumptions for driving. It was Ramadan and this afternoon was worse than normal since everyone was out trying to buy their food for the night's Iftar, or "fast-breaking" meal. The TST/QRF's heavily armored Saxon and Mamba vehicles were having a particularly difficult time linking up with their stranded Raven 7 comrades. The heavily armed Blackwater contractors in the QRF carefully scanned every occupant of every vehicle watching for hostile Saddar militia members or suicide bombers always looking for them. Our DS Special Agent was working with the QRF and was intently watching his sector of responsibility when a roadside IED detonated 100 yards in front of the QRF Motorcade. The Tactical Commander of the QRF immediately ordered a redirection down another street. Overhead, little birds A and B had spotted the QRF Raven 23 and were trying to identify clear routes from up in the air to help them get through to Raven 7 as quickly as possible. The door gunners of A and B were hanging out the doors of their little birds watching for anyone trying to harm the TST. It is easier to see clear routes for them from overhead and within minutes, little birds A and B had linked up Raven 23 with Raven 7 and were now guiding both teams and motorcades through clear routing and away from the smoking craters of the rockets and IEDs. The Blackwater pilots quickly had guided the two Raven units out of the chaos and followed them to ensure that they made it back into the International Zone.

Once back at our HLZ hangars, known as LZ Washington, that was home to the RSO Blackwater air operation, the pilots had little time to relax, ever. They quickly refueled, re-checked their weapons and equipment, and ate some quick sandwiches before launching into the air again. Other Raven Teams would undoubtedly need their help soon enough. As Ramadan began to wrap up the 40 days of fasting, I had advised my teams that we should expect increased violence and attacks from anti-coalition forces and the attack on Raven 7 seemed the validating pre-cursor to that upsurge. Immediately after getting Ravens 7 and 23 back, I called my High Threat Leaders together and notified them that for the rest of today and until further evaluation could be made, we would err on the side of caution and all further Protective Service Details scheduled to go outside of the IZ were put on hold and all teams still out in the Red Zone were called back. We needed to know what was being planned for us by the enemy. We still had several Teams out in the danger zone and we needed to get them home. Raven 27 was a military team from the 1/101st Field Artillery Massachusetts National Guard, who worked for me on protective details, and was still out at the Ministry of Interior.

And Ravens 2 and 9 had dropped off their Principals at BIAP (Baghdad International Airport) and were getting new counter-measures equipment installed in their armored vehicles at Camp Victory. Little birds A and B were redirected to provide overhead support for these ground teams to get them safely home.

The Massachusetts Army National Guard PSD Team was relatively new to our family, having only recently taken over from the departing 1/127th Field Artillery Kansas National Guard one week earlier. The soldiers, cross-trained as Military Police and given classes and training in protective security operations by the RSO and Blackwater staff were on one of their first runs into the Red Zone and we knew how nervous they must be.

The young National Guard Sergeant in charge of the PSD Team was instructed to change radio channels and communicate directly with the supporting aircraft. The experienced pilots of Blackwater A and B easily and quickly established contact with Raven 27 and began to guide them back through the dangerous streets of Baghdad back to the Embassy inside the IZ. Once they were safely inside the checkpoint on the perimeter of the IZ, the tiny aircraft raced out to BIAP to link up with Ravens 2 and 9. Once "on station" they began covering the two motorcades comprised of dark colored armored Suburbans as they moved along the notorious Route Irish to the IZ. The four lane highway that is the principal route from the IZ to the airport had been and was still the scene of countless IEDs and small arms attacks. While it had been relatively quiet for the last couple of weeks due to heavy coalition security efforts, it always paid to be extra vigilant on this deadly route and things were HOT in the city today. The little birds flew orbits over the racing motorcades, the pilots and door gunners scanning the sides of the road and the cross streets for any sign of trouble and feeling that at any second, something was going to come right at them.

Just about the time that the Blackwater crew was thinking that they were almost home-free as the line of Suburbans raced across the dividing line of the Red Zone and the IZ at the checkpoint, the little birds took their final circle-over one of the pre-designated points on the Baghdad streets which corresponded with a traffic cloverleaf that connected Route Irish and Route Jackson. One door gunner, an experienced veteran of the U.S. Army Rangers and Special Forces and countless missions as door gunner of Blackwater B, caught something in his peripheral vision and directed the pilots to bank left. Down below, they saw something that put them into immediate action, without pause or concern for themselves. An Army convoy of Hummvees (HMMWV) had just been hit by an improvised explosive device (IED) and they could see wounded soldiers who needed help. The first pilot in Blackwater B immediately set up close air coverage over the stricken vehicles and provided security for his wingman in Blackwater A, watching for the inevitable small arms attack that follows an IED so that the enemy could finish off any wounded Americans. Blackwater A prepared to set down in the street to render aid and pick up the wounded crew as his radio man contacted the TOC to ask me for authorization to rescue and retrieve, which was immediately given.

The Blackwater crew was now on the vulnerable ground and took up defensive positions to protect their helicopter and everyone's lives. One crew member grabbed his medical aid bag and dashed over to the injured soldiers. This particular ex-soldier was a former 18D Special Forces Medical Sergeant, renowned as the most highly trained Medics in the world. He raced over to assess the wounded. The lead HMMWV in the multi-vehicle motorcade had taken a direct hit by what appeared to have been an EFP (explosively formed projectile). This was an all-too common and extremely deadly form of focused IED. The EFP has at its heart a metal cone that when launched by the explosives becomes a projectile of typically copper that cuts through armor like it was paper. This horrific attack seemed to have been an array of EFPs due to the series of huge holes penetrating the armor of the tough American defensive vehicle. Running up to the vehicle, the Medic saw that less-injured soldiers had already been able to remove two of their wounded comrades from the wreckage and had begun a rudimentary first aid. He ran around to the other side of the damaged vehicle and found three more "downed" troops. He quickly checked the soldier in the front of the vehicle and saw that he had definitely been killed instantly by the explosion. In the rear of the HMMWV, there were two other troops and he helped to remove them from the ruined vehicle. He keyed his radio microphone and advised the orbiting Blackwater B that more helicopters for ambulances would be needed. Helo B called Raven Base in the TOC and we heard the status of the attack. We immediately dispatched the air crews and Blackwater C and D scrambled to get their aircraft into the air.

While the larger Bell 412s, known as a medium lift helicopter, and is an updated version of the Huey UH-1 of Vietnam fame, spun up and began to race to the scene, the Blackwater Medic completed his triage work and began to move the most needy casualties to waiting Blackwater A. He told the young Army Lieutenant, who was now in charge with the death of the Army Major in the front seat, that the RSO Blackwater helicopters could evacuate the wounded to the Combat Surgical Hospital (CSH) in the IZ, which was less than a 3 minute flight away. The shocked

Lieutenant readily gave his OK and Blackwater A lifted off with the first and the most critical need patient-soldiers. In order to do this, the Medic was forced to stay at the attack scene, where he continued to work on the wounded as his "chopper" flew home. The Medic continued to stabilize the patients as Blackwater C and D arrived at the attack site and with the help of the surviving soldiers, picked up the other wounded while Blackwater B continued to provide overhead security coverage. Within a minute, the wounded were loaded and the helos raced for the CSH. The Medic joined the surviving soldiers in their still operating motorcade and together, all drove to the IZ and the CSH where their friends were fighting for their lives.

In that attack which took place on October 22, 2006, two members of the 4th Infantry Division, acting as PSD elements, were killed. Four initially survived the blast and were evacuated by RSO Blackwater Air to the 28th Combat Surgical Hospital in the International Zone. But, had it not been for the alert awareness and the quick response and professional dedication of the Blackwater Air Team and this brave Medic, most certainly many of them could have died out there on Route Jackson that day.

Once again, I was proud to be who we were and to do the job we were assigned. Blackwater Air, operating under the command and control of the Diplomatic Security Regional Security Office of the U.S. Embassy Baghdad, had proven itself invaluable in protecting and saving American lives in the war on terror and in the reconstruction of Iraq. Countless times each day, the "aerial security platforms" helped protect the RSO and Blackwater protected motorcades as they transported Diplomats under the Chief of Mission authority throughout Baghdad and all the other major cities in Iraq. This was not the first time we went into harms way to save fellow Americans. It wasn't even the hundredth time. We were constantly racing to the scenes of injured and dieing American Department of State Foreign Service Officers and Contractors, and all our brave coalition soldiers. It is what we did out there and at the end of the day, there was frequently pain, suffering and even crying by the toughest men on earth. But, there was also great joy and gratification when we saved them and knew they would be going home to their families again. There was no feeling anywhere or anytime like the total engagement with life and death that we encountered every single day.

NOVEMBER 01 THROUGH DECEMBER 03, 2006:

We had entered a new low. Most of the FSNs had either been killed or fled to keep from being killed. The order of the day was Snipers, who seemed to be shooting at our people all the time and from hidden locations. They were killing our soldiers frequently and from quite far away. These seemed to be well-trained and equipped and were killing us from undiscovered hiding places. Not ones typically Iraqi. Perhaps we were seeing assistance from a bordering nation who felt they would benefit from more dead Americans. The Iranians appeared to be training and supplying the Iraqi Insurgents and their skill level and success ratio was going up.

We went on a vendetta against terrorist snipers and had some successes. Our ex-Special Forces Dedicated Defensive Marksmen (previously designated counter-snipers) were the best and we used their capabilities with more frequency when we went into the Red Zone on protective missions.

This particular day we took an Embassy Officer to visit an Iraqi

Minister and since we couldn't trust them nor their entire staff not to tell the enemy that we were coming, it was our custom to place "politically correct" Dedicated Defensive Marksmen (DDMs) in advance to watch for snipers, as well as other attackers, and to eliminate any threats as our motorcades came closer to the venue. On this particular day, one of our DDMs spotted a motorcyclist pull up on the street outside the Ministry next to a parked car and just stop. But while stopped, he was talking to himself or to the trunk of the car. Our DDM spotter zoomed in on the trunk and identified a missing tail light and a barrel of a rifle barely visible in the hole of the missing tail light. Our insurgent snipers had gotten some creative and tricky training from someone and this was how they were killing our soldiers without being spotted. The spotter and DDM both then saw the motorcyclist point up to where our DDMs were to warn the sniper of our position. The sniper quickly fired a shot off at the Blackwater DDM who then carefully placed a round into the trunk of the car, killing the sniper (eliminating the threat). Immediately from another direction to the side of our Blackwater DDM and Spotter, two shots hit the wall right next to his head. Our spotter recognized two more snipers with rifles on a roof top 950 meters away and they were still zeroing in on our DDM. Our DDM fired one shot to gauge his range. His second shot killed one of the snipers. After a moment of cat and mouse waiting, the second sniper poked his head and rifle up to take another shot and our DDM eliminated him. This all took place within 30 seconds of our Principal arriving on venue. On this day, three snipers who had been killing our American soldiers were no more. True credit goes to the skill and calm control of the Blackwater DDM and spotter. We weren't always so fortunate.

My various terrific professional Office Management Specialists

(OMS) who kept me straight and on time for meetings and made sure I was buffered from unnecessary visitations from people who just wanted to discuss their gripes or needs with the RSO. It must be part of their training because each of them during their own tour periods would respond with the same protective tactic. I would hear the door open and someone's voice say they wanted to see the RSO. At that point, I would look up and see the ladies slowly and gracefully and in a non-threatening way, stand and move from their desks toward the individual but in a way that blocked my office door and buffered me from a quick end-run to try and stick their head in my door, knowing I would agree to a few minutes to resolve some normally petty issue. They were the best and I wish I had a video of just once when they would perform this tactical protective measure. In most cases they were successful and diverted the person to my Section Head who dealt with that particular matter but on a rare occasion, the individual would make a quick dash to my door and I would end up being polite. I think those individuals who were able to defeat the OMS defensive line through nefarious means were put on a secret OMS list and typically never succeeded in getting "buzzed" through the door again. I loved my OMS's.

It was time to try and fly all the way to Erbil up north again in the "peaceful and industrious" Kurdish region to visit my RSO who was holding security together in a "neighborhood" compound that literally bordered on the street of the city and incorporated Iraqis and other third-country nationals living inside our perimeter. The DFAC (eating establishment) on the Erbil Consulate site was comprised of two local Iraqis who cooked food from their homes and charged back to the U.S. government for each meal. One intentional poisoning would wipe out our entire operation. I hated this lack of security but at least at this time, the Kurds were being very friendly and they didn't like the insurgents or other Iraqis so they protected us to the degree that one can in a country with a huge terrorist war underway.

We prepped the two medium lift helicopters and took off flying very low over the surface of the earth and as fast as we could. Erbil itself is quite historic. It is the eighth oldest continually occupied city on the planet dating back to about 8,000 years. It's central "old city" or "Citadel" area was unique and reminded me from the air a bit of the old walled cities in Spain except much older and a lot less desirable to be in. In fact, even in less volatile Erbil, we had to fly over the old city and couldn't walk it due to the threats. We spent some time in the desert on the way up and alongside a river as certain planning issues were being taken care of for our arrival, and when we landed, we traveled overland to a Korean Base, where I hoped to move all our people into trailer-type housing and out of that wacky death trap they were in. The real reason for the visit was to push to get our housing project moving on the Korean Base.

The Kurdish people didn't like war but did like Americans. They mostly liked to make money and are very industrious. They were angry at the Iraqis (which they did not consider themselves to be) because they were screwing up their opportunities for commercial enterprise and profits. The most advanced and progressive part of Iraq is the Kurdish area. It was a productive learning experience and we accomplished what I had hoped to.

We left with enough time to get back before sundown when bad things happened with even more frequency. As we approached Baghdad, you could feel the difference in the way the pilots flew. They began a very low, fast and serpentine oriented tactical flying method to maximize our chances of not being hit by ground fire. People would definitely shoot at us. The Pilot's objective was to make it impossible to hit us and they were very good and very experienced at it. Sometimes, even bad shots get lucky and this time, we got hit from rifle fire but no one took a round and we would only have to make repairs to the helicopter. I knew that as happy as I would be when my tour was over, I would be sad to leave. This was either the worst job one would ever love, or the best job one would ever hate.

DECEMBER 04 THROUGH DECEMBER 24, 2006:

December had gotten cold and the nights actually required blankets and the day required a coat. It would warm up during the day to the point of being like winter in San Diego but was pretty freaking cold in that desert at night. The pool still looked great even though no one ever got in it now. I had never been in the pool working so much and I certainly didn't want to now. When the MWR entertainment events took place on stage near the pool at nights, we were huddled in coats and gloves trying to enjoy them. We would have created fires to warm up, but the enemy would have used them to zero in on us.

One of our now routine many daily rocket attacks hit but fortunately there was just one single indirect fire (IDF) projectile. We all knew that a rocket had hit and had hit close because the entire earth shook and the "whump" was loud. We just couldn't find the impact spot. We searched for hours and finally had to admit that it was better at hiding than we were at finding. A couple of hours later, we received a call in our TOC from a KBR contractor who had opened his big industrial food freezer in his kitchen and found a rocket in there he hadn't remembered ordering. As we worked the rocket's path backwards, we found that it had hit a parking lot at a shallow angle, skipped along and penetrated through an air-conditioning unit on a trailer, continued skipping through both walls of another building, went under the Post Office, and entered the freezer where it came to rest without detonating. When a huge chunk of steel flies at the speed a rocket does and impacts the earth, even without detonating, mother earth takes a terrible shaking. I cannot imagine what it must have been like when the asteroid hit the earth creating the Gulf of Mexico. No wonder it wiped out everything on the planet. Our Explosives Ordinance Disposal expert took the rocket out to the river and detonated it as they always did in these cases. Luckily it hadn't caused damage to the post office. Man, don't mess with our Post Office near Christmas. The rocket passed under the Post Office but missed the bags of mail. There were some seriously angry personnel when they heard the insurgents had almost affected the joyful connection to the real world. I think we almost had an assault on Saddar City by bookkeepers and accountants. Later that night, another rocket landed but failed to detonate although it had better aiming success and hit the Iraqi Vice President's home inside the IZ. The shrapnel and sheer force started a fire in his home showing again how unpredictable rockets can be. We were now into the concentrated holiday rocketing period and being hit every day. It was obvious to all of us that the Iraqis weren't very open-minded about Christian holidays. I took them all off my Christmas list.

An Office Manager (OMS) is a professional specialist who runs the daily office operations. You must have leadership skills to be a good OMS and my new one was excellent. She was an attractive "motherly" black woman who always acted in-charge and never got riled by anything. It was her first time under rocket fire but even so, when a rocket hit right outside our office on the front lawn of the palace, I saw her raise her eyes, consider the options and then she gathered everyone and moved them into the inner "Investigations Bull Pen" where they were safer. Then after the "all-clear", she was right back at her desk as focused as ever. She wanted to go to the Airport to greet someone for the experience and helicopter ride but didn't know she would be going out on one of the little birds. This would be her first helicopter ride, not to mention the first time she would be sitting on the open door edge facing out into the wind and with her feet and legs outside braced on two little metal foot pegs. When the little bird banked left, she would be suspended into what seemed like open free-fall and the rush is great, but for many, very disconcerting. When we took her to LZ Washington to depart, she was briefly shocked at the thought of how she would be traveling but quickly recovered and hid her concern and went, as is her philosophy of "no fear". The next time I saw her after she returned, she was walking around trying to hide a big smile on her face and just said "everything went fine". I talked with my pilots and they said that she giggled and laughed and screamed like a little kid on his first trip to Disneyworld all the way and seemed to love it. Now that her hair was repaired and her composure was recovered, she would never admit that to me. She was the consummate professional that could not be ruffled. But, now when anyone mentioned the little birds, I looked at her and I could see her looking away with a private grin on her face remembering the experience.

My Marine Security Guards, and here, also my Marine Security Force, are such good-hearted and brave young men. Our country will always succeed because of the strength and courage of our young people. Every year, the MSGs have a Christmas "Toys for Tots" Program and even though it is a Christian holiday and we are definitely in a Muslim country, the Marines identified a couple of orphanages that could really use our help. It would have to be done carefully and discreetly because if any of the insurgents or radical neighbors found out that the Americans helped the kids, they would kill them all and burn the buildings to the ground. It's not always easy to maintain the spirit of Christmas. These poor orphaned kids had nothing and were often forgotten in the Muslim world but we collected clothing and blankets and 3,000 toys for them. All toys had to be "cleansed" of American tags or any other sign that they might have an American connection, and it took days with 3,000 of them but we got them all cleaned, tagged, and bagged and over to the Iraqi orphans. It must have been quite a morning but I couldn't allow any of us to be there to see their joy for the protection of the kids.

In a dark humor sort of way, we had a funny moment when my TOC got a call and we responded as the only reliable response force around. The Greek Ambassador was driving around in his armored vehicle and with his protective detail and motorcade. He was conducting some business with an Iraqi Minister who was in the car with him. Their entire motorcade was stopped at an Iraqi Military roadblock and when the Iraqis looked inside, they later claimed that they acted the way they did because they were afraid the Iraqi Minister was being kidnapped by the Greek Ambassador. I know, it seems like an unlikely story but the outcome and the key to the story is that the Iraqis took everyone hostage, including the Iraqi Minister. Kidnappings were becoming quite a profit-making industry for bandits and there was virtually no difference between actual bandits or Iraqi Army and Iraqi Police who were doing it after-hours anyway. The difference was that unlike in Colombia or Mexico City, where kidnapping was a "professional" enterprise whose continued operational success depended on returning the individual safe once you got the money, here the

Iraqis were killing the hostage after getting the money just for the personal ease of operation for them. They were dangerous and stupid and that combination is the worst of all. The Iraqi Military element later claimed they were headed back to their base with all the hostages. But to show how inept they were, they never took the cell phone away from the Greek Ambassador who called my TOC and told us where they were and where they were headed. The Coalition Ambassadors all met with me occasionally and we established emergency response procedures for them and this Ambassador responded well and called. We put the birds in the air, sent our ground teams to intercept them and also had "Big Army" put their resources into play, which would pretty much guarantee our strength of control. We all intercepted the Iraqi Army's attempt to make some extra money but listened to their weak story first and then took the Ambassador and Minister back into safe custody and took them home. The Greek Ambassador and the Iraqi Minister both thought they were doomed since they would most likely not be returned alive once the ransom had been paid and were very grateful and sent our Ambassador a nice thank you for our files. One could never gauge what the Iraqis were thinking or what they would try next and they certainly didn't care about their own people, or really any person except their own individual selfish selves.

It was finally Christmas Eve and true to form, the Insurgents and other anti-Coalition Forces were rocketing the IZ and my buildings specifically. I guess I should admit that we expected them to do this since they were hitting us almost every day and night and Christmas must be a holiday that really pissed them off. It became a constant barrage and my perimeter checkpoint number 2 also took 3 indirect fire rockets (IDF). The enemy was getting better and more accurate at selecting targets. The day before, in the warm-up to Christmas, we took 17 rockets in four separate sessions over a 3-hour period. Only pure luck kept anyone from being hurt. We could also hear car bombs going off regularly on the other side of the Tigris River and because of the water, it amplified the sound like it was detonating right outside the trailer or building. The river must be 1,000 meters across near our trailers but it sounded like it was right on top of us. Since it was going to be Christmas, we told everyone to go "home" to their trailers at 1500 hours to make it like a partial day-off holiday. Not many people actually took the time off. There was nothing else to do anyway and we would just end up running to the bunkers to get away from the rocket fire. For me, it was a chance to do some paperwork catch-up between the daily crisis fires. I felt blessed to have the opportunity to take on a challenge the size of this one. We all felt a pride in the job we were doing, and when we rescued or saved someone whose life was in jeopardy, it made everything worthwhile in our own lives at that moment. I was so proud of my entire team, I can't explain it.

DECEMBER 25, 2006 THROUGH JANUARY 29, 2007:

Late Christmas Eve, things went severely downhill and more personal from the rocketings we had been getting earlier in the day and evening. One of our protective security contractors with Blackwater, got too much alcohol in his bloodstream and got into trouble. There are two things that just inherently do not go well together. Alcohol consumption and carrying a weapon. As this man (who was a weapons specialist), left one party at his Blackwater compound, he walked through what had been transitioning to an Iraqi Minister and VIP neighborhood toward Camp Liberty. Another American party was underway poolside at Camp Liberty and apparently it was going "great guns" - including military folks consuming alcohol, which can get them sent home and demoted. As this well-trained but highly-inebriated ex-Special Forces weapons armorer passed the home of the Minister of Interior (MOI), he encountered an Iraqi MOI personal bodyguard outside on the street protecting the perimeter and just looking to create havoc where there was none. No matter how you look at it, at this time, Iraqis, especially those with military or police training, did not like the fact that we were in their country.

So, we have a drunk weapons expert walking past an armed and hostile Iraqi who would love to get "blooded" by killing this American who seems an easy target, and most of the American community is partying and out of sight. It seemed like an ideal scenario for the Iraqi and certain doom for the American. The other side of the coin fortunately is that Iraqis aren't much on the shooting skills. They seem to do a lot of "pointing in the general direction and pulling the trigger". This armed guard waited until the drunk American had walked past him and then pointed and shot. The American was an expert, even drunk, and had been trained to respond in a very specific way. The bullet whizzed past his ear and he heard the shot and felt the air being split near his head. He somehow focused enough to turn and see the Iraqi pointing his AK-47 at him and about to fire again and he drew his weapon and shot the Iraqi dead with one shot. He then continued to Camp Liberty, passing my Peruvian Guards who protected the nearby Consulate compound, which was also the back entrance into Liberty, and as he came up to some of his friends, he told them he thought he had just killed an Iraqi who shot at him. His friends immediately took him back to the Blackwater compound and put him to bed. This is where me and my people came into play. I wasn't at any of the parties since I was the RSO and supposed to be the example of restraint to others. So within an hour, we had pieced together the incident and spoken to my Peruvian Guards, who had diligently logged the drunken defender into the registry when he passed through. I sent an ever-vigilant team of ARSO Investigators over to Liberty and they talked with the others at the party and heard about the self-defense shooting confession and moved on to pick up the shooter who was sleeping it off in his "hooch". The story seemed plausible. We didn't have any reason to suspect that he just shot this Iraqi for no reason. But he had been drunk and that is breaking the cardinal rule when carrying a weapon. No matter what happens, you have fault for being drunk with a gun and drawing the weapon is worse. Its the "vehicular rear-ending" rule for gun-toters. Even if the other car stops like an idiot, you are at fault for hitting him from behind. It was his fault for being drunk with a weapon but he had been defending his own life. There would be Iraqi claims that he shot the bodyguard for no reason, but the truth would always be the truth. And after all was said and done, the truth would be that there were only two people at that shooting. One was dead. The other was claiming self defense. That was my Christmas Eve.

Christmas Day came on the heels of a no-sleep night but the excellent DFAC Manager had taken a lot of effort to decorate the cafeteria in a Christmas way and we were all impressed with his dedication to making us feel a little more at home. I cannot imagine where he found a full-size mechanical Santa Clause playing a banjo. That is truly a sign of a man who knows how to be a professional in his occupation. Yes, it was surrealistic to have it here under rocket fire and we hoped Santa would survive, but it was like much about this place, it was a mix of blood and guts reality mixed with Alice in Wonderland events of disbelief and all sewn up in a never-ending movie of "Ground Hog Day". I decided I would only work 10 hours on Christmas and would take the rest of the day off to relax (if the Iraqi Insurgents were willing). We were so conditioned I felt a little guilty not being at work but briefly enjoyed my sin.

My day after Christmas was highlighted by a phone call from the Actor Will Patton. I really liked talking with him and we talked for about an hour on his dime. I guess he has more dimes than me so it seemed alright. We talked about life and our love of our jobs. He confessed to not understanding how we could do the type of job we did day after day in environments like these and most of my other past assignment locations. He described the life of an Actor and the people he had to deal with and I confessed to him that I didn't think I could live and work in that kind of an environment. His descriptions of the people in the Industry and the way they treat each other was very interesting but a bit cutthroat and discouraging. His is a tough industry to compete in. I'll stick to mine. It may be a bit more dangerous but I understand the risk when it comes at me and I guess I have become to some degree comfortable with this dark side of our existence. But I really liked this guy and his informality and almost family-like relating. Maybe it was just that he is a good actor and able to convince me of his sincerity. Anyway, I told him I would be going to visit my property in Santa Fe, New Mexico, and even though I knew a well-known Actor like him would be always busy with some film or another, I invited him to come out and relax and see Santa Fe. I guaranteed to protect him from movie star stalkers. It would be in February and would be my second of the three short "leaves" we get. I knew I would never be able to squeeze in a third with my work load and since I had lost so much time trying to get out on my first with my Deputy problem. And, it takes at least 2 days to get home and 2 days to get back so there is a lot of wasted time traveling and you are beat when you make it back to Iraq. It almost defeated the purpose of the mini-vacation if you were exhausted when you returned.

A week later we had a pre-New Years Eve gathering at the "Lock and Load" to celebrate the end of the year and we had a pretty big crowd. I don't know how the enemy can time things so well but the rockets started pounding our Palace compound about thirty minutes after we opened and were hitting around the Lock and Load so everyone had to scatter for the concrete shelters. I was deeply impressed to see how fast 100 people can react and run. One would have thought we had practiced it. I guess the couple of hundred prior real-life rehearsals had us all a little on edge but within four or five seconds the place was empty and all you could see were asses and elbows heading for their favorite protective shelter. An hour later, we had all re-gathered to warm ourselves around the "visually-hidden" fire back at the "Lock and Load" to tell our stories over again and abuse those who ran too slowly to the shelters or had tripped or were gaining weight at the DFAC and losing their ability to compete in the field of sprinting. This had now officially become the most dangerous and attack-ridden period of the entire Iraq incursion. There was more violence, street attacks, rocketings and suicide bombings than at any other time since we entered Iraq after the initial U.S. military bombings. Not a day went by that we didn't have rocket attacks on our compound and within the IZ, and we had been experiencing regular ambushes and firefights in the streets of Baghdad, not to mention the other locations throughout Iraq that we had folks in. It can take a psychological toll, which leads to a physical toll when it just keeps happening non-stop, day after day, and worse, night after night. Our morale was good as a group because we supported each other and knew we were doing good work, but individually, we each lay in bed at night and wished it would stop for a few days and give us a break.

The weather had turned cold and rainy and finally brought New Years Eve with it. It was a typically symbolic Iraqi New Year's eve. Right after the midnight hour, the Insurgents launched 12 more rockets onto our compound, injuring several of our people. Again, a serious tolerance gap for our holidays of peace. Muqhtada Al-Saddar, the leader of the main insurgency in Baghdad (though we suspected he was conducting it from someplace comfortable) was becoming a real pain in our asses. Before the rockets fell, the holiday night was also celebrated in a typically U.S. military war zone way with a Karaoke party around the stage by the pool. Most singers were terrible but again, there was a sense of cama-raderie sitting there with the crowd, acknowledging that we were a family of sorts and so everyone listened and supported them. The truth is that probably the only ones who ever told them they were good and had potential were their Moms. Everyone wants to believe Mom.

There was so much bad happening and our days were becoming filled with attacks and killings so I decided I needed to do something good within the community to feel like we were progressing in a positive direction. I found out that Ali, the carpet store dealer, who I visited and looked at his carpets and gave him advice since he knew nothing about carpets, had 15 children and one of them was a 10 year-old girl who was collateral damage from a suicide car bomb blast a year earlier. She had survived but her ear drums were burst and she was having seizures several times a day, and when not in seizure it affected her balance and she would fall down. One of her ears had such a degree of infection that a sub-stance oozed from it that was so repugnant in smell that between the seizures and the smell, she wasn't permitted to sit at school anymore. When he told me the story and introduced me to his sweet little daughter who had come to spend time sitting with her father, it broke my heart. I guess I make a lot of facial expressions when I talk and am a bit animated, so as I was talking with Ali, I noticed her sitting in a corner trying to mimic or duplicate my facial expressions. She won me over right then. I asked my friend, who was the State Department Regional Doctor at the Palace to take a look at her and he gladly did. In fact he is such a great guy, as is the Regional Social Worker, that they took a personal interest. I brought Ali and his daughter to the Embassy and into the Palace to see the Doc. As we entered Saddam's Palace, Ali began to tell me stories about the building and the events that used to take place there. He knew a great deal about the building and the sometimes horrible things that went on in this Palace previously. Both Ali and his daughter were scared and very nervous about entering into this huge place with so many Americans running around and I kept them close to me. The Doc has a great bedside manner and after gaining her trust, he immediately started her on antibiotics for the ear. After his initial evaluation, he also contacted some specialists in the U.S. and asked for their advice and recommendations. Next I went to Ambassador Khalilzad to get permission to have her reviewed and treated at the Combat Support Hospital (CSH). In his usual oblivious way, he approved it and I am not even sure he heard what I said. That was alright with me. So, with the Doctor "conferencing" for a few days with specialists while she kept putting drops in her ear, I began to set up the appointment with the CSH. I ended up spending two days of my limited time in the hospital working out arrangements for the CT scan and overall review but it was worth it. The Doctors were actually thrilled that they were going to get to help. None of us usually got to see kids that weren't dead and the Doctors, who were all married and missing their kids back home actually got very enthused about working on her. I think we all felt that somehow this connected us to the good side of life again.

The first day I took her and Ali to the CSH, they sat close to me and again were very nervous, but Americans have a special sense for making people feel welcome and as the Doctors would walk by us sitting in the hallway and see this pretty little 10 year-old girl sitting there, they just couldn't walk by without smiling and saying hello and trying to get her to smile and remembering their own kids back home. She was to all of them, like a surrogate daughter. Two very busy Doctors actually stopped and touched her cheek and talked with her (but in English) and then immediately went down the hall and brought her back stuffed animals as gifts. Everyone was falling in love with this injured and suffering brave little girl. That is what Americans are all about. We love our kids and in my case, I do my job to hopefully make life better for the kids. I had tears in my eyes when I saw her face as she got these gifts but when I looked at her father Ali, he was sobbing his eyes out. Water was just running. The Doctors ran a long series of very expensive tests and exams and identified the damage and treated it. She would still need to have skin flaps sewn over her ear drums in the future so she could hear properly again but that would be after the infection healed and that would be treatable in Amman. Over the next months, the Palace Doctor and I continued to monitor her progress and kept up with fighting what had been a terrible infection. When I last saw her, she had gone 12 days without a seizure and was becoming a happy little girl again. We had become friends and she would stand holding my hand at Ali's carpet shop, looking up at me and still mimicking my expressions. She eventually went off to have the ear drum operation but I never saw her after that. I did hear from Ali in an email after I left Iraq that she was fine and back in school and his carpet business was booming. Sometimes you just have to have these good moments to remember to compensate for the others.

The other bad experiences were still getting worse and more frequent. It was becoming a daily tragedy and lives of friends were being lost. A 28-year old girl working for the National Democratic Institute (NDI) was traveling in a convoy in the Red Zone and the entire convoy came under fire in an Insurgent ambush. The attack was complex and coordinated and involved heavy weapons, including grenades, rockets, and large caliber machine guns. They killed most of the convoy but their objective seemed to be to kidnap her and we all knew (apparently including her) how nightmarish her life would become if they took her hostage. They tried to get her to open the door of the armored vehicle she was locked into and she refused. No one else was alive to help her but we had received the emergency call and were rushing to her with our attack helicopters. The Insurgents knew they only had a moment to get her out before we would arrive and rain down damnation on them so they tried one more time to get her to open the door and she apparently made the conscious decision to accept her fate. She refused. The Insurgents placed grenades under her car and blew it up. The grenades probably killed her but the car became an inferno and burned literally for hours. We took six hardly-recognizable bodies back to the compound for shipping home. She had been a pretty and sweet little blond-haired girl who just wanted to save the world a little bit and they took that from her. She was harmless and had been very helpful to the local citizens, which is probably how they targeted her. These Insurgents seemed to be lacking in humanity and I had lost any compassion for them.

Piling extreme distress upon extreme distress, I next had one of the worst days of my life.

On Tuesday , January 23rd, 2007, while in support of a U.S. Embassy Baghdad diplomatic mission, five brave and devoted Blackwater security personnel working for me were killed in a single long-running and complex battle in the streets of Baghdad by Anti-Iraqi Forces (AIF) while doing their duty protecting and saving an American Officer who was the target of an ambush. All RSO Security personnel involved in this particular incident were members of the Blackwater organization or the U.S. military, who joined in later, with the exception of the RSO assigned to their team as part of his regular duties.

At 0940 hours on January 23rd, one U.S. Embassy Baghdad employee working as a senior advisor for the Iraq Reconstruction Management Office (IRMO) was attending a meeting with her Iraqi counterparts at the Iraqi Ministry of Public Works Annex. We had selected an armored sedan for this venue rather than the big Suburbans or Toyota Land Cruisers in order to reduce the targeting profile. The Protective Services Detail (PSD) we assigned to her was Raven 7. As standard protective measures, we assigned a Dedicated Defensive Marksman (DDM) to Raven 7, to observe and monitor any enemy activity in the area that might need to be neutralized in order to protect the Principal and get the team into and away from the venue safely. This area of Saddar City was very dangerous and could be very unpredictable and was known to have numerous well-armed small enemy cells creating havoc and pulling hit-and-run operations.

At 1110 hours, a firefight developed in the general venue neighborhood between undetermined Iraqi Government Forces and

Anti-Iraqi Forces (AIF). The AIF spotted our DDM, which probably meant that they had specifically been targeting and monitoring our venue and team, and they engaged the Raven 7 DDM with accurate small arms fire (rifles). Because of the initial firefight between the Iraqi pro and anti forces, the DDM had already taken the proper precautions and called the TOC, requesting additional security support including RSO helicopters to evacuate the Principal from the venue. Two of our Hughes 530 helicopters identified as "Little Birds" One and Two were immediately dispatched from the RSO Air Wing as we began our Tactical Operations Center (TOC) oversight operations to get our people home safely. An RSO Tactical Ground Support Team for this report identified as Raven 23 also immediately responded to the Raven 7 request for back-up. From the TOC, we also requested "Big Army" provide us with military support and they notified us that both Army ground and air support units had been dispatched to the venue.

By 1120 hours, Little Birds One and Two were providing overhead suppressive fire against the enemy so that Raven 7 could safely depart the venue. During this cover fire, one of the two Door Gunners on Little Bird One was shot in the head by the Anti-Iraqi Forces from an undetermined location and both Little Birds quickly flew the injured Blackwater Warrior to the 28th Combat Support Hospital (CSH) as two more little Birds, numbers Three and Four, took their place providing cover fire for Raven 7's escape and trying to eliminate the attack elements.

At 1135, as Tactical Support Team (TST) Raven 23 was proceeding to the attack site, they became engaged by small arms fire (SAF) at another location and one of their tires was shot out, temporarily disabling their movement. An RSO Counter-Assault

Team quickly responded to Raven 23 to lend cover fire support while they replaced the tire. The CAT Team was immediately engaged by the small arms fire, which began to demonstrate to those of us working the oversight in the TOC, that there was a large coordinated effort in various parts of the city that had been pre-staged and had been waiting for a venue visitation to this Iraqi Ministry or perhaps another nearby. The size of the enemy's forces and the number of locations they were ambushing our people from, as well as the substantial firepower was more like an anti-U.S. Military operation rather than a simple Embassy motorcade attack. We had to escalate our resources quickly and checked to see where the Army support was. Raven 23 was able to replace the tire as the CAT took their fire and both elements were now moving in the direction of Raven 7 to lend support.

At 1137, we were notified that Big Army Attack Aviation had arrived on the venue and was lending substantive support.

At 1140 hours, because of what appeared to be a large coordinated enemy effort in the area, larger and more coordinated than we had ever seen before, I put out the word through my TOC that all Teams on venues were to stay at those venues and off the streets, and those in transit, return immediately to the IZ to await further evaluation of all activities in the city.

At 1150 hours, Little Bird Three took damaging gunfire to the helicopter and the exceptional pilot was forced to make a controlled "hard" landing at the Iraqi Ministry of Health. At the same time, Little Bird Four disappeared off our grid and did not respond to communications. After evaluating the damage, Little Bird Three was able to return on its own power safely to LZ Washington in the IZ. But Little Bird Four was missing and presumed to have crashed. We immediately initiated search operations through the dirt streets and alleyways and dusty parks and dirt soccer fields in the area where they had last been tracked on our monitors. Both RSO and U.S. military elements aggressively proceeded to the general area and began a fast search. In that chaotic city environment, it is very difficult to find anything even as substantial as a little helicopter. We had control over 2 RSO-dedicated unmanned aerial vehicles (UAVs) that provided critical and highly tactical information to my TOC daily and we redirected their efforts to finding our Little Bird.

At 1210 hours, the RSO Tactical Support Team identified as Raven 26 arrived on Venue and linked up with Raven 7 to lead them out and to safety. Within five minutes, Raven 7, supported by Raven 26 were moving out of the Ministry to what was hoped to be a safer area and back to the relative safety of the IZ and Palace grounds. At 1233 hours, Raven 7, with the IRMO Principal, and Raven 26, all arrived back in the IZ without further incident. Raven 26, then turned around and headed back to support the other elements in the search for our downed helicopter and four crew members and friends.

At 1308 hours, a combined Iraqi Army and U.S. Army unit located the missing Little Bird about 500 meters south of the original venue. It had crashed and bodies were reported seen on the street near the "bird".

At 1325 hours, Raven 22, Raven 23 and Raven 26, as well as the CAT, all converged on the crash site and linked up with a U.S. Army Stryker Company already attempting to secure the crash site and planning to recover the bodies laying exposed near the Helicopter. During this attempt at getting to the bodies, another massive firefight developed involving the U.S. Army, RSO, and Blackwater elements against a very large contingent of Anti-Iraqi, Anti-Coalition Forces apparently waiting to ambush us at the crash site. They were positioned on multiple floors of several high-rise buildings surrounding the area as if they had been staged and waiting. The attack from the enemy was so complex and substantial that once on-site, it was impossible for all our units to even evacuate the area. They were all "pinned down" and fighting back against a strong force with heavy weapons. We were forced to "up" our response and called-in stronger weaponry including the Stryker-mounted MK-19 40mm automatic grenade launchers and Apache AH-64 Attack Helicopters with Hell-Fire Missiles. The Apache Helicopters are a beautiful but fearful weapon, not just in strike capacity but even their design to make one believe that they have chosen the wrong path. The Apache's fired missiles into the buildings where the attackers shot at us from and that ended the resistance and brought the "abandoned" building down pretty much to rubble.

Even from a distance while trying to get to them, it appeared obvious that the four bodies of our men, lying in the open and stripped naked of their equipment and clothing, were dead, probably from the crash and stripped by the Insurgents after being dragged from the helicopter. During the battle to reclaim the bodies of our friends, seven U.S. Army soldiers had been wounded as well.

As the four bodies were recovered to be taken home, the seven soldiers were being treated for their wounds and some were flown out for rapid treatment at the CSH. No RSO personnel had been wounded but our Blackwater brothers had suffered terrible losses and that meant our family had tragically been diminished that day. All four in the crashed helicopter were dead and at 1335, we received word that the Door Gunner of Little Bird One had died of his head wound at the 28th CSH.

At 1356 hours, Raven 26 returned to the Embassy with the first two recovered dead bodies from the Little Bird Four crash site. At 1435 hours, Raven 22, Raven 23, and CAT departed the crash site. Prior to departure, in order to keep the Insurgents from gleaning any equipment from the helicopter or using it as a propaganda tool, our Teams and the U.S. Army units destroyed what was left of the badly damaged Little Bird Four helicopter airframe.

At 1445, Raven 22, Raven 23, and CAT arrived back at the Embassy with the remaining two bodies of our fallen friends.

By 1541 hours, we had safely recalled all our remaining PSD Units not involved in the firefight from their venues. Numerous RSO vehicles were damaged, another Blackwater vehicle crew member suffered a concussion from an explosion during the battle and the mechanics went to work immediately on repairing the Little Birds in case other recovery emergencies came up. We still needed to be able to save other lives if called upon. This was my darkest day. I had lost five of my men, my friends, our associates. I was ultimately responsible for all our lives and this broke my heart. One of the men was the twin Brother of another of our Blackwater helicopter pilots. We would not recover soon from the losses this day.

Our lost comrades, whose bravery cannot be over-stated, were shipped back to the U.S. for family funeral and burial services and on January 25th, we held a memorial service in the IZ, across from the Palace grounds. Several of us spoke and we talked of what it means to give up your life protecting the innocent whose lives are entrusted to us, and their closest friends told stories about their personalities and we all, every experienced old war dog, cried without shame. It is a selfish act because we are actually mourning for our own loss. We are suffering knowing that we will not have that personality and character to talk with or laugh with again. We had over 1,000 people in attendance outside in the cold and several of us, certainly me included, had a hard time getting through our speeches while maintaining any control over our emotions. Every one of my people are like sons and daughters to me and I constantly preach to them about how we are "family". When your sons or daughters, or husbands or wives, or friends return from their deployments, remember what they might have gone through, seen, or lost, and be patient with them and compassionate. You will not understand and they will not be able to explain it in most cases. Give them time to purge their grief and resolve their inner issues. My DS Agent had performed as a true hero and I sat down and wrote a recommendation to the Department of State for him to receive The Award of Heroism. I hoped they would concur.

The day after the loss of our 5 Blackwater brothers, while still in deep shock and carrying out our work like walking zombies whose training kept us functional but removed from outward emotion, the enemy launched multiple rocket attacks throughout the day landing their rockets on our Palace grounds in the midst of all our people going about their business. Six of our/my people were wounded. One of my Army guys who worked for me on the Protective Security Details and who had been getting a lot of real-time experience in firefights lately, was playing volleyball and when they all heard the whistling, everyone dove for cover. But, as one of the rockets hit just 50 yards away, the Sgt. caught a huge hellish looking jagged piece of metal about the size of half a sandwich that went through his lower leg ripping out part of his leg bone and a massive amount of tissue. He survived but with serious damage. The medics reported after his initial operation, that he can be repaired but it will take several more operations to complete the entire rebuilding process and some serious recovery time. He was flown to Germany where he could receive better care for the long term operations and recovery period. I went over to the hospital (CSH) to see him before he was flown out that day and he was so drugged up that he was actually smiling and cracking jokes. The strength of our nation lies in the courage of our young people. We were told that he will recover almost 100 percent.

JANUARY 30 TO MARCH 17, 2007

On January 30th, so soon after the loss of so many of my Team, we had two medium lift helicopters returning from a day trip to Al-Hillah, south of Baghdad. It was a PRT headquarter located in a renovated small hotel with a landing strip across the street from it and barriers and Texas Walls (T-Walls) by the thousands blocking off the perimeter from an attack. Unfortunately, the enemy was very capable and pretty accurate at landing rockets on their compound and the landing strip. As the Medium lifts completed half of the approximate one-hour trip back to Baghdad, by a bad stroke of luck, they traveled over what was a surprise ambush on the ground and one of the helicopters took machine gun damage sufficient to force it to make an emergency landing. The second medium lift kept overview as a lookout. Once the damage was evaluated, it was obvious that the helicopter would need to be air-lifted back to Baghdad for massive repairs.

Unfortunately time was against us and the enemy troops had followed the helicopters path and were in hot pursuit. At the TOC, we called in Big Army to lend support and try to get a huge lifter helo to come out to bring back my $3 million dollar bird. The support troops were on the way but the lift helo was not available. The Army was interested in fighting the Insurgents and they would also try to protect our helo until the lifter became available. We landed our second medium lift and loaded all the passengers from the first, minus some of the "shooters" who would work with the Army forces, and flew it back to our hangar in the IZ. The Army and our few men engaged what turned out to be a substantial force for as long as they could, but after several of the Army soldiers were injured protecting the helicopter, their Commanding Officer called me and asked if the bird was worth some of his men's lives and I told him no – get your men out of there but blow up my helicopter before leaving so the enemy would not be able to use it against us later. It was a hard decision to make about the helicopter but an easy one to make about the men's lives, which took precedence. They blew it up as the Insurgents got close to it in order to hopefully inflict casualties and then were out with their wounded being taken to the CSH. I was later apologetic for the loss of the expensive helicopter but not for saving some men's lives. We all had lost enough lately.

In an early February protective mission for one of our PRT Officers out near the notorious Railway Station, again near where we lost our helicopter crew, we had placed a DDM on a building to watch for the bad guys trying to sneak in to set-up another ambush. He was a big guy who worked out with me in the gym every morning about 0500 hours and I had been told he was an excellent shooter. We also had two other DDMs placed in the area in the hopes that we wouldn't find ourselves in a tough spot again.

Men were seen coming down the side streets with weapons from various directions and getting established in defensive positions. My work-out friend was watching one through his scope and was spotted by an insurgent on the ground who began to shoot at his position. This initiated a firefight that went on for a little over an hour. During the battle, my DDMs identified several enemy snipers on other rooftops who had begun to "pepper" their positions. Before the battle was over, three enemy snipers were dead, as were many of the enemy forces on the ground who had hoped to set up an ambush for the motorcade that by this time had been redirected out safely and was home in the IZ. As we called in our little birds to rapidly pick up our DDMs from the roof tops, my gym associate, who was now staying low and behind the roof top wall, turned to race to the hovering helo and a 50 caliber round went right through the wall and penetrated his stomach at an angle. For any who might not know, a 50 caliber round is enormous and usually fatal. My friend went down but was alive. His Spotter and a gunner from the helo pushed and pulled his body toward the bird but he was so big and heavy, they had a devil of a time lifting his limp large form up to the helicopter platform. With the help of the co-pilot, the three of them got him inside and away to help as another of our DDMs killed the one who had made the lucky shot through a wall. He was given immediate care and stabilized and 2 days later was to be sent to Germany for long term recovery. I went to his room at the Combat Support Hospital to see him before he left and in his wounded and heavily drugged state of mind, he surprised several of us by being awake and in morphine-type happy spirits but slurring his words. His final words to us before sleeping were that he had just gotten his trailer the way he wanted it and no one better mess with it because he was coming back. We all did something that was a cross between laughing and crying to hear him express his only concern for his now perfectly laid-out trailer. What a terrific guy.

A few days later, we ran another protective mission to the Iraqi Ministry of Justice. It was in that same Saddar City area where we had taken beatings in so many battles lately and we were beginning to over-compensate with greater forces to prevent any more surprises with large enemy numbers showing up. We were also seeing greater use of enemy snipers and their skill level and tactics were improving. Obviously, they had completed some special training somewhere and were back to demonstrate their new skills and abilities. They would never equal the skill and experience of my guys though, who had done this job as members of one of the several U.S. Special Forces groups.

As anticipated, a battle erupted and while the forces on the ground were fighting it out with our guys, my DDM had his hands full on a central roof top. The enemy had placed five snipers on various roof tops to try and gain an advantage at wiping out our ground forces. As one would shoot at one of our troops, our Spotter and DDM would zero in on him and take him out. Then another of the enemy snipers would detect our Dedicated Defensive Marksman (DDM), as the Department and DS preferred to call them, and try to get him. Our DDM then took him out with an expert shot. It went like this for about 45 minutes and at the end of it. Our DDM had killed 5 enemy snipers who would have wreaked havoc on our men and killed many of them. It was a miraculous and heroic act and we worked to find a special award that could be presented to him for the exceptional bravery and skill he demonstrated. This was one of our better days when we could enjoy our success without mourning any of our men being lost.

I had purchased the home in Santa Fe, New Mexico, just before coming to Iraq in the hopes of it being a good investment for me and I had never spent a day in it. The market had tumbled, home values were falling, and I had a nice unused home that was costing me an arm and a leg. It was time to take what would end up being my second but also last rest leave of the three we are offered. I decided I should go to Santa Fe for 2 weeks and rest up and see what my home was all about in the cold season. I arranged for the purchase of a bed to put in the house and sheets and pillows. Anything beyond that, I could get when I arrived or just ignore it and live sparsely like I was doing in Iraq. I have mentioned before how difficult it was to get in and out of Iraq but the trip to Santa Fe took me four full days to arrive. I was a wreck and felt out of place in a beautiful community that seemed to be completely unaware and unaffected by the helicopters, rockets and enemy attacks that I had been experiencing every day. I actually felt like an alien in an environment not designed for me. I wasn't sure how to behave or what to do. I had gone from commanding a large force to standing alone on my silent 5 acres of trees and rocks in an instant and it was confusing. I didn't speak to many people or socialize since I didn't know anyone but I did walk the art galleries and nice comfortable and expensive boutique stores. I worked in the yard digging through the light layer of snow and frozen ground just to try and get a feel for my place, but it was odd. I was lacking the helicopters who 10 times a night flew what sounded and felt like two feet over my trailer roof, shaking my entire little home and practically knocking me out of bed. There was an unnatural lack of rockets and car bombs detonating across a river that was now on the other side of the world. No battles, no snipers, no wounded or dead, no blood, no constant demand for me to make life and death decisions. I missed it. I tip-toed through this environment like I was trying not to be discovered for who I was at this moment. The skies were beautiful at night. The town plaza allowed me to sit quietly on a bench and listen to live bands play free music for anyone who wanted to listen, and I quietly ate alone in cozy restaurants watching the people go about their apparently busy and meaningful lives. I wasn't sure this would ever be right for me again.

I spent my time more or less resting and hanging out at Harry's Roadside Bar and Restaurant and then returned through Frankfurt. The entire trip back took 2.5 days and I was exhausted by the time I got back to the comfort of what I knew. An interesting note for my trip return though was that in the Frankfurt airport, I was watching a man flirt with the Business Class Lounge hostess and while just standing there, his sport coat burst into flames. It was either the first case of spontaneous combustion I have ever witnessed or the hostess was a witch and didn't like his flirting. Either way, it was unexplainable and was a good beginning for my surrealistic journey back to Iraq.

One afternoon, two soldiers on the palace grounds were off-duty in one of their trailers playing what was one of their favorite pastimes – a war-oriented video game, where they shot their way through ninjas and enemies who were trying to shoot them to keep them from progressing to the next level or something like that. They were seated on their couch electronically fighting for their lives against the game when a stray bullet from across the river came through the wall of the trailer and through the TV and penetrated one of the soldier's stomach. His partner told me he sat there with his mouth open, not believing the game had actually shot him and then he slumped over and his buddy called us and we rushed him to the CSH. He lived but must have been shocked to have the game shoot back. The random shootings from across the Tigris were increasing along with the rocket and mortar attacks.

We had begun protecting the Iraqi Ministers as well as Dignitaries from other countries who had come to Baghdad as part of a "Donors Conference" to see if the neighboring countries could begin to pull part of their weight on helping out the reconstruction of Iraq instead of leaving it almost entirely to the Americans. The truth was that many Arab countries thought of Iraq as sort of the bastard son of their world and had no respect for them or their poor ethics. Iran had been attacked by and attacked them on various occasions so what was their motivation? I didn't have personal high hopes for the success of the Conference but it was our job to keep them alive while in the IZ at the discussions. We also anticipated a lot of rocket fire trying to hit the Conference Center and knew there would be "spotters" nearby watching to see where the rockets hit so that they could redirect fire by cell phone, hoping to "walk-in" a direct hit on the meetings. And, true to form, there were rockets coming regularly, in between our military trying to run down the launch locations, which always seemed to have moved by the time they got there. The no collateral damage rule was holding us back from winning this war. It had gone from military tactics to win, to political decisions made by committee sensitivity, and that meant we just took the hits without recourse. The rockets were typically launched from a range of about 12 kilometers away and pin-point accuracy was difficult. One of the 122mm rockets landed about 60 yards from my office window in the front yard of the Palace. For those never close to a rocket hit, 60 yards is like the world has ended and it throws you from your chair as if you had firecrackers in your pants. The rockets have a 30 yard kill ratio and shrapnel goes 100 yards or more with killing capability. Saddam had built an atrociously ugly huge fountain in the front and the one good thing was that the rocket hit it and partially destroyed some of its hideous nature. The rocket had obviously been intended for the Conference but was short by about ½ mile and created a 5 foot hole. After enough time to ensure that no more were "in-flight" following the one, we were back at work.

It was now mid-March and I had just received the formal confirmation of my next assignment. I had been asked to be the Senior RSO in Islamabad, Pakistan. But I had 11 weeks left in my Iraq tour and besides the battles and rocketings to come, I still had to write 60 evaluation reports and at least 40 award recommendations for my Team.

MARCH 18 THROUGH APRIL 14, 2007:

General Casey, the Force Commander in Iraq had departed and I had my first meeting with General Petraeus, his replacement. He seemed like a very bright guy and very personable, a clear thinker, and had a great reputation. We would see how it went.

Due to the unfortunate ever-creasing political sensitivities, we had been advised to use caution on inspecting the Official Iraqi's vehicles when going into and out of the IZ. Our goal was to prevent explosives, weapons, and terrorists from entering the IZ and carrying out attacks against us and vehicle inspections were the most basic of access control procedures. We decided that we would comply but that we would, along with the Military Police perimeter control forces, inspect cars on a random basis or when we knew of potential imminent threats. So, if we felt there was a threat, we would do a 100% check on certain days. On a few occasions, we randomly searched vehicles, including the Iraqi ambulances that were suspected of smuggling bombs, guns and terrorists into the IZ and from this, we found numerous AK-47s, explosive devices already made up and ready to use, and even terrorists hiding in car trunks and ambulances.

One week after one of these vehicles was caught, a suicide bomber wearing a bomb vest worked his way into the Iraqi Deputy Prime Minister's home, which only had Iraqi security at their insistence, and the bomber detonated himself and several other people, but the Deputy PM survived. The investigation showed that some of his personal bodyguards were involved in planning the assassination. They had allowed the bomber in through the kitchen entrance. Things were definitely going to get worse before they got better in the IZ and in Iraq.

In addition, as we prepared our largest Embassy in the world for occupancy, what would this mean for those who would be working in it? If there were now bombers and explosive supplies and who knew how many weapons inside the IZ, how could we protect ourselves even inside the massive compound. Any time anyone left the gate to conduct business they were susceptible to being killed in any number of ways. I began to plead my case that we needed to enlarge the IZ and make it air tight, which would start with a complete house and building purge and cleansing of the IZ. Then a total access control check of all vehicles entering (and departing) the IZ. Some of the Iraqi Ministers who knew they were targets were in favor of it as well. But, it was just NOT going to happen. The original agreement was that we would return parts of the IZ to the Iraqis and the time was coming to comply or put our foot down to save our own people. It seemed clear to me what the outcome would be but those who came after me would suffer the consequences. It was a very frustrating point for myself and various Military associates we worked closely with on these matters.

It was finally time for Ambassador Khalilzad to leave and we planned the security for the huge farewell party that would take place in the large high-ceiling, gilded conference hall that housed recreation and eating space for everyone and included the famous "Green Bean" coffee shop. It was our version of Starbucks and we all loved it. Although, there was always free coffee at points around the Palace in order to keep us working zombies on our feet 20 hours a day. When we wanted something that more resembled the U.S., like a caramel mocha latte, the Green Bean was our normality break and the prices were only slightly better than at Starbucks. It was actually one of the very few places one could spend any money in-country. It consisted of the PX, a couple of fast food restaurants that stood next to the PX, and the Green Bean. It was our corner of the world we left behind.

Khalilzad's party was going to be many hundreds of Iraqi VIPs and other Mission Officers and it was a certainty that the enemy knew the time and date and would make every attempt to refine their trajectory skills to land the rockets on the Palace to kill a few of the VIPs, if not the Muslim "blasphemer" Khalilzad himself, as a recent Fatwa had labeled him. We used almost 500 of my men and the military forces as well to secure the outside event but with our "no-collateral damage" policy, the sky was open territory to any rocket or mortar that they wanted to lob in. And they did. We started taking rocket fire about 20 minutes into the event. Most traveled the 12 kilometers and landed far enough from our Palace that it only shook the ground and made us run and jump for cover. The event continued. However, odds being what they are, one rocket found its way near to Saddam's large ugly fountain in front of my office again and hit the earth just about 8 feet in front of it. It was close enough to shatter some of the fountain concrete and send shrapnel and rocks and dirt flying at the speed of death out in 180 degrees of direction. One of my young Agent ARSOs was posted in front of the building about 40 yards from where the rocket hit. A rock from the earth became a projectile and hit my Agent, going right through his suit jacket and pants and hit him in his upper thigh. It knocked him down and we thought we had a fatality but the stone had been roundish and other than creating a huge bruise and destroying his only suit, we were blessed that day with extreme luck. The Agent had received his onward assignment to work on the Secretary of State's Protective Detail and this "good" suit was going to be his big ticket item for his assignment. When we lifted him up to work on his wound and check him out, he looked at me and said, "sir, what am I going to do about my suit". It is odd what people say first when they are experiencing shock and I couldn't help it, but I burst into laughter, now that I knew he was alright and that his main concern was the loss of his "Hollywood suit". I wrote him up for an award for exceptional dedication to duty under fire with a $500. monetary reward so he could use the money to buy a new quality suit. He was bruised for weeks but happy and a very lucky young man.

The above attack was just the first of a hellish series that plagued us for the next four days. I guess it was their way of expressing how they felt about Khalilzad. Eleven rockets, including some of the largest we had seen, all landed in my compound with a new-found accuracy. A 120mm rocket can hit a mile away and practically knock you off your feet. A huge old Russiam 240mm rocket fell into one of our KBR compounds and absolutely decimated several buildings, freezers, generators and other working equipment. It also wounded five persons. It was so powerful, it seemed the world had ended when it hit. The next day, 5 more rockets hit inside our compound, all around my office and one smashed into a pillar on the outside of the building itself, sending stone shrapnel into the building. Eleven more people were wounded.

The next day it went horribly worse. It was March 27th, 2007, and early evening. I was still working in my office when the first whistling noises could be heard, which meant it was directly overhead and very close. You were either going to be very lucky again or dead. The louder the whistling in that few seconds of the world standing still, the more you realized you needed to be deep in a hole immediately. To be able to hear a rocket split the air and make that whistling meant that someone or some few of our people were going to be in trouble. The first 122mm rocket slammed into the sand volleyball court between the DFAC and the pool and impacted with such force that life came briefly to a Hollywood slow-motion stall just for a second but it seemed longer. The rocket buried itself 12 feet deep into the sand and soil and not too much shrapnel had exploded outward. The blast was so powerful, it was like we were moving in slow motion, unable to force ourselves back into rapid mode. Then the air rushed back in and we knew that it had hit within our protected Palace grounds and we needed to get moving to see if anyone needed to be saved or repaired. My Team had far too much experience with these now and as I ran from my office to respond, my men were right with me and we were going as fast as we could toward the back exit to get to where we thought it had hit. We had no time to think about our own protection or condition. That one had hit on top of us and people would be in need. We just ran for the exit. Our real time experience, following the exceptional High Threat Tactical Training we had received prior to our deployment was what took over entirely right now. Our focus was total. As we ran down the 150 yard-long hallway, the second rocket hit and it was apparent that it had hit inside the wall and closer to the door we were heading for. Our momentum continued to carry us forward. We had the sense though to realize that they might be "walking" the rockets in right to where we were about to exit. It also meant there was an enemy spotter out there reporting the success back to the launch site. The second rocket had hit a large communal bathroom and shower trailer and later we would find nothing but splinters in that big hole. It had been only seconds now since the first rocket had hit.

Almost the same instant of time that we reached the back exit door, the third rocket came down in front of the KBR Housing office across the street from us. It was about 1930 hours, and this rocket was a 107mm. As it came for the sidewalk in front of the Housing Office where Americans always stood or sat to converse and pass the time with the friendly people in that office, it struck a tree about 6 feet above the ground and detonated at head level, sending an "air burst" shock wave and massive shrapnel out in all directions. We exited the door as it detonated and shrapnel struck the walls around us. We forced onward across the street to the detonation site. Three people were seen immediately down. Two soldiers in uniform and one young lady we all knew as the perpetually happy Manager of the Housing Office. Medics, Nurses, and other trained personnel were joining us at the site evaluating the injuries. Once we cleared the blood off the soldiers, we recognized them as men who worked with us in security daily.

We set up a protective cordon around the scene and began to coordinate urgent medical treatment. This was where the RSO shop could ensure that exactly what needed to be done was, and that it was done efficiently and as quickly as it could. We were in charge and made sure medical personnel got in and all others stayed out. We also had the resources to get the personnel to the CSH faster that waiting for the ambulances. We began the overall coordination. We also began to coordinate with KBR Fire to deal with the damage and fires from the various rocket blasts, the damaged buildings and the five cars that were destroyed. There were a lot of varied situations that had to be quickly remedied and we still had no idea who else we would find in the buildings or trailers, or under equipment or buildings that were injured and needed treatment. My Team worked fast to get a thorough evaluation and to get help to the wounded.

We looked over the Housing Officer Manager and evaluated her for injuries. She was unconscious and unresponsive to our attempts yet initially we couldn't find a single wound or shrapnel penetration on her body. There was no blood but we couldn't get her to respond. We continued to try and found a person who said that after the blast went off, she had still been standing about 20 feet from the blast. She screamed loudly once, then dropped straight down. We prepped her for transit to the CSH with proper braces and controls and put her in our own vehicles over to transport her to save on the ambulance response time. Within a couple of minutes that seemed like hours, she was on her way to the Doctors at the CSH along with medical personnel to monitor her condition.

We were also hands and knees deep in the blood of our military friends and we had numerous professional medical people doing the best they could. If one is going to get injured, this is the environment where everyone will try to help and there is an abundance of trained people. Some of my team began to search for any other injured who might have been further away from the blast and not identified yet in the dark and in between the trailers and other equipment. One of our friends, a Master Sergeant with the Joint Area Support Group (JASG), who worked with us on all security matters in the IZ including the access controls, was hit with multiple lethal shrapnel penetrations. He was the comic in the JASG and everyone knew and loved him. We treated him and placed him on a gurney and transported him to the CSH within a few short minutes, along with military medical personnel who were monitoring his wounds.

The third injured was a soldier and he actually seemed to have the most severe obvious wounds. Blood was everywhere and numerous medical personnel were working on trying to temporarily patch up about 8 holes in his body from a lot of brutal shrapnel pieces. We all did the best we could and put him in one of our armored vehicles with medical personnel and shipped him to the CSH for urgent treatment.

On the way to the CSH, the Housing Manager stopped breathing and the Medics were unable to save her. Upon a thorough medical review later, it was discovered that she had died from a penetrating fragmentation wound to her lower back. She had been working in this environment for almost 3 years and just days before, due to the intense rocketings lately, had decided she was finished and was making plans to go home. She had been a morale builder for all of us and was greatly loved and would be intensely missed.

Our Master Sergeant friend stopped breathing on the way to the CSH as well. The medical personnel tried cardio pulmonary resuscitation all the way to the CSH but he died from too much trauma to his upper body.

The third seriously wounded victim from the sidewalk, the soldier with 8 holes punched into his body, survived and after being stabilized for a number of days, was shipped off to Germany to receive long term recovery care.

We found others. A civilian contractor with Raytheon, standing only 23 feet from the point of impact, was seriously wounded but stabilized at the CSH and survived. Also, another soldier and an American working in the Office of Iraqi Reconstruction Management (IRMO), were located about 85 feet away from the point of impact and treated for minor wounds. We also found people with minor wounds under trailers and behind large equipment. We worked most of the night to cover all ground until finally we felt we had located all injured and had the damage under control and could start repairs.

The Memorial Service was a heart breaker for all of us and once again, there was not a dry eye in the crowd. The war-hardened, the newly indoctrinated, the old war dogs like myself, we all had tears pouring down our faces at our loss of friends of such value and grace. None of us will ever forget that night or the friends lost.

Our new Ambassador arrived the day after the deaths of our two friends and the wounding of the third soldier. We were already back working hard but inside still going through the grieving process. He hit the ground running without the full understanding of what his people had been experiencing and that would require a period of adjustment with him. He arrived with a reputation of having been successful in several hard assignments and was thought of highly by the Department and I think his peers. We were told that he had a very supportive stance on security and I was initially enthused but would find out later that there were some kinks in that profile. He had just left Islamabad, pulled out early to take Khalilzad's place, and my assignment to Islamabad had been with the understanding I would be working for him there. As it was now, I would be working for him for a few months in Iraq and then moving on to Islamabad and an unknown Ambassador. One positive sign of his similarity to the philosophy of my Agents was his love of working out and especially running. He started with 8 miles a day around the controlled area within the Palace grounds but we warned him that the environment was not always healthy and also the heat could cause illnesses. He stubbornly refused to listen to advice and wanted to run as he had in Islamabad, a city with a clean, low mountain air and pleasant humidity part of the year. We had our Marine Security Guards run with him thinking they could keep up. The pace wasn't fast, just persistent for 8 miles, and the first time out, only one MSG and one Agent finished with him. From then on, we had the bodyguards ride bikes around him to stay with him and still be able to protect him if something should happen. It is hard to do both when you are tired. Within about 3 weeks, the new Ambassador had developed some bronchial disruption and was having a hard time with his strength. No one wants to believe us at first about the bacteria and munition ions in the soil but it gets everyone who runs too much outside. He was forced to cut down to about half his normal distance and not run every day. There were also days of course when the sky was pink from sand in the air and the quality of air was so destructive, we prohibited everyone from exercising outside completely.

Being early April, I had begun to think about my departure and what my life would be like away from this challenge. It seemed the hardest job a person could possibly do but because it was so meaningful and significant every day, and it was as close to true life as we will ever know, it was hard to move on to something that would be less – and everything we did would probably be less than this assignment. I would worry about all my people who would still be here after I had gone. For as long as I lived, I would feel a bond with all of them and would try to help them in any way I could.

The World Premier release of the movie, "A Mighty Heart" had been scheduled for about 5 days after I returned to the U.S. in New York City and I was invited as one of the seven main movie characters. The book had not been accurate from the perspective of what we actually did during the investigation, but it was a love story of Danny and Mariane. I now wondered how different or varied the movie would be from the truth, but I wanted the opportunity once in my life to experience a New York City Premier and DS was beginning to make plans for me to do some interviews on live TV and with some of the press. I would need to get over my war zone adrenaline crazies before I got too involved with the Media.

Then on another typical day, we had an incident where we were needed once again to rescue military forces. A military convoy was hit by an EFP (explosively formed projectile) and three soldiers were killed immediately. One other was seriously wounded and five military and the civilians they were escorting were stranded in the Red Zone with an enemy force moving in on them. My TOC got the call and notified me. I ordered one of our ground rescue teams in to look over the situation and they reported the 3 apparent dead and one badly wounded and the rest of the group huddled hoping for rescue from the military. We overheard the military radio transmission which said they were

30 minutes from being able to respond. We knew they would all be dead by that time so I immediately dispatched two Little Birds to provide overhead cover fire and one Medium lift to get the injured and others. The medium lift picked up the wounded soldier and packed on the stranded survivors and within 40 seconds, was overhead and on the way to the CSH, bringing the soldier in for life-saving treatment. Then the others were dropped off safely. Our Ground Forces recovered the three dead bodies and brought them home. It was satisfying to be able to help and the seriously wounded soldier survived but all of us wondered why our military had insufficient resources.

On April 7th, around midday, as the heat was beginning to reach intolerable levels and everyone had already been soaked with sweat for 4 hours, a Chief of Mission Protective Security Detail (PSD) positioned at the State Oil Management Organization in Baghdad, reported an explosion in the vicinity of their venue. Our DDM reported seeing another Western Contractor PSD Team being attacked. We checked our records for other teams out on venues for the day and recognized this as an Aegis Team transporting multiple U.S. Military Officials. For some reason, certain U.S. Generals had decided to use outside contractors for their own protection. The Aegis Team had been struck by an Anti-Armor Improvised Explosive Device (AAIED) resulting in three killed; one American military, one Colombian PSD Team member, and one South African PSD Team member. Aegis was primarily South African and had a reputation for risk and frequent casualties. Also, the Iraqi Interpreter had received some minor injuries.

One of our RSO Tactical Support Teams (TST) in the vicinity was dispatched to secure a landing zone so RSO Air Assets could land and provide a medical evacuation. The wounded were taken by my Medium Lift helicopters to the IZ CSH (28th Combat Surgical Hospital). The TST picked up the three dead and brought them back to the CSH for disposition, and the five remaining Aegis Principals were also transported to Camp Liberty by other RSO Air assets. The Iraqi interpreter survived and was released the next day. My Team then began an investigation of the unique device used to create the devastation. It appeared it was a steel-plated shape charge with copper components for maximum collateral damage. I hated it when I recognized a more sophisticated type of constructed device that was more effective and destructive. That was a bad sign of possible cooperation between two devious enemies.

Back in our IZ, which had been penetrated by weapons, explosives, and terrorists, but according to the politicians had to be allowed to happen – a suicide bomber wearing an explosive vest, walked into the Iraqi Council of Representatives (their Congress) and detonated, killing himself and others including several key Iraqi government officials. Since security for their Congress had been turned over to the Iraqis, we were not allowed access or involvement in any form of security including screening the vehicles or people who entered the site or the building. All indications were that the blast had assistance from the inside but the Iraqis just couldn't get any security that was reliable or trustworthy. Anyone could be working for the enemy, even if only because their families were being threatened or from the offer of money, or actually by a sense of loyalty to the enemy or hatred for the current Iraqi politicians. The options for disaster were endless.

The Council of Representatives had adjourned for lunch and Iraqis sat together at tables in the small cafeteria area near the

Council meeting room. As with all explosions, instantaneously it went from calm to chaos when a loud explosion ripped through the eating hall. The room filled with smoke, toxic fumes and residual dust from the matter that had disintegrated from the blast. Some people recovered and ran for their lives. Those wounded remained where they fell or staggered around helplessly. The dead were lying scattered around. Our IZ Police partners notified me and the TOC of the incident as we were already gearing up to respond from what sounded to us like a substantial nearby detonation. We instantly knew this was not going to be good because it had taken place inside our unfortunately compromised protected zone. It wasn't the time to point fingers and tell the politicians that I told them so, but that would definitely need to come later to try and protect those who would come here after my tour finished. Our RSO Office in Baghdad was the biggest in the world and our resources of manpower, helicopters and armored cars of varying types and designs, allowed us to perform missions never anticipated by the State Department or DS before.

Once the bomb went off, the attack seemed significant enough that I decided to ignore the fact that the Iraqis were in charge of security over there and I began to dispatch people to get control of the place. I immediately dispatched 15 Medical Teams to set up a Triage, which eventually became 30 teams. The helicopters were put on alert to be used as emergency CSH transport. I sent as many security teams as we could let go to get perimeter and building control and to protect our medical personnel, who would be focused on their wounded and not on an assassin walking up behind them. I sent over 100 men and women to deal with the urgent care aspects and an additional 25 Blackwater Medics and other specialists.

As the Medics quickly made their way to as many injured as they could find in the rubble, my Security Response Teams fanned out across the venue, setting up the cordon of security for my focused medical personnel to be able to work in safety. We set up a shuttle of our ambulances and armored cars to transport the wounded to the CSH and various other Iraqi Clinics in the vicinity.

I also had two of my Investigators from the RSO "Bull Pen" begin to do a Post Bomb Blast Investigation, searching for the components that would have made up the explosive device. As they made their way through the bodies and rubble, there were cell phones everywhere in the dust going off from family and friends trying to locate people they knew had been at the Council meeting.

The most-seriously wounded were taken out first, followed by the walking or stumbling wounded. One of my Teams actually climbed 13 stories of the nearby Al-Rashid Hotel in response to a report of a woman who had staggered away from the scene and gone into the hotel. They finally found the traumatized woman and got her to medical attention. We located others sitting in chairs staring out the windows of nearby office buildings and treated them for shock. The wounded and traumatized were everywhere.

We brought in our partner U.S. Army K-9 Teams and the Embassy's Explosive Ordinance Disposal Teams, and we scoured the building for any further explosive threats. Before long, we were able to turn the inside of the Council meeting hall back over to the Iraqi Army but we were going to maintain control of the perimeter access points to ensure a level of comfort zone. We had American political folks who attended these meetings as well and it was in our best interest to take back access control.

Cameras had recorded the bombing and I ordered them to be confiscated and brought to our headquarters so that we could evaluate it and try to establish who, what, where and why of the attack. I also didn't want the tape to get into the wrong hands and become an Al-Qaeda propaganda tool. We took all the Press footage as well and that stirred up a hornet's nest with them until we reviewed it all and then returned it for their transmission. A couple of hours later and minutes after returning it, the bombing was on CNN. A total of 10 died. We remained in control of the Iraqi Congress at their request for the next two months while they re-analyzed their strategy on staying alive and operational in their Congress. Later, when I was interviewed about why I got my people involved in an Iraqi venue issue, my response was that it was a moral issue, like when we send out forces and resources to rescue U.S. Military wounded. We have the ability to help and save some of the people and if we don't, people are going to die, and that is just not acceptable. Following that response, the Press, who wanted to challenge what I had done, left me alone, not seeing any positive considerations in trying to make us look like we had overstepped our boundaries. I also gave the press a quote to walk away with – "There is not another Diplomatic Security Team or operation like this in the world, and the privilege that we all have is phenomenal. When they leave Iraq, they will leave with great pride and self-respect for the work they did, because they literally saved lives every single day". Then we all went back to work.

This period was harsh, brutal, bloody, and we lost a lot of friends. I was scheduled to leave in June but there was talk that I could be leaving later now in order to maintain senior coverage until my replacement arrived. I still had so much to accomplish before I left. I needed to get my other 12 helicopters in-country. I still had some new security posts to open in the south and the north and I had a couple to close down as well. The new Embassy was finishing construction and by all appearances had some problems that would delay our moving in on time although our Overseas Building Office (OBO) still assured us everything was on track. It is a mile long compound bordered by a mile-long wall on what would become a dangerous street if the U.S. Military actually pulled out. And, the Tigris River is on the back side where anyone could shoot at us from across the river. It was going to be a challenge like no other for the 2,000 who would live and work here every day.

April 15 through May 28, 2007:

My departure schedule was falling into place and as happy as I was to think about leaving this place, I now couldn't imagine not doing this substantive work and felt that I would be less than I was currently if I wasn't saving people on a regular basis. I was afraid of not being there to do what needed to be done. I knew my replacement could handle the job but I guess I wanted to feel that I was a critical and necessary component. Once I stepped off this high-profile stage, would it ever be the same again? If something happened to my 7,000 people, would I blame myself for not being there? Yes, I would, but really had no option and had to come to some type of personal closure on this horribly miraculous and strangely exciting experience. At this point, I was to overnight at Camp Sully at the airport the night of June 5th and depart Baghdad International Airport to Kuwait on a military C-130 cargo plane June 6th, arriving in time to catch the midnight commercial flight to Washington, D.C., and arriving to what would certainly be a surrealistic civilization at 0640 the morning of June 7th. My first out-brief was at the Department of

State with our excellent and supportive DS Assistant Secretary at 0900 hours right after arrival. Following that but the same day, and certainly in a state of serious jet-lag, I was to begin a series of interviews with CNN and other news media related to the Daniel Pearl case and the Hollywood Premier of the movie "A Mighty Heart", to be in New York City one week after my arrival out of the war zone. I was going, no matter how strange I would feel or how out of place I might be among them all. I knew Mariane Pearl would be there and Will Patton, and that would be enough to provide some basis for normalcy. Who knew, I might even get a chance to see Angelina Jolie, who was playing the role of Mariane, or one of my favorite actors, Brad Pitt. The State Department and DS Public Affairs people had also arranged other live television interviews in New York around the Premier and DS's prime rule was to "NOT talk about Iraq, stick to the Pearl case". After what I had been through, how bad could live TV be.

My final days in Iraq were not going to be any easier than the ones before. My constituent post furthest south was Basrah and they had been literally averaging 15 rockets a day. It was the location I was most concerned about in the country but I had arranged for the best man to be placed there as RSO. I knew my RSO in Basrah was stronger than most others, mentally and maybe even physically, and even though it would take a toll on him, I felt he was the most stable and our best chance for handling the day-to-day excessive stress. As in many highly stressful environments, people develop their own sense of dark humor that compensates for some of the harsh situations and ludicrous rules and guidelines. They get pounded every day by rockets, mortars, and machine gun fire and have little opportunity to respond to a rocket launched from 8 to 12 miles away. It can be frustrating. Also, if they shoot back at the enemy with their rifles or other weapons, they have to account and explain every round and where it went and where it landed. The reporting goes something like "I fired 2 well-placed rounds down range". That usually keeps the politicians off our backs as our people die and can't respond due to the "no collateral damage" policy. On one particularly frustrating day, after having been pounded by every type of enemy weapon possible for four straight days and nights, my RSO in Basrah provided me 5 minutes of actual out-loud laughter from the dark sense of humor derived from extreme frustration and stress. On this day at this time, the enemy decided to shoot at them from several hundred yards away with large caliber machine guns. Our RSO forces; American RSO and Colombian Guards, spotted them. Big mistake being seen considering the frustration level of my guys. The report I received from my RSO stated "we took incoming fire and spotted the enemy so we fired 400 well-placed rounds down range". There was no more shooting by the enemy that day.

The Vice President of Iraq asked us to take him and his two sons out to the RSO firing range for some shooting practice. I was happy to further the political relationships and if this would help, it would be done. The VP was actually a nice and courteous man with a large contingent of solemn and "seemingly angry" Iraqi bodyguards, who all insisted on standing right next to him as we tried to assist with upgrading his style and skill in shooting. His bodyguards were stiff and suspicious and never offered a moment of relaxing conversation or a smile but I suppose they were just doing their jobs and had no real reason to trust the people who invaded their country, even if we had gotten rid of a vicious murdering Dictator for them. His sons were well-behaved but obviously afraid of Americans and I can only imagine what stories they had been told about the child-eating, two-headed monsters that Americans were. Eventually, working hard to joke with the kids and showing them that we were nice guys who just wanted to help them enjoy a couple of hours, they began to loosen up.

We had a wide variety of interesting weapons for them to sample and they all migrated to certain ones that they preferred. Some, because they had probably seen them in a movie. Others, because they had lots of "gadgets" on them. And of course some, because they could "rack off" a lot of rounds in a heartbeat. For those, we maintained a "hands-on" approach so they wouldn't be knocked over backwards and accidentally kill a bodyguard. It went well enough and they left with the bodyguards looking at us like they still wished we would turn our backs on them for a second. That wasn't going to happen.

The following day after the Iraqi VP and sons did their shooting practice, a large Russian 240mm rocket soared from 12 kilometers away and landed inside my shooting range, right smack on the spot the Iraqi VP and his sons had been practicing the day before. This day though, we had a training course going on with about 30 men. They heard the air-splitting whistling sound and it was significant considering that this enormous car-length size rocket was coming in hard and fast on top of them. They knew what to do and ran for the front berm of the range which had a protective lip. Others knew they had only a second or two and dove to get as flat as they could and prayed it would not be a direct hit. It was. The huge rocket hit in the middle of the large firing range and shrapnel and blast effect wounded 11 men. We were only lucky in that none died. Some injuries were significant enough to send some men home to the U.S. and others were allowed to return to work in a couple of days. Life just seemed so random with who gets hit and when and by what. Did someone across the river hear about the VP's visit?

There was apparently interest by top Embassy leadership in gaining entry to certain religiously significant Iraqi cities and this day would be my "career-riskiest" and most disillusioning of this tour. A terrorist-controlled city in the south is called Najaf. We didn't go there and neither did our military. It is referred to as the Holy City of Najaf and carries some religious (and apparently political) significance, which was not lost on our Ambassador. We knew that the Aegis organization had been making some runs over the highway that leads to Najaf and their South Africans Protection Teams had been suffering substantial deaths and injuries in doing so. It was getting so that when we heard about another devastating loss of personnel in the south, we knew it Aegis. They were taking risks to meet the needs of some organization or an individual who likely would end up dead or captured with them. We were very disappointed in their approach. None of us had the resources to successfully traverse the single, death-trap road to Najaf and I was not going to sacrifice my men. We knew also that the weapons and additional terrorists were being supplied out of Najaf and it seemed to us that it should be hit by a major military operation. However, the "Holy" city of Najaf was a political situation and our politicians preferred to allow them to continue supplying the enemy rather than hit a Muslim Holy place.

Interested political leadership had an objective of being the first to get people into the Holy City. I informed the Ambassador that to go to Najaf would entail a U.S. military-sized operation with 30 or more gun trucks and overhead cover by Apache helicopter gunships, and even then, the roads were lined with EFPs and IEDs, and from past actions with Aegis, some of the soldiers were definitely going to die. I advised him that if it was critical to meet someone from there, it would be better if they came up to Baghdad or we met them in another neutral and safe location in-between but that it was a definite loss of life mission to go to Najaf. I left it with him as a U.S. military resource operation only, if the Army was willing to risk their men. Big Army with big weapons was the only way and even that was a terribly bad idea, which, after details that cannot be discussed, was fortunately dropped for the next year or so.

It was hard to fathom, but we were being barraged by rockets now to an even greater level than previously. Every time we thought things couldn't get any worse, we had a greater number of rockets beat us literally to death for days without end. We had all become jumpy, and at a loud noise, most people were getting under the DFAC tables, or diving into the sand, or at least falling with some focused speed to the ground. It was like a perpetual adrenaline rush. We were all on edge. At the same time, it brings on that strange sense of dark humor and it was rife on the compound. It also affects sleep patterns substantially and the Doctor and Psych at the Palace, who were terrific and I called my best friends, were seeing a lot of people coming in for some form of assistance. I watched my men and women closely but they were rocks of strength. I couldn't have been more proud of any people on earth. Truly our RSO T-shirt slogan of "Resistance is Futile" fit this group. They just continued to run, bombing after rocket attack after killings, like energizer rabbits. On one day we had 10 rockets fall on us in just a few seconds. They fell directly on our compound wounding 4. The next day 8 more rockets fell, wounding 6 more. Two days later 6 more rockets fell on top of us killing 4, and the next day 4 more rockets fell on us killing 1 and seriously wounding 3 and moderately wounding 4 more. Our lives and our trailers and offices were being shaken and rocked every day and night and we found ourselves rolling and diving on the ground quite a bit now. During one such series, I was sprinting from concrete bunker to bunker, checking on any wounded or scared and as I was sprinting between detonations, I actually pulled a muscle in my buttocks that would bother me for the next 6 months. Was this a sign of age or stress? A butt-muscle pull? How does a 56-year old skilled athlete and professional warrior explain that. During dinner one night, the Rocket alarm went off. It was astounding to see 400 people simultaneously dive beneath their tables. It was impressive to see and I saw it from under the table.

Being a thoroughly experienced "Pakistan hand", I had also begun tracking trends and patterns in Pakistan and had been closely monitoring the reporting of terrorist movements and actions. It seemed clear to me that there was a new move toward escalated hostilities in Pakistan and my prediction to my DS folks was that I would be arriving at just the right time for a new level of terrorism and violence. It truly appeared that terrorist troops and emphasis was headed that way. Never during the U.S. action in Iraq had it ever had the level of violence that we had witnessed during my year here. And, we were hoping that the Surge, which was beginning now, would reduce the violence after I left. It all made sense to me from my career perspective. The golf clubs in Pakistan might not get much use.

This environment and the type of impact it has on the psyche of those not accustomed to a life of this type of stress and risk, sometimes can cause people to do strange things, beyond anything they thought they would ever do. In fact, this type of risk situation also attracts strange people who might not have any business being here in the first place. There are more unusual characters and misfits here than any other single place on earth. When you think about it, who are those 60 and 70 year old people who volunteer to come here and why would they do that? We even have one 84 year old man shuffling around the halls of the Palace. What kind of civilian requests to come to a war and blast zone to live in a flimsy trailer that is atomized when it gets hit by a 122mm rocket? The other odd thing is that we all get along and there are few personality problems. That might also need to be psychoanalyzed. A few days ago, one man slipped a little too far over the edge though and he got drunk, jumped in an ATV-type Gator, and began driving all over the IZ raising hell and letting the wind refresh his soul. I understand his need for it but he was so drunk that he also drove out into the Red Zone, which is what caught our attention. He finally hit a speed bump he didn't see at about 20 mph and it threw him out of the Gator and onto his back, where he lay until we and the IZ Police picked him up a few minutes later. Fortunately, no enemy personnel saw him and he would survive. But, we spoke with him to get an idea of his mental state and afterwards decided that he needed to go home to the U.S. and not come back. The experience in Iraq had exceeded his mental parameters and his time was up.

Vice President Cheney came for a visit again as the heat began to climb; now reaching 120 degrees during the day. We put on the big security operation but nothing stops rockets and sure enough, it was an invitation to the enemy to launch on our compound. VP Cheney had a gaggle of Press that were even less polite than the usual group. They also seemed to want to appear like they "had been there and done that" to our group of battered tough people. They all talked the talk, using the words that would make them seem experienced, but in their newly bought cargo pants and 86-pocket media vests and perfectly clean shirts, we frankly didn't give a crap, if I may say that. We parked all of them in one of our large conference rooms outside but near the north wing's

Classified Access Area (CAA), keeping them out of the classified operations and in a room set up with electronic access to the real world just designed for them.

Almost as if it was what the Press wanted, a rocket fell about a mile away, but in the IZ. As I have stated before, even a mile away, the earth shakes and howls at the harsh penetration of solid earth. But it was a mile away and none of us even left our desks after evaluating the sound, repercussion effect, and realized we were alive. But, much to our delight and humor, which was greatly needed, the entire Press pool came running out of the conference room like panicked children and began heading for the stairs down to the basement. Everyone else in the halls came to a halt to watch this comical lemming-like sprint, enjoying what seemed so out of proportion. We let them run it off and then went downstairs to get them a few minutes later after getting full enjoyment of talking about it with others and brought them back upstairs to their "down room". We told them it was a mile away and not to worry inside the palace but they all had that first-timer crazed "I was just almost killed" look in their deer-headlight eyes and just sort of looked at me like I was creating some conspiracy. Well, to make them all heroes I guess, the next day, all their stories in their papers told of how they and the VP were almost killed. VP Cheney came out of his meeting and didn't even know the rocket had hit until he read their articles.

The Department of State was beginning to experience a shortage of volunteers to fill the ever-increasing number of job slots for Iraq, especially in the PRTs and they decided that a promotional DVD would inspire people and increase recruitment motivation. We held a Country Team meeting to discuss their intentions and I said I would assist with my resources to make the film.

The Producer/Director had some good credentials and a very attractive (female) Assistant so of course I volunteered. One must always recognize the need for stimulus. They evaluated all the working areas and took footage of various aspects of the operation but realized that the real interest and perhaps the glamour and adventure niche would come from the security section. We would need to assure those considering volunteering that we would take care of them and protect them and they needed to see how tactical and proficient our operation was. So, I was asked to do a number of interview "takes" and they ended up in the recruitment film. But one of the unique aspects was to show those considering the adventure, what the place looked like and what they would see and encounter when in Iraq, or Baghdad specifically. So, I agreed to take them up for filming from our medium lift helicopters but only within the IZ. I wasn't going to have a dead film crew doing a motivational film.

One of the highlights was to fly over the new impressive Embassy site and see what a massive "self-sufficient city" it was going to be and the very nice apartment buildings people would be living in. As we flew over the apartment buildings getting the footage we (they) hoped would increase volunteer excitement, we felt and heard a loud impact sound that felt like we had taken a 50 caliber round to the helicopter. It jolted us. I looked at my door gunner and he looked at me and we both shrugged our shoulders. I watched our passengers to see if anyone slumped forward or a pilot lost control but nothing happened. We did not appear to be hit although it seemed like a strong smack. Then out our left side, we all noticed a cloud of fire and smoke coming out of one of the new embassy fifth floor apartments. As we had flown over it, a rocket had traveled from Saddar City and struck a direct hit into the apartment. We had been so close to the traveling hunk of steel as it hit the building, we had experienced the impact and shock wave. Since the rockets usually traveled in series, it meant we were a flying duck target for others and the pilots reacted instantly, pulling the helicopter into a G-Force banking maneuver that I didn't think was even possible for a helicopter. Literally, out bodies were pinned to our seats and the blood was forced back as our skin was pulled back. It was a forceful and impressive action to save our lives and they quickly angled for the LZ to get out of a sky with potential 70 pound bullets of steel with high explosives in them. I thought my head would explode from the blood rush from their clever highly-skilled move but I liked it. The professionals they were though, the camera people got some great shots of the smoke billowing out of the apartment.

About at this time, our truck convoys of supplies coming up from Kuwait in the South, were being repeatedly attacked and we were running low on basic food stuffs. I was not happy about our contractors being attacked and too often killed in these attacks that should be able to be prevented by our military elements, but the food issue has brought a cognizance of another issue. I understood clearly that within this microcosm we lived in where our meals were there for us when we walked in, and we just dropped off a bag of dirty laundry and then picked up clean and pressed clothes two days later, the entire focus of all our faculties was to work those 16 or 18 hour days and not to have to think about anything else distractive. But, with the shortage of food, we realized that we only had one comfort in our entire lives right now; the food. For those 3 20-minute meals we took, that was the only comfort we experienced and it was critical to our daily rejuvenation and salvation to continue on. These freaking terrorists in the south were affecting our morale and we were all getting testy about our military's lack of focus on a very essential issue. Our comfort zone was damaged and we were all pissed – including the soldiers who ate in our DFAC and in all the others. I will say that the food and facility manager was the most creative and exceptional I will ever meet. He did the most with so little that it did impress the entire Palace contingent and we even took a photo with him in thanks. Eventually, the food began to make it back in again but we could see this was going to be a real problem with the insurgents in the south now eating our supplies. Maybe we should try the old poison food supply truck and let them capture it to reduce their forces.

I was "short" and the thought of leaving this addictive and all-encompassing environment was more surrealistic than the thought of being in a place so unusual. But, on the other hand, the arrangements had been made for me to go to the New York Premier of the movie "A Mightly Heart". I was a bit excited to have an opportunity like this and to possibly meet some stars – as long as no one made any loud noises and made me look foolish diving under the dinner table. I was also scheduled to do live TV interviews on major shows and as an adrenaline junkie, I liked that too. The question was really whether I would seem like a maniac, doing live interviews so few days out of an active war zone.

In the final few days before I departed, tragedy struck again to remind me of where I was and what we were facing. An Iraqi employee working for the Political Section was kidnapped by the terrorists. He was also the husband of my Iraqi Investigator, a sweet older woman who had really put her heart into the job to help us. It was not known to anyone outside the Embassy that they worked for the Americans of course or they and all their family members would have been executed after being brutally tortured. They both had been in a market and been kidnapped for ransom.

But as the terrorists looked through her purse and his papers, they found an Embassy ID in her purse she had forgotten to take out. This is a fatal mistake. They realized now though that maybe they could get more money for them from the Americans and they released her to get her family's money and hopefully more from the Americans. While it is true we don't negotiate with terrorists, personally we loved these two nice older people whose children had already migrated out of Iraq and we wanted to try to recover him alive.

The insurgents/terrorists were asking the family for a million dollars. Everyone always starts with a million dollars. It is moronic but it always starts with that magical amount. The family pulled together what meager funds they could get in the hopes that they might actually let him go. We knew that the odds were not good and that these unsophisticated criminal/terrorists did not understand the concept that stated that if you want this kidnapping industry to succeed, you have to return the hostage when you get the money or people won't pay the next time you kidnap someone. Certainly the two main kidnapping industry-centers of Bogota, Colombia, and Mexico City, had done exceptionally well following that basic principle. These idiots were clueless so all we could do was hope for the best.

But, in the most of optimistic hopes, we did place some undercover elements out there at the money transfer spot, hidden so that if the terrorists didn't follow the rules and let him go, we might be able to track them to their headquarters and get him back through an assault. Then, they shut the lid hard on us and said that they would only let him go if the wife, our employee and friend, delivered the money. This was an exceptionally bad option with pretty much only one anticipated conclusion – her death as well. This was not an American operation and it was a personal matter, one that officially we were not supposed to interfere in, but we told her it was a bad idea and that as hard as it was to face, she might have to let it go in order to still be alive for her children. Damn, these things were never easy to discuss and seemed so brutal no matter how you present it. She said she understood but that she was his wife and by culture and obligation and love, she had to make the money drop to get her husband back. Now we really had to hope that the undercover operatives in the worst enemy territory could keep an eye on her, as hopeless a wish as that was.

She went off to make the drop and the last our "spies" saw of her was when the kidnappers put her in another vehicle and drove off through a narrow enemy alley that was immediately blocked to our undercover people at gunpoint. They were able to save themselves but we lost track of her movements. We all sat and worried throughout the night. At one point in the early morning hours a call was made to her family's cell phone. They received a call from her saying in tears and horror that she was taken by them and that they had taken the money and then showed her the husband dead inside a freezer. Two days later we recovered both bodies by a riverside. These Iraqis are brutal and uncompassionate with their own people to such a degree that it is impossible to understand. I have grown to dislike the Iraqi enemy more than any other enemy I have ever faced. I am so jaded now I will never be able to trust most Iraqis again. We lost two beautiful sweet Iraqi friends who only wanted a better life for themselves and their families and who had sacrificed everything in order to try and obtain it. We were all heartbroken and some of my staff who worked daily with our investigator were devastated.

Two days later, on June 6th, 2007, I got on an airplane to fly to the United States to re-enter an environment that seemed totally incongruous with where my focus was at the time. I was forever changed but knew with even more conviction that I was a Special Agent doing what I did for all the best and right reasons. I had throughout this tour, and still have posted on my office wall today, a statement that seems particularly appropriate – "People sleep peaceably in their beds at night only because rough men (and women) stand ready to do violence on their behalf." It was however, becoming harder to maintain my Zen composure. Iraq was now behind me, but would never be out of me. I was going to take 5 weeks to try and assimilate it all. Later, I and some of my team would receive an Award for Heroism for one of our rescues, signed by the Secretary of State. There had been a lot of growing up being done here by some young exceptional Agents who would take my place when I retired in a few more years.

Chapter Twenty-Two
THE "RETURN FROM IRAQ" PRESS TOUR AND REST STOP, JUNE - JULY, 2007

I arrived on a commercial flight in Washington, D.C. at 0700 hours after traveling for 48 hours to get "home" and I was dirty, sweaty, jumpy, tired and a wreck. My first meeting was at 0900 hours with the Assistant Secretary for Diplomatic Security, Richard "Grif" Griffin, a man I respected a great deal and who had given me his total support and confidence while I was commanding in Iraq. Fortunately at least, they allowed me to check into a hotel, take a shower and change out of my travel clothes and into a clean 511 shirt and pants. I had brought a suit I quickly had made in the Red Zone of Baghdad by an Iraqi tailor who was looking to make some dollars and then intended to leave the country through Amman, but it was wadded up and needed to be cleaned and pressed. Apparently, they had also set up several interviews with U.S. Government Press Agencies for this morning who wanted to know about the Daniel Pearl case and the upcoming premier on the 13th in New York. They were advised not to ask any questions about my service in Iraq. In addition, a CNN interview was arranged with the beautiful Zain Vergee for that afternoon and I would need my suit for that one. That part, I would enjoy and hoped not to make a fool of myself, although that wasn't cut in stone either at this point.

I made the cleansing ritual and changed into my human being disguise and we were off to the State Department. Before leaving for Iraq, I had out-briefed with our DS Assistant Secretary and he had made a request. He said "Randall, right now we have almost 500 armored vehicles paid for by DS over there and we can't account for about half of them. Please take as a priority assignment, the accounting for where those cars are, whether destroyed by the enemy, by our own troops so the enemy wouldn't get them, or exactly where in Iraq they currently are." I had put some very qualified people on that upon arrival in Iraq and every car had been identified by status. When I walked into his office, he seemed genuinely glad to see me home alive and knew what I had gone through in detail. We discussed things that still needed to be done and I found myself also telling him frankly about the problems he was going to face with the new leadership and the trends of the terrorists. While there, friends I knew and had been close to for years and others I had become friends with over the email system and phone, who backed me up and supported my needs over there, came in to say welcome back. Though I am a jaded and hardened individual, and often like to think of myself as emotionless, I began to sense a "Kodak Moment" coming on and realized that I was definitely in need of some sleep and emotional adjustment time. I slapped myself several times and got back on track, finishing the out-brief with the Assistant Secretary and then was escorted down to the Public Affairs recording studios in the State Department that I had never seen before. Of course, with how hard I had worked to stay out of Washington for the past 20 years, that wasn't surprising.

The studio was freezing. I suppose that is a requirement for all the equipment but brother, after adjusting to the severe heat of Iraq, I could feel my shirt standing up and a chattering beginning. The interview, primarily for the GSN (Government Security News), but also to be used in other USG publications and web sites, was well orchestrated and professional and evolved into a 45-minute, three-part interview that went into a number of publications, videos, and web-site productions. The reason I was doing all this was that for almost my entire career, DS had wanted to be low profile, and there was so much that needed to be said about the work DS carries out domestically and overseas, and the successes we have had protecting America and our people. It was time DS got some recognition as the most capable and professional, elite Federal Law Enforcement Organization in the world. I was also seeing the personal side for me and it couldn't hurt my ego to have some exposure for some of the things I had been able to accomplish. But mainly, this was the golden apple time for DS recognition and all the other Agents who risked their lives and sometimes lost them protecting our nation. The GSN 3-part interview later hit You-Tube, which I was totally unfamiliar with, and apparently during one week, had the number one most hits of any item on the site. I wasn't really sure what that meant. I just repeated what I was told. The headline in their publication was "The real investigator behind the reel character in "A Mighty Heart". Frankly, I was looking forward to seeing Will Patton in New York to talk to him about the filming experience. I didn't understand his industry at all but found it curious and wanted to know more. We had already set up breakfast the morning of the Premier.

The professional Officers running DS's Public Affairs (PA) were giving me good guidance throughout on how to interview, how to deflect the bad questions, how to dress with a blue shirt so I wouldn't look deceased, although I wanted to wear all black as always. They were terrific. A PA Officer stayed with me at all times and guided things in the right direction. After I would go home to see the family in Tempe, Arizona, for a few days, my PA Guide would meet me in New York to assist with the live TV, radio and press events. I also gave him my second ticket for the premier since neither of my two choices of Halle Berry or Beyonce were available (or cared). Although I am keeping a life-long invitation open for Halle.

I couldn't believe that after 48 hours without sleep, I was still awake and moving but here I was, living off the remains of my adrenaline. Washington, D.C., was hot and humid and I had just been told that the afternoon recorded interview with CNN's Zain Vergee was going to be held outside in a park for that "natural look". I had been doing a lot of natural-look sweating for the last year and believe me, I loved air conditioning and if it hadn't been for Zain, and my biological drive, I might have declined the sweat-fest in my new Iraqi suit.

In the afternoon, we showed up at the park and after wandering around too much in the heat, we found her and her crew. She was gorgeous even with a glow of the heat. I, on the other hand, could go through a Hollywood make-up session and on my best day, would still look like someone they wouldn't want on their film. She asked her questions as we sat at a small table and then suggested we continue the interview walking through the park. She had also been advised that there could be no Iraq questions but Zain is a clever aggressive career woman and couldn't resist. So, as we were walking in the park, my PA Guide was having a hard time staying with us to monitor every question and every answer without looking like a stalker on film in the background, so Zain sprung the question. I have a 151 IQ and am street-smarter than I look, as well as being a trained salesman so there are not many journalists who can outwit or trick me. Zain said, "so Randall, I understand that you have just returned from Iraq. What was it like and what did you do there?" I looked over at my PA guy in time to see his expression of career-disaster and smiled. I looked at Zain and on film with my full Bennett smile, said, "Zain, I am not really at liberty to discuss the Iraq activities I was involved in but I would love to take you to dinner tonight where we could discuss it or anything else." Yes, I asked her for a date on film. Zain didn't miss a beat minus a brief non-visible stunned pause. She said something to the effect that she would think about it and we moved back to the subject she was allowed to talk to me about. Honestly, I really wanted a date with her. I wasn't interested in just deflecting her Iraq question. I was thinking a nap, shower, and a dinner date with this beautiful lady. Zain and I developed a nice friendship by email and occasionally see each other when she comes to a country I am in but there has never, much to my unhappiness and not for a lack of trying, been any development of an intimate relationship. On the positive side I guess, the interview ended up getting a lot of exposure and play for DS and myself.

I suppose the non-date was the best call since later that day, I went to bed and woke up about 12 hours later in time to go to the airport and fly to Phoenix, Arizona, to see my immediate family for a short but large reunion in our family HQ, the town of Tempe. I spent a few days there seeing them before flying to New York City for the premier and a number of other pre-premier live interviews. My intentions after the premier were to fly back and rent a car, drive to the west coast to see some wonderful friends, and then drive up to the beautiful home I had bought in Santa

Fe, New Mexico. It was about time I spent a few weeks in the over-priced, value-crashing home that I bought at just the wrong time. At least it would be very quiet and my sister Barbara had promised to come out to visit.

So, after the family reunion, I boarded a plane with my now much-appreciated Iraqi black suit and black shirts and required blue shirts and headed for the Big Apple. Everyone seems to know New York. I don't know anything about it. I know Cairo, Bogota, Baghdad, Buenas Aires, Luanda, Nairobi, Santiago, Bangkok, Madrid, Karachi and a hundred other exotic cities, but in New York, I was a stranger in a strange land. But I was excited to experience it this time and I was beginning to catch up on rest and almost getting over my jet-lag.

I checked into the hotel and my PA Guide was there to greet me and act as my "handler". I can at times be a bit to handle, especially if I feel like it, but I was beginning to like him and I enjoyed his company and so it became more of a focused partnership on these interviews.

DS had also agreed to pick up my expenses and that made it all the better since originally, this movie premier thing was only a personal side trip and it was going to be expensive. Now that there was some serious mileage to gain for DS, they took on the expenses, which also obligated me to abide by most of their rules and stay within their guidance, which I am sure they knew I would only to the extent that I felt it made sense. They had also assigned me a female DS Agent as my protection and driver and she was enthusiastic and terrific. She was a relatively new Agent assigned to the New York Field Office and still had that appreciation for every new experience. It certainly made life easier though having a law enforcement vehicle and driver to get around. She also seemed excited about the whole movie thing and that enthused me.

Over the next two days preceding the premier, I interviewed live on Fox and Friends on the morning show with those three lively personalities. I also interviewed live with MSNBC, Tucker Carlson, but remotely, sitting in a room with make-up on looking at a screen with Tucker on the other end, staring at him on screen to give the impression that it was a direct interview. And, I even gave an interview over the phone to Roe Conn of WLS in Chicago during the evening rush hour period, which apparently captured a good group of listeners. It was all a very interesting experience. I think the PA guy and my female Agent assistant were enjoying it as much as I was, but every time I walked out of a studio interview and hadn't destroyed my career or my PA Guide's by making some comments about killing people in Iraq, or god knows what else he was worried about me saying, he took a deep breath and seemed very pleased that we had survived another possible titanic disaster.

In addition to doing the live TV and radio, I interviewed with a couple of print press folks. DS had thought I had some connection to Santa Fe, New Mexico, so they had arranged for the largest newspaper to do a Sunday insert special article. It was nice and fun but no one in Santa Fe had any idea I lived there or had ever met me. The Washington Post also did a nice article and then it spread to NewsMax.com, The New Yorker, USA Today, the NPR News Blog, CNN printed transcripts (minus the invitation for a date with Zain), various DS publications, spreading out to a multitude of home town newspapers in the U.S. and of course the You-Tube thing. I enjoyed it but it was a bit overwhelming and I realized it was my 15 minutes of fame and very soon, it would be over and I would be focusing on life-saving issues again, this time in Islamabad, Pakistan, and no one but me would remember all this attention.

The morning of the Premier, Will Patton had invited me to breakfast and we were meeting at a hotel restaurant near his home with his Agent present as well, who had wanted to meet me and probably was looking out for Will's interests. I was happy to see Will again. We had exchanged quite a few phone conversations over the past year and I truly liked the guy. He had a good heart and character, was quite a bit more shy than I thought Actors could be and was not flashy or abrasive at all. He was just a good guy, besides being one of the best Actors in the world without question.

The female DS Agent was very excited this morning about the possibility of meeting the famous Will Patton so I worked out a strategy with her. She would drop me off in front of the hotel, park the car, wait 30 minutes and then come in and find me to tell me where she would be when I finished. That way I could take the opportunity to naturally introduce her to Will. I walked in and found him sitting inconspicuously with his Agent in a booth that had a draw curtain for a sense of privacy from the gaping eyes. He got up with a big smile leading me to believe he was happy to see me and introduced me to his Agent. We discussed life, Iraq, the filming, and some of the interesting experiences he had in India with Angelina Jolie and Brad Pitt and the ruckus they always caused when people knew they were nearby. It was an insight to an industry I know nothing about but like everyone in America, have always been curious about. It was just damn good to see him again. I asked him what time he was going to the Premier and he asked if he really needed to go. He said he hated those kinds of things. I thought he was kidding but he was dead serious so I had to convince him that he needed to come in order to support me. He said he thought he had a suit somewhere that he bought in 2000 and again I thought he was kidding but was wrong. He was actually wondering if he had a suit. He said his mother was in town and he would bring her as well.

At that time, my fellow Agent walked in, "radioed up", armed, in a nice pant suit and with all her equipment on her belt and walked over to our table, which caught the eye of Will. At first he looked concerned but when she gave me the line about where she was parked when I finished, Will looked pleased, so I introduced them and Will stood up and in a true southern gentleman manner, greeted her and talked with her for a couple of minutes about who she was and what she did. It went well. After she left, Will looked at me and said, "I had no idea you had Agents who looked like her". We agreed on a time to meet at the Premier and I went off to do some more interviewing. I will never forget what a nice guy Will Patton is and will always feel I owe him a favor.

To show what a small world it can be even in New York, I went to lunch in a small rapid-service diner across the street from the hotel I was staying in and while I was sitting there about to eat, in the front door of the diner walked the FBI female Agent who had worked with me in Pakistan for a short while on the Pearl case. She was also portrayed in the movie briefly but I had heard it was not a kind portrayal and she was actually a very nice lady. The Director Michael Winterbottom had a reputation for disliking the FBI. Personally, I had enjoyed our dinner together in Santa Fe and we were planning to get together in New York for dinner if we could swing the time. What a shock to see her though at this place and at this specific moment in time, just hours before the Premier and we hugged and for the few minutes she had for lunch, we caught up on our lives and current status and she told me how some of my FBI friends were doing. It was a moment that could never happen without some external syncronistic higher power but it made sense right now that it should occur.

The night came, and as is my fashion comfort zone, I wore my black Iraqi "lucky" suit with a black buttoned up shirt and a silver Hopi Indian pin at the collar, with a design representing the power of the Bear. It made me feel relaxed, black on black. My PA partner was suited up and ready to go, camera in hand, and our DS escort was excited about who she might see this night. We arrived at the Zeigfeld Theater, famous for its premiers, and I suddenly felt a bit lost and out of place with the long lines of people on both sides of the streets, hoping to catch a glimpse of Angelina and Brad. They calmed down as we exited our car and they saw that we were just some lucky unrecognizables. We walked to the end of the red carpet stretch and were greeted, thank heavens, by people who seemed to know who we were and were very kind to give us some directions. It was at this entry to "the walk" that I ran into Michael Winterbottom and other Producers and some of the Actors who were playing people who I had become so close to during the investigation. They had done a good job on cast selection because I could pretty much guess who was playing who. Then I saw the Indian actress, the beautiful Archie Punjabi, who was playing Asra Nomani in the movie and wow, I knew who I was going to hang out next to for awhile. She turned out to be very kind and interesting to talk with as well. In my momentary stun and loss of focus, I forgot to ask for her number or at least an email address. What a dummy. Ah, those lost opportunities that haunt us.

I now had to begin my walk down the red carpet past the gaggle of press that usually I was checking and monitoring for weapons, and this was where our PA guy showed what a cool professional he was. He knew DS should maximize this opportunity and he preceded me by a ways telling all the press that I was the real character portrayed in the movie and all of a sudden, they all wanted me to stop and do an interview. Also, the annoying photographers were all yelling "hey Randall, look over here". How surrealistic was this? One week ago, I was dodging rockets, repairing wounded, and mourning over the loss of wonderful Iraqi employees. Now I was walking a movie premier red carpet with people calling my name. Fortunately or unfortunately, I knew I wouldn't remember much of it in the morning. It was just too out of perspective. I interviewed with quite a few reporters on my walk including CNN again, and even some music channels like MTV and V. The DS PA guy was terrific at his job and seemed to be having fun. At the end of the walk, I met up with Archie and now I could do what I really wanted to – spend time flirting with her. She was terrific and as I have since learned watching her on film, she is a talented Actress.

Mariane Pearl finally showed up and after hugging her for awhile, we talked and caught up on her life and how her son Adam was doing. Maybe the thing I regret most is that my job has not allowed me to spend time with Danny and Mariane's son Adam. We made plans to spend time in NYC after this hurrah was over but I suspected that she was going to be much too busy at this juncture in her life and that turned out to be true.

About half my brief stint of fame had expired when a limo pulled up and the crowd went wild. It was Angelina and Brad, and as they walked around giving the crowd what they wanted, I went in with Will to get settled into my seat. I met Will's sweet Mother and told her what a terrific son she had. She was absolutely delightful. Angelina and Brad came in and sat on the front row and the movie began. This was my first viewing of the film and I didn't know how I would take it or feel about it. I had no idea how it would portray me or even how accurately it would follow the true storyline. As it turned out, it was an excellent drama and it gave the essence of the story but not with accuracy of course. After all, it was a Hollywood movie. The Director had told me that after the cutting of the film, Angelina had said she needed more time portraying her role as Mariane and that meant the rest of us were on less of the time. The movie also made it appear that the investigation sort of took place out of Mariane's home, which is of course not true. This was an international terrorism investigation and they didn't have the clearance for what we were doing day and night. The investigation had as you would imagine, taken place out of my office. In fact, Mariane and Asra used to get upset with me because I wouldn't or couldn't tell them everything that was going on. Nonetheless, Will was excellent and I was honored that he portrayed me, and Angelina – my god, she really became Mariane. I now saw what it meant to be an Actor. They were all exceptional. I don't think I could do that.

The movie ended and I sat back up from where I had been scrunching further and further down in my seat as I relived the case in my head. It was hard to watch, especially the moment we told Mariane that Danny was dead. When Angelina walked into the back bedroom just as Mariane had and slammed the door and screamed, besides reliving the wet eyes, I almost had to leave the theater. It was like honestly having to do that twice and no one should ever have to do it even once.

Once we got to the party, the group sort of dissipated. I began to wander around looking for a glass of red wine, which didn't take long to find and then just walked through the crowd seeing what and who I could see. It was a very interesting time and I would cross paths with those I had met, in between seeing some of my favorite stars like Ed Norton. This was impressive but I was mostly staying to myself, taking it all in and trying to maintain focus. I ran into our PA guy and he told me Will was looking for me in another room and that was definitely the guy I wanted to hang around with. I felt comfortable with him.

I was still sipping my first glass of wine when I found Will and we talked and hung out for awhile. Eventually, I noticed people looking at us, I guess because we looked a little like brothers, and then they started to come over and ask for autographs. Yes, they were asking for Will's autograph and wanted to take pictures of us together, but they were also asking for my autograph. I told them that with my autograph and if I paid them $4, they could buy a cup of coffee but they insisted. Then I could see people pointing subtly and mouthing the words "that is the real Randall Bennett from the movie". It, and life, had reached an all-time new level of bizarre.

Across the room, swamped by crowds of admirers, were Angelina and Brad. Will asked me if I had introduced myself to Angelina yet and I smiled thinking he was teasing me. As much as I was inclined to do so, why on earth would I want to embarrass myself to such a degree? He was serious though and dragged me over. I waved at to our PA guy to get his camera ready. It didn't matter whether this went well or poorly, it was going to be a photo to remember.

As we neared, a lot of people were clamoring for their attention and we sort of just stood to the side until Angelina saw Will and she grabbed him and hugged him as a real friend. What a lucky guy. Then she saw me standing there most likely looking like a stalker or at best a person out of his element. I realized my silence could only worsen things so I decided I better at least introduce myself. I said hello and that my name was Randall Bennett. To my total surprise, her eyes got big and she said, "the real Randall Bennett?" I was so stunned I wasn't sure if I was the real Randall at that moment but with the sound of rockets detonating in the background of my mind I said yes. She then hugged me and again, though she is an amazing actress, had tears coming from her eyes. The hug was long enough to be memorable for me and then she took my hand and led me to a table and we sat while she continued to hold my hand and she wanted to ask about the movie, the real case, and how her performance had been in respect to the real events. I told her that the two times my heart had been broken were when Mariane had slammed the door and screamed and then again when she did it on screen. She was so perfectly beautiful and poised I was having a hard time delving into her character. I am usually very adept at recognizing the inner self of people from all my experience with investigations but she was tough. Either that or I was smitten. I suppose it could have been both. After all, I had only left the battlefield one week before. Then Mariane came over and so did Will and the four of us sat at the table talking together. Mariane was the one to point out that here we were; the two real case individuals and the two who portrayed us sitting together. It was kind of cool. Looking outward, I could also see many people who were just dieing to end my moment and get close to Angelina themselves. Then, while my hand was still being held, Brad Pitt came walking casually over with his tie undone and his hands comfortably in his pockets and that winning smile he is famous for and stood smiling at all of us. I realized I should probably identify whose hand was being held by his girlfriend so I stood up and said my name was Randall Bennett and held out my hand. Will mysteries never end? Brad got big eyes and said, "the real Randall Bennett?" I guess so. He then hugged me, which was pretty cool but didn't generate the same reaction as with Angelina. Then he took my arm and sat me down and wanted to know about the case and my interpretation of the movie, which he was a co-Producer of through his Plan B Productions along with Paramount Vantage. Then Ed Norton walked over and Brad introduced him to me and told me how Ed was one of the truly great actors. I could hardly believe the 15 minutes of fame I was sharing and was thrilled to look up and see our trusty PA guy clicking away with the camera. Thank goodness there would be some form of verification that this really occurred. I also dragged our DS PA representative over to get a photo with Angelina so that the moment and opportunity wouldn't be missed. He emailed it that night to his DS office and by the time he returned, there was a full size poster of he and Angelina hanging in the office to greet him.

As with all things, this magic moment ended and Mariane and I said we would try to get together in the city the next day but I knew it was going to be tough. She was with her two new close friends Brad and Angelina and would be very busy. Will and I walked across the room and stood out of the shark fest to take some deep breaths. The next moment, every man's fantasy at some point, The Nanny, Fran Dresher, walked up and started to talk with Will. It was interesting to see how shy Will was and when Fran talked to someone on the other side, he actually asked me what he should do. I told him to get her number and then let me know everything later. I was kidding, but not really. Then I was distracted by two girls who walked up to me, and again, not really understanding that I wasn't famous, asked for photos and an autograph, which I am sure if I searched the trash later, I could have recovered. Out of the corner of my eye, I saw Will and Fran exchange numbers. That made me very happy because I think the world of Will. He is truly one of the good guys.

Well, I continued to wander the party completely out of place, Will took his mother home, Brad and Angelina left, Mariane went back to her hotel and waiting little Adam, and eventually my PA partner and I got the sense that our New York adventure was over. It was an experience I will never forget and I appreciated how nice Brad, Angelina, Ed, Will and everyone had been to me. I am not much of a "star watcher" but these folks have my respect and admiration. Now it was on to several week's quiet recovery in Santa Fe, New Mexico, and some psychological "backstopping" and normalizing from a visit by my wonderful, understanding and always-supportive sister Barbara, and then back into the fire in Islamabad, Pakistan, for what might be my final true terrorism tour.

Before I move on to Pakistan, I need to mention one of my mini-trips between Iraq and my departure to Islamabad. I had not seen my Madrid Ambassador and friend and his wife, for a couple of years now, nor my other close friends from Madrid who were the Ambassador's Assistants. I didn't really have many actual friends since I had moved around so much but these people are the best and I would sacrifice anything to keep them safe. These good folks had maintained communication with me while in Iraq and had been a source of morale and support and encouragement. The Ambassador is one of the most successful businessmen in the world and I have never been more impressed with anyone I have ever met. He is one of the finest people, and most caring, people-oriented the world has produced, and his extreme business success with such a fine strong character seemed conflictive to me, which impressed me even more about him. He was the person I wished I could model myself after. Yet, he sort of watched over me in a way and maintained his support and friendship to me by telling me in his emails that I was his hero. I have never understood that but it picked up my spirits to such a degree that I would ride high on it under rocket fire for days and would read his email several times. I suppose in his wisdom, he understood what it would mean to me.

The Ambassador had asked if I could come by his southern California hang-out between my assignments to say hello and the fact that he would even care to make the offer was an enthusiasm boost. His wife was much the same way and had always been a good friend. I made up my mind that after the New York episode, I would fly back to Phoenix and drive over to pay my respects as part of my mental restoration period.

I arrived in his Southern California town and my good friend from Madrid told me to check into a particular hotel and that he and his wife were coming down for the dinner event as well. This would be such a great reunion. I checked into the hotel that I couldn't afford but made up my mind that for this two night event, I would splurge. The first night I walked around the calm, manicured, and commercial environment around the hotel, silently, alone and inconspicuously moving though expensive malls where everyone seemed to have an agenda but I just wasn't in the frame of reference yet to understand it.

The next day I met them and they told me the Ambassador had

coordinated a small dinner with us and a few of his friends at an exclusive Club/restaurant next to a Music Hall named after his wife. WOW! When we arrived at the dinner, there were a dozen of the most powerful people in his circle of friends. I was a bit confused by its appearance and wasn't sure of the agenda for this type of dinner until the Ambassador began to speak to open the dinner. His opening was to relate my resume to everyone present and to highlight my accomplishments and to offer praise down upon my head. I was embarrassed, shocked and so touched that if I hadn't just been presented as a tough guy, I would have let a tear or two loose. How could a man who had become and done so much, and was the person I most idolized in all ways, say such praising comments about me. I was just a crazy field operative who seemed to always be in trouble with the bad guys in every country I went to. A vague figure who earned civil servant pay and would upon the day I retire, be forgotten forever. I don't ever remember being more affected by a group's appreciation, which they all went along with and after each of the items the Ambassador mentioned, would commend me and tell me how great a job I had done for our nation. It is not possible for me to properly express the impact this evening had on me. They even asked me to relate some of the details of various experiences and I accommodated them from the sheer shock of the event. I will never forget this, and the Ambassador will forever be MY hero and the man I most respect.

As I drove away the next morning to go rest silently and alone in my home in Santa Fe, New Mexico, I was stunned, elated, euphoric, and perhaps even more committed to the work I do for my country. I do what I do for the future of the children but also for people like these who are the heart and soul of our nation. My life is full.

Chapter Twenty~Three
RSO ISLAMABAD, PAKISTAN, JULY 2007 - AUGUST 2008

I arrived in Islamabad during an auspicious full moon that seemed to fill half the sky and made the land as visible as the middle of the day but with deep and long shadows. I landed early in the morning to very familiar smells, sights and sounds that included the confusing constant stream of thousands of people no matter what time of day or night it is. I have always wondered where so many people with children are going at 2 or 3 o'clock in the morning. It is just the way their lives are. The recollection of Pakistan was so familiar it was almost like a strong déjà vu sensation and I knew I was back to a country that had been as much or more my home than most of the U.S. had been for the past 20 years. In total, I had spent almost 5 years here and knew the culture and thought- process pretty well. I hoped it would serve me well as an advisor to the Ambassador and in the protection of my people. I knew things were going to get progressively worse on the terrorism front and took a deep breath out loud as we traveled the airport road into the casual downtown "suburb" housing area where my house was. I would try to sleep a few hours, shower, and get into work early to begin my evaluation of the Programs and security in-place.

Islamabad is a very big Mission, both physically and in personnel. It covers 65 acres that includes apartment buildings for some employees, baseball and soccer fields, several tennis courts, lots of wooded areas to walk around in, a large American Club facility with restaurant and bar, a large pool and gym facility, and of course the various Embassy office buildings and parking. It had been designed to be basically self-sufficient following being burned to the ground in 1979 by radical Muslim students from a University near the Embassy, who heard a rumor that the U.S. had bombed Mecca. We lost American lives that day and we would never forget it. Security was now tight and we were fully capable of defending the compound. The Embassy was located in what is called the Diplomatic Enclave. In most countries that would mean it is a controlled and protected region where the enemy cannot penetrate. In this case as in many similar situations in Pakistan, it was mostly façade and could be entered without much resistance (or any) from multiple directions. So, we ran our own security and didn't count on the Police controls for the Enclave. The complicated risk was several pronged, but one sharp fork was that we had over 400 homes out in the city where the majority of our people stayed each night and that meant they traveled to and from home and work every day, as this job was another 7 day a week challenge. That is a huge number of moving targets and a pretty easy and soft scenario for the enemy. We would have to work on improving that, or better yet, reducing it substantially and getting more of the Americans on the Embassy compound somehow, even if we had to sacrifice the soccer field. It had been suggested before and rejected by management but times were about to change and with greater violence comes clarity and cooperation from the fear in the hearts of the innocent and inexperienced.

Islamabad is nothing like Iraq but has its own extreme volatility and when one looks back over the past 3 decades, there is some nexus to Pakistan with almost all international terrorist acts. It has always been a country on the brink. The brink of a failed state, the brink of anarchy, the brink of being the home to all radical elements in the world, the brink of economic failure, which brings on greater devotion to fundamentalist religion, and the brink of self-destruction as a Nuclear State. It has always been one of, if not the, most dangerous places in the world and is the breeding ground for the worst and most radical terrorist elements including a large percentage of the world's suicide bombers. That was to a large extent why I liked it. It was the perfect place for an RSO who likes to be in the middle of the "Big Show" and have a chance to make substantive contributions fighting the worst enemy in the world. Mother, I'm home.

One of the most substantial differences between the terrorist actions in Iraq and those in Pakistan is that Iraq is a war with the U.S resources to fight a war, and the protective IZ to give the good guys a chance to retreat and recover and be relatively safe in. Islamabad had the same kind and level of terrorism and especially suicide bomber-type terrorists but we had none of the resources nor an IZ with U.S. military for our protective bubble. We would be fighting this war without my Iraq RSO Air Wing, without my 450 up-gunned armored vehicles, without my heavily armed escort resources, and without the massive amounts of money to do whatever we needed to do to protect the people. We were almost on our own with only our creativity and experience to keep us all alive. A perfect place for me to operate. It would be hard but I knew I was going to like this tour because I would be totally engaged and knew the terrain well and already had Pakistani friends in high places.

On the northern edge of Islamabad are the foothills of the Himalayas, called the Margalla Hills. They are not too high but rugged to climb and good exercise with dense tree coverage and monkeys and other wild animals running around them. But on the northern side of these foothills, beginning with the town of Abbottabad, began the Northwest Frontier Province (NWFP) and that meant territory that became wild and unpredictable leading up into the high mountains or going west directly toward Afghanistan and the Pathan tribe's, gun-cultured always-volatile city of Peshawar and then further into the off-limits Federally Administered Tribal Area (FATA), essentially controlled by the terrorist leader Baitullah Mehsud and his capable Al-Qaeda-affiliated operational cell. One faced Al-Qaeda and the re-surgingTaliban elements when you approached those areas and even the police stayed away and hoped they would self-destruct. Unfortunately, it was a launching platform for the terrorist acts of Baitullah Mehsud against the westerners in Pakistan and the Pakistani government. Each act he successfully carried-out was further emboldening him and making him more of a legend to his followers.

It was 110 degrees and 95% humidity when I arrived and like sucking water to get the air out of it. Iraq was very dry. Islamabad was very humid except during the winter when it got nose-bleed dry. I also arrived during the Monsoon and it was raining like hell frankly and smelled of rich dark earth that could grow anything. Entire hillsides were washed into the streets when I tried to get to work in the mornings and I had to turn around and try another route. At least it seemed the terrorists didn't like rain. The rain was so dense, one couldn't even see the road. It was driving by feel and very slowly. The good side is that Islamabad has the tropical rain forest appearance and is lush and green and plants and flowers are cheap. You can buy a dozen roses for $3.

As I began my work and my interfacing with the Ambassador, DCM and the other Political and Intelligence folks, I found that the many years spent in Karachi and the knowledge I had gleaned from those hard years stuck with me and provided me with an insight and understanding the others didn't have. It was easier for me to read between the lines when something was happening and to know what it actually meant. That turned out to be an amazing asset to me in serving the Ambassador and in providing the proper protection of our facilities and people. The Pakistani conspiracy theories could drive foreigners crazy but they seemed clear to me for what they really were and I already knew that their inane debates over meaningless matters were insignificant but just something they liked to do to hear themselves talk. I clearly remember it frustrating me at first in Karachi but it just sort of seemed comical now that I understood.

I started writing this memoir when I arrived in Islamabad. I wrote mainly only on weekend mornings for a couple of hours before going off to my office to stay caught up on security threats and the constant backlog of Programs and Projects that needed to be taken care of. I didn't anticipate anything coming from this written record other than a genealogical account of part of the life of one of the Bennett family.

I hate stereotyping people but I am afraid that in order to explain certain aspects of the Pakistani culture, I am going to be forced to portray some things in what seems to be profiling or stereotyping.

All the jokes made about Pakistani drivers; they are basically true. The driving tactics here are totally insane and follow no discipline or understanding. I have just discovered that many of the "country folk" who come to the big city, such as it is, interpret the white dotted lines on the roads not as lane dividers, but rather as the line they should track down the center of their car as if it is a guideline. I wondered why they always seemed to be driving two lanes, and a Pakistani friend explained to me that they have no formal driving training and use the line as a center guide. It creates an interesting caution when they decide to make a turn. It also creates 5 lanes of cars instead of 3 at a stoplight, everyone assuming they will rush out to take the right of first passage when the light changes, though some decide not to wait to eliminate the question.

There is a serious lack of control on the part of the drivers (and pedestrians for that matter) and the other day I witnessed a man sitting on the curb of a main road with his feet facing out in traffic. I have no idea what he was doing but the rush of competing cars ahead of me were four cars wide on a 3 lane road and as they got to this man, the outside car simply ran over the squatter's feet in order to maintain his competitive position. The damage to the hapless citizen must have been massive but the cars ahead of me never even slowed.

My first impression of my new Ambassador Patterson, was extremely positive. She is intelligent and acutely perceptive and seems to understand big picture Washington from every angle. My third day in Pakistan, the Ambassador decided she needed to visit Karachi and since it was "my town", I was to go with her to act as guide and of course her protective Agent. I left the day before the Ambassador to conduct an "Advance" of the trip. I hadn't even unpacked my bags yet but grabbed a few things and excitedly looked toward the possibility of meeting with my old friends while I was back in Karachi. When I arrived at the Consulate, all my Pakistani friends who had served with me before were there to hug me and greet me with bright, wet eyes and questions of whether I remembered them or not. Of course I did, from FSNI Z to the car mechanics, and it was a huge reunion. They all kept reciting how I had saved their lives by preparing them for the suicide bomb that took down part of our building but allowing them all to escape. Though Karachi is possibly still the most dangerous city in the world, I will always have a soft spot for it and the friends I made. I even made time for a quick trip over to see Mohammad K, my Brother in the carpet business. When I walked in, it was like I had never left. Mhd K was the same K and our relationship had not changed a bit. Once bonded, always family.

The Ambassador's trip went well and I even took her over to see the Mohatta Palace Museum, that I had helped to open by installing all the security and providing excess expendable equipment to secure the millions of dollars of prize historical artifacts. It had been a successful and beneficial act of social responsibility to the Karachi community and the Ambassador loved it. Looking back and seeing something you did like that which has now prospered into more than you could have hoped for is very gratifying. Something besides just catching or killing terrorists that makes a positive contribution.

The threat situation in Islamabad was already worse than I thought it would be. Reporting by our own people and warnings by my police friends all indicated that Al-Qaeda was heavily involved in orchestrating plans to attack our Embassy and other Consulates in Peshawar, Karachi and Lahore. I began an orientation with my American and Pakistan security team where in our twice-weekly meetings I gave them a scenario of an attack or a bombing, or other incident, and we talked about all the things that we could expect to see and feel and that would need to be done rapidly in response to the incident. I needed their heads to be on straight and for them to already know how to respond if and when the "bad thing" occurred. For me, it would just be a repeat of many times before but I needed them to automatically move quickly to begin the countering, saving, and contacting of support elements. The mental preparation is as important if not more important than a physical walk-through. If your frame of mind has not already accepted and planned for a crisis, it can take too long to get the wheels moving. This was a good team and they were thinkers and doers so I felt good but would continue to "test" and "orient" them to the vicious possibilities. We had already had a recent suicide vest bombing at the airport in the area outside where everyone greets the arriving passengers and another terrorist with a suicide vest bomb attempted to enter the Marriott Hotel staff entrance and a guard stopped him and died for his valiant efforts. This was only the beginning. I could feel it coming like a dark cloud of locust. We needed to get prepared.

SEPTEMBER 2007 – ISLAMABAD, PAKISTAN

This was turning out to be another all-consuming 7 day-a-week assignment and the amount of work was never-ending. The list of projects and Programs that needed to be properly set-up or caught-up would take me the entire year and maybe then some. I began fighting to get additional Surveillance Detection Team members for all our posts in Pakistan, additional ARSOs for Islamabad and Peshawar, additional Pakistani Investigators for all posts and even another Office Manager to help my OMS, who did the work of 10 but would be leaving when I did. I knew what was going to happen to the terrorism activity at this Mission and I needed to get more people here to deal with it as quickly as possible. The reality was that with our bureaucracy, it would probably take my entire year.

I was still ducking and diving when I heard the right loud noises, so Baghdad still had a grip on me but it was getting better. It was probably good to retain that edge anticipating what was coming and we had a shooting recently in the Diplomatic Enclave, so that was another sign that the Enclave was not the protective perimeter our own walls were.

In addition to the terrorist preparations, we still had other investigations we were conducting including an interesting double murder. An American Minister and his wife, who were precariously proselytizing in this strict and non-permissive Muslim environment, received a knock on their door a couple of blocks from my home and two of their "friends" from the church (a male and female Pakistani couple) plus one unknown Muslim man were there and were invited into their home. The guard at the gate had verified that the Minister knew them and welcomed them so he allowed them to enter. Minutes later, several shots were heard and the guard saw the Muslim man burst out with a hand gun and ran past him out the gate. Then the Pakistani couple came out and the guard tackled the pair and held them both while calling for help. The guard handcuffed them and then peered inside the house to witness the Minister and wife dead on the floor. These were the original facts we had to work with. The story turned out to be quite different from all our speculating, as we all sort of bet on what had happened based on the rarest of facts only. It involved secret Affairs, blackmail, and the misappropriating of large sums of money from the church. The Pakistani couple hired a notorious "hit man" from a tribe and village known for specializing in "death for hire" contracting. The whole story was very "hole in the wall gang" stylish. Negotiations did not go well for the Pakistani couple so the hit man completed his assignment and killed both the foreigners and ran out the door. The Pakistani couple was charged but the killer made it back to the "hole in the wall" village and the police said they don't go there out of fear and being outnumbered so he was safe.

The level of suicide bombings had been escalating around the country and even in what used to be a peaceful and virtually untouched Islamabad. On September fourth, we had two suicide bombing incidents near our Embassy Enclave in a "semi-off limits" neighborhood where "The Red Mosque" was located. They killed 29 persons and wounded 66. There was also discovered a suicide bomb vest hidden in the brush near the U.N. gate entry point to the Enclave. It was ready to be strapped on and detonated. We can only surmise that someone was going to use it by throwing themselves on one of our vehicles as we exited the Enclave at some point during the day, but that he must have had a change of heart and decided to live. It shows us though how vulnerable we are every day and how easy it would be to successfully target us. We tried working with the police again at our Enclave entry points and emphasized that if they didn't pay attention, they would be the first to die - but with their Insh-Allah attitude (if God wills it, it will be so) we realized we could be left a bit susceptible.

In order to try and keep our Enclave a little safer, we devised a method for screening and controlling the hundreds of visa applicants that come on a daily basis, any one of which could be coming to deliver their package rather than collect a visa. To enter the Enclave (in theory), a vehicle must be given clearance by an Embassy prior to the police allowing it in. Of course that was a joke with the Pakistanis but at least we made it more random and lessened the odds. There were also Pakistani police Intelligence Agents who watched these applicants to screen out any that they didn't want coming in to give us sensitive Pakistan information or to pass anything that might embarrass them. It made doing our job more difficult. Three Afghan men, who had been interpreters for our U.S. military in Afghanistan had completed their service with our military and had been scheduled for visa interviews to go to the U.S. as their reward. While waiting at the Convention Center in their typical Afghan attire, they were noticed by Pakistani Intelligence and of course this raised both suspicion about why they were there, and interest in what they might be there to tell the U.S. The Pakistani Intel guys grabbed them, hooded and handcuffed them, and threw them into car trunks and drove off with them to a location to be "interrogated". After five very serious hours of questioning, during which time we were harassing the Pakistani Police to let them go, assuming that they were missing from the Convention Center for that reason, they were deemed to be there simply for visas and returned to us to complete their transactions. They came into our Consular Section and we interviewed them on what had happened. These guys had seen so much bad happen in Afghanistan and had been involved in so much horrible stuff themselves, they were hardly phased by the Pakistani's attempts to break them. It turned out that it had been the ISI who took them (Pakistani version of the CIA) and I met with local police to wage a complaint and voice my concern. Knowing the power of the ISI in Pakistan, having worked with them under dire circumstances in Karachi, I realized it was only a façade but had to get it down on the books that we were watching. No police officer is stupid enough to file that report against the ISI and risk their career or their family's safety by drawing the attention of the ISI, so it just went away. It was just the way things were done here.

We began to hear dissent from the local people about the current President, General Pervaiz Musharaff - not having done enough for his people since he took over in a bloodless coup in 1999, in Karachi when I was there. Frankly he is the only one I have seen who has ever worked to do anything for the people. But humans are cursed with an inability to hold a focus for more than a few years and they were looking for fresh and faster hope. And, President Musharaff was still wearing his Army Commander uniform in the President's position and the people didn't like it and felt it sent the wrong signal. Up to this point he had refused to give up that proud symbol of where he came from but the handwriting was on the wall. Two former Prime Ministers, Nawaz Sharif and Benazir Bhutto, were both now smelling the blood in the water and were trying to get back into the country and into power. They had both been expelled at different times from Pakistan for corruption on a massive scale but Pakistanis don't seem to hold that against anyone for very long and now the political parties of both corrupt officials were making noises to try and get their folks back into the country again.

Nawaz was the one Musharaff took over from and he was banished for treason and corruption. He had refused to allow Musharaf's plane to land back in Karachi after a trip and the plane was very low on fuel. It optioned-out to only crashing and dieing or having his troops seize the airport and take over in a coup. He chose the coup and was quite benevolent about it. Anyway, Nawaz decided to try a run to get back into Pakistan and flew to Islamabad, where for two hours, he and his Press circus were held incommunicado in the airport before being cast back out of country on the plane they arrived on. It entertained the country for a couple of hours and then for days after in the press like a sitcom. The Pakistanis love their politics and conspiracy theories.

We entered Ramzan (known as Ramadan in Arab countries), where all good Muslims fast from sunrise to sunset for 40 days. And that is supposed to include no food or water. It is not a healthy thing to do for those infirm or old or young, and for the others, it is a very big risk and danger for all of us. When their blood sugar begins to drop in the early afternoon, their driving going haywire, their anger goes through the roof and they begin to do things totally abnormal and risky – that is to say riskier and less safe than normal on the roadways. And god help anyone in their way on the roads between 1700 to 1730 as they race home to get ready to break their fast (Iftar). You will only be considered an expendable speed bump. The Iftars also become quite a social event and every Embassy or Ambassador puts on an Iftar during this period to host their Pakistan Ministry friends - but the food has to be ready to go on time or politics will suffer. We also get invited by our friends to break fast with them at their homes and it also is the social thing to do. I knew enough to never try to approach the table until they had all first obtained some food and drink to quench their hunger and thirst from a very long and difficult day. 40 days of this (and usually in extreme heat) takes a serious toll on their patience and their work ethics. Supposedly, the principle is that the money saved from not eating is to go to the poor and is called Zakat. It is a nice idea but the rich stay rich and the poor get poorer.

The extremist Taliban elements in our countryside, especially in the Waziristan western border regions next to Afghanistan, had begun their own surge to retake the region for their backward and stifling, religiously restrictive Sharia law ways. They were conducting their efforts as they always did, through fear and killing. They had begun a large campaign of assassinations of anyone in control of a village or a region so the people would not be able to contest their onslaught. Their goal was to return to 600 A.D. and to implement Sharia Law, which makes women less than cattle and allows the men to regress to an attitude of doing whatever they want to, to anyone they feel like it. No women's rights, no education, no books, no western ideas, clothes or materials or conveniences. And, they could and would kill anyone who wished to offer an opinion or suggest an alternative. It becomes the stone age. The other day, in one single effort, a force of 500 Taliban just over-ran 300 armed and "trained" Pakistani soldiers, took them hostage, killed some because they felt like it, and began negotiating for returning the rest. Not one single shot seemed to have been fired by a Pakistani soldier in the "attack".

I had been waiting for my shipment of household effects to come so that I could have my suits and shoes and dishes etc…, what I needed for my life. It had been a couple of months and the shipment finally arrived. Unfortunately, and any Foreign Service Officer can relate to this, they shipped to me what I had asked to be stored and stored what I needed. So instead of my suits, I now had a nice outdoor patio table, umbrella, and chairs for some purpose I could not imagine, and which I guessed would become a center point in the living room downstairs.

As in Baghdad, although on a much smaller scale and with limited serious assets for defense, I had an excellent and dedicated team working with me here. They were all highly-motivated, good-hearted and bright young people who worked without much needed oversight and just wanted to perform well. Their focus was as it should have been and with them running their assigned Programs, it allowed me to do more of the big picture work, looking at what was coming down the road at us from the Al-Qaeda/Taliban operation on the western border, run by that psychopath Baitullah Mehsud. I was impressed by the caliber of individual coming out of the DS selection process lately. They were overall a better quality individual than the majority when I was recruited. Of course the needs have changed as well with a much greater understanding of technical capacities, and those of us who operated "at loose ends" and a bit rogue in the old days, doing what needed to be done and reporting it back in the most positive light possible, were becoming a thing of the past. But, we were what was needed to make this organization succeed and we took great risks to achieve the goal of saving our people on a shoe string. I always got attached to my people and I felt very protective of them.

Pakistan was heating up with almost daily bombing incidents, assassinations, and tribal and political murders taking place in each of the cities we had representation in. Those included of course Islamabad, which had never seen violence like we were seeing now; Peshawar, which could self destruct in the next year or two due to its vicinity to the western border and its desirability to the Taliban and terrorist elements. It is a totally tribal city and would be a perfect capital for them; Lahore, situated near the Indian border and though it is their city of culture and arts and Pakistan's movie industry called Lollywood, it is the softest and ripest of targets and would soon see its own share of disaster as well as always being in the India/Pakistan nuclear threat picture; Karachi, which would always be the most dangerous city on earth, but at this time with its current level of killings and bombings, was still less than it was during my four year tour there, and would continue to be a breeding and recruiting ground for dangerous suicide killers; and Quetta, one of the wildest tribal-ruled cities ever on the planet, where we had a DEA operation in the middle of a scenario involving smugglers, terrorists, Iranian spies and killers, and tribal lords who long for the old days when they could (and really still did) just kill off anyone competing with them. Now, much of the assassination or other illegal action must be sanctioned by one of the two big families, the Bugti's and the Marri's. This was a nice step down from the Iraqi absolute war, but still a serious assignment to keep me interested and as stated before, almost every terrorist act in the last 30 years ha some nexus to Pakistan. And, one always had the curious politics for entertainment. With concerns about possible demonstrations for the upcoming elections, the current government picked up 3,000 political activists and political competitors and locked them up until the election was over. They also feared that the political party based in Peshawar might stir up trouble in Islamabad so they closed down the road that connected the two cities, creating a 1,000 truck jam-up. It took two full days to untangle the truck mess, further complicated by the Pakistani drivers trying to push their way through the mess, thus squeezing the knot tighter. At least it would keep things a bit calmer, though the "human rights" issues had been smashed to pulp.

OCTOBER 01 THROUGH NOVEMBER 04, 2007, ISLAMABAD, PAKISTAN

With so much violence going on now, I was very lucky that the prior Inspector General of Police in Karachi during my tour there (K), was promoted to the Secretary of the Ministry of Interior and was here in Islamabad, where I had relatively easy access to him, and he was being terrific about allowing me to get deeper access to information the Pakistanis had than my predecessors ever got. This was allowing me to be better prepared to protect my people and to obtain support when I needed it, not to mention that it was great to see my old and close friend again. When we first met again in the Ministry, K hugged me and actually had tears in his eyes. It was very touching and I felt the same way about him. In the meeting, he would go between tearing up and laughing as he would remind me about the numerous crazy adventures we shared in those dark and violent days in Karachi. With tears and a sparkle in his eyes, he told me that those days working with me were the best days of his life, and that hit home so deeply with me that I knew I would always give loyalty and friendship to this good-hearted friend. We had survived so many attacks and bombings, including the Pearl case, and been through so many killings together, there could never be a tighter bond between brothers. He had been very protective of me in Karachi and always worried with there being so many attempts to take my life by Al-Qaeda elements. He told his Police Officers that they were not to let anything happen to me and they knew he meant it. I could never thank people like he and Captain and "D" enough for what they did to keep me alive and involved in the investigations with them. Secretary K held a briefing for the Ambassadors posted in Islamabad and he discussed the upsurge in terrorist attacks and the investigations they were conducting and one Ambassador asked if they wanted or needed outside assistance. He looked at my Ambassador and told them all that only once had they ever permitted a foreigner to be a part of their terrorism investigations and that coincidentally, that man was back in-country as the Chief of Security for the American Embassy. When the Ambassador told me what K said, I hoped she did it with a bit of pride and appreciation. I always tried to do my best for her. And, I never betrayed the trust with my friend.

Former Prime Minister Benazir Bhutto, now smelling the blood in the water from the national unhappiness with President Musharaf, arranged, with strong pressure from U.S. Senators and Congresspersons she had befriended, to come back to Pakistan. She wanted to return with her husband, Asif Zardari, known during her reign as "Mr. Ten Percent", for his demands that everyone who wanted any contract or business deal pay him 10% off the top to his private account. Allegations put their ill-gotten gains robbed from the Pakistanis at 1.5 Billion dollars but who knows how much it was. Zardari eventually served 11 years in prison for his actions and this is the same Zardari who is now President of Pakistan. He eventually had become known as "Mr. 40 Percent" because of his ever-increasing greed. Benazir was thrown out of country and charged and Zardari served the time. But, here they were again because of U.S. political pressure, being allowed to come back in and stir up a hornets nest. The U.S. was recommending that a convicted criminal be allowed to come back and try to gain the same position held before. Who could have figured that one out.

Benazir was loved by many, but hated by others and was as juicy a target as one could ever identify. She was told by the Police and personal security advisors that if she was coming into country, she needed to do it quick and quiet and get from the airport to her compound post-haste. She told everyone to back off and that she would be doing a slow motorcade from the airport to her home in Karachi so that all the people who loved her could see her and know she was back to save them from Musharaf. In fact, the schedule she had laid out for her drive literally showed it to be an inch by inch trip taking about 18 hours to traverse the 12 miles. That was a death wish in anyone's book and the police were in a panic knowing that this scenario would certainly contain some terrorist attack. Still, she refused to listen and at the 12-hour mark on her slow highway journey home, two suicide bombers detonated in the crowd close to her motorcade, killing 140 people and wounding another 500. Her refusal to be concerned or to listen to security professionals had cost 140 people their lives. At this point, common sense took over and they drove fast the last 5 miles to her compound where she "holed-up" in a panic trying to blame the police and Musharaf for trying to assassinate her. She had also told the police that they could not set up a protective circle around her home or motorcade to keep bombers back and she refused their assistance stating that she did not trust the police and would use her own untrained political associates to handle her security. Without the police controlling and protecting her, it was open to these bombers and many police gave their lives trying to compensate for her political arrogance. Her husband Zardari, took over security and hired thugs he had served time in prison with to run her protective security. Protective Security is an art and a science. Special Agents train for years to be professionals who can protect the President, VP, or in our case, the Secretary of State, most foreign dignitaries visiting the U.S. as well as our Senators and Congresspersons when they travel into foreign countries (CODELS). These thugs had no training and worse, no understanding of what protection was all about. It made one a bit suspicious about the motive and actual level of concern for Bhutto's safety to allow untrained criminals to protect such a vital asset and prime target.

There were a couple of responsible people in Bhutto's entourage who understood something needed to be done, including an

American attorney and friend who was traveling with her. They contacted my Ambassador and asked what they could do and whether the RSO, the U.S. Government, or U.S. Special Forces could protect her in-country. Obviously, the U.S. had no authority or jurisdiction to protect her in her own country and that left me, the RSO. No way! Not only did I not have resources sufficient to properly protect her, but her stubbornness to listen to guidance that was for her own good, and her ego, that led her to a blindness to any danger, would mean that if I took the advisory job, it would be a lose-lose venture, because at some time, her obstinance and refusal to listen to the security professionals would mean that she would be killed. The U.S. could not be a part of that kind of scenario. If she continued to behave the way she was, and remained surrounded by ill-prepared and questionable-loyalty thugs, and also kept the police from doing their jobs, it was only a matter of time before she would be assassinated. That was a simple fact in Pakistan.

My Ambassador was as politically smart and savvy as anyone I had ever known and she picked up on this risk instantly and we concurred on this dead-end request. What was decided though was that the Ambassador would briefly loan me out to the Bhutto loyal few and her "security" chiefs. I would fly quietly into Karachi, meet with her people and give them strong advice as well as the names of several indigenous private protection companies that I had dealt with before, all based in Karachi but with nation-wide coverage. These were companies who were professional and capable but truth be told, it all depended on her listening to what they said. Better a Pakistani company fail her than the U.S. government. The conspiracy theories would never end and we would be attacked by Pakistanis world-wide.

So, I flew to Karachi and we asked them to meet me in the Consulate, where they could enter virtually unseen and never be linked with me in order to keep our relationship private and segregated. Benazir's American friend who was with her, and several Pakistani "security" and Administrative people, including one retired Pakistani Ambassador, who we tried to keep out of most of the meeting due to his reputation for loose lips, met with me and my Karachi RSO, who would derive benefit from this experience, in a conference room out of the way and inconspicuous.

In as clear, firm, but friendly and specific a manner as I could, I explained why the U.S. Government could not and would not take on this assignment and why Blackwater could not operate in Pakistan because of their high profile and lack of familiarity with the streets, as well as their raising the threat profile and targeting on Benazir just by being here. They seemed to understand that so I moved on to the methods and tactics they should be employing to protect her and explained to them what a specific and highly-skilled profession "Personal Protection" was. They also seemed to understand that. I then told them about the weaknesses I had witnessed on Zardaris thug patrol including how they watched Benazir instead of the crowd, which allowed the terrorists to get right up next to their target to act. Their focus was simply backwards. They understood that as well. After going through a long list of things they needed to think about, I told them they needed an indigenous Protection Service that understood the lay-of-the-land, the streets, the cultural and political implications, and would recognize local aspects and concerns outsiders would not. This job had to be done by Pakistani Protection Professionals. They "got it". Then we brought in the ex-Pakistani Ambassador, spoke courteously for a few minutes and disbanded the meeting.

I quietly returned to Islamabad and briefed Ambassador Patterson, who seemed happy with the approach and hopeful receptivity to the concepts. I then at about 2000 hours, went down to my office and typed up the same information into a cable for Washington (you have to feed the beast) to document that we had done and said what was needed in order to keep Benazir Bhutto alive. We had shown her the way to have the best chance of staying alive. Both the Ambassador and I feared that the attitude we had witnessed with Benazir might have dangerous or fatal consequences and we wanted it known and documented when or if Congress came asking, that we had done everything we could plus more. Our arranging this meeting and providing them with guidance as well as the local company contact information for professionals who could provide the best chance for her survival, was beyond what we normally did, but since we cared, and I was an asset with experience, it was the responsible thing to do. Now we waited to see what would happen.

Within a few days, Benazir's American friend got back to us, frustrated by not being able to convince Bhutto of the requirements for her safety. She had stated that first, she only trusted her own party people to be around her and that her husband's security folks could do the job. Strike one. She also decided second, that she was going to keep the police away from her while in movements and put them only on the outer-most perimeter of her security ring because she felt they might try to kill her. That was total foolishness and strike two. But strike three came when she stated (and only god knows why she would say this certainly knowing better), that no one was going to kill her; that her people loved her and that the Holy Koran prohibited the killing of women and children so she would be safe. How many women and children had already been killed in this idiotic "holy war" and she had already been targeted upon her arrival? What was she thinking? I began to believe she wanted to be a martyr yet the size of her ego seemed to contradict that. Her stubborness and blindness to the facts was almost certainly going to get her killed at some point. The American returned to the U.S. frustrated and concerned for her safety and we watched closely for the next problem.

It was only a couple of weeks later, about 8 weeks after her initial arrival back in Pakistan that the inevitable occurred. Benazir Bhutto was in Islamabad/Rawalpindi, still politicking her intentions to run for the Prime Minister position. She had again, against all recommendations, had some local mechanics cut out a top hatch into the roof of the fully-armored car she had been given to keep here safe. Everyone told her not to do it because it meant the benefit of the full armoring against bombs and attacks was ruined. But, she wanted to be able to stand up through the roof and show off to "her people" who loved her and be able to wave at them. Leaving a meeting in the early evening, she was progressing in her vehicle very slowly through the huge crowd that had gathered to see her and she was standing in her socks on the seat, through the hatch, waving to everyone. The idiot bodyguards were as usual watching her and not the potential enemy when a man standing 20 feet from the car pulled a gun and had the time to fire two shots at her from an awkward and unprofessional one-handed stance. No one doing protection fired a shot back. He should have been dead the second he reached for his weapon and metal was detected in his hand. The inept ex-con bodyguards dove for cover. Both shots missed since firing one-handed is the act of an amateur and as Benazir began to duck back through the hatch, the man then detonated his vest bomb practically next to her vehicle as he walked toward it. The forceful blast threw her head into the edge of the locally-cutout hatch and she hit so hard, the steel hatch broke skull fragments that stabbed into her brain and her brain began to bleed internally. She was dead within minutes.

Later, through my police contacts, I quietly obtained absolute verification pointing to who had orchestrated the act (Baitullah Mehsud) and also was allowed to review Benazir's body and skull X-rays. I personally saw on the X-ray the bone chip spikes that had penetrated the brain and caused her death. Contrary to the rumor mill, no gunshots hit her. It was that stupid cutout hatch and faulty security that had brought about what was logically predicted to happen. This was a senseless tragedy. We all knew also that this event would be used by Zardari to further his position and power in politics. Some days it was just harder to accept incompetent loss of life to stupid politics than others. This was one.

The DVD, "A Mighty Heart" about the Daniel Pearl investigation I ran in Karachi, had just hit the streets in the cities of Pakistan, including Islamabad, and though it was nice to get a copy for my file, this meant my profile and possible value as a target just went up about 500 points. I decided that I would now never be without my hand gun and would have to take extraordinary precautions until I could evaluate what this reminder to some folks who didn't like me would mean. One thing we had learned about Al-Qaeda and terrorists in general was that they held a grudge forever and made their plans on a very long-term scheme. They celebrated and mourned over battles and people lost a thousand years ago. I wanted to see if they were going to identify that I was back in-country and then decide that I had been given too much free time since the Karachi anti-terrorism successes and try to remedy that.

November 05 through December 09, 2007, Islamabad, Pakistan

I had been working seven days a week, about 12 to 14 hours a day and I needed a break so I went to Thailand and spent just short of 2 weeks walking freely on the streets, eating at friendly open-air restaurants, working out every day at the hotel gym (but somewhat cautiously and in pain with my still broken shoulder) watching actual Hollywood movies and doing some shopping, and reminding myself how lucky I was going to be working next in this friendly environment. I flew back to Islamabad and one hour later, the first of many bombs to come, detonated. I was instantly returned to my proper serious focus and Thailand was only a vague memory of things the way they should be.

Pakistan had just been declared "the most dangerous country in the world" by another weekly news magazine and hundreds of mostly innocent people were being killed daily, with an emphasis in the western border region. Anyone who resisted the Taliban or Al-Qaeda efforts to take over their village was publicly tortured and killed along with his family. That pretty much worked as a strategy every time with uneducated, defenseless farmers and goat herders with no weapons to fight back, and who had been brutalized most of their lives for generations. And the Pakistani military and police seemed to have limited capacity and maybe limited motivation to do anything about it. The Waziristan area was following Tribal Law under a Federally Administered Tribal Authority (FATA) and there was some question as to how much authority the Pakistanis had over that region. An old agreement had given them self-rule rights. This was allowing the terrorists to use it as a staging and training area for their maniacs who were going out on missions to kill all of us or other government authorities and doing it successfully. When you intend to kill yourself in the act, you have a certain sense of freedom and fearlessness in your action. That really gave them the upper hand. Recently, women were volunteering and being used as suicide bombers, which was a change and even more complicated for police to react to or prevent since men and women ignored each other and scrutiny was prohibited. A woman could pretty much walk into a place unchecked. Two mornings ago, our day started with two suicide bombings in our city. Things were heating up as I had predicted.

Looking back over at Iraq now, it appeared that things had significantly slowed down on the violence and attacks. We had received over 300 rockets during my year and now, they were almost not occurring at all. On the other hand, the Pakistan western border with Afghanistan had erupted like a firestorm and it seemed that many of the Insurgents from Iraq had come over for the battle. The Americans told the Iraqis that they wouldn't leave until things got under control and I guess the Insurgents realized that if they wanted the Americans out of Iraq, they should go somewhere else to fight for awhile and let the Americans leave Iraq before coming back later and destroying it to take over power and rule their own way.

DECEMBER 10, 2007 THROUGH
JANUARY 09, 2008, ISLAMABAD, PAKISTAN

Pakistan was in the midst of plans for their upcoming national elections. The whole country was spun up over who would win and who would cheat who and the conspiracy theories and accusations were coming so fast and furious that no one could keep up with all the allegations being thrown around. And, massive demonstrations were occurring all the time screwing up the traffic patterns and country's productivity (such as it was). I know I hadn't been very favorable in my discussions previously about the Congressional Delegations (CODELS) that came out to visit our Embassies and Missions and I still wasn't particularly, but we needed their support and funding out here to fight the Al-Qaeda/Taliban surge and they controlled the budget. There were of course those who did vital work and I respected them for what they did and the efforts they made. But, during this Christmas period, when we might have gotten our first day of rest in many months, it was also when Congress closed down for the holidays so they used it to travel out and show us how much they were supporting us. Just during this Christmas period, we had 8 CODELS in a two-week period. Not only did it kick our behinds from the added work-load during the crucial election period, but no other work got done as we shuttled them around in vehicles and our precious USAID helicopters that were supposed to be doing humanitarian work. My security resources were stripped clean and with all the killings and bombings, there was no rest and a great deal of stress trying to keep them alive when they asked or demanded to do various precariously unsafe things. It generally made for horrible holiday periods for us.

The terrorist activity and numbers of deaths continued to pick up and we watched a constant daily death toll. In 2007, over 600 innocent people we were aware of died from just the suicide-type terrorist attacks alone. I could almost guarantee that 2008 would make that number look insignificant. We now had in early January, some days where more than a hundred died in a single day, with the emphasis on the western border of course. Suicide bombers in our cities were my daily bread and butter and fortunately the police had been catching some. But, assuming that those they captured were just the tip of the iceberg, it meant we had a major network trying to assault our community and at some point, they would be successful. The greatest asset I had was my Ambassador. She seemed to trust me enough to allow me to do what I needed to do and kept the bureaucratic stuff off my back for the most part. There had been so much terrorist killing and political infighting, which in Pakistan generally leads to political assassination and with the murder of Benazir Bhutto, that the January 8th elections were postponed to February 18th. So, for me, it meant there would be an ever-increasing amount of bombings and killings now for an extra 5 weeks as everyone tried to make their violent points known.

With the killing of Benazir Bhutto in a manner we told her would occur if she didn't get serious about her security, the other former Prime Minister who was kicked out of Pakistan after his conviction on corruption and treason charges, Nawaz Sharif, had returned to try his hand at being elected and taking control of the country again. There was talk that because of some point in his conviction, he would be unable to run for office, but he could still run things from the shadows if he could stay in Pakistan. He saw how serious conditions were from Benazir's killing and when our Ambassador met with him, she offered to have me meet with him and give him the same guidance and resource references I gave to Benazir's people. So, showing that he understood survival, he agreed and the Ambassador sent me on another quiet low-profile visit to Lahore to meet with his people and discuss the measures they needed to take if they hoped to keep their political leader alive. The meeting actually went pretty well and they took a lot of notes, asked a lot of focused and insightful questions, and gratefully accepted my list of indigenous Pakistani Protective Services companies. I quietly flew back to Islamabad and within the next couple of weeks, watching Nawaz on TV, we noticed that certain security measures and tactics I had recommended to them were actually in play and they were creating a strong protective perimeter with sensible professionals forming his line of defense. Who knows, he might survive if he stayed smart.

January 10 through February 07, 2008, Islamabad, Pakistan

I have mentioned the many killings and attacks but have not commented on the specific details so perhaps that leaves you wondering if things were really that bad. So, I listed some of the more significant events within a one month period of time to provide an example of the daily level of violence and terrorist-inflicted death that we dealt with. In Iraq, the press covered the rocket attacks and ambushes so the world was somewhat informed. Here, the press can't survive if they try to report it and they either hide in the hotels or report from another country after having their Pakistani contact tell them what is going on. I took a sampling of about 2 weeks worth of activity to show you what my days were made up of in this truly worsening terrorist environment. The rapid surge of violence was becoming precarious and necessitated security policy changes for all our people that would restrict their movements and eliminate many of their freedoms in order to keep them alive.

January 9 – Soldiers were patrolling in the area of the once beautiful and culturally unique tourist destination of SWAT, when terrorists ambushed them and killed all 9 of them.

January 10 – A large terrorist suicide truck bomb in Lahore, the artistic center of Pakistan where their movie industry is centered, and one of the first big suicide vehicle bombings for Lahore, killed

28 persons and wounded more than 30.

January 14 – A large bomb detonated in Karachi killing 10 and wounding over 50.

January 14 – Terrorists ambushed several drivers near Peshawar, killing all 7 people.

January 14 – In the Northwest Frontier Province (NWFP) that borders the Islamabad Margalla Hills, the Taliban surged into a village and destroyed all western-type schools, medical clinics and shops that had anything of any western influence. They also killed the owners to make a point.

January 14 – In Islamabad, a husband killed a man who had sex with his wife and got her pregnant. The court ruled that once the baby was born, the husband could kill the wife as well. The court also ruled that a female friend who knew about the affair may also be killed by the husband. In fact, the court asked the friend's family to kill her as an act of "honor restitution".

January 15 – In the city of Multan, 6 suicide bombers were captured with their pre-constructed bombs and 36 other suspects were arrested as they prepared to do the same.

January 15 – Again in the beautiful SWAT Valley, an all-night gunfight raged and in the morning there were 36 dead and 72 injured, some of which died later. Many more from the valley were missing and presumed taken for later torture and execution by the Taliban.

January 16 – In SWAT, a roadside bomb detonated and killed 6 and wounded 9 more. The use of roadside bombs as in Iraq, signaled a dangerous change of Modus Operandi and also suggested an influence from Iraq or more probably Iran.

January 16 – In South Waziristan, home of the Waziri Tribe, 700 terrorists attacked and seized a military fort killing 37 soldiers and losing 40 terrorists in the process. I met with a major Waziri Tribal Leader, to discuss his options and concerns and his only concern was that I help his son get to the U.S. to become a Dentist.

January 17 – A Sunni suicide vest bomb-wearing terrorist walked into a Shia Mosque in Peshawar and detonated himself in the middle of a group of praying Muslims. 12 were killed and 22 were wounded.

January 17 – Rashid Rauf, a terrorist in police custody for plotting to blow up transatlantic flights, was taken from the courthouse back to his cell and on the way the police helped him to escape. However, first, they took him to McDonalds for lunch and he left from there.

January 18 – Three rockets destroyed a western-influenced café in Quetta.

January 18 – In Islamabad, two terrorists who had been sentenced to death for killing a large group of individuals, miraculously escaped from the courthouse after the sentencing.

Ali Zardari announced to no one's surprise that he would now run for Prime Minister in place of his dead wife, former Prime Minister Benazir Bhutto.

During this 2 weeks of violence, we also worked 11 CODELs,

trying to keep them from becoming part of the statistics.

January 19 – Muharram was celebrated. This commemorates a large massacre of Muslims in the year 644 A.D. Hundreds of thousands took to the streets and whipped and cut themselves so that their bleeding reflected the events of the massacre 1400 years before.

January 19 – In the NWFP, 8 terrorists were captured and identified as Al-Qaeda. When captured, they were in possession of preconstructed suicide bombs, designed with high explosives and cyanide. What they must not have known is that the intensity of the blast might have destroyed the cyanide as a disbursable gas.

January 19 – Terrorists launched 10 mortar rounds into the city of Peshawar and they landed in the neighborhood where the U.S. Consulate is located but missed our compound. However, several local homes were hit and many deaths resulted.

January 20 – the Taliban and Al-Qaeda made an announcement that all Americans interfering in the upcoming Election Monitoring Process on February 18th were to be killed. Against my strong recommendation, the Mission decided to send out teams of American Officers to remote towns to monitor the fairness of the election so I had to find a way to keep them alive without the required resources.

January 20 – In Islamabad, the Police captured 2500 kilos (5500 pounds) of high explosives, along with a huge load of ball-bearings and 13 vehicles painted to resemble Government of Pakistan vehicles. They also confiscated 6 guns and 2 grenades. The intent was to create 13 large and highly lethal suicide vehicle bombs. If the police caught these, how many had they missed?

January 22 – A Pakistani Army fort in the NWFP was attacked and taken over by terrorists. 42 Pakistani Army personnel were killed and the rest were to be executed for propaganda advantage.

January 22 – In another stroke of luck, the Islamabad Police captured 6 more terrorists as they were entering the city, loaded with all necessary explosives and equipment to create more suicide vehicle bombs.

All these and more were just from a two-week period and from the pattern here, it was clear something big was in the works and that it was inevitable. This represented the intent to perpetrate a series of devastating attacks against the western community and Pakistani authorities. Obviously they had substantial explosives and a waiting list of volunteers to commit suicide. Everyday was just preparing for the shoe to drop and hoping it didn't drop on any of my people. Also, the Ambassador had been loaning me out to the entire diplomatic community and I had begun doing security consulting at the other Embassies to identify for them where their attack weaknesses were. I had already consulted with almost a dozen other Embassies. Many were in completely untenable positions and in venues along streets. I gave them the best recommendations I could based on their weaknesses, and limited funding, and then walked away with my fingers crossed. And it all just continued on.

I had been in contact with an old friend in Karachi, who was Pakistan's most accomplished and well-known sculptor and jewelry designer. My now ex-wife "A" and I had been friends with him when we lived in Karachi. I called to find out how he had been doing and he told me sobbing that both his famous painter parents had been brutally murdered 2 weeks prior and that the police weren't doing anything to find the killers. Apparently the killers had taken valuable jewels and a large sum of money. It was common in Pakistan to have the police pursue thieves and murderers who got away with a high-value "take" and never be caught. They actually were caught but after turning over their cash and jewels, the police let them go or they disappeared. I told him I would come down and intercede in the investigation.

The Ambassador needed to make a 2-day trip to Karachi January 25 and 26, so I went with her as her guide to Karachi and her protection. While there, she went to a safe and controlled lunch with attending bodyguards so I left the Karachi RSO with her and I split off to go see my friend and look into the double-murder investigation. As I walked through the murder scene and heard all the facts, besides identifying it as one of the most violent and hateful personal killings of humans I had ever heard of, it became clear without much work that it had been an inside job. The method of their deaths was so brutal, it could not have been anything else and they knew exactly where things of value were and left untouched and unruffled, all the other areas. I told my friend I would deal with it and when I returned to Islamabad the next day, I went to see the Secretary of the Ministry of Interior. I laid out all the facts to him and the insights I had from what I saw and told him what I surmised and who I thought committed the act. He agreed, picked up the phone, called the Police Inspector General in Karachi and yelled at him and demanded a resolution. Within 48 hours, the Parent's chauffeur, maid and their two murdering psychopath friends were caught, interrogated and confessed. Much of the money was gone but many of the jewels, which my friend's Father had collected, were located and returned. He was very grateful and at least now could begin to seek closure. The details of the murders are so ugly and sick that I won't describe them in this writing.

My days weren't getting any easier. On January 28, I received an early morning call at my office in the Embassy that we might have an American suicide at a residence. My first thought was that it was more likely to be a murder and maybe even terrorist influenced but left my options open until after I inspected the scene, the body, and the circumstances. The address given me seemed odd though, it was the home of a U.S. Embassy employee I knew well and I thought that he had left country having finished his tour a couple of weeks prior. I wondered if we didn't have a household staff member or perhaps the replacement for our comrade who had found it all a bit too much for him in Pakistan. I looked around for one of my young Agent ARSOs to take with me for the experience and possible follow-up procedural investigating. This was something they would all most-likely face in their futures and if I had one who seemed strong enough and ready, I wanted to give them this training opportunity. I found my female ARSO, who was as solid and mentally strong as they came, and she was tested already with a tour in Cairo so I waved her over and told her she was going with me to the scene and to come prepared. She was always up for any new experience to expand her portfolio and make her a better DS Agent and RSO so she eagerly jumped and grabbed her "go" bag.

We arrived at the residence, which we had ordered sealed until we arrived. Though there are many other Federal Law Enforcement Agencies represented at Post, DS has jurisdiction in these matters affecting American citizens. We try to be sensitive to involving any affected Law Enforcement Agency if it is "their" man, and with the uniquely qualified FBI in matters of evidence collecting and processing, we try not to be jealous guarders of territory and allow them to get involved in that process.

My ARSO and I walked into the residence. In order to minimize interruption of the scene and to gauge how grisly it truly was going to be for her, I told my ARSO to first wait outside and let me get a perspective of the scene and conditions. I found him dead on the floor and there was the usual blood splatter and tissue matter in various places, with concentrations in the tub. I called her in and she stayed by the door while I reached into the tub and pulled out the handgun. When a shot is fired, the slide ejects the empty shell casing and inserts a new round all as part of the "gas blow-back". Thus, it is called an automatic handgun. I opened the slide and found an empty expended shell casing in the weapon. The gun had been fired but had not recycled another round. That meant that when it was fired, the barrel had been placed tightly against something and held the slide there so that it was not permitted to be pushed back by the expended gas to re-cycle the next round. The answer most likely was suicide, with the weapon held tightly against his head. There was no direct wound in the front but the body was in the first-phase of mess condition and would have to be cleaned up and viewed by a Coroner to get the true picture. I laid the now-open weapon and shell case on the bathroom counter. I did a cursory inspection of the upper torso talking my way through it with my ARSO, who seemed to still be in control and not changing color. She was going to do well.

After the initial inspection, we exited the bathroom to get organized for the forensic collection and found the FBI in the TV room. They mentioned that they should be handling the evidence scene and I clarified jurisdictional matters. They then stunned me by asking if I had any experience with dead bodies. My blank stare at them made them remember my history. Nonetheless, I saw an opportunity to advance my ARSO's learning curve and told them that she would be handling the investigation but that we would like an FBI Agent to work evidence collection and processing with her on the case. Fortunately, they agreed and assigned a female Agent who had been in Iraq with me and I respected and liked her very much. She was one of the more capable FBI Agents I had ever met and was also sensible. She and my ARSO would not only work well together but would end up being friends. She was great. I had sort of convinced her to come to Islamabad after her Iraq tour and I felt responsible for her safety and happiness on the job. She was a bit frustrated by the usual bureaucracy but was bright enough to know how to handle it well.

They both negotiated the complexities of the case extremely professionally and worked well together. The FBI Agent got what she needed to feed the FBI and my DS Agent got her big case and high-profile learning curve experience. The victim had actually never planned to go home. Unknown to anyone his depression had been covered well by a joking sunny personae that everyone in the Mission took to be a well-adjusted happy guy. The family knew Senator Kerry so the Senator flew out as part of a CODEL and met with me and asked me to fill him in on some of the "inside" investigation information, which I did in hopes it would stop the parent's fear that a terrorist sniper had shot their son in the head. Senator Kerry asked for my cell phone number so he could call with any follow up questions but he never did. It was a tragedy for all of us who knew him and we all remained confused as to how we could have been so blind to our friend's true pain.

The Ambassador to Pakistan from the Netherlands asked our

Ambassador if they could borrow me for security consulting and she agreed. They had an Anarchist fool Political Party leader in their country who was threatening to release a 10-minute video insulting Islam and the Holy Quran. We all knew that after those cartoons the Dutch had allowed to be printed portraying Muhammad in an allegedly less than respectful light, this video was sure to bring the mobs to all our doors and for the Netherlands, probably bombs to their walls. I visited their residential-Embassy and was truthful with their Ambassador about their inability to prevent destruction of their building in the location and condition of limited security it was currently in. They were all concerned and took my advice seriously but commented that their "Home Office" had told them that if the threat became that bad, they would all be brought home and the Embassy would be closed down. It was just another situation of "Political Will" superseding common sense and threats. I did what I could by giving them the truth and telling them they could contact me anytime. Now we would wait to see if the video got released.

FEBRUARY 08 THROUGH MARCH 15, 2008, ISLAMABAD, PAKISTAN

It was time I took a trip and re-visited Peshawar to get a feel for the environment and what appeared to be a serious degrading of security conditions. Almost every day, there were multiple reports of radical Muslim-oriented attacks taking place in the city and suggestions that Peshawar was about to fall to the Taliban and Al-Qaeda elements. The total loss of a key city like Peshawar that acts as the gateway to the old silk route and now Afghanistan, including some re-supplying efforts of the U.S. military such as fuel, seemed impossible. But, the Pakistanis had a history of being late to respond and even though Peshawar was a pretty good-sized city, it wasn't impossible that the enemy could get a substantial Insurgent presence that could turn Peshawar into an active war zone, eventually razing it totally through constant guerilla bombings and attacks.

Peshawar is an exotic classic old Hollywood-type movie setting located just 55 kilometers from the Khyber Pass. Its dusty narrow alleys screamed of danger and risk but also of adventure, its 400-plus year old Arabic mixed with Mughal design museums, shopping suks, homes, massive ancient brick forts, with an almost total female population wearing black Burkhas, and open display and wearing of rifles and hand guns by men with two and three-fist-long beards, made this city one of the most stimulating memories I had. There had been some great experiences and close calls in this primitive city straight out of the dark ages. I loved it, but hated it for the risk it now posed for my people. If it was just me to worry about, that would have been one thing. But now I was the one in charge of keeping everyone alive and my perspective had to be wider and more cautious. It wasn't just big smiling Pathan warriors anymore. Now, we had the perverted hatred by the Taliban.

The Consulate was a physical disaster from a security perspective. It was located in a residential neighborhood, where we had to close off the streets and driving to and from work was a disaster waiting to happen. This visit convinced me to eliminate the personal vehicle driving policy and go much more restrictive on movements. A major disaster was just around the corner for this place and we needed to try and make sure it didn't happen to our people. The whole city was moving backwards instead of progressing. It literally was racing to reach back to the dark ages and had as an example of their devolution, recently passed a local ordinance outlawing women from wearing sandals that make a flip-flop noise when they walked. The basis for this new and important style change was that the men felt it was "too sexy" and provoked them to think of sex. Excuse me?

The time for the Election Observer Teams to go out finally came up and bit me. I had to make it work with a minimum of risk and injury. For us to send our people into the same villages and towns where the enemy was killing local Pakistanis on a daily basis, in order to verify that the elections were fair, would be precarious and logistically a challenge.

My only choice was to find the best way for this to happen and fight for compromises to minimize our exposure. Fortunately (in a dark way), more madness and mayhem occurred in Pakistan and our excellent and astute Ambassador was swinging more my way on the safety of our folks and she was responsive to my suggestions. First, I reviewed the 65 locations and eliminated all Taliban and Al-Qaeda-controlled cities and villages. I also eliminated villages that were just too far away to have any hope of getting a police response team in to help them if there were demonstrations or shootouts. I needed the ability to get overland rapidly without too many ambush sites or bad roads that could create scenarios for easy capture. This initial review brought us from 65 to 22 cities/villages. Then we used up our favors with our Police contacts to get them to give us a police support vehicle in each of the towns and to have observer police monitoring the "highways" or main roads, radioing in to let us know when our vehicles had passed, as well as when they were safely in their sleep accommodations for the night.

We set up a 24-hour Command Post that ran for 3 days from the initial departure of our teams until every one of them were home and through my Embassy gates safely. We also coordinated to have USAID earthquake relief planes and DEA helicopters ready in case we had to call upon them for us to use as an Emergency Response Team. In addition, DS was still supporting my position and pushed to install a high-speed satellite-focused GPS vehicle tracking system for us covering mainly Pakistan, but it could be expanded to monitor all movements of USG in the region. The "Blue Force Tracker" GPS system was basically the same that I had in the TOC in Iraq and had been a key to life-saving response. So, we trained the civilian Observer Teams and placed the GPS units in each car and I set-up RSO teams to constantly watch everyone's movements in Pakistan and hope that a 911 alarm never went off. The system worked well and we were allowed to keep the system afterwards for use in tracking all future movements of our people. This was a useful resource addition to our portfolio and since we were now the "most dangerous country in the world", it made sense.

The operation, with all the police resources reporting in, and with their escort assistance on highways and in the towns went successfully and we got everyone back within 48 hours. There was only one couple who tried to go "rogue" on me and decided after their day of observing they were going to sneak out at night without the police knowing and go on a sightseeing tour of an unsafe and uncontrolled area. Thankfully, the police were secretly watching from a hidden place and called me to tell me they had snuck out. I had the police apprehend them and escort them back.

For about two years, a Pakistani-American we'll call "the Doctor", had been transferring around in the Pakistan prison system without the U.S. Government even knowing he was missing. No one in his family, which was living in the U.S., had reported it to us. He was a political radical who had been stirring up trouble in the Karachi area, while his family lived in the U.S. without a source of income or fatherly support. One day he just made too many Pakistani officials nervous with his threats and he was picked up and incarcerated. First he had been held in Karachi; then he was transfered to another more remote town to reduce his visibility to his political party friends, and finally, to make him sort of disappear, he was sent to a District Prison in a town called Zhob, in the rugged, mostly untraversible (except to smugglers on camelback) Province of Baluchistan, about 20 miles from the Afghan border. Two years after he first went missing, the matter came to our attention and we finally tracked him to Zhob, which is a smuggling conduit, and totally Taliban-controlled town that is about as dangerous a place for an American to go as there is on this planet. The likelihood of an official USG American going into that primitive Tribal Taliban town and returning was zero. We heard that the Doctor was suffering from a condition but that he was fine and content. Well, once the U.S. government folks sitting at their Washington, DC desks hear about something like this, it doesn't matter what we have to do to show their constituents that they take care of all Americans, and they begin to apply pressure to get the Consul General or someone in the American Citizens Services Section to visit the AMCIT for the record and to file a report on his condition. I vetoed this visit entirely to Zhob. I wasn't about to lose American Officers on the chance that we might be able to see the Doctor. Plus, there was no way to get to him over that enemy-controlled terrain. I did, however, promise to try and work the issue with the Secretary of the Ministry of Interior, or his number two, the General to see if there was some way we could get the prisoner moved to a location of greater safety like Quetta (hard to believe Quetta would ever be safer than someplace else). We felt that might make life better for him in a larger town and we would have periodic visiting rights as required by our USG. It was comical to think though that we were moving someone to Quetta for safety reasons; Quetta being a conduit for drugs, weapons, enslaved people, terrorists, and Taliban, and controlled by several War Lord families. The approach was to tell the Ministry that we were obligated to visit him, and that it could be in Zhob, or they could move him to Quetta or maybe even a safer place, in order to back them into a spot where they had to decide. I felt quite certain they would never in a million years allow us to die in Zhob, even if we could figure out a method to get in and out. After literally a month of negotiations, believing we would never accept the risk, the Ministry of Interior folks said that we could fly into the tiny dirt-field airport of Zhob. This was their reverse psychology approach of trying to get us to say thanks anyway and back off. Unfortunately, the eyes of Washington were blindly upon us and I was forced to reverse their psychology and call their bluff and say OK, and that we would fly in on one of the USAID small Caravan planes. The Ministry of Interior was caught off guard and temporarily reversed their decision and said they would get back to me. I kept pushing and told them we wanted to do it soon. They craftily agreed to move him to Quetta, which would allow me to also make an inspection of the Serena Hotel for our occasional official use, and they set a date. They apparently never intended on allowing us to see him. Because of the clear threat on making this trip, the Consul General, a good-humored young man, felt he had to do this himself. Because he was going, I had to go to protect him. I couldn't allow anyone to place themselves in danger unless I was willing to do it myself, and certainly not any of my younger Agents in this case. Some had families. This scenario always seemed to bite me in the ass. The risk had to be mine to take.

We landed in Quetta and received a call from the Police saying that they were unable to bring the Docto to Quetta. So in obstinance, I told them we would go to Zhob the next day and that they should make preparations for our protection and our visit. I thought this would get the Doctor to Quetta post-haste but instead, they agreed and said they would call back with directions and clearances for the pilots, who were Pakistani Police pilots contracted out for the anti-narcotics work. When the Pilots heard the decision was Zhob, there was sheer panic in their eyes and they began searching for any way possible to not go. They knew it was unlikely we could get in and leave alive. In addition to Americans, the Taliban loved to torture and kill Pakistani Police. My Pakistani Investigator, who was with us on the trip for translation of Urdu or Farsi or Pushto or Baluch, whichever might come up, received the directions for landing in Zhob the next day from the Ministry. I have never seen Pilots more reluctant to fly in my life and I have to say that I had some reservations about whether we would survive. My one hope was that my friend Kamal would not let me die on his watch.

The next day as we flew from Quetta, approaching the town of Zhob, everyone was tense and the Pilots said that they would have to stay very high until right over the airfield to avoid surface to air missiles (SAMs) and that then we would steeply and quickly circle down into the field and hope for the best. Again, Zhob is considered to be under the control of the Taliban and recently a key Al-Qaeda leader had been captured coming from there, which meant that those hard-core terrorists were directly linked to Zhob. I was hoping that all the confusion on when or if we were coming would not have allowed any coordinated plans to be made by the Taliban or by Al-Qaeda, who would not be very nice to me if they caught me and learned who I was.

As we circled steeply down into Zhob, it looked like a village from the dark ages. Everything was of a mud-hut construction except a couple of official buildings we could see in the distance and with one "wall-ringed" fort, and with limited cars, which were all strong 4-wheel drive types, obviously used for smuggling and other nefarious purposes. As we circled down closer to the dirt landing strip, I could see there were large numbers of Police, Frontier Constabulary, and even Pakistani Military posted all around the field and extending far out into the perimeter desert and hills. There had to be hundreds. And, we spotted a string of up-armored vehicles with large caliber machine guns surrounding a few sedans, which I hoped were for us. I cannot imagine how my friend got this many resources out here to protect us. This was a wasteland in the middle of nowhere. I would again forever owe him for this.

We landed and were introduced to the key officers of each Pakistani protective faction and we were served the customary hot sweet tea and then they told us we had to go to the other side of the town where the prison was. A formally-rigid and tense individual told my Senior Investigator that we all needed to fill out Profile Forms, which could have been in case we died to identify us but I knew he must be Intelligence and was just doing his job. The other side of town meant we would be driving through this narrow street dirt road town with at least a hundred perfect ambush scenarios. Here is where all we could do now was to sit back and hope for the best and observe closely in case there is a need or chance to respond, escape, or to fight back. The Consul General, who was also my friend, was taking it well and I respected him for that. Maybe he just didn't comprehend how bad it could be to be captured and tortured, but he maintained his usual constant smile.

With almost 300 Police, Frontier Constabulary, and Pakistani Military protecting us, we moved through the "dark ages" town to the Prison without incident. Again, we drank the hot sweet tea with the Prison Police Chief, who seemed to have become a bit looney being posted out here too long, and while the Consul General interviewed the Doctor, I kept the Intelligence Officer (who had been assigned to regulate the questions) busy talking about America, which he was fascinated with all things of. The Prison Chief kept waving at the Intel Officer, telling him to listen to what was being said since the Intel Officer was the only one who spoke English. But, I kept him entertained so the CG could get true responses from the Prisoner, and the Prison Chief just sat there unhappily out of the conversation, wondering if his life and career were over.

The Doctor was in decent condition and was actually treated with some deference since he had been helping the injured and sick at the Prison. There were no medical personnel and maybe they kept the Doctor in Zhob to fill a void. But one thing was certain, he was a little extreme and most likely a trouble-maker. If they released him, we felt he would go right back to doing the same things he was now in prison for. He even told us flat-out that he would. He was charged on three accounts; possession of firearms, possession of explosives, and possession of a stolen vehicle. When you put those three things together, one can hear a loud explosion somewhere in the future. It seemed his goal was to be a martyr. CRAP!

We finished our visitation and the CG and I went out for our return journey to the airport, which I worried about even more since bad people would now have had a chance to "gear up". I was pretty happy though with the huge numbers of armed men protecting us. We made the traditional photo-ops in front of the Prison with the Prison Chief (the Intel Officer at least knew to stay out of the photos) and various protective elements who all smiled widely. Then we made the run back and though the streets felt tense and any ambush would have been a total disaster for us, we made it.

Once back at the sort-of Airport, the Military Intel guys wanted to know why we had a Chinese person with us and they were very concerned about it. The "Chinese looking guy" was the Consul General. We had a devil of a time explaining to them that the U.S. was made up of ethnic people from all over the world. Thank heavens my Senior Investigator was there to translate and explain. I think the CG might have had to stay in Zhob otherwise or be deported. Besides surviving another great little adventure, the best part for me was looking down from the plane at the twisted geological terrain of Baluchistan. I have never seen any more unique and bizarre landscape in my life. It was unbelievable and virtually impossible to traverse by vehicle or on foot.

No one was happier to get out of there than the Pilots, who made a steep, circling exit up and away, still expecting SAMs to be launched at us. The massive numbers of protective personnel Kamal had put in place were the only reason we survived that trip and knowing now what I knew about Zhob following our visit, I put it on the "never to be allowed to be visited by anyone again" list. Great photos and proof again that I was blessed to be lucky!

MARCH 15 THROUGH APRIL 13, 2007, ISLAMABAD, PAKISTAN:

Tragedy struck Islamabad again the night of March 15th, 2008. At 2045 hours, in the middle of the peak dinner hour, a terrorist bomb comprised of approximately 7 kilos of high explosives, was placed in a satchel or computer-type bag and thrown over the wall of an Italian restaurant popular with foreigners called Luna Caprese and located across from the residential F-6 Market area known simply as "the supermarket". Without any prior "announced" planning or coordination, four of our Embassy FBI Agents in the Legal Attache Office, including my friend who had worked in Baghdad with me, had decided to go to this restaurant together, this night, at this time. That eliminated any thought of specific FBI targeting but random violence can still have the same outcome. The first recognition that something was going wrong was when the explosive satchel landed on the plastic table in the outdoor dining courtyard, breaking the cheap table and making a very loud crashing sound. Every diner turned to look. Seconds later, the bomb detonated and was heard and felt for a couple of miles, including by myself, sitting in my residence in the F-8 residential area. I was way too familiar with the sound and effect and knew immediately that we had a detonation near the market area. I jumped up and began to put on my boots and weapon, expecting a cell phone call before I could get out the door. It came from our Marine security Guard at Post One as I left the front door advising me that an explosion had happened somewhere in the F-6 Market. I began driving as fast as I could, watching and listening for a secondary bomb or an ambush on the road. As I drove, I called my ARSOs and my excellent Deputy RSO, who was already beginning to set up the Command Center in our offices at the Embassy since he lived on-campus, and he had called our Pakistani Investigators and our DS and State Department Command Centers in Washington DC. Our superb Office Manager was also fortunately on campus and had quickly gone to the office to begin the call-out procedures in order to get 100% accountability of all our people. We were like a smooth-functioning machine, unfortunately because we were gaining so much experience doing this. About 4 minutes after I left my residence, as I came down a side street to the F-6 market, I could see the chaos and beginnings of movement of people covered with blood and the crowd of curious Pakistanis pouring in. I quickly parked, scanned the area for any obvious or hidden threats for me specifically and headed toward what was obviously the center of the attention, the Luna Caprese Restaurant. As I walked, I received a call telling me that it was thought we had four Legat (FBI) personnel in the restaurant. Then in front of the Luna Caprese, I ran into one of our Embassy Nurses who lived close by, also coming to assist and we both wanted to know the status of any Americans who had been there. I got a brief look into the walled compound but the bomb had gone off in the back courtyard and it was now being conveyed to us that the four Embassy Americans and a fifth American who worked for the Red Cross, had limped and been dragged out to the street, apparently (in broken Urdu and English) by my FBI friend, who was bleeding but was virtually carrying two of her FBI friends. The best translation we could get was that she had commandeered a police truck, put everyone in it and directed the surprised driver to take them to the PolyClinic Medical Center. That was her. A former Marine, disciplined to the core and an excellent Agent for the FBI. I was proud of her as I had been in Iraq. She is one of those "good ones" who want to save mankind.

I called into the Deputy's line and told him what the Nurse and

I had found out and we directed the Pakistani Investigators and the Medical staff to get to the PolyClinic ASAP. As I now headed for the Embassy, we had the Doctor and several Nurses (which fortunately included an additional visiting Nurse from Kabul, Afghanistan), my Investigators and some "Special Element" armed personnel all heading to the clinic. And every one of my ARSOs were responding to the Embassy quickly and without needing guidance.

I arrived at the Embassy five minutes later and we began to get all our operational requirements in order. My Deputy, who was by now quite capable of dealing with major disasters and threats from all he had experienced over the past 9 months, had things in order, and my OMS, who was just simply a Super Star, had the accountability of almost every American finished. She maintained a calm essence under the worst conditions. The Pakistani Investigator Team had made contact with the Police and we were getting a security cordon around our wounded at the clinic immediately. Our fear now, besides how badly our friends were injured, was that a secondary attack would be perpetuated against our folks.

Two of my young ARSOs came into my office with grim looks on their faces and made a pitch to go to the clinic also to protect their FBI friends. I paused briefly as I weighed the additional risk but it only took 5 seconds to tell them to go, and to be careful, but that I wanted constant status reports from them. It was what we did and though I always placed myself at risk, I was a bit protective of my other people. But this was their time and they needed to do this for our friends and for themselves; for their own self-respect and sense of value as to who they were, and for their career experience and skill development And these young Agents were highly trained, some of the best in the world. Their faces sort of lit up and they got quickly armed and practically ran out the door. There are times when a father just has to let his kids go and this was certainly one of them.

The reports received on our FBI friends were conflictive and that worried me. Some said that they were not badly injured. Others said that a couple of them were seriously injured and possibly close to death. I needed facts. One of my ARSOs called me from the Clinic and told me that the Doctors were saying that they were OK and could go home to recover. The ARSO said the Pakistani Doctor was an idiot and described some of the injuries and symptoms to me, which seemed pretty serious. We decided to ignore the Clinic Doctor and to get them moved immediately in ambulances to the Shifa Hospital, which was the best in the city but had been a greater distance and initially we wanted emergency care and stabilization. We had patient stability to a degree now and we needed the best medical attention. My ARSOs and the Special Forces guys worked to get the entire group moved and the Embassy Medical Staff were "sent from God" as usual. The Pakistani police also set up a substantial force outside Shifa Hospital to deter secondary terrorist problems.

A thorough re-evaluation was done at Shifa Hospital and as we suspected, the injuries were significant and life-changing if not life-losing. If they had gone home as the first prognosis suggested, at least two would have died before the sun came up. At the hospital, wherever the four were being worked on, we had armed protective Agents guarding the halls and doorways. At 0230 hours, my FBI friend, who had suffered a burst ear drum and was having a problem with constant ringing in her other ear, and also had some minor lacerations to her face and scalp, had been released, but had come straight to the Embassy where we all were still working the issue. We all understood why. The other three were being kept at least overnight, if not for quite a few days.

Throughout the night, the RSO operation, the Front Office, and the remaining Legat personnel remained in contact with each other and our various Operations and Command Centers in Washington DC. The Management Section began contact with a Medevac service for the 17th to fly them to one of our top-level medical service locations and by the morning of the 16th, the injured were stable and protected in their rooms, but badly damaged.

Besides my friend having a burst ear drum that would require a later skin flap operation in the U.S., one other Legat person suffered the same burst ear drum but also had his entire front of his scalp cut and lifted up creating a scar across his forehead that seemed about 6 or 8 inches long, though many months later when he was allowed to return, we kidded him that it wasn't even noticeable. One other FBI Agent sustained multiple serious facial lacerations and swelling so bad that he wasn't even recognizable when I visited him the next morning. He had received many shrapnel penetrations to his body and such serious wounds to one leg that it was without feeling and had deep cuts all over it. He had become a close friend of mine as well but would not be returning to duty. His recovery period would be planned out over years. The fourth FBI Agent sustained serious facial wounds and the complete loss of one eye and the possible loss of his other eye as well. Time would tell on that. He also had numerous other shrapnel penetrations to the body. He would be retired and never work as a Field Agent again.

The RSO Team had worked all night until the sun came up to make sure that everyone was taken care of and that the Washington information beast had been fed sufficiently. We got them all Medevac'd over the next two days and this incident meant I had to change the policy on the freedoms and lifestyles of all our people in Islamabad. There would be no more public restaurants permitted. We still allowed the restaurants inside the two primary hotels we used but only randomly and unpredictably. Things were getting worse and they would continue to get more dangerous probably for the next couple of years before there might be any hope of improvement. We needed to do some hunkering down for awhile until we could get a true feel for what was in the works for our Americans and other westerners. I imposed tight movement policies and placed other controls to hopefully reduce our footprint and "track-ability". In the end, the bombing had killed one woman and wounded twelve other innnocents but it could have been much worse. The investigation revealed that the bomb had been packed on only one side with ball bearings, intended to maximize deaths. When the satchel hit the plastic table, it had flipped the bomb upside down landing on the grass with the majority of the ball bearings now directed to focus the blast into the earth. Such was the luck of everyone there that night or the huge number of ball bearings would have killed most or all of the people. Still, as bombs work, everything it impacts turns into shrapnel, so the plastic table and chairs all became small projectiles that ended up creating the hundreds of penetrations into everyone's bodies, along with rocks and miscellaneous matter and 50 to 100 or so of the ball bearings.

My FBI friend had been a hero that night and later, she and another wounded FBI Agent received medals from their Headquarters, and they were well-deserved. My team had done an incredible job and once again, proved that DS is truly the most capable federal law enforcement organization in the United States, which means the world. I was so proud of all my people. And even though the FBI sometimes feels that I don't fully appreciate them as an organization, it is really just some of the small-minded people in their organization that I object to as in many organizations. This particular night, though they might not make a reference to it or comment about their appreciation for my people, this success story could not have been done without the DS Agents who went to protect and watch over their FBI friends, along with the superb Medical Staff and the exceptional Special Element people who always make us feel better and safer.

This bombing meant that the Embassies located in "residential-type" structures, essentially streetside and with no set-back or what we would call physical security measures, began to call and meet with our Ambassador, looking for guidance. She in turn, referred me to them or them to me and I began a busy "out-sourcing" of my time to help them each understand their own particular vulnerabilities. The Americans, which means DS, are considered to be the leaders on security, although we are at a level most can-not match with funding or governmental support. Nonetheless, they like to have us look over their operations and controls so that they know exactly, or reasonably closely, how much threat or risk they face. I tried to be non "sky is falling" when I gave them their feedback but usually, it wasn't good. I usually started off my review by voicing my understanding of their financial limita-tions and ask them to give me a figure of what they might have to spend on upgrades. It is usually staggeringly low. I then told them what the best use of that limited money is like Shatter-Resistant Window Film (Mylar), or changing their personnel and vehicular access controls. But then, I have to tell them what their overall weaknesses are and what it would mean if a comparatively similar bomb was thrown over their wall or a vehicle bomb was parked next to their wall. This was usually the moment of shock and the famous "deer in the headlight" look. The damage from a satchel bomb is significant enough to turn their lives upside down but when they hear about virtual total destruction from a car bomb, the Ambassadors and Administrative Officers begin to think about early retirement or career changes. The truth is the truth and I owe them that. They get the good, the bad and the odds from me so that they can make the best judgments for their people. I can't personally protect them all but I do want them to know where they stand. At moments like this bombing, even capable and experienced Embassies want to discuss with others to compare their thoughts about vulnerability. I must have met with 25 different Embassies including the Germans, Italians, French, Turkish, Canadians, British, Japanese, Dutch, Danish, Australians, Ukrainians and a host of others as well as many other businesses including the Serena and Marriott Hotels. The Serena Hotel had excellent set-back. The Marriott was just too close to the road but had taken outstanding and diligent measures to reduce their liability like barriers and dogs and eliminating all shops to reduce foot traffic but they still faced a proximity risk. It was a busy time.

Reports of Suicide bomber-terrorists roaming the city looking for targets of opportunity were coming at a rate of several per day. Unfortunately, some of them were true and we were witnessing regular attacks against the Pakistani government (GOP), mostly in the form of vehicular suicide attacks. Trucks with 500 kilos of high explosives would ram GOP buses filled with employees. Motorcycles with 20 kilos would pull up next to a VIP car and detonate. It unfortunately had begun to go the direction of my predictions. Pakistan had now become the new "war zone" and Iraq had gone quiet. All attention from Washington seemed to be focused on our activities and that meant we might get more "development" funding and support for the FATA, which seemed to me to be money down a black hole. We definitely would be further plagued by CODELS who all wanted to have "been there and done that" when their re-elections came up. Military people would want to make "touch and go's" or one-day stops so that they could claim their 30-day danger pay bonuses, and I was still certain that I was not going to get any heavily-armored weapons-mounted vehicles or helicopters. We would still fight a war-front level operation on a security shoe-string. It just meant I had to restrict the actions and movements of my people and hope for the best with using greater unpredictability. I did still love my job though. There was nothing like being on the front of the Global War on Terrorism, and I would know since it seemed to follow me or get there before me no matter where I went. There is nothing more satisfying than actually being able to look substantively at the end of the day at successes that saved people's lives. And I wouldn't have traded my job or the opportunity to work with these quality people like Ambassador Patterson for anything.

The world of our industry is truly small and one never knows when they might run into someone from a bizarre part of their past. That is especially true in my line of work. Earlier in this saga, I mentioned an adventure in Zaire where my Team that included U.S. special military elements, the SAS, the RCMP, and the GSG9s took over Kinshasa and ran it following a massive evacuation due to Zaire Presidential Troops shooting up the city over a denied pay increase. It had become a city of burning, looting and canabalism and we evacuated the 1,100 westerners and took over what became a massive city-ghost town for a couple of months. I had become close friends with the SAS Team leader and for about 3 years after that event, we maintained contact to the degree one can, working through secret unidentified Postal Mail Boxes and both of us always being sent off to rectify some other rebellion or posting in another foreign country. Fifteen years had passed since we lost contact with each other.

As part of my open door policy to briefing all companies who have a security concern in Pakistan, I was briefing a western Pakistan border region USAID-funded Non-Governmental Organization (NGO) in my office and they had the usual bug-eyed stare at my stark and honest depiction of what they could expect to happen in the Northwest Frontier Province and FATA areas. They mentioned they took security seriously and had hired a security consultant to work for them in a full-time advisory capacity and "Bob" would be coming to Islamabad in a few days and would I be willing to meet with him. I asked if this "Bob" was a Brit, retired from the SAS, and they said they didn't know but would ask. The next day they called back and confirmed it was my friend from Zaire and that he was looking forward to seeing me after 15 years of no contact and 18 years since the Zaire adventure. This reunion turned out to be pure synchronicity and we now maintain close contact, I am Godfather to his new son, and as a couple of the last survivors of our various groups, we swore a pact to never let this bond of "old surviving war dogs" disappear again. He began spending about 2 weeks per month in Pakistan and it was nice to have a friend who understood what we had both been through and he was a true security professional. Frequently the strangest things happen.

April 14 through May 30, 2008, Islamabad, Pakistan

The daily terrorism threat maintained its course and we were searching the city for 10 suicide bombers who allegedly had entered the city of Islamabad with plans and resources to do some serious devastation. They were known by name and ranged from 10 years old to 20 years old. How can any man of conscience send a 10-year old boy to his death before the boy even knows any better. Perhaps the "man of conscience" is the problem. I don't see them killing themselves, just sending others. No conscience, no soul. We had also begun another Shia versus Sunni war in the city and just the other day one sect walked into the mosque of the other sect and while they were kneeling and praying, opened up on them with machine guns, killing dozens.

In the midst of all this death, destruction and threats of more to come, a new METRO store opened up on the outer fringes of Islamabad, on the way to Rawalpindi. It is a huge wholesale chain that makes a SAMS or a COSCO look like babies. This European chain allegedly has tens of thousands of stores worldwide. I went to inspect it to see if it was safe for our people to access and as we approached, I saw that across the street from it, stretching into the horizon was where the Afghan mud-hut settlement was located. Now I knew that Metro must have gotten a good deal on the land. For heavens sake, they built their store across the street from 20,000 Afghans living in huts and shanties, where terrorists came to hide as a safehaven before carrying out their bombings and killings. This would make it a bit of a problem for our people to shop and that was a shame since we really needed a place like this. I talked with the store management and the police and both told me that there were imminent plans by the city planning board to do a "community resettlement". Translation – They would bulldoze the entire community into non-existence and send them fleeing somewhere else. This would be a "community relocation opportunity" as they put it. Their answer was clear to those of us who knew how to read between the Pakistani lines. I was torn - my ethics were bothered here. On the one hand, I wanted the store to be available to my people and I wanted the bad guys hiding in the village to get out and run away and to lose their organization for awhile. On the other hand, I felt bad about the long-term suffering Afghan refugees who had nothing to begin with except what would be bulldozed. Life was so much more complicated and conflictive than the surface level view. I could picture the incident clearly. They would just role in unannounced one morning early with bulldozers and other heavy equipment along with a large contingent of police. With loudspeakers blaring, they would give them just minutes to grab their meager possessions and run before having their mud-huts flattened. I felt sort of like a bad guy supporting the element that would be responsible for the community destruction. I gave my people authorization to shop there, but only on certain days and at limited times to minimize exposure and threat.

Pakistan was a tough and raw-minded culture with primitive rules and sometimes barbaric punishments. The previous week in Karachi, three teenage boys tried to rob a home and foolishly got caught. The neighbors don't have respect for police or the laws that have been created for everyone and they tied the boys up in the street and poured gasoline on them and lit them on fire. The newspapers were also there watching it happen and the front page of all papers showed the three young alive boys on fire, dieing a horrible death. I guess they believed that you only get one mistake with no forgiveness. The crude nature of life here and in other places on the planet can sometimes be very disturbing and I have seen too much of it in the last 20 years.

The burnings of books, western clothing and CD stores continued in the western border region and the Pakistani government had suggested that they might allow the region to revert to primitive and soul-stifling Sharia Law if they would quit conducting terrorism against the rest of the country. How foolish could one really be? The only thing that this would do was to give the terrorists another stable area to get stronger and conduct their operations from. If they did this, it would be the beginning of a long struggle trying to reverse it, maybe taking years. I would like to believe sane minds would prevail. It would be like the old horrible Taliban era being given authorization to conduct their mindless and barbaric acts again.

During May 25 to May 30, there was a regional celebration called Urras. This strange and delinquent celebration is of a local Saint for the Sufis. This "Saint" relished the smoking of hashish and of dancing all night long and being a dirty vagabond apparently. 200,000 badly dressed and unwashed people poured into Islamabad, where the Saint's monument is located and smoked hashish all day and night and danced and played kind of horrible music all day and night. They blocked traffic on the roads and the police just allowed them to get it out of their system. I wondered if the music was supposed to be so bad or if they were all just so high that they sucked at playing stoned. With dreds in their hair and jangling jewelry all over their bodies, especially wrists and ankles to make more noise, they roamed the city for 5 days, dancing the whole time until they collapsed from fatigue. I guess the drugs kept them moderately passive but it was one of the strangest celebrations I have witnessed.

MAY 30 THROUGH JUNE 30, 2008, ISLAMABAD, PAKISTAN

Realistically, the western border region, which was feeding the suicide and assassination attacks in Islamabad, Rawalpindi and even Lahore, had officially become totally off the "scale of control". This year, already the number of suicide bombings had reached 800 for the country. This was in comparison to 67 for the same time period in the previous year. If anyone doubted before that things always seem to go to hell when I arrive, here was a statistic to back up that myth spread as a joke by my DS friends.

The case to identify, locate, and capture those responsible for the Luna Caprese restaurant bombing and the serious injuring of the four FBI Agents, had been progressing and I was able to make a substantive contribution to identifying the people behind the planning but cannot discuss it due to the sensitive nature of the methods and means. But one advantageous point had been that as the case progressed, the Pakistani Police either did something right or got lucky and caught four suicide bombers with four very large vehicle bombs, rigged to go off, as well as three of the bombers "handlers". The vehicles were rigged with 1700 kilos (3740 pounds) of high explosives and would absolutely have destroyed everything within about a 100 yard radius. These were enormous bombs and this signaled that something very big was in the works. Two days after the first lucky capture, the Police (probably from interrogation of those they captured) caught two more suicide bombers and explosive-laden vehicles, also ready for an act of terrorism. If luck had not prevailed, the total destruction caused by these vehicles might have sent some foreign Diplomatic Missions packing for their home countries.

Unfortunately, one vehicle bomb slipped through. The only blessing was that it was the smallest of the set. A suicide driver brought the vehicle up next to the Danish Embassy wall, and exactly as I had advised them weeks before that the incident would occur if they got targeted, he detonated and took out their wall, all windows, cracked and shattered their building/residence structure, seriously damaged and burned out nearby homes, and wreaked havoc on the interior offices and personnel, killing eight (8) innocent people. We immediately had the police seal off their dead-end road and provide police officers to guard the crime scene. The Danes called for their special security team to come to Pakistan to study the incident and I did what I could to get our people, including the FBI Forensic personnel involved. About the only evidence we (and the police) had to work with was six fingers we found. But with a virtually non-existent forensic database in Pakistan, the fingers weren't going to help. So, for me, I was left with providing grief and psychological trauma counseling and advice to the Danish Embassy Staff (which was suffering the usual mental shock) and offering to coordinate police assistance with their visiting investigative team. I am not sure at what point in my life of many disasters I stopped going through the shock and awe phase but as I looked and listened to their confused and rapid disjointed conversations that ranged from guilt to grief to total confusion and collapse, I remembered many years ago when the adrenaline might have done something similar to me. It was painful to watch as they began their pain, grief and guilt cycle to start on their path to psychological and emotional recovery and I discussed the many phases they would repeatedly go through with them in hopes that they would understand that what they were feeling was natural and actually part of the healing process.

The bombing of the Danish Embassy had led to an even greater demand for security advice by the other Embassies and between calls to me and the pleadings to the Ambassador, I kept a very busy schedule telling people at other Diplomatic Missions things they didn't want to hear. Essentially, "get inside the Diplomatic Enclave immediately or be susceptible to the same outcome". At our Ambassador's request, I went to the Swedish Ambassador's home to discuss the security for their Swedish National Day celebration scheduled for one week later. They were in a residence just like the Danes and were rightly concerned. I explained that in order to still have the celebration, they would have to clear away all cars and close off the entire street and set up a large contingent of security, but that it could be done and I would help with the police. In the end, they rightly decided it wasn't worth the effort or risk.

Meanwhile out in the uncontrolled Tribal Zone of North and South Waziristan (the FATA), the Taliban continued their campaign of fear and forced-obedience through killing, maiming, destruction and torture. We were trying to support the primitive "tribal self-policing" elements out in the FATA such as the Levys and the Kazadares, who are essentially sheriffs trying to protect their own little villages, but they were barefoot men and boys who had to use whatever personal weapons they had like old Enfield rifles, and they had almost no ammunition. So, the Taliban came into their towns in large numbers with their AK-47s. They tortured some, they killed the tribal elders so that there would be no leadership to resist, and they forced the Levys and Kazadares to join them or they killed them too. The Taliban also destroyed everything "western" in the towns such as burning down 10 girl's schools and killing all the teachers. They told the girls that they could only go to Madaris (religious schools) or that they and their families would be killed. Since the Pakistanis seemed disinclined to use any real force to stop this, it did not bode well for the poor people of the western provinces for at least the next couple of years.

In the middle of all this, I received an "Award for Heroism" for an act in Iraq. It showed up in Pakistan in a mailed package from the State Department, signed by the Secretary of State. Somehow, the significance of being told you are a hero and receiving an award loses some of its import, when it comes unannounced in the mail. Oh well, frame it, center it on the wall, and stay focused on the job of protecting your people. I had put the same sticker I put on my computer screen in Iraq on my computer screen in Islamabad to make me stay on track. It simply read, "regain your focus". Everyday I tried to regain my focus on what was truly important and ignore the nonsense like that it was monsoon season again and the hillsides were washing out into the streets, or that it was 115 degrees and 99% humidity, or that we had 36 Congressional Delegations (CODELS) in the past 6 months and were burned out on visitors. Oddly, I knew I would miss it every day. I would just have to bear the burden of peace and tranquility.

JUNE 30 THROUGH AUGUST 15, 2008, ISLAMABAD, PAKISTAN

As I began my final couple of months in Pakistan, I reflected on the almost 6 years I had spent in this country since 1990, the majority being the four years in Karachi, and I felt a deep frustration with the absolute ineptitude and lack of forward momentum that this place had made. From time to time, the fact that it never changed made me feel comfortable in that I always knew what to expect and could pretty well predict what their responses would be to most political or terrorist actions. It's predictable foolishness and failed focus on helping their own people, and the greed of those who ruled the country had tired me out. Just like every group who took over control of this country, their goal was never so that they could make positive change for progress (with the exception of Musharraf who actually tried). Their attitudes were always "oh boy, now its my turn to rape this country for everything I can get". My journey here had become something different now for me after all this time. Even many of those people who I call my friends and have known for so long and even risked our lives together and had my life saved by them, frustrated me with their personal and selfish goals to "get theirs" while they can and "to hell with the poor" or the advancement of their nation and cities. Perhaps one of the only exceptions to this awful and failed attitude is my close friend, the Secretary of the Ministry of Interior. He had been consistently a man of honor with a heart that beats for the principles that Pakistan was constructed upon and he continually beat his head against every changing regime's greedy attitude, yet still tried to make his country safer for the people who got sacrificed in the game-playing. He had become broken and disheartened by what he had to endure with the changing governments, and after all the many years he had fought with everything he had to make change, he now had the drained appearance of a man who had given up. In a personal meeting with me, he voiced a desire to move to New York, where his family and specifically his grandchild lived, and to try and enjoy a few final years with those he loved. He appeared ill from the long hours and constant barrage of death with few substantive results being seen.

The SWAT Valley and the villages within it are, or were, so beautiful. It was in the late 90's, when people could travel there as tourists. The culture was colorful and native and used to be friendly. When people talked of SWAT, their eyes lit up and everyone had a great story of their trip with the smiling people and the hospitality that was shown and the food and the nighttime dancing by firelight. Then, a few years back, the Taliban began moving into SWAT and Pakistan allowed it to happen in their blind lack of understanding and lack of concern. The SWAT Valley is only about 100 miles from Islamabad and one would think that the close vicinity to the Capitol City would have been concern enough. SWAT had now been decimated and all dancing and music came with a death penalty. No colorful clothing could be worn. No jewelry could be made or worn, and no women could be seen except covered completely in Burkhas, mostly black. Anything suggesting industry or progress had been destroyed. Their unique and beautiful culture appeared to have been lost. SWAT now had an average of 100 people killed per day either by the Taliban or as they were caught in the local conflict. An indigenous and unique populace was being wiped out and may never be seen again. Besides the Taliban, Al-Qaeda had moved in with their intentions of gaining a stronger grip on other areas of Pakistan. And the greedy War Lords saw the chance to make money off people's misery and they ran the guns, drugs and even smuggled human slaves. From this new base of operation, the Taliban and Al-Qaeda had begun to slip out through the region and into other areas to plot and plan and carry out terrorism to gain more territory for "the cause". And no one saw anything being done about it by the Pakistan government, army, or police. Up to now there had been no political will exhibited to save their nation. Any and all moderates being found in villages were being executed and we saw the result first hand through this now-constant, almost daily barrage of suicide bombings aimed at getting all westerners out of Pakistan so that they could take Pakistan over and declare it for primitive Sharia Law.

In one stubborn village, the Taliban publically beheaded 12 people to get their point across. When a police officer was posted in a village to try and give it stability, the Taliban would kidnap them and return them a piece at a time to their police headquarters to put enough fear into the police that they wouldn't resist their movement. Recently a suicide bomber who came from the western border region walked up to a bus stop in Islamabad that was filled with Pakistani women and children and blew them all up. What was his plan? What did he hope to accomplish? Why did he kill his own people, and all of them being non-combatants? Even with my experience, I can't find any solid between-the-lines basis or justification for killing all these innocents.

We had begun seeing more black flags with swords on them, which is the flag of the militants, being posted around the city. This was a clear indication of the frustration of the people at remaining poor for so long without any window of hope for progress or improvement, and it was forcing them toward a more radical support of elements that might at least change what is bad, even if it did actually mean change for the worse overall. I advised Ambassador Patterson that as bad as things had been this past year, unfortunately, the next couple of years were going to be worse. Two weeks previously, every Pakistan military officer living in a secure protected military housing cantonment in Quetta, awoke to find on their doorsteps, a package of documents and a DVD, selling them on joining the militant movement. This was an obvious signal of the will and frustration of the people.

I awoke on Pakistani Independence Day, with news that nine more suicide vehicular bombs and bombers were roaming around town looking for a western or Pakistani government target to annihilate. The fact that everyone was still driving to and from work and home in Islamabad and most of our other constituent posts was going to shortly become intolerably dangerous and would have to be stopped. The risk was just too high and the targets of opportunity too plentiful. But we had to find an alternative other than just closing down and walking away or sleeping in the halls of the Embassy. This was the strange and sometimes dangerous balance that Foreign Service Officers live with in their jobs and that those living in the United States and working in a normal environment don't understand. Every day for all of us is complicated by risk just getting to the office and having to think about the safest way to get into a grocery store and get out alive. We all have to think in a manner that is far outside the cube of normality or civilized existence. The previous night in Lahore as the people were preparing for today's Independence Day celebration, a suicide vested-bomber walked into a crowd of people and detonated, killing seven besides himself and wounding 30 others. Everyone was just innocent neighbors.

As it does occur in Pakistan with some level of regularity, I was hit with horrible food poisoning and it almost totally incapacitated me for 2 days while it worked its way out of my body through cramps, vomiting, and a reasonable amount of pain while I sat at my desk and worked. As I recovered from the food poisoning, a group of big angry yellow wasps attacked me outside the Embassy front entry and before I could respond, they stung me twice on the neck and injected quite a painful toxin. Also, the mark from the stings, or scar as they have now become, seem to remain. What a way to finish up a tour. It seemed perfect.

I suppose out of a need for more sacrificial victims, The Taliban had begun to actively kidnap young boys between the ages of 13 to 16 in the Taliban-controlled area on the western border. They had been known to kidnap them for sexual interests previously but this time, it would seem that it was as a source to be used as forced suicide bombers. Many had recently been grabbed as they were either going to school or on their way home from school. They just snatched them off the street and the parents had no hope of ever seeing them again, no matter the purpose or intent of use. They then began a dehumanizing process with them, beginning with a total brainwashing and then when they were ready, or needed for a suicide mission, they were drugged with "the water of Allah", which put them into a semi-catatonic state where they would follow orders with little resistance. It must be a scapalomine-type drug. Any who were able to resist the brainwashing were killed to eliminate any suggestion of resistance. In just the last month, 25 young boys meeting this profile were kidnapped by them. The Taliban really had to be stopped. They were heartless, souless demons from hell itself and could not be written as more evil in the worst Hollywood movie. It broke my heart when I thought of the loss of those young people's lives with no one fighting for them.

Two of Pakistan's most well-known moderate Journalists, who are married to each other and live in Lahore, began to receive death threats. Threats were not so new to them but the level of hatred and sincerity of the language brought the case to our Public Affairs Section, then to our Ambassador and onward eventually to my door. The Ambassador asked me to fly to Lahore to meet with them and give them counsel and guidance as well as to evaluate their physical security. I was to see what they could do to better protect themselves during this precarious period and to stimulate police interest in watching over them. As I might have voiced once or twice, I am not the biggest fan of the Press, which seems to promote their own agendas these days and manipulate what they want to be their own outcomes. But when I met these two individuals, I liked them both. They were an older couple, whose names I will protect, and they lived in a nice home with decent security but certainly not enough to stop anyone who actually wanted to kill them. We talked for two hours about their routines and self-awareness, as well as the measures they currently took and now needed to take. Then I looked over their physical security of home and work and the routes they took to and from, and made recommendations for them. One recommendation was to go visit their kids who live in Europe until things cooled down a bit and the angry faction looked elsewhere to vent their hostility. This would also give the police some time to get a grip on the situation and hopefully deal with it. I love it when people are sensible and they took my advice and left for a vacation with the family. Upon their return, they would still need protection for a year or two to allow a certain measure of safety but for now, they had extended their life expectancy.

Things were getting very close to my departure and I still felt like I had too much to do to get things secure prior to my future permanent absence and my not being able to monitor things every minute and juggle security issues as needed daily. When I left, I would be leaving my friends alone, and even though I trusted the new crew to watch over things, I didn't trust anyone as much as I trusted myself. Yes, I might be a bit of a control freak but my control is for the safety and comfort of those I watch over, not for myself.

Before coming here, I also remembered that in the past, Islamabad had some good golf courses and I had bought clubs and shipped them here thinking I would play. Well, that had certainly turned out to be a pitiful hope. I had virtually worked 7 days a week and

14 hours a day. Thinking about Thailand coming up, and how much I was told the Police Generals liked to Golf, and of course the amount of good will and liaison that can be accomplished on the golf course, I decided to take 2 hours off on a Sunday and go to a range to see if I could still hit a golf ball after about 15 years without playing. I hit two buckets of balls and realized that though I had no game at this point, at least I could still drive a ball fairly well. That was enough. I took my blisters and went back to work.

Within the final few days prior to my departure, the Deputy Chief of Mission, who had become a good friend and who was married to my exceptional Office Manager, arranged for an executive helicopter trip up into the northern high mountain range to visit the Agha Khan's Foundation and Medical Clinic in the Hunza Valley. This was where the legendary Shangri-La was located, where people never aged and lived forever, and nearby were the mountains K2 and Nanga Parbat. The helicopter trip took us past them and it was a sight never to be forgotten. This was the perfect ending to an exciting but violent tour. I at least felt that it had been a success since none of my people had been killed and the Mission was safer overall due to the things that we had done on the physical security and emergency preparation end like our Secondary Defense Force that I had created and implemented.

My replacement finally arrived and needed 2 of the 3 days I had left to get his wife and dog settled in so I had a couple more days to wrap up loose ends, then gave him his in-brief, such as it was with so little time left for our actual transition. Luckily, as was an RSOs' procedure, I had put everything in writing in a large classified notebook for him. Then, as it always happens in its surrealistic manner, one minute you are in the constant line of fire thinking about preventing death, and the next, you are on a plane headed back to a place that has no comprehension of the dangers faced and type of life you have been living. I was taken out to the chaotic Islamabad airport and away I went from what would more than likely be the final critical threat posting I would ever work. This was possibly the end of an era, my era, and as one might expect, I left with regret and a smile.

I spent my two weeks of Congressionally-mandated personality readjustment in the U.S. and got to be close to my sweet mother and some of my brothers and sisters again. It was nice but I was almost always thinking about Pakistan and my next encounter in Thailand. In an attempt to pass the time, I took a trip and spent three days in the Grand Canyon alone, hiking everywhere I could go and going out on every small ledge I could find to look into the abyss. I loved the beauty and silence of the Canyon. Then, back to the Phoenix airport and off to my next assignment for DS.

Chapter Twenty-Four
ADJUSTING TO BANGKOK, THAILAND

I arrived at Thailand's new Suvarnabumi Airport about midnight and the familiar smells, sounds and sights came back and I found myself smiling for no particular reason. Here were the beautiful petite Thai girls all trying to get you to use their taxi services and the clean orderly operations that make Thailand such a happy place to be. I was met by my new Deputy RSO and our Thai Residential Security Program Manager and was taken to my temporary residence, until mine was prepared.

This was a big city that I could now walk freely around in almost any time of the day or night without being armed or fearing an imminent attack. I could sit outdoors at cafes and eat in peace while watching the people happily walk by, enjoying their lives, not suffering through it in constant misery and anguish. This was a city of life, music, activity, and beauty, not to mention exceptionally beautiful and friendly women. It was going to be a shock for me but one I felt I could readily adapt to.

Having carried the reputation with me of my assignments always "blowing up" and becoming "the most dangerous places on earth", I had taken teasing from my DS associates and their jokes that I not allow it to carry over into Thailand. I planned to change my Karma and to bring a different sense to this assignment. When, after being in Thailand only a few weeks, political demonstrations broke out and there were some shootings and small bombings, I took a teasing from DS again over it being my fault. A month later, when both Bangkok airports were seized for 8 days by political activists and no one got in or out of the city, it also gave cause for DS to wonder if it was somehow my fault and I took heat for that as well. Personally, if I was trapped in Bangkok for 8 extra days, I wouldn't consider that a hardship – rather a lucky break. But, I suppose others had different perspectives.

The Royal Thai Police Generals who I began to make my calls on were all very friendly and as it is my habit to joke and tease my way into a friendship, they responded perfectly and to the point that the Deputy Commissioner General of Police told me that I needed a good Thai wife and he would be working to find the right one for me, as in his opinion, Farangs (foreigners) always picked the wrong Thai women. He said he would happily do police and background checks on any girls I wished to date and we laughed about that though I suspect he meant it. Other Royal Thai Police Generals actually started introducing me to their favorite appropriate single Thai women and my social readjustment into a "normal" life began. I really liked the personalities of these Thai Officials.

As a lucky break, shortly after arriving, I escorted two dozen high-ranking Royal Thai Police and Royal Thai Government Officials back to Washington D.C. for a two week DS Anti-Terrorism Assistance Training Conference. The diverse group made a very interesting mix as well as creating a terrific liaison opportunity. I found I had walking pneumonia during the 2 weeks and it took a great deal of my energy away but the trip paid off substantially and we all became close friends and permanent contacts, as well as Karaoke partners. One might not suspect it, or understand it, but singing Karaoke with them established a bond of trust and family.

After returning from Washington and getting over the Pneumonia, I began to play golf and attend parties with my Royal Thai Police friends and to sing more Karaoke, which I had never expected I would ever do. The job was busy but administrative, and though I missed being "in the action", it was time I focused on the next phase of my life. This was the perfect place to do it. I was again lucky as I always had been, and I actually smiled just walking to work. We would now see just where life was to go.

And what I had always known was true, was re-validated by my new Thai Senior Foreign Service Investigator Khun Aor, when she said, "You are a lucky man Khun Randall. You are a free man in Bangkok and the styles have changed. All the girls are wearing short dresses now". I guess it all came down to timing and luck.